The Civil War
Generals

The Civil War Generals

Comrades, Peers, Rivals —
In Their Own Words

Robert I. Girardi

"The painful warrior famoused for fight

After a thousand victories, once foiled,

Is from the book of honor banished quite

And all the rest forgot for which he toiled."

—William Shakespeare

First published in 2013 by Zenith Press, an imprint of MBI Publishing Company, 400 First Avenue North, Suite 400, Minneapolis, MN 55401 USA

Zenith Press titles are also available at discounts in bulk quantity for industrial or sales-promotional use. For details write to Special Sales Manager at MBI Publishing Company, 400 First Avenue North, Suite 400, Minneapolis, MN 55401 USA.

To find out more about our books, join us online at www.zenithpress.com.

Library of Congress Cataloging-in-Publication Data

Girardi, Robert I.
  The Civil War generals : comrades, peers, rivals—in their own words / Robert I. Girardi
      pages cm
  Includes bibliographical references.
  ISBN 978-0-7603-4516-0 (hardback)
  1. Generals--United States--Biography. 2. Generals--Confederate States of America--Biography. 3. Generals--United States--Quotations. 4. Generals--Confederate States of America--Quotations. 5. United States. Army--Biography. 6. Confederate States of America. Army--Biography. 7. United States--History--Civil War, 1861-1865--Biography. I. Title.
  E467.G526 2013
  355.0092'2--dc23
  [B]
                        2013020315

Editors: Scott Pearson and Madeleine Vasaly
Art Director: Rebecca Pagel
Designer: Kim Winscher
Cover Designer: Kent Jensen, knail

References throughout this book indicate the individual to whom a quotation is attributed and the source in which it appears. The quoted individual is not necessarily the author of the source work.

On the cover: *Prominent Union and Confederate Generals and Statesmen as they Appeared during the Great Civil War, 1861–5*, Kurz & Allison, Chicago, 1876./LOC

Printed in the United States of America
10 9 8 7 6 5 4 3 2 1

CONTENTS

INTRODUCTION

The Civil War was the great American epic, a tragic conflict, full of high drama and intrigue. Though North and South shared a common heritage and history, their outlook on the future had grown progressively disparate. As the conflict escalated over the issues of slavery and its expansion into the territories, compromise became less viable. The political process ultimately broke down when Abraham Lincoln was elected president, despite not appearing on the ballot in a single southern state and with only a plurality of the popular vote in a four-way contest. The election of Lincoln was the catalyst for seven states to secede from the Union and form the Confederate States of America. Just six weeks after Lincoln was inaugurated, war broke out in Charleston Harbor, with the bombardment and surrender of Fort Sumter.

Millions of men fought in the war, but only a handful of these actually rose to command. At the beginning of the war, the United States Army consisted of approximately 16,367 soldiers and officers, comprising ten infantry regiments, five cavalry regiments, and four artillery regiments. Of the 1,108 officers, there were only five generals—one major general and four brigadier generals—with an average age of seventy years old. Major General Winfield Scott was seventy-five, suffered from narcolepsy, and was so fat he had to be hoisted into the saddle. John Wool was seventy-seven, David Twiggs seventy-one, and William S. Harney was, by comparison, a spry sixty. Joseph E. Johnston, at fifty-four, was just a kid. The officer corps was comprised of both Northern and Southern men. Of the 270 from the South, 202 resigned to fight for the Confederacy. Additionally, fifty men of Northern birth, or from the border states, joined the Southern cause. Some others resigned, and the balance remained loyal to the Union.

By the end of the war, more than a thousand men (not counting those of brevet rank) served as generals, leading the brigades, divisions, corps, and armies of the North and South. But none of those men had any experience leading large bodies of men in combat. The pre-Civil War army was divided, with most regiments serving only in detachments, scattered between the coastal fortifications, frontier forts, and recruiting and staff posts. Among the high command, none had ever commanded a full regiment; most had commanded little more than a company-sized unit. Aware of this deficiency, the Confederacy's Richard S. Ewell wondered why he was elevated to the rank of lieutenant general. Ewell, a veteran of the old army, explained that in his years in the cavalry, fighting Indians on the Plains, he had learned everything about commanding fifty United States dragoons and had forgotten everything else.

None of these men had practical experience of the kind that would be necessary in the war. From a theoretical standpoint, they were not much better off. The United States Military Academy at West Point did not teach tactics and troop management in its mandatory curriculum. This meant that Civil War generals would have to learn on the job—and it meant the men they commanded would pay with blood until they did. This professional deficiency was recognized by some, who had supplemented their formal training and made their reputations by observing foreign wars or engaging in studying and translating tactical and training manuals. "Naturally the West Point officers were placed at the head of the army in the beginning, as they were the only persons supposed from their education and experience, to have much military knowledge," wrote John Pope. According to Benjamin F. Butler, a Democratic politician who rose to the rank of major general of volunteers and commanded an army, "[W]ith the exception of the Mexican [War] veterans, there were no West Pointers at the breaking out of the war who had had any experience in the field . . . It was assumed that West Point officers knew the whole art of war and were ready-made generals. A few—but not too many—of those officers read military books."

It was not always the best men who became generals—often it was the best available or the best connected. They were brilliant and amateurish, decisive and bumbling, capable and jealous, ambitious and cowardly. Some were promoted from the old army; the balance came from the general populace and included former soldiers, politicians, teachers, lawyers, engineers, inventors, businessmen, alcoholics, thieves, and some who were failures in every other endeavor. Some were promoted for strictly political purposes, and some, like Alexander Schimmelfennig, because of their nationality. The men who commanded Civil War armies were a mixed lot to say the least.

In any event, once placed in command, these men held responsibility for the outcome of the conflict and the lives and well-being of the men serving under them. Most of them appreciated this responsibility, but because so many generals were promoted beyond their capacity, it was not surprising that some of them were not regarded highly. When President Abraham Lincoln learned on March 3, 1863, that the Confederate raider John Singleton Mosby had captured Brig. Gen. Edwin Stoughton and fifty-eight horses, Lincoln professed more concern for the loss of the horses. "I can make brigadier generals," he said, "but I can't make horses."

Civil War armies were composed predominantly of volunteers. This was true both of the rank and file and the officers who led them. Leadership was of paramount importance. Civil War soldiers would follow a leader; they were less inclined to go forward while their generals remained in the rear. Thus, many generals exposed themselves under fire. For example, at Gettysburg, when cautioned that he was putting his life in jeopardy, Maj. Gen. Winfield Scott Hancock told his men that there were times when the life of a corps commander does not count. Men were more likely to go where they were led than where they were bidden.

One of the compelling characteristics of the Civil War is the fact that many of the officers on both sides were familiar with one another. Many of the leaders shared a background of similar education, religious values, and social or even family ties. In many instances, Civil War generals had a long acquaintance, either at the U.S. Military Academy at West Point or comparable institutions such as Virginia Military Institute (VMI) and the Citadel, in South Carolina. Others were comrades in arms against the Seminoles in Florida or had served

Carte de visite featuring famous Union generals killed during the war.

together in Mexico, on the Plains, or in Texas against various Indian tribes. The tedium of frontier duty, mixed with slow promotion and the high drama of impending sectional conflict, presented a large canvas upon which to draw the measure of one another. Like a large, dysfunctional family, these officers lived and worked together, sharing a multitude of trials and dangers, but they were not at all harmonious. Petty jealousies and bitter rivalries that germinated in this environment had long-lasting implications.

This makes the Civil War a fascinating study of interpersonal relationships. Character traits and flaws, bad habits, scandalous behavior, weaknesses as well as strengths, all were common knowledge in the old army. Civil War generals were thus often able to base their tactical considerations on intimate knowledge of the personality of their new opponents. These insights, however, could be just as problematic among officers who were supposed to be on the same side. Generals now in positions of authority had the ability to materially affect the careers of their peers: advancing pets or squelching (if not destroying) their rivals. There are numerous examples of such behavior in the pages of Civil War history. Ulysses S. Grant and Philip H. Sheridan were among the most ruthless practitioners of this policy.

Some generals were too proud, or too vain, to willingly subordinate themselves to officers whom they had previously ranked, or whom they personally disdained. The perceived unfairness of the promotion system took precedence in their minds over cause and country. Confederate General Joseph E. Johnston feuded with President Jefferson Davis over just such an issue. On the Federal side, Maj. Gen. John C. Fremont resigned his commission rather than serve under Maj. Gen. John Pope, whom he had previously commanded, and Fremont never got another command. This selfish rank discord exhibited itself even on the battlefield. According to Ulysses S. Grant, "The worst excuse a soldier can make for declining service is that he once ranked the commander he is ordered to report to."

As a result of their previous relationships, the Civil War generals were able to form snap judgments about one another that were widely accepted as gospel. For example, in the spring of 1862, when Henry W. Halleck wired George B. McClellan after the capture of Fort Donelson that Ulysses S. Grant had resumed his former bad habits, he knew that McClellan would understand him—Grant was a drunk and had resumed drinking. Braxton Bragg's irascibility was legendary, he argued with everyone including himself; testy Gen. George Gordon Meade was a "damned, goggle-eyed old snapping turtle"; Joe Hooker would lose his nerve under pressure, he always did when playing poker; and John Pope was a braggart and a liar, all the Popes were. General Sam Sturgis pulled no punches expressing his opinion of Pope, declaring, "I don't care a pinch of owl dung for John Pope."

When a new enemy commander was appointed, a general, Union or Confederate, would seek out classmates or those who had served with the newly appointed adversary to find out about him. Thus William T. Sherman quizzed John M. Schofield at Atlanta to learn that John Bell Hood was "bold to the point of rashness." James Longstreet warned that "That man Grant will fight us every day and every hour until the end of this war." And a dubious Confederate officer was advised that far from being cautious, Robert E. Lee's very name might be audacity.

Rival generals were like schoolboys at times, sending each other messages through the lines, safeguarding each other's wives and properties, playfully taunting each other, or saluting each other on the battlefield like knights errant. In 1864, during a bloody campaign in the Shenandoah, George A. Custer rode out in front of his men, took off his plumed hat and made an exaggerated sweeping bow to the Confederate commander, Thomas L. Rosser. The two

Carte de visite featuring Confederate generals killed during the war.

cavaliers had been West Point classmates and friends. Gouverneur K. Warren taunted Ambrose Powell Hill after delivering a bloody repulse to Hill at Bristoe Station. Warren was married to Hill's erstwhile sweetheart. Louis A. Armistead was mortally wounded at Gettysburg, but before he died he sent a message to his close friend, Winfield Scott Hancock, whose men were responsible for the wound. Hancock was also seriously wounded. First Lady Mary Todd Lincoln was visited in the White House by her sister-in-law, the widow of Confederate

Gen. Benjamin Hardin Helm, who was killed at Chickamauga. Experiences and relationships such as these add depth to the story of the generals' relationships to one another.

Union Major General John Gibbon wrote, "In fighting battles, there is but one object in view—to beat the enemy. In writing of them . . . the writers are induced to turn their 'guns' upon their own friends and tell what might have resulted if others had acted differently or worked as assiduously as themselves." This is very true in the aftermath of the war, when many of the generals rehashed the conflict with ink, attempting to redeem tarnished reputations. Some of these memoirs devolve into meticulous rehashing of battles, weighing and placing blame, and justifying failure. For example, Joseph E. Johnston's *Narrative of Military Operations* and John Bell Hood's *Advance and Retreat* are hundreds of pages long and filled with dissections of each other's actions, statements, and failings.

In the pages that follow, the generals will speak out about each other, rendering their impressions of their colleagues. Although most of the quotes are from generals, in some instances I have allowed staff officers and selected others to speak out as well. The multitude of opinions rendered here varies as much as the men who voiced them. Some are self-serving, some vindictive; some flattering, some damning. Ben Butler, for example, spares no effort to denigrate West Point generals. Others, like William F. Smith, cannot help to place their own misfortune, fairly or not, upon the shoulders of others. David S. Stanley is especially bitter when referring to William T. Sherman. David Hunter is reviled by his Confederate adversaries for his destructive campaign in the Shenandoah Valley.

Many of the quotes presented are the opinions of staff officers. A general's staff was his military family; they ate, slept, fought, drank, and bled together. General Charles F. Smith stated, "It is not possible for a general to always see with his own eyes, or be in two places at the same time: hence the device of a staff. . . . Staff-officers should be men of aptitude and experience, not figureheads or mere pretty men . . ."* The insights of staff officers are often far more revealing than the frankest writings of a brother general. Because of their varied duties, staff officers observed close hand many of the generals in the heat of battle and in the aftermath of camp. Thus they saw generals leading troops in battle, cowering behind trees, or drinking themselves into a stupor. Staff officers tended to speak more freely about generals than other generals did and their wartime observations provide some of the most biting and insightful observations we have. Some of the more prominent staff officers quoted here are G. Moxley Sorrel, Henry Kyd Douglas, Horace Porter, Theodore Lyman, Thomas J. Goree, and the British observer, Col. Arthur J. L. Fremantle, of Her Majesty's Coldstream Guards.

Also included are quotes from and pertaining to various naval commanders. The rank of admiral in the navy has parallel standing with army generals and so, under this loophole I chose to include these as well. Besides, some of the opinions expressed are very telling and add to our glimpse into the character of our Civil War commanders.

Several army war correspondents were also consulted. Among the more prominent are Sylvanus Cadwallader and Charles Page. These men were if

Quoted in Lew Wallace: An Autobiography, *1:345*

nothing else, very opinionated, and tended to safeguard the reputations of the generals they admired at the expense of others. Cadwallader can be especially pernicious in his judgments. Nonetheless, these opinions have come down to us through the years as eyewitness testimony of the nature of the generals of the war. The opinions of these men shaped the public perception of who those generals were to the Civil War generation.

In addition to those previously mentioned, I have also included the opinions of several select government officials, including Assistant Secretary of War Charles A. Dana; Secretary of the Navy Gideon Welles; President Lincoln's secretaries, John Nicolay and John Hay; and the rebel war clerk, John B. Jones. I have also allowed the commanders in chief, Abraham Lincoln and Jefferson Davis, to have their say.

All of them are windows to the past, allowing us to view these commanders in the eyes of their peers. Their biases are telling—often revealing more about the source than the target. This is not meant to disparage these writings; even the most vitriolic description of a rival has some basis in truth, and conflicting perceptions can provide a more nuanced, if murkier, sense of the personality of these generals. For that reason, I have included multiple quotes about generals where available. Predictably, those who garnered the most press were those who were particularly prominent or controversial. Thus there are numerous opinions voiced about George B. McClellan, Joseph Hooker, Ulysses S. Grant, Robert E. Lee, Stonewall Jackson, George Gordon Meade, and William T. Sherman, among others.

Surprisingly, and somewhat disappointingly, there is silence from a number of the great leaders. Some, like Stonewall Jackson and Albert Sidney Johnston, were killed in action, and thus left no memoirs; others, like Robert E. Lee, studiously avoided leaving a written record or saying anything negative about their subordinates. Braxton Bragg and Nathan B. Forrest give us nothing. There is actually a surprising dearth of commentary about the Confederate generals, hence the almost two-to-one disparity represented in this work. On the Federal side, Ulysses S. Grant and William T. Sherman both left lengthy memoirs, but they rarely praise or criticize others. Grant especially is reticent, except insofar as he mentions someone he wronged or hurt in some way; for example, he goes out of his way to praise Gouverneur K. Warren and then condemns him in the same breath. It was Grant, using Philip H. Sheridan as his tool, who wrecked Warren's career at the height of his triumph at the Battle of Five Forks. Although we hear from George B. McClellan, Philip H. Sheridan, and Benjamin Butler, there is a virtual silence from other army commanders. William S. Rosecrans, Don Carlos Buell, and George H. Thomas are mute. One wonders what delightful memoirs would have come from the pen of Joseph Hooker, Ambrose E. Burnside, Nathaniel P. Banks, or Daniel Sickles, but we will never know.

In a work of this sort, some limitations are necessary lest the work collapse under its own weight. Space and time prohibit examining in detail the relationships between the various generals and their staffs, and much of the underlying story in each relationship. The quotes themselves are lifted out from the larger context of whatever memoir or papers they appeared in. The reader should keep these things in mind, and I strongly encourage anyone seeking to learn more to examine the original material in its entirety. I have not consulted the numerous treasure troves of personal papers of these generals, but have limited my selections to those accounts readily available to the general public.

I have omitted opinions voiced by junior officers not attached to headquarters and the rank and file in general. Many such opinions exist and are worth reading and knowing, but they are beyond the scope of this work. I have chosen to minimize opinions which are mere eulogies or hero-worshipping idolatries of the person mentioned. Also, I have not included laudatory comments meant only to secure promotion or advancement for the subject. Thus the *Official Records* have not been extensively consulted for the purpose of this book. Rather, I have endeavored to find opinions that actually convey a sense of who the man referred to was, both positively and negatively. I also sought to include quotes of substance and have mostly omitted single line summations, attesting to one's bravery, drunkenness, or other characteristics. The purpose has been to bring insight into the personalities of Civil War generals.

Because the comments were written over a wide span of time, both ante and post-bellum, I have not included the rank of the writers and the subjects as these changed frequently over the course of the war. Additionally the opinions of some of the writers changed over time. I have endeavored to present the opinions as accurately as possible within these confines. It would have required extensive annotation to remedy this entirely, which was both beyond the intent and purpose of this work.

In addition to the opinions about one another, I have also included one section that describes how Civil War generals viewed their profession; i.e., quotations about generalship or the qualities that made for successful generalship. Further details appear in the appendices. I have also included an appendix of the contributors, being a list of those quoted with a brief description of their official roles and capacity. An additional appendix features a partial list of Civil War battles along with the names of people from this book who fought at them.

Though many who read and study the Civil War tend to revere some generals over others, and admire the monuments erected in their memory, we should never forget that they were mortal men, with talents and flaws, honor and prejudice. In no way does this diminish their service and sacrifice. Instead, their achievements stand out in greater luster, for they were able to rise above their shortcomings. Commanding Civil War armies was a difficult task under the best of circumstances. No officer who rose to the rank of general had ever commanded so many men before. Generals learned their trade on the job, some sacrificing their lives in the process—123 generals died in the war, 78 Confederates and 45 Union, including 2 army commanders, Albert S. Johnston and James B. McPherson, and a variety of corps commanders. Despite the battle of words presented here, one should recall the wisdom of Confederate Gen. John B. Gordon who wrote, "It is easier to criticize a general, than to command an army."

Prominent Union and Confederate Generals and Statesmen as they Appeared during the Great Civil War, 1861–5, *Kurz & Allison, Chicago, 1876.*

ON GENERALSHIP

"If a general can only inspire his men with the feeling that he knows what he is about, he will have good fighters. He can put them anywhere on any field, and in the face of any fire!" —James Longstreet, *Battles and Leaders*, 5:689

"Our generals should, undoubtedly, do more, but our people should certainly expect less." —John Beatty, *The Citizen Soldier*, p. 189

"Skillful generalship and good fighting are the jewels of war. These concurring are difficult to overcome; and these, not numbers, must determine the battle." —Frank Haskell, *Haskell of Gettysburg*, p. 112

"He who does *something* at the head of one Regiment, will eclipse him who does *nothing* at the head of a hundred." —Abraham Lincoln, *Lincoln on War*, p. 123

"A single life, even that of a distinguished general, in time of war is of slight consequence to the general result . . ." —Josiah M. Favill, *The Diary of a Young Officer*, p. 248

"It is well known that the personal character of a general officer in moments of difficulty has a powerful influence upon the result." —Andrew A. Humphreys, *The Virginia Campaign*, p. 4

"It has been said that one bad general is better than two good ones, and the saying is true if taken to mean no more than that an army is better directed by a single mind, though inferior, than by two superior ones at variance and cross-purposes with each other." —Abraham Lincoln, *Speeches and Writings*, p. 295

"In war men show how vastly they differ in character and the skillful commander uses his troops in accordance with such characteristics." —John Gibbon, *Personal Recollections of the Civil War*, p. 292

"A commander may be a great captain compared with his military predecessors, and yet some of his operations be regarded as very faulty by more modern commanders." —John M. Schofield, *Forty-Six Years in the Army*, p. 357

"The spirit of obedience, as distinguished from its letter, consists in faithfully forwarding the general object to which the officer's particular command is contributing." —Alfred Thayer Mahan, *Mahan on Naval Warfare*, p. 125

"It does not look like good generalship to lose a battle and a cause and then lay the responsibility upon others." —James Longstreet, *From Manassas to Appomattox*, p. 405

"For the success of war, offense is better than defense; and in contemplating this or any other military measure, let there be dismissed at once, as preposterous, the hope that war can be carried on without some one being hurt ..." —Alfred Thayer Mahan, *Mahan on Naval Warfare*, p. 340–341

"There is a curious jealousy in our army, a grasping after power which does not rightly belong to them, which must be owing to our new-fledged generals not knowing the exact duties and powers of their position, and consequently being afraid that they will not get all they are entitled to ..." —Charles S. Wainwright, *A Diary of Battle*, p. 262

"The chief duties of a general to his command may be classified—the enforcement of discipline—tactical instruction—care of the health of his men—and they are all important because tending to efficiency, the measure of which is the exact measure of his own efficiency." —Charles F. Smith, in *Lew Wallace: An Autobiography*, 1:344

"So much of the efficiency of troops depends upon the character of those who command them, that it behooves a government to take every means to secure the best officers possible." —William B. Hazen, *A Narrative of Military Service*, p. 384

"The character of a leader is a large factor in the game of war ..." —William T. Sherman, *Battles and Leaders*, p. 4, 253

"One of the most difficult lessons a commander has to learn is when to offer or accept battle, and when to refrain or decline—that is, to be complete master of his own natural combativeness." —John M. Schofield, *Forty-Six Years in the Army*, p. 362

"It is a striking proof of the evil effect of war upon the minds and passions of men, not only of those who are engaged in it, but even more upon those who see it from a distance, that commanders are often severely condemned for prudent care of the lives of men under their command, who have no choice but to march blindly to death when ordered, while the idiotic sacrifice of the bravest and noblest of patriotic soldiers is loudly applauded as a grand exhibition of 'gallantry' in action." —John M. Schofield, *Forty-Six Years in the Army*, p. 182

"The great commander is he who makes his antagonist keep step with him." —D. H. Hill, *Battles and Leaders*, 3:651

"I think our generals betray in some instances total ignorance of human nature. They fail to appeal to the emotions or passions of their men." —Emory Upton, *Life and Letters*, p. 80

"War, once declared, must be waged offensively, aggressively. The enemy must not be fended off, but smitten down." —Alfred Thayer Mahan, *Mahan on Naval Warfare*, p. 128

"In the movement of numerous bodies of troops errors and blunders will naturally be made, even with the best digested plan; they are of frequent occurrence, and ever will be, either emanating from the commander himself (for 'he who never made a mistake never made war'), or a staff officer misunderstanding the orders he may receive, or through an inferior officer taking upon himself an undue responsibility. Nor is it desirable that it should be otherwise; for errors committed, which are always quickly detected, afford the practical—the best of all lessons." —Arthur William Alsager Pollock, *The United Service Magazine*, 98:1, p. 184

"With the exception of the Mexican [War] veterans, there were no West Pointers at the breaking out of the war who had had any experience in the field . . . It was assumed that West Point officers knew the whole art of war and were ready-made generals. A few—but not too many—of those officers read military books." —Ben Butler, *Butler's Book*, p. 863

"Now a West Pointer if he graduated very high never was employed in the army in managing troops until our war. He was simply assigned to public works . . ." —Ben Butler, *Butler's Book*, 2:863

"I am very sorry to say I have seen but little generalship during the campaign. Some of our corps commanders are not fit to be corporals. Lazy and indolent,

The high command of the Army of the Potomac—Grant, Meade, and the corps commanders—in the autumn of 1864.

they will not even ride along their lines; yet, without hesitancy, they will order us to attack the enemy, no matter what their position or numbers." —Emory Upton, *Life and Letters*, p. 109

"Men will fight very well under a commander they do not love provided they have confidence in his ability to command." —John Gibbon, *Personal Recollections of the Civil War*, p. 122

"It is so easy to fight battles on paper, so different from fighting them successfully on the ground." —John Gibbon, *Recollections of the Civil War*, p. 272

"The war is over, but the fighting has just begun." —John Gibbon, *Recollections of the Civil War*, p. 386

"An army commander, to be successful in the field, must be as near a despot as the institutions of his country will permit." —John Gibbon, *Recollections of the Civil War*, p. 417

"I am disgusted with the generalship displayed. Our men have, in many instances, been foolishly and wantonly sacrificed." —Emory Upton, *Life and Letters*, p.108

"The desire for higher command, greater power, and more unrestrained authority exhibits ambition inconsistent with due military subordination and good citizenship. It is a dangerous ambition in a republic." —John M. Schofield, *Forty-Six Years in the Army*, p. 480

"It sometimes takes a civilian to 'teach a soldier his place' in the government of a republic." —John M. Schofield, *Forty-Six Years in the Army*, p. 7

"Great wrongs as well as great evils were also done in the appointment of officers, more especially General officers" —John Gibbon, *Recollections of the Civil War*, p. 420

"But military brains—a natural aptitude for arms and the best culture West Point can give him—that is what an army commander needs …" —James F. Rusling, *Men and Things I Saw*, p. 107

"A general who has gained the hearts of his soldiers has only to plan well and execute well to bring abundant success …" —Oliver O. Howard, *Autobiography*, p. 167

"Naturally the West Point officers were placed at the head of the army in the beginning, as they were the only persons supposed from their education and experience, to have much military knowledge" —John Pope, *Military Memoirs*, p. 210

Carte de visite depicting Gen. Robert E. Lee and other Confederate generals in Virginia in 1864.

"I am thoroughly disgusted with our generals + think we had better give up the struggle at once unless we can have a radical change. You have no idea of the imbecility of management both in action + out of it." —Francis C. Barlow, *Fear was not in Him*, p. xxxii

"The capacity of preserving one's presence of mind in action is among the highest attributes of an efficient commander or subordinate officer ..." —Jubal A. Early, *Narrative of the War Between the States*, p. 14

"I know there is an awful amount of jealousy among our leading generals. But hardly think it can go so far; at the same time, it is equally hard to suppose they are actual fools." —Charles Wainwright, *A Diary of Battle*, p. 57

"In war there is a critical instant—a night—perhaps only a half hour, when everything culminates. He is the military genius who recognizes this instant and acts upon it . . . there is thus good reason why great soldiers should be so rare. . . . A great soldier must have, in addition to all usual traits of intellect, a courage unmoved by the greatest danger, and cool under every emergency, and the quickness of lightning, not only in conceiving, but in enforcing an order . . ." —Theodore Lyman, *Meade's Headquarters*, p. 162–163

"It did not occur to me that wounds and death, even of the commanding general himself, were of any consequence except as they might influence the progress and final result of the battle. This is the feeling that must dominate the action of every successful commander." —John M. Schofield, *Forty-Six Years in the Army*, p. 364

"Officers of all grades and of the highest character fall into the error of memory which modifies facts according to one's wish and feeling." —Jacob Cox, *Reminiscences*, 2:286

"How strangely stupid our generals and Government have been! How slow to learn even from the enemy!" —Charles Francis Adams Jr., *A Cycle of Adams Letters*, 2:7

"We do not need geniuses; we have had enough of brilliant generals; and give us in the due course of promotion an honest, faithful, common-sensed and hard-fighting soldier, not stupid, and we feel sure of success." —Charles Francis Adams Jr., *A Cycle of Adams Letters*, 2:14

"It requires a deal of figuring to keep the '*political*' colonels out of the way of these Regular Army gentlemen. I grant there is an advantage in favor of the man who has made the art of war his study, but that is only the advantage of theory. And where that theory has never had any better opportunity to develop into practical knowledge than the lazy limited routine furnished by the little standing army of this Republic, I must say that the advantage is not very great over a thorough, intelligent, practical business man." —Alvin C. Voris, *A Citizen-Soldier's Civil War*, p. 128

"The worst excuse a soldier can make for declining service is that he once ranked the commander he is ordered to report to." —Ulysses S. Grant, *Battles and Leaders*, 4:99

"The military profession is made up of trivialities and the enforcement of trivial things is fully justified by the results produced—obedience to orders, discipline and military efficiency." —John Gibbon, *Recollections of the Civil War*, p. 38

"No general who is influenced by a council of war is fit to command an army." —David Hunter Strother, *A Virginia Yankee*, p. 206

"The best material for commanders in this civil strife may have never seen West Point. There is something in the remark that a good general is 'born to command.' We have experienced that some of our best-educated officers have no faculty to govern, control, and direct an army in offensive warfare." —Gideon Welles, *Diary*, 1:85

"All war is destructive of human life, and that which is most destructive is soonest ended. The general who takes great risks wins great victories or suffers disastrous defeat. That is the general for the weaker party." —William C. Oates, *The War Between the Union and the Confederacy*, p. 169

"The President is too easy with . . . do nothing Officers . . . a General or Admiral may defeat the end of an entire campaign by his blunders & neglect, and perhaps be retained in his command, at most only relieved of his command with full pay & allowances, and nothing under Heaven to do but eat, sleep & enjoy himself at the expense of the Country. This is all wrong." —Alvin C. Voris, *A Citizen-Soldier's Civil War*, p. 140

"As the preacher knows his bible, as the lawyer knows his statutes, every general should know the regulations and articles of war. . . . In battle, a general's duties . . . are—first to fight, second, to fight to best advantage." —Charles F. Smith, in *Lew Wallace: An Autobiography*, 1:344

"An individual in an obscure position may give his life, indeed, to the public cause; but he hazards no more. He scarcely at all brings the cause itself into danger. This cannot be said of a commander; and I hold it a crime in any one to seek, and it may be even to accept, a position involving vast interests without a realizing sense of ability and suitable preparation for it." —Ethan Allen Hitchcock, *Fifty Years in Camp and Field*, p. 435

"The first quality of a good soldier is obedience and discipline. The first quality of a good officer is a sense of the indispensible need of order, and of discipline as the condition of order." —William B. Hazen, *Narrative*, p. 390

"Graduation at West Point does not make one a good general. A man must have natural aptitude or adaptability, or he will not succeed." —William C. Oates, *The War Between the Union and the Confederacy*, p. 302

"No commander of any army does his whole duty who simply gives orders, however well considered. He should *supervise their execution*, in person or by staff officers, constantly, day & night, so that if the machine balks at any point he may be most promptly informed & may most promptly start it to work." —E. P. Alexander, *Military Memoirs of a Confederate*, p. 110

"The sight of a general officer, let alone the privilege of speaking to one, was an event to be recounted to one's friends. In those days the title of general was not so familiar as to be encountered on every hotel register." —George A. Custer, *Battles and Leaders*, 6:15

"No general ever won a permanent fame who was wanting in these grand elements of success, knowledge of his own and his enemy's condition, and personal superintendence of operations on the field." —D. H. Hill, *Battles and Leaders*, 6:642

"If the Republic goes down in blood and ruin, let its obituary be written thus: 'Died of West Point.'" —James A. Garfield, *The Wild Life of the Army*, p. 153

"Without the discipline, organization, and tactics of the old army, the new army, generals and all, would be but a loose mob." —Ethan Allen Hitchcock, *Fifty Years in Camp and Field*, p. 322

"But enough about Generals, that I know does not interest you." —William Dorsey Pender, *One of Lee's Best Men*, p. 57

FAMOUS UNION COMMANDERS OF THE CIVIL WAR, 1861-'65.

Postwar lithograph of prominent Union generals. Premium for The Pivotal
Battle of the Civil War.

UNION GENERALS

JACOB AMMEN
Brigadier general. West Point (1831). Colonel of 24th Ohio Infantry. Served in the western theater, in administrative capacity.

"He is somewhat superstitious. He never likes to see the moon through brush. He is to some extent a believer in dreams. . . . He is a strange combination of simplicity and wisdom, full of good stories, and tells them against himself with a great deal more pleasure than any others. . . . He talks incessantly; his narratives abound in episode, parenthesis, switches, side-cuts, and before he gets through, one will conclude a dozen times that he has forgotten the tale he entered upon, but he never does. . . . After all I have said about General Ammen, it is hardly necessary to remark that he does most of the talking." —John Beatty, *The Citizen Soldier*, p. 156, 158

"When on duty, General Ammen was a stern, unbending disciplinarian. When off duty he was ever among his men, listening to their complaints and supplying their wants. No officer in the field was more beloved by the soldiers, and the name 'Uncle Jake Ammen' will ever be held in grateful remembrance by thousands of brave men who had the honor to serve under him." —Whitelaw Reid, *Ohio in the War*, 1:903

ROBERT ANDERSON

Brevet major general. West Point (1825).
Veteran of Black Hawk, Seminole and Mexican
wars. Commanded Fort Sumter. Commander
of Union forces in Kentucky, 1861.

"Of all my acquaintances among men, Anderson
had the fewest vices of any one of them. In fact,
I doubt if he had any quality which the world
ordinarily denominates *a vice* ... In all things
he was rigorously temperate and moderate,
and he was as honest and conscientious as it is
possible for a man to be. He was a pattern of
order and method, and worked out his plans
slowly. He always had a reason for what he did,
and generally he proclaimed his reasons, and his
frankness sometimes rubbed me *contre poil.*"
—Erasmus Keyes, *Fifty Years' Observations*, p. 367–368

"Anderson ... had many ties and associations which bound him to the South.
He performed his part like the true soldier and man of the finest sense of honor
that he was ..." —Jefferson Davis, *Rise and Fall*, 1:216

GEORGE L. ANDREWS   Brevet major

general, West Point (1851). Brigade commander,
Army of Virginia. Chief of staff to Nathaniel P. Banks
in Louisiana.

"Gen'l Andrews I like very much & is really doing the right
thing & is very strict, has a school of the officers himself so
that the drill shall be uniform in the Corps, putting him
at the head instead of Ullman is a change for the better."
—Cyrus Hamlin, *Cyrus Hamlin's Civil War*, p. 47

ALEXANDER S. ASBOTH   Brigadier general. Hungarian

revolutionary. Chief of staff to John C. Fremont in 1861.

"General Asboth was a tall, spare, handsome man, with a gray mustache
and a fierce look. He was an educated soldier, of unquestioned courage, but
the responsibilities of outpost duty bore rather heavily on him, and he kept
all hands in a state of constant worry in anticipation of imaginary attacks.
His ideas of discipline were not very rigid either ..." —Philip H. Sheridan,
Memoirs, 1:168

WILLIAM WOODS AVERILL Brigadier general. West
Point (1855). Served on the Plains. Commanded cavalry division in Army
of the Potomac.

"It is curious to notice the nicknames that get applied to men in the corps
and how obstinately they cling to the person to whom they are applied . . . In
our class there is Swell Averill, very appropriate too for you can not name a
subject with which he is not acquainted or tell a story he cannot double, with
an AIR, too." —Cyrus B. Comstock, *Diary*, p. 162

ROMEYN B. AYRES Major general.
West Point (1847). Mexican War veteran. Brigade and
division commander, Army of the Potomac.

"Ayres . . . bluff and gruff at questions about the lateness of
his column; twitching his mustache in lieu of words, the
sniff of his nostrils smelling the battle not very much afar;
sound of heart, solid of force, all the manly and military
qualities ready in reserve—the typical old soldier." —Joshua
Lawrence Chamberlain, *Passing of the Armies*, p. 122

EDWARD BAKER Major general. Lawyer.
Black Hawk and Mexican War veteran. U.S. Senator and
friend of Abraham Lincoln. Killed at Ball's Bluff, 1861.

"Baker's moral and physical courage was so great as almost
to entitle him to be called intrepid, and yet in social life,
he was the easiest and most amiable of men. He possessed
the gift of eloquence to an extraordinary degree, and his
perceptions were quick." —Erasmus Keyes, *Fifty Years'
Observations*, p. 302

NATHANIEL P. BANKS Major general. Massachusetts
Congressman and governor. Commanded Union volunteers in the
Shenandoah, 1862 and captured Port Hudson, Louisiana, 1863.
Commanded Red River Expedition, 1864.

"Banks has some ready qualities for civil administration, and if not employed
in the field or active military operations, will be likely to acquit himself
respectably as a provisional or military governor. He has not the energy, power,
ability of Butler, nor, though of loose and fluctuating principles, will he be so
reckless and unscrupulous." —Gideon Welles, *Diary*, 1:210

"With all General Banks' faults, he had some striking good qualities. He was a gentleman in his manners . . . He looked well in his uniform, and kept himself always scrupulously neat, though rather theatrical in his style of gloves and boots. With a better surrounding he would have had more success as a general. He had not much force of character, and lacked nerve in time of danger . . . Banks always preferred to be considered a soldier rather than a statesman. He never had sufficient military force to properly occupy the country under his immediate command, much less to make expeditions into hostile regions." —David Dixon Porter, *Naval History of the Civil War*, p. 547

"It is plain from Admiral Porter's account that Banks is no general, has no military capacity, is wholly unfit for the position assigned him. He has never exhibited military capacity . . . Banks has much of the demagogue, is superficially smart, has volubility and a smack of party management . . . Banks is not only no general, but he is not much of a statesman. He is something of a politician, and a party man of his own stamp, and for his own advancement, but is not true and reliable." —Gideon Welles, *Diary*, 2:18

"General Banks was a fine representative of the higher order of Yankee . . . His personal graces were equaled by his energy, and his ability was considerable." —George A. Townsend, *Campaigns of a Non-Combatant*, p. 233

"It is well known that Banks always saw things with very largely magnifying glasses when 'Stonewall' Jackson was about." —Jubal A. Early, *Narrative of the War Between the States*, p. 156

FRANCIS C. BARLOW   Major general. New York lawyer. Lieutenant colonel of the 61st New York. Brigade and division commander, Army of the Potomac.

"He looked like a highly independent mounted newsboy; he was attired in a flannel checked shirt; a threadbare pair of trousers, and an old blue kepi; from his waist hung a big cavalry saber; his features wore a familiar sarcastic smile . . . There, too, was General [David] Birney, also in checked flannel, but much more tippy than Barlow, and stout General [Winfield S.] Hancock, who always wears a clean *white* shirt (where he gets them nobody knows); and thither came steel-cold General Gibbon, the most American of Americans, with his sharp nose and up-and-down manner of telling the truth, no matter whom it hurts . . ." —Theodore Lyman, *Meade's Headquarters*, p. 107

"He was not at first sight an impressive looking officer. He was of medium height, of slight build, with a pallid countenance, and a weakish drawling voice. In his movements there was an appearance of loose jointedness and an absence of prim stiffness ... Francis C. Barlow was a great soldier. He was, in my judgment, fully equal for a corps commander. He knew the details of his business; he had the military instinct; and he was fearless." —Charles Augustus Fuller, *Personnel Recollections of the War of 1861*, p. 7

"It's pleasant and refreshing to meet a man like Barlow among the crowds of mediocrity which make up the mass of an army. Here's a man who goes into the army and in everything naturally recurs to first principles. The object of discipline is obedience; the end of fighting is victory, and he naturally and instinctively sweeps away all the forms, rules and traditions which ... in the hands of incompetent men, ultimately usurped the place of the ends they were calculated to secure ... I am more disposed to regard Barlow as a military genius than any man I have yet seen ..." —Charles Francis Adams Jr., *A Cycle of Adams Letters*, 2:167

"General Barlow was still a young man, but with his beardless, smooth face looked even much younger than he was. His men at first gazed at him wondering how such a boy could be put at the head of regiments of men. But they soon discovered him to be a strict disciplinarian, and one of the coolest and bravest in action. In both respects he was inclined to carry his virtues to excess." —Carl Schurz, *Reminiscences*, 3:7–8

JOHN G. BARNARD Brevet major general. West Point (1833). Chief engineer, Army of the Potomac.

"Gen. Barnard of the engineers; an ungainly, studious looking man, with a stoop in his shoulders. He is as deaf as a post, extremely ill-bred; vastly book learned and thoroughly unreliable. In fact, a time serving critic and a military pedant, only fit to write disquisitions. Here, he is simply in the way, and he is here, only (as Meade said afterwards) to "make another book" and to try and glean a little credit for himself." —Theodore Lyman, *Meade's Army*, p. 195

JOHN BEATTY Brigadier general. Ohio banker. Brigade commander, Army of the Cumberland.

"General Beatty was never absent, during his entire term of service, from any command to which he had been assigned ... He was thoroughly impressed with the duties and responsibilities of his position, and his soldierly reputation was stainless ... His power of endurance was wonderful. When occasion demanded he could perform the longest and most fatiguing marches without complaint, and seemingly without suffering the slightest inconvenience from want of food or sleep." —Whitelaw Reid, *Ohio in the War*, 1:926

HENRY W. BENHAM

Brevet major general. West Point (1837). Mexican War veteran. Chief engineer, Department of the Ohio until 1862. Commanded engineer brigade, Army of the Potomac, 1863–1865.

"I was very glad to hear General Sedgwick speak so highly of General Benham ... He said that he considered him the smartest man in the army, although he did not possess so much general information as some others ... Although I have got along very well with General Benham, I don't think I should like to be his adjutant-general permanently. He is not at all well posted in regard to office business, and keeps doing things which are irregular, and the blame of which, if any mischief should ensue, would fall upon the adjutant-general ... and from seeing General B. not disposed to stand up for his staff ... I feel somewhat anxious ... he is very incautious in what he says about others, and censures the acts and abilities and doings of other generals ... He is very ambitious, and very conceited ... He is unfortunately very quick-tempered, and pitches into officers without giving them the slightest chance to tell their side ... he is a man that I have no respect for at all. He loses his temper and becomes so violent that it is ludicrous to see him." —Stephen M. Weld, *War Diary*, p. 160, 172, 174, 180, 181

"Benham is to be made the scapegoat for all our misfortunes—and the last is the only item of news which gives us any satisfaction ... Everything here but honor has been sacrificed to the fussy incompetence of Benham, the unmilitary amiability of Hunter, and the misplaced philanthropy of Edward L. Pierce ..." —Charles Francis Adams Jr., *A Cycle of Adams Letters*, 1:160

"On Sunday there arrived General Benham, one of the dirtiest and most ramshackle parties I ever saw . . . You ought to see this 'Ginral.' He has the face and figure of Mr. Briggs and wears continually the expression of Mr. B. when his horse sat down at the band of music." —Theodore Lyman, *Meade's Headquarters*, p. 23, 241

DAVID B. BIRNEY

Major general. Lawyer and businessman. Brigade, division, and corps commander, Army of the Potomac.

"Birney was one who had many enemies, but, in my belief, we had few officers who could command 10,000 men as well as he. He was a pale, Puritanical figure, with a demeanor of unmovable coldness; only he would smile politely when you spoke to him. He was spare in person, with a thin face, light-blue eye, and sandy hair. As a General he took very good care of his Staff and saw they got due promotion. He was a man, too, who looked out for his own interests sharply and knew the mainsprings of military advancement. His unpopularity among some persons arose partly from his promotion . . . and partly from his cold covert manner . . . I always felt safe when he had the division; it was always well put in and safely handled." —Theodore Lyman, *Meade's Headquarters*, p. 266

"In person General Birney was a strikingly handsome man. He was tall, straight and lithe, and of the pure Saxon complexion. His face was remarkably intellectual. His manners were kind and courteous and his voice was as gentle as a woman . . . esteemed as a man by all who knew him, and honored by his country as one of her best and noblest soldiers." —Benjamin Butler, *Life of David Bell Birney*, p. 282

"General Birney is undoubtedly a loss to the army. He was a very good soldier, and very energetic in the performance of his duties. During the last campaign he had quite distinguished himself." —George G. Meade, *Life and Letters*, 2:235

FRANCIS P. BLAIR Major general.
Lawyer and politician. Brigade division, and corps commander, Army of the Tennessee.

"General Blair joined me at Milliken's bend . . . a full-fledged general, without having served in a lower grade. He commanded a division . . . I had known Blair in Missouri, where I had voted against him . . . when he ran for Congress. I knew him as a frank, positive, and generous man, true to his friends even to a fault, but always a leader. I dreaded his coming. I knew from experience that it was more difficult to command two generals desiring to be leaders, than it was to command one army . . . It affords me the greatest pleasure to record now my agreeable disappointment in respect to his character. There was no man braver than he, nor was there any who obeyed all orders . . . with more unquestioning alacrity. He was one man as a soldier, another as a politician."
—Ulysses S. Grant, *Battles and Leaders*, 3:537

"General F. P. Blair . . . has done good service in the field and in politics also. He was a fearless pioneer in the great cause of the Union and breasted the storm in stormy Missouri with a bold front . . . Frank is as bold in words as in deeds, fearless in his utterances as in his fights; is uncalculating—impolitic, it would be said—rash . . . but sincere and patriotic to the core."
—Gideon Welles, *Diary*, 1:405

"Frank Blair is about the same as an officer that he is as a politician. He is intelligent, prompt, determined, rather inclining to disorder, a poor disciplinarian, but a brave fighter." —Charles A. Dana, *Recollections*, p. 66

Major General Francis P. Blair Jr. and staff, 1864.

"He has abundant talent—quite enough to occupy all his time, without devoting any to temper. He is rising in military skill and usefulness. His recent appointment to command of a corps, by one so competent to judge as Gen. Sherman, proves this." —Abraham Lincoln, *Abraham Lincoln, Speeches and Writings*, p. 531

LOUIS BLENKER Brigadier general.
Bavarian officer and revolutionary. Brigade and division commander, Army of the Potomac.

"Blenker proved that a man can be a perfect stage-general and at the same time a very efficient soldier. He was a thoroughly brave man, an excellent organizer, and an efficient commander. The regiment he had formed was a model regiment ... While he amused his friends by his theatrical oddities as a type, he still enjoyed their sincere respect." —Carl Schurz, *Reminiscences*, 2:235–236

"He was in many respects an excellent soldier; had his command in excellent drill, was very fond of display, but did not, or could not, always restrain his men from plundering ..." —George B. McClellan, *McClellan's Own Story*, p. 138–139

JAMES G. BLUNT Major general. Doctor. Abolitionist and
Kansas Jayhawker. Commander, Army of the Frontier.

"Although I had at first esteemed General Blunt much more highly than he deserved ... I became satisfied that he was unfit in any respect for the command of a division of troops against a disciplined enemy. As was my plain duty, I suggested confidentially ... that he be assigned to the District of Kansas, where I permitted him to go, at his own request, to look after his personal interests." —John M. Schofield, *Forty-Six Years in the Army*, p. 63

JOHN M. BRANNAN Brevet major
general. West Point (1841). Mexican War veteran. Commanded Department of the South, 1862–1863. Division commander, Army of the Cumberland.

" ... he is the senior general now since General [David] Hunter left ... the youngest looking general I have yet seen—very sturdy ... He is, of course, a West Pointer; served all through the Mexican War; sore at being relieved by Mitchel ... he seems a very frank officer-like man, very young for a brigadier and quite a soldier." —Samuel F. P. DuPont, *Civil War Letters*, 2: 224, 226

WILLIAM T. H. BROOKS
Major general. West Point (1841). Seminole and Mexican War veteran. Brigade and division commander, Army of the Potomac.

"The old and tried commander . . . was one of the most energetic and brave brigade commanders in our army, and notwithstanding his abrupt and sometimes very stern manners, had endeared himself by his excellent discipline and fighting qualities, not only to his brigade, but to the whole division." —George T. Stevens, *Three Years in the Sixth Corps*, p. 160

"Gen. (vel 'Bully') Brooks, a tall strong man, with a heavy, rather sullen face. He has a great reputation as a valiant man & steady soldier, but seems to quarrel plentifully." —Theodore Lyman, *Meade's Army*, p. 191

CATHARINUS P. BUCKINGHAM
Brigadier general. West Point (1829). Adjutant general of Ohio.

"His services through the war were not of the kind that figure largely in the public eye or in the newspapers of the day, but a large share of the credit which Ohio won for her promptitude in filling her quotas, and for the admirable organization of her troops is due to General Buckingham . . ." —Whitelaw Reid, *Ohio in the War*, 1:889

DON CARLOS BUELL
Major general. West Point (1841). Seminole and Mexican War veteran. Commander, Army of the Ohio.

"General Buell was a brave, intelligent officer, with as much professional pride and ambition of a commendable sort as I ever knew . . . He was not given . . . to forming intimate acquaintances. He was studious by habit . . . he was a strict disciplinarian and perhaps did not distinguish sufficiently between the volunteer who 'enlisted for the war' and the soldier who serves in time of peace." —Ulysses S. Grant, *Personal Memoirs*, 1:358

"I have at all times said and believed that General Buell was the best general the war produced. He was a victim to the demand for success; and the confidence of the country, so necessary for a commander, was in his case greatly impaired . . . Probably his removal could not have been avoided, but the army was never as good again tactically as while under Buell." —William B. Hazen, *Narrative*, p. 67

Buell "was a fine soldier, a brave patient man. He was persecuted by the ultra-abolitionists because he did not rush in and free all the slaves . . . It was something like McClellan, although he was not theatrical like McClellan. If it had not been for him there at Shiloh, there would have been no Grant." —David S. Stanley, *Generals in Bronze*, p. 190

"Gen. Buell was not particularly popular with political soldiers, newspaper correspondents and others who were carrying on the war from safe distances in the rear. He was eminently and emphatically a soldier, with no ambition or expectations outside the line of his duty, and with honor and integrity . . ." —Milo Hascall, *Personal Recollections of Stone River*, p. 3

"Don Carlos Buell was a very capable general . . . He was brave and laborious, and, despite accusations to the contrary, loyal . . . however, he was either too cautious or too rigidly methodical to be great or successful in the hour of battle." —*Lew Wallace: An Autobiography*, 2:644–645

"Notwithstanding his coldness and austerity of manner and seeming indifference to the private soldier and distrust of volunteers, the Army of the Cumberland owe much to Gen. Buell for their discipline and education in the forms and technique of the profession of arms." —Benjamin Scribner, *How Soldiers were Made*, p. 63

"He was always looked upon as a quiet, methodical, and 'safe' officer . . . His deportment is gentle and soldierly; he thoroughly understands his business, and despises that coarse vulgarity so common among Federal leaders of the present day." —An English Combatant, *Battlefields of the South*, p. 157

"Few officers in the service possess more reticence, terse logic, and severe habits of military discipline than General Buell . . ." —James A. Garfield, *Battles and Leaders*, 6:117

"He long remained unpopular with the great mass of the people who supported the war. He was accused of undue lenity to the Rebels, of too much sympathy with them, and, indeed, disloyalty to the cause. This last slander he himself did something to encourage, by the publication of a letter, obviously designed to aid the Democratic opposition to the war . . . Personally, General Buell . . . is cultivated, polished, and reticent; disposed to have but few warm friendships; exclusive and somewhat haughty in his bearing. He is one of the most forcible and pungent writers among the officers who rose to distinction during the war." —Whitelaw Reid, *Ohio in the War*, 1:724

"The only redeeming trait of Gen. Buell . . . was his order and system. I heard of that long before I knew anything of him personally. I failed to discover any such quality in him in the management of his troops." —Hans C. Heg, *Civil War Letters*, p. 181

"He is a direct, martial-spirited man and has an air of decision and business which I like." —James A. Garfield, *The Wild Life of the Army*, p. 49

JOHN BUFORD

Major general. West Point (1848). Frontier service. Commanded cavalry brigade, Army of Virginia; reserve cavalry brigade and cavalry division, Army of the Potomac.

"Buford's coolness, his fine judgment, and his splendid courage were known of all men who had to do with him ... His quiet dignity, covering a fiery spirit and a military sagacity as far-reaching as it was accurate, made him ... one of the most respected and trusted officers in the service." —John Pope, *Battles and Leaders*, 2:491

"General John Buford was a healthful, hardy cavalry officer, born in Kentucky, a graduate from the Military Academy in 1848. He especially distinguished himself during the war for boldness in pushing up close to his foe; for great dash in his assaults, and ... for shrewdness and prudence in the presence of a force larger than his own." —Oliver O. Howard, *Autobiography*, p. 406

"He is one of the best of the officers ... and is a singular-looking party. Figurez-vous a compactly built man of middle height, with a tawny mustache and a little, triangular gray eye, whose expression is determined, not to say sinister. His ancient corduroys are tucked into a pair of ordinary cowhide boots, and his blue blouse is ornamented with holes; from one pocket thereof peeps a huge pipe, while the other is fat with a tobacco pouch. Notwithstanding this get-up he is a very soldierly looking man. He is of a good-natured disposition, but not to be trifled with." —Theodore Lyman, *Meade's Headquarters*, p. 21

"To this officer the young hair-brains of our Headq'rs attached themselves, as he has a great reputation for cool daring, and is good hearted withal. He is a man of middle height with a yellow mustache, and a small, triangular gray eye; his expression is sinister, though his reputation is the contrary." —Theodore Lyman, *Meade's Army*, p. 34

"He was decidedly the best cavalry general we had, and was acknowledged as such in the army, though being no friend to newspaper reporters ... In many respects he resembled Reynolds, being rough in his exterior, never looking after his own comfort, untiring on the march and in the supervision of all the militia of his command, quiet and unassuming in his manners." —Charles S. Wainwright, *A Diary of Battle*, p. 309

"He is a Kentuckian ... Buford, as you may suppose, is hardly calculated to shine in any ballroom except a Mexican fandango, where he seems in his element. Here the natives call him 'Hell-roaring Buford.' He is over six feet and out of proportion, large in other respects." —Richard S. Ewell, *The Making of a Soldier*, p. 77

NAPOLEON BONAPARTE BUFORD Brigadier general.
West Point (1831). Civil engineer. Brigadier general in western theater.

"I see the name of N. B. Buford for Maj. Gen. He would scarcely make a respectable hospital nurse if put in petticoats and certain—is unfit for any other military position. He has always been a dead weight to carry, becoming more burthensome with his increased rank. . . . There are here worthy men . . . whose promotion would add weight to our cause where it is needed . . . Conspicuous among this latter class is Brig. Gen. John A. Logan. He has proven himself a most valuable officer and worthy of every confidence he is entitled to and can be trusted with a command equal to what increased rank would entitle him to. There is not a more patriotic soldier, braver man, or one more deserving of promotion in this department . . ." —Ulysses S. Grant to Abraham Lincoln, February 9, 1863

STEVEN G. BURBRIDGE Brigadier general. Graduate of
Kentucky Military Institute. Lawyer and farmer. Brigade commander, Thirteenth Corps. Commander, Department of Kentucky, 1864. "Butcher of Kentucky."

"General Burbridge, who commanded the 'District of Kentucky,' was a native of the state, and extremely unpopular, as any native and resident of the state would have been who had attempted to enforce martial law at his home. He was charged with cruelty and favoritism." —John M. Palmer, *Personal Recollections*, p. 226

"General Burbridge . . . I judge to be a mediocre officer, brave, rather pretentious, a good fellow, but not destined to greatness." —Charles A. Dana, *Recollections*, p. 65

AMBROSE E. BURNSIDE Major general.
West Point (1847). Mexican War veteran. Inventor.
Rhode Island Congressman and major general of militia.
Brigade, division, and corps commander, Army of the
Potomac. Commander, Army of the Potomac, 1862–1863.

"Of course we had to have our inevitable 'Review,' and Burnside, portly and handsome, smiling and courteous, with his side-whiskers, mustache, and beautiful white teeth, but without dash or grip in his face, sat erect on his dark-brown bobtail horse, while a hundred thousand of us marched part, scanning him closely. I do not think there was an officer or a man of us that felt safe in his hands . . . I do not want to be unfair or unkind to poor General Burnside. He was certainly loyal and patriotic, and meant to do his best. But I think history will declare he was utterly incompetent for such a great command." —James F. Rusling, *Men & Things I Saw*, p. 60, 65

"Burnside was the idol of the class, our leader in everything but studies. Benny Havens worshipped him next to Andrew Jackson. Burnside was tall, commanding, and manly . . . mature-looking . . . He was the soul of 'fun, frolic and friendship,' a model soldier in appearance, and so frank that everybody trusted him." —Orlando B. Wilcox, *Forgotten Valor*, p. 53

"We all thought we knew Burnside well, and while we did not think him a strong man we knew him to be cautious, and thought him amenable to advice from those he knew had his interests at heart. The result was we knew nothing of him—of opinions he had none save the reflection from the last person with whom he talked. With all this there was the intense stubbornness which sometimes takes hold of weak minds . . ." —William F. Smith, *Autobiography*, p. 59

"He was rather a large man physically, about six feet tall, with a large face and a small head, and heavy side whiskers. He was an energetic, decided man, frank, manly and well educated. He was a very showy officer—not that he made any show; he was naturally that. When he first talked with you, you would think he had a great deal more intelligence than he really possessed. You had to know him some time before you really took his measure." —Charles A. Dana, *Recollections*, p.138

"A large, brave, prepossessing man, popular with his associates, he was accustomed to defer greatly to the judgment of his chosen friends." —Oliver O. Howard, *Autobiography*, p. 314

"He was preeminently a manly man . . . His large, fine eyes, his winning smile, and cordial manners, bespoke a frank, sincere, and honorable character, and these indications were never belied by more intimate acquaintance . . . I learned to understand the limitations of his powers and the points in which he fell short of being a great commander; but as I knew him better I estimated more and more highly his sincerity and truthfulness, his unselfish generosity, and his devoted patriotism." —Jacob Cox, *Reminiscences*, 1:264

"I think Burnside a first rate man & I think there is no doubt he will be much more active than his predecessor. If so, it is a Godsend to the country. 'Nuff sed." —John W. Geary, *A Politician Goes to War*, p. 69

"Whatever may have been the failings of General Burnside, it cannot be charged that he was characterized by any large amount of self-conceit . . . Burnside had not the system and order which distinguished McDowell, and his idea of practical operations were sometimes very crude."—Herman Haupt, *Reminiscences*, p. 306

"He was always a striking figure, and had a dashing way with him which incited enthusiasm among his soldiers. Without seeming to care for his costume . . . there was apt to be something picturesque about him. He had a hearty and jovial manner, a good-humored cordiality toward everybody, that beamed in his face as he rode through the camps or along the lines . . . His bearing under fire was good, and his personal courage beyond question. He shrank from responsibility with sincere modesty, because he questioned his own capacity to deal with affairs of great magnitude." —Jacob Cox, *Reminiscences*, 1:389–390

Cabinet card photo featuring Abraham Lincoln and prominent Union leaders. (Collection of Robert I. Girardi)

"I like Burnside as a man ... He is noble in generosity and heart, but his letter assuming the whole responsibility of this movement, seems to me to show a disregard of the consequences of his acts that astonishes me." —Gouverneur K. Warren, *Happiness is not My Companion*, p. 64

"Burnside ... is patriotic and amiable, and, had he greater powers and grasp, would make an acceptable and popular, if not a great, general." —Gideon Welles, *Diary*, 1:182

"Burnside is a good General, but he has not the brains of Mac and what is a great deal more he has not by far the confidence of his men ... Everything before us seems darker than before." —Alfred Sully, *No Tears for the General*, p. 157

"Look at Burnside. A good fellow certainly, manly honest and comely. But of only moderate mind and attainments. Who has made our cause suffer more in battle than any other Genl ... neither blunders & inefficiency—personal animosity in higher sources—nor friendship with the prescribed has lowered him ..." —Gouverneur K. Warren, *Happiness is not My Companion*, p. 69

"Burnside had ... some operations on a comparatively small scale to his credit ... He was also a very patriotic man whose heart was in his work, and his sincerity, frankness, and amiability of manner made everybody like him. But he was not a great general, and he felt, himself, that the task to which he had been assigned was too heavy for his shoulders." —Carl Schurz, *Reminiscences*, 2:397

"I can't help feeling sorry for Old Burnside—proud, plucky, hard-headed old dog. I always liked him, but I loved little Mac, and it was a godsend to the Confederacy that he was relieved." —George E. Pickett, *The Heart of a Soldier*, p. 66

"He was believed to be a frank, manly, modest, brave soldier, conscious of his own deficiencies ... but not possessed of capacity for an independent command. Burnside was never a pretender ... and had many staunch friends." —Henry Kyd Douglas, *I Rode with Stonewall*, p. 202

"He was dressed so as to be almost unrecognizable as a general officer; wore a rough blouse, on the collar of which a close look revealed two much-battered and faded stars, indicating his rank as major general. He wore a black 'slouch' hat, the brim well down over his face, and rode along with a single orderly, without the least ostentation ... He was not only popular with his own corps ... but with the whole army ... because of his modest, quiet way of going about." —Frederick L. Hitchcock, *War from the Inside*, p. 39

"Burnside was a man of remarkable enthusiasm with which he was but too apt to be carried away ... for his characteristic defect was to trust too many things to chance, exemplified by a favorite expression of his, 'Trust to luck.'" —John Gibbon, *Personal Recollections of the Civil War*, p. 252

"On every occasion during the war, when there was need, Burnside displayed the same heroic self-abnegation. His ability has been questioned, his strategy criticized, and sometimes even his vigor denied; but the purity of his patriotism and the loftiness of his public spirit were unsurpassed." —Adam Badeau, *Military History of Ulysses S. Grant*, 2:261

"We may look for any disaster from Burnside. He is unfit to be in any separate command." —Marsena R. Patrick, *Inside Lincoln's Army*, p. 311

"General Burnside was an officer who was generally liked and respected. He was not, however, fitted to command an army. No one knew this better than himself. He always admitted his blunders, and extenuated those of officers under him beyond what they were entitled to. It was hardly his fault that he was ever assigned to a separate command." —Ulysses S. Grant, *Personal Memoirs*, 2:539

"The designation of Burnside to succeed McClellan was a great surprise to old army circles, both in the Federal and Confederate armies; and was, perhaps, an unpleasant one to Burnside himself. He was popular, but not greatly esteemed as a general. He had commanded a brigade at the first battle of Bull Run, but had in no way risen above, even if reached, the average of brigade commanders." —E. P. Alexander, *Military Memoirs of a Confederate*, p. 282

"Ambrose E. Burnside, was the soul of good-fellowship, an amiable officer, and a kind-hearted gentleman. He possessed those qualities as a cadet." —Fitzhugh Lee, *General Lee*, p. 221

"Those of us who were well acquainted with Burnside knew that he was a brave, loyal man, but we did not think that he had the military ability to command the Army of the Potomac." —Darius Couch, *Battles and Leaders*, 3:106

"He is quite different from McClellan in his manners, having great affability and a winning way with him that attracts instead of repelling strangers." —George G. Meade, *Life and Letters*, 1:304

"Burnside somehow is never up to the mark when the tug comes." —Charles S. Wainwright, *A Diary of Battle*, p. 352

BENJAMIN F. BUTLER Major general.
Lawyer and Democratic politician from Massachusetts.
Brigadier general of Massachusetts militia. Military
governor of New Orleans, 1862. Commander, Army of
the James, 1864–1865.

"He is the strangest sight on a horse you ever saw; it is hard
to keep your eyes off him. With his head set immediately
on a stout, shapeless body, his very squinting eyes and a
set of legs and arms that look as if made for somebody
else, and hastily glued to him by mistake . . . Add to this
a horse with a kind of rapid, ambling trot that shakes
about the arms, legs, etc., till you don't feel quite sure whether it is a centaur,
or what it is, and you have a picture of this celebrated General. Celebrated he
surely is, and a man of untiring industry and activity." —Theodore Lyman,
Meade's Headquarters, p. 192

"General Butler . . . developed remarkable ability in civil organization, and
showed courage and determination in any project in which he was interested.
While just and even generous in dealing with the men in his department his
manner was decidedly autocratic. He rarely tolerated conduct savoring of
insubordination, and yet under peculiar circumstances, he overlooked it."
—Joseph B. Carr, *Battles and Leaders*, 2:146

"General Butler . . . is a remarkable looking man. Stout in person, nervous and
peculiar in manners, he has a large head and a striking profile not wanting in
dignity and greatness. His manner is affable and his conversation bright and
agreeable . . . Butler's countenance is altogether indicative of more refinement
than I expected to see. His drooping left eye gives his face a somewhat sinister
expression and his nervous manner is somewhat disturbing, but altogether
the impression he made on me was favorable and strong." —David Hunter
Strother, *A Virginia Yankee*, p. 136

"As an administrative officer General Butler has no superior. In taking charge
of a department where there are no great battles to be fought, but a dissatisfied
element to control, no one could manage it better than he . . . I liked Butler and
have always found him not only . . . a man of great ability, but a patriotic man,
and a man of courage, honor, and sincere convictions. Butler lacked the technical
experience of a military education . . . as a general was full of enterprise and
resources, and a brave man." —Ulysses S. Grant, *Butler's Book*, 2:852, 862

"General Butler was not a professional soldier and he did not appreciate that
there was anything in the profession more than could be acquired in a few
hours by a good lawyer. His experiences in the field . . . were small, and without
knowing much he yet thought he knew enough not to be compelled to ask
for advice and had a suspicious disposition which prevented him from taking
honest opinions." —William F. Smith, *Autobiography*, p. 89

"Looking back, the thing which stands prominently forth ... is my sense of the utter incompetence of Major General Benjamin F. Butler of Massachusetts, and the terrible disasters and loss of life that incompetence directly involved ... Grant's campaign went absolutely to pieces at the very outset because of Butler's utter military incapacity, and his inability either to see an opportunity, much more to seize it ... The military element did not enter in any degree into Butler's composition, and the Army of the Potomac ... paid the penalty." —Charles Francis Adams, *Autobiography*, p. 159–160

"I had never met that gentleman before, and although he was at the time a prominent politician, I had not felt interest enough in him to watch his proceedings ... after being with him six days I saw plainly that he possessed phenomenal activity and persistence of brain power, and that he considered himself fit to be the leader in all the pursuits, callings, professions and occupations of men whether he had studied them or not." —Erasmus Keyes, *Fifty Years' Observations*, p. 402

"I do not like General Butler, but I can do him justice ... I feel a certain conviction that he was especially suited to govern New Orleans under the circumstances and probably but few could have done so ..." —Samuel F. P. DuPont, *Civil War Letters*, 2:327–328

"He is not the grossly fat and altogether ugly man who is presented in the illustrated weeklies. He is stoutish but not clumsily so; he squints badly, but his eyes are very clear and bright; his complexion is fair, smooth and delicately flushed; his teeth are white and his smile is ingratiating. You need not understand that he is pretty; only that he is better looking than his published portraits." —John William De Forest, *A Volunteer's Adventures*, p. 9

"I am fearful that Gen. Butler is a failure ... He has had no military experience in the field. His operations in the early stages of the war were not of such a sort as to develop skill & ability for operations of the kind undertaken by his army. That he has acquired reputation as a General is true, but it has been rather on account of administrative ability connected with civil rather than military matters. To me it is singular that the War Department should entrust to such a Gen the supreme command of as important an enterprise as this ..." —Alvin C. Voris, *A Citizen-Soldier's Civil War*, p. 178

"Butler has shown ability as a police magistrate both at Baltimore and New Orleans, and in each, but particularly at the latter place, has had a peculiar community to govern ..." —Gideon Welles, *Diary*, 1:210

"While Butler has talents and capacity, he is not to be trusted. The more I see of him, the greater is my mistrust of his integrity." —Gideon Welles, *Diary*, 2:81

"He was a good administrative officer, though often given to severe and unusual methods in enforcing discipline and in dealing with the dissatisfied element of the population living within his department; yet he did not possess the elements necessary to make an efficient officer in the field. As he was inexperienced in fighting battles, Grant felt reluctant to give him charge of any important military movement." —Horace Porter, *Campaigning with Grant*, p. 246

"Besides commanding a large army in the field, he is Major-General commanding a large Department and Commissioner of Exchange. His great aptness and inexhaustible industry enable him to give personal attention to all the details of these three distinct orders of affairs and duties. He is like Frederick the great in his personal attention to subordinates as well as to the ruling affairs within his control." —Charles A. Page, *Letters*, p. 250

"He is a stout, middle-aged man, strongly built, with coarse limbs, his features indicative of great shrewdness and craft, his forehead high, the elevation being in some degree due perhaps to the want of hair; with a strong obliquity of vision, which may perhaps have been caused by an injury, as the eyelid hangs with a peculiar droop over the organ. The General, whose manner is quick, decided, and abrupt, but not at all rude or unpleasant . . . A vivacious, prying man, this Butler, full of bustling life, self-esteem, reveling in the exercise of power . . . a tall, saturnine, gloomy, angry-eyed, sallow man, soldier-like too . . ." —William Howard Russell, *My Diary North & South*, p. 201–203

"Butler was notoriously a military charlatan, who had been forced upon Grant . . . by political considerations. During all of the summer campaign, he knew and felt his importance, and had been able even successfully to bully Grant himself . . ." —E. P. Alexander, *Military Memoirs of a Confederate*, p. 582

"General Butler . . . is an energetic, cursing and swearing old fellow." —Robert Gould Shaw, *Blue-eyed Child of Fortune*, p. 77

"Butler . . . was fertile in resource, energetic in will, and not apt to be long cast down. He was always ready to adapt himself to the situation, no matter how disagreeable, when once it became inevitable. His administrative ability was conspicuous, and no one questioned his earnestness. He had many of the qualities that go to the making of a good or even a great soldier . . ." —Adam Badeau, *Military History of Ulysses S. Grant*, 2:259

DANIEL BUTTERFIELD Major general. Lawyer and businessman. Brigade commander, Army of the Potomac, 1862; Chief of staff, Army of the Potomac, 1863. Division commander, 20th Corps, 1863.

"That lying little knave. He is one of the most corrupt, scheming, lying scoundrels. And he is one of those fellows that when he's found out in his lies, it doesn't seem to phase, he will brazen it out. He pretends he was wounded at Gettysburg . . . He was hit in throat with the branch of a tree. He tied a handkerchief around it with the bloody side out . . ." —Alexander Webb, *Generals in Bronze*, 148–149

"I have been annoyed very much by Butterfield being in command. He thinks himself very smart, but is in reality nearly a fool about some things—I am utterly disgusted with him—He would keep me doing nothing but answering his follies." —Marsena Patrick, *Inside Lincoln's Army*, p. 221

"General Butterfield is a very rigid disciplinarian and never can endure ignorance of the simplest military movements ... His very strict discipline made him personally unpopular with his whole Division, but all had great confidence in his military ability ..." —Harvey Reid, *The View from Headquarters*, p. 127, 167

"I have just come from Butterfield's tent and am very much disgusted with his manner and the view he takes of our affairs—his Ex Cathedra way of speaking, & the flippancy of the whole head Quarter[s] establishment ..." —Marsena R. Patrick, *Inside Lincoln's Army*, p. 210

"Beware of Butterfield, he will lead you astray; he is a dangerous man. He was chief of staff to Gen. Hooker; Meade took him, but did not intend to keep him. Meade offered the position to Gen. Warren, but Warren did not wish to have it, so Butterfield remained, although he was removed after Gettysburg." —Martin Thomas McMahon, *General in Bronze*, p. 85

"General Butterfield was Assistant Foreman on a fire-engine, when he was young in Utica; and he set fire to a church thinking to get there first to put it out; but the church burned down before they got there, and his father had to build a new church to keep him out of jail." —Gouverneur K. Warren, *Generals in Bronze*, p. 87–88

"Butterfield has not made so good a chief of staff as I expected. Much to my surprise he does not seem to have practical common sense in all points, the very trait of character in which it was supposed he would excel. He is most thoroughly hated by all the officers at headquarters as a meddling, over-conceited fellow. They say that Hooker would be a delightful man to serve with if he would only get rid of 'the little Napoleon.'" —Charles S. Wainwright, *A Diary of Battle*, p. 215

EDWARD R. S. CANBY Major general. West Point (1839). Seminole and Mexican War veteran. Commander, department of New Mexico, 1862; commander, department of Military Division of West Mississippi, 1864.

"He was affable and courteous in his manner, tall and fine looking, soldierly in his bearing ... He was very entertaining in conversation; had a thorough knowledge of the details of the service; and [was] especially well versed in regard to the duties of the various staff departments of the army ..." —Benjamin Grierson, *A Just and Righteous Cause*, p. 325

"Canby was, I think, the most accomplished and best informed officer I ever met, only excelled by that prince of soldiers . . . C. F. Smith, the model soldier of our army . . ." —Henry Heth, *Memoirs*, p. 138

WILLIAM P. CARLIN

Major general. West Point (1850). Brigade and division commander, Army of the Cumberland.

"Carlin was one of the most thoroughly reliable men I ever met in the service. Whenever you had decided what was to be done, Carlin was the first to rise in your mind as the man to do it. And when you had given him an order, you might go about your business with perfect assurance that it would be obeyed to the letter if it was in the power of a human being . . . if it could be done, he'd find a way to do it . . ." —William S. Rosecrans in *Memoirs of Brigadier General William Passmore Carlin*, p. 2

"His courage, skill, and ability had been tested . . . and I confidently relied upon his cordial co-operation and support . . . I found him prompt to obey orders and always ready for any service however dangerous or disagreeable. Wherever he was ordered he went without question, and when he led his gallant brigade into action, he did so intelligently and fearlessly . . . and earned for himself the reputation of being one of the very best division commanders in the army." —Richard Johnson, *A Soldier's Reminiscences*, p. 241

EUGENE ASA CARR   Major general. West Point (1850). Plains
Indian wars. Brigade and division commander, western armies.

"He is a man of more cultivation, intelligence, and thought than his colleagues generally. The discipline in his camps I have thought to be poor and careless. He is brave enough, but lacks energy and initiative." —Charles A. Dana, *Recollections*, p. 65

JOSEPH B. CARR   Brigadier general. New York businessman and
colonel of militia. Brigade and division commander, Army of the Potomac.

"Carr is a splendid man, a good General, and his heart is in his work. He is a grate Union man . . . and a warm supporter of the administration.

He wished to stay in the Army to do or die for his country. A great friend of the Volunteers and opposed to Regulars, he is a very kind and sociable man—ever ready to do an act of kindness to those who needed it."
—Robert McAllister, *Civil War Letters*, p. 279

SILAS CASEY Major general. West Point (1826). Mexican War veteran. Authored tactical manual. Division commander, Army of the Potomac, 1862; brigade commander Washington Defenses until 1865.

"The man of our class who has left the most monuments of his work behind him was General Casey, Chief of Engineers, and yet he originated nothing . . . a man of wonderful ability, he was without desire for any human fellowship."
—David S. Stanley, *Memoirs*, p. 23

"We were in the command of General Silas Casey, a noble specimen of a man and a soldier. His manly dignity and kindly bearing impressed all with profound respect for him . . . we never ceased to remember him with pleasure."
—George T. Stevens, *Three Years in the Sixth Corps*, p. 11

"Brigadier General Casey of New York, probably 55 years of age, badly bald, hair and whiskers white, the latter consisting only of the underchin growth. He has a florid countenance, blue eyes, a very long slender Roman . . . [nose] and a very large mouth. He is a microscopic sort of man of the bookish persuasion much wedded to the school of precedents and res judicata, and the minutest matters of form." —James A. Garfield, *The Wild Life of the Army*, p. 188

AUGUSTUS L. CHETLAIN Major general. Galena businessman. Brigade commander, army of the Tennessee. Commanded Defenses of Memphis and raised regiments of United States Colored Troops.

"He proved a most valuable officer, for I found him to possess both intelligence and zeal, with a rare qualification for the organization of troops. He never failed in any duty he was assigned, either as superintendent or inspector, to which latter duty I assigned him." —Lorenzo Thomas, in Chetlain, *Recollections of Seventy Years*, p. 107

JOHN COCHRANE Brigadier general. Lawyer and Democratic Congressman. Brigade commander, Army of the Potomac until 1862.

"He has been wayward and erratic. A Democrat, a Barnburner, a conservative, an Abolitionist, an Anti-abolitionist, a Democratic-Republican, and now a Radical Republican. He has some, but not eminent, ability; can never make a mark as a statesman." —Gideon Welles, *Diary*, 2:43

JOHN M. CORSE Brevet major general. West Point dropout, 1855. Iowa Lawyer. Brigade and division commander, Army of the Tennessee.

"Six or eight years ago he was dropped from the roll of cadets at West Point for incompetency, inability to maintain the required rank in his class ... He couldn't do the mathematics of West Point, nevertheless he was a natural soldier, and, as young as he is, has won his present rank by sheer fighting, by sheer *ability* in fighting." —Charles A. Page, *Letters*, p. 396

DARIUS N. COUCH Major general. West Point (1846). Mexican War veteran. Division and corps commander, Army of the Potomac until 1863. Commanded Pennsylvania militia.

"He was an honest, faithful, and laborious man, a brave, modest, and valuable officer." —George B. McClellan, *McClellan's Own Story*, p. 139

JACOB D. COX Major general. Lawyer and abolitionist. Brigade and division commander, temporary corps commander, Army of the Cumberland.

"He was not a great General. He was not even a great corps commander. He never seemed brilliant, but he was generally safe. He never displayed the inspiration of war, but he generally followed sound rules of war. He was too cold to be loved by his troops, but ... they never failed to respect him. He was too tame and methodical to be admired by his commanders, but ... they never failed to trust and to advance him ... In personal appearance General Cox is trim, compact, and elegant ... Without a spark of genius, he was still ... the most many-sided man in the army ... He was too cold for friendship or popularity. In war, his soldiers had no enthusiasm for him; in politics, his party regarded him as a dead-weight." —Whitelaw Reid, *Ohio in the War*, 1:776–777

SAMUEL W. CRAWFORD Major general. Surgeon. Brigade and division commander, Army of the Potomac.

"We don't think too much of Crawford. He was a tall, chesty, glowering man, with heavy eyes, a big nose, and bushy whiskers; and he wore habitually a turn-out-the-guard expression, which was, as we knew, fairly indicative of his military character." —Abner Small, *The Road to Richmond*, p. 149

"He is a strong anti McClellan, and, of course, powerful for the Administration. Don't know exactly what to think of C.—brave, perhaps dashing, untiring in his endeavors to introduce order and discipline, but specious, & talkative; unpopular with his officers also." —Theodore Lyman, *Meade's Army*, p. 283

"Crawford, a conscious gentleman, having the entrée at all headquarters, somewhat lofty of manner, not of the iron fiber, nor spring of steel, but punctilious in a way, obeying orders in a certain literal fashion that saved him the censure of his superiors—a pet of his State, and likewise, we thought, of Meade and Warren, judging from the attention they always gave him—possibly not quite fairly estimated by his colleagues as a military man, but the ranking division commander of the corps." —Joshua Lawrence Chamberlain, *Passing of the Armies*, p. 122

THOMAS L. CRITTENDEN Major

general. Lawyer, Mexican War veteran. Brigade, division, and corps commander, Army of the Cumberland.

"Crittenden was greatly beloved by his men. He was always genial, kind, just, and brave to a fault . . ." —William B. Hazen, *Narrative*, p. 152

"Surely in the annals of warfare there is no parallel to the coolness and nonchalance with which General Crittenden marched and counter-marched for a week with a delightful unconsciousness that he was in the presence of a force of superior strength." —D. H. Hill, *Battles and Leaders*, 3:643

"He is the queerest-looking party you ever saw, with a thin, staring face, and hair hanging to his coat collar—a very wild-appearing major-general, but quite a kindly man in conversation, despite his terrible looks." —Theodore Lyman, *Meade's Headquarters*, p. 116–117

"I like Crittenden much, and shall be with him for some time . . . He is 45 years old, rather tall and slim, and somewhat Western looking, with, I regret to say, long hair. He is, as far as I have been able to find out yet, an excellent officer and a very genial, pleasant, kindly man . . ." —Charles J. Mills, *Through Blood and Fire*, p. 85, 89

GEORGE B. CROOK Major general. West Point (1852).

Brigade and division commander, Army of the Cumberland and Army of the Shenandoah.

"A man of medium size, with light hair and sandy beard, his manner was rather diffident and shy, and his whole style quiet and reticent. His voice was light, rather than heavy, and he was so laconic of speech that this, with his other characteristics, caused it to be commonly said of him that he had been

so long fighting Indians on the frontier that he had acquired some of their traits and habits. His system of discipline was based on these peculiarities."
—Jacob Cox, *Reminiscences*, 1:205

"Major General George Crook . . . was a soldier of high training and tried courage, making no war on women and children, houses and barns."
—G. Moxley Sorrel, *Recollections of a Confederate Staff Officer*, p. 275

"Crook was a classmate of mine . . . We had known each other as boys before we entered the army, and later as men, and I placed implicit faith in his experience and qualifications as a general." —Philip H. Sheridan, *Memoirs*, 1:474

NEWTON M. CURTIS Brevet major general. Farmer and postmaster. Brigade commander, Army of the James.

"A finer specimen of physical manhood it would be difficult to find. Six feet six inches in height, erect as the typical Indian, he weighs two hundred and thirty-two pounds; but if he were six feet twelve and weighed twice as much his body would not be big enough to contain the great soul which inhabits it. He had one eye shot out by a Confederate bullet, but if he had lost both his lofty spirit would have seen as clearly as now that the war was fought in defence of inherited belief, and that when it ended the Union was more closely cemented than ever." —John B. Gordon, *Reminiscences of the Civil War*, p. 115

GEORGE A. CUSTER Major general. West Point (1861). Cavalry brigade and division commander, Army of the Potomac and Army of the Shenandoah.

"This officer is one of the funniest-looking beings you ever saw, and looks like a circus rider gone mad! He wears a huzzar jacket and tight trousers, of faded black velvet trimmed with tarnished gold lace. His head is decked with a little gray, felt hat; high boots and gilt spurs complete the costume, which is enhanced by the General's coiffure, consisting in short, dry, flaxen ringlets! His aspect, though highly amusing, is also pleasing, as he has a very merry blue eye, and a devil-may-care style." —Theodore Lyman, *Meade's Headquarters*, p. 17

"He was . . . a slim, long-haired boy, carelessly dressed . . . Custer was simply a reckless, gallant boy, undeterred by fatigue, unconscious of fear; but his head was always clear in danger, and he always brought me clear and intelligible reports of what he saw when under the heaviest fire . . . In the latter days of the war . . . he displayed a degree of prudence and good sense, in conducting the most dangerous expeditions, that surprised many who thought they knew him well." —George B. McClellan, *McClellan's Own Story*, p. 364–365

"I had known Custer well at West Point. He was an indifferent scholar, but a fellow of tremendous vitality and vigor. Six feet tall, with broad shoulders, deep chest, thin waist, and splendid legs, he had a perfect figure and was one of the best horsemen of his day . . . He was known in his cadet days and always afterward by his familiars as 'Cinnamon,' because he was partial to cinnamon hair oil . . . Custer was never rated as a great general, for, although full of dash, enterprise, and experience, he never acquired the habit of properly measuring the endurance of his men and horses. Besides, some thought him overconfident and occasionally jealous . . ." —James H. Wilson, *Under the Old Flag*, p. 101–102

"He was a most striking picture; a rather young man, dressed in a blue sack with the largest shoulder-straps of a major general I ever saw; with long, red hair hanging in oily curls down near to his shoulders, a gorgeous red scarf in which there was a gold pin, nearly two inches in length and breadth, with big letters, 'George A. Custer, Major General.'" —John Haskell, *The Haskell Memoirs*, p. 94

"Custer lost his life in not doing what I told him. I used to tell him 'Don't be so anxious to fight yourself—fight your command.' He was so anxious to fight himself he would forget his command—that is not a general's business. That is what he did with the Indians. He was so anxious to fight himself that he lost his command and got killed." —Alfred Pleasanton, *Generals in Bronze*, p. 120

"Custer never required more than simple orders . . . for he had in himself the vim which insured a prompt response to the wishes of the commanding general . . ." —Frederick C. Newhall, *With Sheridan in the Final Campaign*, p. 36

"At the time of his appointment as Brigadier and Major-General, General Custer was the youngest officer of his rank in the army. He never lost a gun or a color; he captured more guns, flags, and prisoners, than any other General not an army commander . . . General Custer's career was active, highly energetic, and honorable; but he gave no evidences of great generalship. As a subordinate . . . he was in his proper sphere. In such a capacity, for quick dashes and vigorous spurts of fighting, he had no superiors, and scarcely an equal." —Whitelaw Reid, *Ohio in the War*, 1:782–783

"He was one of the most enterprising, fearless cavalry leaders the great war produced . . . He was most ambitious and enterprising and soon rose to the command of a regiment and brigade, and later commanded, with great success, one of the active cavalry divisions. We were very near the same age—rivals in the military profession, but the best of friends." —Nelson A. Miles, *Serving the Republic*, p. 110

LYSANDER CUTLER   Brigadier general. Surveyor and schoolmaster. Brigade commander, Army of the Potomac.

"Cutler . . . was a natural soldier though somewhat inclined to arbitrary and dictatorial measures. He soon became a good tactician . . . Cutler was an old grey-headed man . . ." —John Gibbon, *Personal Recollections of the Civil War*, p. 28

JOHN A DAHLGREN, USN   Rear admiral. Career navy man. Established U.S. Navy Ordnance Department and invented the muzzle-loading Dahlgren gun.

"We are not at all satisfied with the conduct of Admiral Dahlgren. He is represented as having chronic sea sickness, a chronic dislike to do anything . . ." —Alvin C. Voris, *A Citizen-Soldier's Civil War*, p. 139

"Dahlgren is very proud and aspiring, and will injure himself and his professional standing in consequence. With undoubted talents of a certain kind he has intense selfishness . . . he is less devoted to the country than to himself . . . he never acts on any principle of self-sacrifice . . . He has intelligence and ability without question; his nautical qualities are disputed; his skill, capacity, courage, daring, sagacity, and comprehensiveness in a high command are to be tested. He is intensely ambitious . . . He has the heroism which proceeds from pride and would lead him to danger and to death, but whether he has the innate, unselfish courage of the genuine sailor and soldier remains to be seen." —Gideon Welles, *Diary*, 1:317–318, 341

JEFFERSON C. DAVIS   Major general. Mexican War veteran. Brigade, division and corps commander, western armies. Murderer of Gen. William "Bull" Nelson.

"General Davis was noted for having mastered the vocabulary of the 'Army in Flanders' more completely than any other man of his rank." —Carl Schurz, *Reminiscences*, 3:79

"Yesterday I had quite a spat with Jeff. C. Davis—our Division Commander—he is a proslavery general, and he is down on the Abolitionists . . . I have no good feeling for him, and I have made up my mind that I will not go into another Battle under his command." —Hans C. Heg, *Civil War Letters*, p. 178

RICHARD DELAFIELD   Brigadier general. West Point (1818). Chief engineer of the U.S. Army.

"Delafield was the embodiment of able administration; very exacting in his requirements, and, like the just judge, precise and severe in his awards of punishment—so much so that he appeared to us subordinates at times to have eliminated all feeling from his action; but this was his view of discipline." —Oliver O. Howard, *Autobiography*, p. 1:100

ELIAS SMITH DENNIS   Brevet major general. Illinois legislator
(house and senate). U.S. Marshall in Kansas. Brigade commander in 17th Corps.

"He is a hard-headed, hard-working, conscientious man, who never knows when he is beaten, and consequently is very hard to beat. He is not brilliant, but safe, sound, and trustworthy." —Charles A. Dana, *Recollections*, p. 71

THOMAS C. DEVIN   Brevet major general. House painter and
lieutenant colonel of New York State Militia. Cavalry brigade and division commander, Army of the Potomac.

"Devin was a good soldier and a hard fighter, but he had one defect—he was quite deaf, and like most deaf people, he did not like to admit he could not hear you. So I was never sure he understood an order . . . [John] Buford was a very laconic man. He would never tell enough in his reports, but I could always read between the lines and fill them up. While [David M.] Gregg would ka-plunkity, plunk write down the truth. If he got licked, he would say so. While [Hugh Judson] Kilpatrick would exaggerate, he was a good fighter, but it was for Kilpatrick . . ." —General Alfred Pleasanton, *Generals in Bronze*, p. 116

JOHN A. DIX   Major general. U.S. Senator from New York,
railroad president, Secretary of the Treasury under Buchanan. Garrison duty.

"He is a pure man, I think, of reputable scholarly attainments, but without much force or energy. He has abilities to fill any station respectably, but can give character to none." —Gideon Welles, *Diary*, 2:608

GRENVILLE M. DODGE   Major general.
Railroad engineer. Brigade and division and corps commander, western armies; commander, District of the Mississippi; commander Department of Missouri and Department of Kansas.

"He possessed rare practical intelligence, intense and untiring energy, was courageous to a fault, resourceful and efficient and as a soldier in the civil war, a railroad engineer and manager . . . he proved himself a most valuable officer to the service in the West." —Augustus L. Chetlain, *Recollections of Seventy Years*, p. 107

"Who could build a trestle bridge like . . . General G. M. Dodge, who was not only a superb commander of men in battle, but was already an eminent practical engineer?" —Oliver O. Howard, *Autobiography*, 1:602

"General Dodge, besides being a most capable soldier, was an experienced railroad builder . . . General Dodge had the work assigned him finished within forty days after receiving his orders. The number of bridges to rebuild was 182 . . . The length of road repaired was 182 miles." —Ulysses S. Grant, *Battles and Leaders*, 3:692–693

ALFRED N. DUFFIE Brigadier general. Decorated French army lieutenant. Cavalry brigade and division commander, Army of the Potomac.

"I had so little confidence in anything he said or did that I placed but little confidence in his report." —George Crook, *Autobiography*, p. 133

EBENEZER DUMONT Brigadier general. Lawyer and legislator. Mexican War veteran. Brigade commander, Army of the Ohio.

"He is a small man, with a thin piping voice, but an educated and affable gentleman . . . The General is an eccentric genius, and has an inexhaustible fund of good stories. He uses the words 'damned' and 'bedamned' rather too often; but this adds, rather than detracts, from his popularity. He dispenses good whiskey at his quarters very freely, and this has a tendency also to elevate him in the estimation of his subordinates." —John Beatty, *The Citizen Soldier*, p. 90, 96

SAMUEL F. DUPONT, USN Rear admiral. Mexican War veteran. Superintendent of U.S. Naval Academy. Commander, South Atlantic Blockading Squadron.

"DuPont is getting as prudent as McClellan; is very careful; all dash, energy and force are softened under the great responsibility. He has a reputation to preserve instead of one to make." —Gideon Welles, *Diary*, 1:247

"DuPont has ability, pride, and intrigue, but he has not the great essentials of a naval commander —heroic valor, unselfish energy, and devotion to the country. Thinks of himself more than of the country and the service . . . He has too much pride to be a coward, —would sooner die than show the white feather, —but the innate, fearless moral courage of Farragut or John Rodgers is not his." —Gideon Welles, *Diary*, 1:477

"Eminently adapted to command, he knew well how to secure the best services of his subordinates. Intelligent, cheerful in manner, of tall and commanding mien, he naturally invited and obtained the confidence of those who were fortunate enough to serve under his orders . . . Though fitted by nature to be a leader among men, he thoroughly appreciated the necessity for study to make himself equal to every professional requirement." —Daniel Ammen, *Battles and Leaders*, 1:691

"All of the qualities of a great commander were possessed in an eminent degree by Dupont. He was well informed in everything relating to naval matters, had great influence in naval circles . . . Dupont was a man of fine presence, and there was something so winning in his manner to all with whom he came in contact, that no man in the Navy had more friends and admirers." —David Dixon Porter, *Naval History of the Civil War*, p. 60–61

WILLIAM H. EMORY Major general. West Point (1831).

Mexican War veteran. Brigade, division and corps commander in various theaters and armies.

"General Emory was a veteran . . . and in the war of the rebellion had exhibited the most soldierly characteristics at Port Hudson and on the Red River campaign . . ." —Philip H. Sheridan, *Memoirs*, 1:473

DAVID GLASGOW FARRAGUT, USN Vice admiral. Career navy. Veteran of war of

1812. Commander West Gulf Blockading Squadron.

"The Admiral is low in stature, about five-feet-five, a very handsome, gentlemanly face, soft in manner and speech, and womanly except when aroused. He is a fine representative of the glory of the Old Navy." —David Hunter Strother, *A Virginia Yankee*, p. 161

"Farragut has prompt, energetic, excellent qualities, but no fondness for written details or self-laudation; does but one thing at a time, but does that strong and well; is better fitted to lead an expedition through danger and difficulty than to command an extensive blockade; is a good officer in a great emergency, will more willingly take great risks in order to obtain great results than any officer in high position in either Navy or Army, and, unlike most of them, prefers that others should tell the story of his well-doing rather than relate it himself." —Gideon Welles, *Diary*, 1:230

"He stood high in the navy as an officer and seaman, and possessed such undoubted courage and energy that no possible objection could be made of him . . . In whatever position he was placed, Farragut maintained his reputation as a fine officer and genial, cheery companion. He was esteemed by all who knew him, and no one in the navy had more personal friends or fewer enemies." —David Dixon Porter, *Battles and Leaders*, 2:26–27

ORRIS S. FERRY Brevet major general. Lawyer and judge, U.S.

Congressman. Brigade commander, Army of the Potomac and Army of the James.

"Gen. Ferry was cautious, conservative, honest, careful of his men. Had firmness to a fair degree, & would fight if necessary with stubborn energy, but would not fight for the fun of the thing. He acted from a sense of duty & would modestly do all that he felt he was required to do whatever the cost might be is a straight forward way without ever thinking of artifice or intrigue, and after all was over would not mount in a balloon to blow his horn." —Alvin C. Voris, *A Citizen-Soldier's Civil War*, p. 115

CLINTON B. FISK Brevet major general. Businessman. Commander, District of Southeast Missouri; Department of North Missouri.

"General Fisk . . . whom the President personally knows is, I am convinced, an able, prudent, and sagacious officer. His policy has been to conciliate—to induce men to cease wrangling and fighting, and to promote peace and quiet . . ." —John G. Nicolay, *With Lincoln in the White House*, p. 148

JOHN G. FOSTER Major general. West Point (1846). Mexican War veteran. Brigade commander, 9th Corps and commander, Department of North Carolina.

"About Gen. Foster I know but little, save that he was very zealous in our behalf while he thought we were an integral part of the 18th Army Corps, but neglected us with a vengeance when he found our status was in doubt. Through his instrumentality our payment was deferred some two months. In personal appearance he was head and shoulders above any of the Generals I have lately seen and is much beloved by his officers." —Alvin C. Voris, *A Citizen-Soldier's Civil War*, p. 115

WILLIAM B. FRANKLIN Major

general. West Point (1843). Mexican War veteran. Brigade, division, and corps commander, Army of the Potomac and Army of the Gulf.

"Franklin, with fine abilities, is neither a great General, nor either an ordinary good officer . . . he is time serving, and not safe, talented perhaps, but no General." —Philip Kearny, *Letters from the Peninsula*, p. 50, 90

"Franklin was one of the best officers I had; very powerful. He was a man not only of excellent judgment, but of a remarkably high order of intellectual ability. He was often badly treated, and seldom received the credit he deserved. His moral character was of the highest, and he was in all respects an admirable corps commander . . . he would have commanded an army well." —George B. McClellan, *McClellan's Own Story*, p. 138

"General Franklin had fallen under the displeasure of the authorities in Washington as a friend of McClellan. As a commander of troops he proved himself cool and brave, and of great ability. No one then serving in the army could have commanded it better." —Thomas W. Hyde, *Following the Greek Cross*, p. 116

"General William B. Franklin is of the highest class of Pennsylvania gentleman. Like McClellan and Hancock, he was well born and educated, and combined the versatile capacity and attainments of the former with the sturdy character of the latter." —Dabney H. Maury, *Recollections of a Virginian*, p. 68

JOHN C. FREMONT　Major general. Engineer and explorer. Mexican War veteran. U.S. Senator and presidential candidate. Commander, Department of the West, 1861; commander, Mountain Department of Virginia, Tennessee and Kentucky, 1862.

"My first impressions of him were that he was a handsome and graceful man, short and slender, with black eyes and black curly hair, rather of the 'ringlet style.' He talked very little and appeared to be as reserved in character as he was frugal in words. I admired him as one of the most notable and successful young officers in the service . . . I never could, without an effort, regard him as an American. In his appearance and manner and his habits and ideas he was essentially a foreigner . . . He appeared to be dazed with the confusion and excitement around him, and but imperfectly to realize the situation and its necessities. One may look in vain for any acts of a practical character for evidence that he was a practical man or that he possessed that robust common sense . . . essential in his position." —John Pope, *Memoirs*, p.10, 12

"Fremont was not only ambitious, but also vain, lending a ready ear to sycophants. He had very little knowledge of the nature of men . . . I believe him to have been a brave and dashing soldier. He was more than six feet high and of corresponding robustness, of dark complexion and features indicating resolution and energy. He had 'an eye like Mars to threaten and command.' When in full regimentals on a powerful black charger he paraded the streets, he looked the very ideal of a soldier." —Gustave Koerner, *Memoirs*, 2:169–170

"Fremont has totally neglected the important duties of his station and given himself up to California speculators, flatterers, etc . . . Ab. Linc. [Lincoln] was miserably in error when he had Fremont called from Europe to take command in Missouri." —Franklin Archibald Dick, *Troubled State*, p. 18, 20

"Major General Fremont—a middle-sized, middle-aged man with a weatherbeaten face and a grizzled beard, shot and thin. He looked like a man who had seen hardship." —David Hunter Strother, *A Virginia Yankee*, p. 61

"I am perfectly disgusted with the service and if I had anything else in the world to do would not remain in it one hour to be ranked and commanded by citizens who have not been in the service as many weeks as I have years, or by officers far my juniors whose only reputation in the army has been remarkable for avoiding all duty in the field—nice, good-looking, gentlemanly fellows who through political influence have been able to spend all their time in cities while others have had to do their work, and through that same influence are now put over our heads; and even some of them have been made Brigadier

Generals. Fremont is a shining example. A bigger humbug never lived. The country will find it out before long at their expense. So far he has done nothing but blunder." —Alfred Sully, *No Tears for the General*, p. 132–133

"Fremont has gained no reputation during the War. In power his surroundings have been awful. Reckless, improvident, wasteful, pompous, purposeless, vain, and incompetent. In his explorations, however, he showed perseverance and endurance, and he had the reputation of attaching his men to him . . . On all occasions he puts on airs, is ambitious, and would not serve under men of superior military capacity and experience. Fremont first and country after." —Gideon Welles, *Diary*, 2:42

"He sorely disappointed the sanguine expectations of his friends. He displayed no genius for organization. There was much sluggishness and confusion in the assembling of troops . . . There was no unity of command . . . He was surrounded by a body guard consisting mostly of Hungarians . . . It was my first meeting with Fremont. I saw before me a man of middle stature, elegant build, muscular and elastic, dark hair and beard slightly streaked with gray, a broad forehead, a keen eye, fine, regular features . . . There was an air of refinement in his bearing. His manners seemed perfectly natural, easy and unaffected, without any attempt at posing. His conversation . . . had a suggestion of reticence and reserve in it, but not enough to cause a suspicion of insincerity. The whole personality appeared rather attractive—and yet, one did not feel quite sure." —Carl Schurz, *Reminiscences*, 2:342, 344

"'The Pathfinder' is a strong Republican and Abolitionist . . . a man with a dreamy deep blue eye, a gentlemanly address, pleasant features, and an active frame, but without the smallest external indication of extraordinary vigour, intelligence or ability; if he has military genius, it must come by intuition, for assuredly he has no professional acquirements or experience." —William Howard Russell, *My Diary North & South*, p. 197

"The universal opinion is that he has entirely failed, (and that he ought to be removed)—that any change will be for the better." —John G. Nicolay, *With Lincoln in the White House*, p. 60

"Gen. Fremont needs assistance which it is difficult to give him. He is losing the confidence of men near him, whose support any man in his position must have to be successful. His cardinal mistake is that he isolates himself, & allows nobody to see him; and by which he does not know what is going on in the very matter he is dealing with. He needs to have, by his side, a man of large experience." —Abraham Lincoln, *Abraham Lincoln, Speeches and Writings*, p. 267

"Won't it be disgusting if Fremont is superseded?—the only man who has really shown that he knew what he was about. Who could replace him? . . . The only thing I have thought about lately, as (very) desirable . . . is a place on General Fremont's staff." —Robert Gould Shaw, *Blue-eyed Child of Fortune*, p. 142

WILLIAM H. FRENCH   Major general. West Point (1837). Seminole and Mexican War veteran. Brigade, division and corps commander, Army of the Potomac.

"French . . . was also thick-set, probably upwards of sixty years old, quite gray with a very red face. He had an affection of the eyes which kept him winking or blinking constantly, from which he earned the sobriquet, 'Old Blink Eye.' . . . Of General French, bronzed and grizzly bearded, we had seen much; all our work had been under his supervision. He was a typical old regular, and many were the cuffs and knocks we received for our inexperience and shortcomings . . . We felt especially pleased with the praises of General French, because it revealed the other side of this old hero's character. Rough in exterior and manner of speech, he was a strong character and a true hero." —Frederick L. Hitchcock, *War from the Inside*, p. 39, 240–241

"General W.H. French . . . was a man advanced in years . . . He had a mind of unusual quickness, well replenished by a long experience in his profession. French somehow was able to take more men into action and have less stragglers than any of his parallel commanders . . . He was often imperious and impatient, but no one ever saw his troops . . . go into action without a thrill of admiration for him and his command." —Oliver O. Howard, *Autobiography*, 1:187, 339

"He looks precisely like one of those plethoric French colonels, who are so stout, and who look so red in the face, that one would suppose some one had tied a cord tightly round their necks. Mounted on a large and fine horse, his whole aspect was martial, not to say fierce." —Theodore Lyman, *Meade's Headquarters*, p. 10

"Gen. French is a thorough soldier and doubtless an excellent division commander, but his capacity does not rise to a corps, and it is said on good grounds that he sometimes drinks too much." —Theodore Lyman, *Meade's Army*, p. 117

JAMES B. FRY   Brevet major general. West Point (1847). Mexican War veteran. Staff officer. Provost marshall general of U.S. Army.

"Fry is the firmest and soundest man I meet. He seems to combine great honesty of purpose with accurate and industrious business habits and a lively and patriotic soldier spirit that is better than any thing else, today." —John Hay, *Inside Lincoln's White House*, p. 5

JAMES A. GARFIELD   Major general. Politician and U.S. Congressman. Brigade commander, army of the Ohio. Chief of staff to Rosecrans, Army of the Cumberland.

"Garfield . . . who became an 'Old Man of the Sea' on Rosecrans' shoulders, was everlastingly meddling. Rosecrans was in many respects a man of genius and disposed to do right, but he was easily influenced, and Garfield's blarney and deceitful tongue captured Rosecrans ... His sitting complacently, cheerily at Rosecrans' table whilst writing daily letters to cut his throat occurred upon this Chickamauga campaign." —David S. Stanley, *Memoirs*, p. 158–159

"Garfield ... was a man who learned quickly and possessed a comprehensive mind. Without being a handsome man, he was fine looking, and robust and vigorous far beyond the average of men; his face then presented all the freshness of youth; his eyes were bright and large; his gaze penetrating ... He was industrious and capable of much labor of any kind—in the office tent or in the field. I think he gained considerable influence over Rosecrans and that he had his entire confidence." —William P. Carlin, *Memoirs*, p. 90

"General Garfield's military career was not of a nature to subject him to trials on a large scale ... But he always enjoyed the confidence of his immediate superiors ... As a Chief of Staff he was unrivalled. There, as elsewhere, he was ready to accept the gravest responsibilities in following his convictions. The bent of his mind was aggressive; his judgment of purely military matters was good; ... and his far-reaching, soldierly sagacity; and his conduct at Chickamauga will never be forgotten ... In political life, he is bold, manly, and outspoken ... Personally, he is generous, warm-hearted, and genial ... In person is nearly or quite six feet high, with a broad chest, and somewhat heavily-moulded figure. His head is unusually large, and his round, German-looking face, seems the very mirror of good nature." —Whitelaw Reid, *Ohio in the War*, 1:763–764

JOHN W. GEARY Major general. Businessman and lawyer. Mexican War veteran. Brigade and division commander, Army of the Potomac and Army of the Cumberland.

"He was a tall, rawboned man, with black hair. He seemed disposed to give me his military history as soon as I met him ... He told me he was the only Federal general who had ever beaten Stonewall Jackson." —William P. Carlin, *Memoirs*, p. 113

"He was a tall, athletic man, upwards of six feet in height ... He was a fine exemplar of the American gentleman, preserving the better individualities of his countrymen ... Geary could not do a mean thing, and his courage came so naturally to him that he did not consider it any cause of pride. The bias of party ... had in some degree affected the General. He was prone to go with his party in any event, when often ... his fine intelligence would have prompted him to an independent course ... I wish that all our leading men possessed his manliness, for then more dignity and self-respect, and less 'smartness' might be apparent in our social and political organizations." —George A. Townsend, *Campaigns of a Non-Combatant*, p. 268–269

JOHN GIBBON   Major general. West Point (1847). Seminole and Mexican War veteran. Commander of Iron Brigade. Brigade, division, and corps commander, Army of the Potomac and Army of the James.

"He is compactly made, neither spare nor corpulent, with ruddy complexion, chestnut brown hair, with a clean-shaved face, except his moustache, which is decidedly reddish in color, medium-sized, well-shaped head, sharp, moderately-jutting brows, deep-blue, calm eyes, sharp, slight aquiline nose, compressed mouth, full jaws and chin, with an air of calm firmness in his manner. He always looks well dressed." —Frank Haskell, *Haskell of Gettysburg*, p. 134

"He is an off-hand, soldierly man, of middle height; sharp nose, light brown hair, and rather stern of aspect. He is remarkably outspoken." —Theodore Lyman, *Meade's Army*, p. 118

QUINCY A. GILLMORE

Major general. West Point (1849). Engineer. Commander, Department of the South. Commander 10th Corps, Army of the James.

"Gillmore has high qualities as an engineer, but very little as a general in command. Lacks administrative ability, powers of organization, and has not that talent which relies on itself and keeps its own counsel." —Gideon Welles, *Diary*, 1:547

"I have a good opinion of Gillmore as a second officer and as an engineer or artillery officer, but his skill and strength in other respects and particularly in organizing and controlling men and planning and carrying out details of an important movement as chief are questionable . . ." —Gideon Welles, *Diary*, 2:128

"He never displayed remarkable merits as a leader of troops in the open field. He was a good, but not a brilliant, corps General. If he committed no grave faults . . . he never shone conspicuous above those that surrounded him. He was prudent, judicious, circumspect, not dashing, scarcely enterprising . . . he was never tried on a large scale or under favorable circumstances. But in his province as an engineer and artillerist, he was as bold as in the field he was cautious. He ignored the limitations of the books . . . General Gillmore is among the handsomest officers of the army. He is above the medium height, heavily and compactly built, with a broad chest and general air of physical solidity. His features . . . are regular and expressive. The face would be called a good-humored one, the head is shapely and the forehead broad and high. He speaks with nervous quickness . . . He is an excellent talker, and is familiar with a wide range of subjects outside of his profession. In social life he appears as an elegant and accomplished gentleman." —Whitelaw Reid, *Ohio in the War*, 1:654–655

GEORGE H. GORDON
Major general. West Point (1846). Mexican War veteran. Brigade and division commander, Army of the Potomac.

"We hear that Colonel Gordon is likely to be made Brigadier. There is not a man in the regiment . . . who will not be very sorry not to go into action under him. As far as we can judge, he is a man who would be cool and clear-headed in a fight. He has, besides, the affection of the men, and, when he takes hold, can make them do what he chooses." —Robert Gould Shaw, *Blue-eyed Child of Fortune*, p. 167

GORDON GRANGER
Major general. West Point (1845). Mexican War veteran. Brigade, division, and corps command in various capacities in western theater.

"Gordon was always an interesting person to meet. He had no reverence for rank or position. He came out bluntly with whatever he wished to say, and he didn't hesitate to tell of his own gallant deeds as well as other people's." —William P Carlin, *Memoirs*, p. 51

"Granger was a man of brains and courage, but I think a coarser grained man, both in looks and manner, I never saw . . . His broad flat face and rugged, angular features and an expression which he always wore on his face, half insolent and half familiar, indicated pretty clear his character and disposition and did not endear him to those brought into relations with him. His manner was not only blunt to a degree, but well nigh intolerable to strangers. . . . The trouble with him was, that he could not help severely criticizing, indeed abusing, those to whom he professed friendship . . . his tongue wagged at both ends and from both issued little except vitriol . . ." —John Pope, *Memoirs*, p.103

"Gordon Granger was rough in manner, but he had a tender heart. He was inclined to insubordination, especially when he knew his superior to be wrong. Otherwise he was a splendid soldier. Rosecrans named him well when he wrote of him 'Granger, great in battle.'" —J. S. Fullerton, *Battles and Leaders*, 3:667

"Gordon Granger was a cavalry officer of the old school . . . he had an ideal figure with a fine head, a fierce moustache, and a withering glance. While his port and bearing were those of the traditional swashbuckler, he had natural parts and professional acquirements far above the ordinary. Imprudent and reckless in behavior, he would do himself more harm by a day of senseless braggadocio than he could repair by a month of irreproachable conduct. A compound of opposites, inconsiderate, overbearing, and profane to a degree rarely surpassed, he knew how to be a gentleman of the most courtly manners. Brave, brilliant, and aggressive, a bolt of steel in action, he occasionally fell into fits of indolence and wasted hours when minutes were of inestimable value." —James H. Wilson, *Under the Old Flag*, p. 307

"Some of his characteristics did not impress me favorably, and I sometimes wished the distance between our camps greater. His most serious failing was an uncontrollable propensity to interfere with and direct the minor matters relating to the command, the details for which those under him were alone responsible. Ill-judged meddling in this respect often led to differences between us . . . Yet with all these small blemishes, Granger had many good qualities, and his big heart was so full of generous impulses and good motives as to far outbalance his shortcomings . . ." —Philip H. Sheridan, *Memoirs*, 1:170

ULYSSES S. GRANT Lieutenant general.
West Point (1843). Mexican War veteran. Commander, Army of the Tennessee, Military Division of the Mississippi, general in chief of U.S. Army 1864–1865.

"Grant's telegrams . . . show that he had a good memory for injuries, real or fancied, with an utter lack of sympathy or active friendship for Thomas . . . They also disclose a willingness, if not a settled purpose on Grant's part to cause Thomas' removal and downfall, provided the authorities at Washington could be induced to take the responsibility for such radical action . . . When told . . . he would have to do it himself and take the sole responsibility, he hesitated . . ." —James H. Wilson, *Under the Old Flag*, 2:66–67

"It is hard for those who knew him when formerly in the army to believe that he is a great man; then he was only distinguished for the mediocrity of his mind, his great good nature, and his insatiable love of whiskey." —Charles S. Wainwright, *A Diary of Battle*, p. 329

"Yesterday I got a sight of the new lieutenant general as he was poking around the house he has since moved into. He is not so hard looking a man as his photographs make him out to be, but stumpy, unmilitary, slouchy, and Western looking; very ordinary in fact." —Charles S. Wainwright, *Diary of Battle*, p. 338

"He was slight in figure and of medium stature, whose face bore an expression of weariness. He was carelessly dressed, and his uniform coat was unbuttoned and thrown back from his chest. He held a lighted cigar in his mouth and sat in a stooping posture . . . His trousers and boot tops were spattered with mud." —Horace Porter, *Campaigning with Grant*, p. 2

"Grant is a man of a good deal of rough dignity; rather taciturn; quick and decided in speech. He habitually wears an expression as if he had determined to drive his head through a brick wall and was about to do it. I have much confidence in him." —Theodore Lyman, *Meade's Headquarters*, p. 81

"From the first his silence was remarkable. He knew how to keep his temper. In battle, as in camp, he went about quietly, speaking in a conversational tone; yet he appeared to see everything that went on, and was always intent on business . . . In dress he was plain, even negligent; in partial amendment of that his horse was always a good one and well kept." —Lew Wallace, *Battles and Leaders*, p. 1, 404–405

"General Grant was not endowed by nature with the impressive personality and soldierly bearing of Winfield Scott Hancock, nor with the peculiarly winning and magnetic personality of William McKinley—few men are; but under a less attractive exterior he combined the strong qualities of both." —John B. Gordon, *Reminiscences of the Civil War*, p. 463

"You ask me about Grant . . . I knew him as a young man in the Mexican War, at which time he was considered a clever young officer, but nothing extraordinary. He was compelled to resign some years before the present war, owing to his irregular habits. I think his great characteristic is indomitable energy and great tenacity of purpose. He certainly has been very successful, and that is nowadays the measure of reputation." —George G. Meade, *Life & Letters*, 2:162

"Grant is emphatically an executive man, whose only place is in the field. One object in coming here is to avoid Washington and its entourage. I intend to give him the heartiest cooperation . . . I believe Grant is honest and fair, and I have no doubt he will give me full credit for anything I may do, and if I don't deserve it, I don't desire it." —George G. Meade, *Life & Letters*, 2:182, 183

"Gen. Grant is not a very fine-looking general, but he has the appearance of a man of determination. He seemed to be thinking of something else than reviews, for he often forgot to return the salute of officers in passing. No doubt he was thinking of the great work before him and forgot that he was the reviewing officer of the day . . ." —Robert McAllister, *Civil War Letters*, p. 408

"I met Grant . . . and, although somewhat disappointed at his simple and unmilitary bearing, his friendly welcome met my heart at once . . . While he showed but little of that smartness of carriage and dress and none of that

Lieutenant General Ulysses S. Grant at Cold Harbor, Virginia, June 1864.

hauteur or affectation of rank and superior knowledge which were so noticeable in McClellan . . . he seemed self-contained, simple-minded, and direct in all his thoughts and ways." —James H. Wilson, *Under the Old Flag*, 1:138–139

"General Grant is a thick-head but a fighting man. Rosecrans is a clear-headed soldier and equally a fighting man, the most promising soldier we have in the field." —David Hunter Strother, *A Virginia Yankee*, p. 137

"General Grant made a flying visit here last week. I spent the evening with him, and was most agreeably disappointed, both in his personal appearance and his straightforward, common-sense view of matters." —John Sedgwick, *Correspondence*, 2:177

"That he was bold and aggressive, we all knew, but we believed it was the boldness and aggressiveness that arise from the consciousness of strength . . . General Grant's method of conducting the campaign was frequently discussed among the Confederates, and the universal verdict was that he was no strategist and that he relied almost entirely upon the brute force of numbers for success. Such a policy is not characteristic of a high order of generalship, and seldom wins unless the odds are overwhelmingly on the side of the assailant." —Evander M. Law, *Battles and Leaders*, 4:143

"It was at General Pope's headquarters . . . that I first met General U.S. Grant. He was then a slender, straight, bright-eyed, and young looking man. I was much more pleased with his appearance and manner than I had expected to be. There had been much talk in the army and the newspapers about his alleged intemperance. He did not look like a drinking man. His mind seemed too alert and active to belong to a man addicted to that indulgence. He talked freely and with perfect frankness." —William P. Carlin, *Memoirs*, p. 50

"Grant was an uncommon fellow—the most modest, the most disinterested, and the most honest man I ever knew, with a temper that nothing could disturb, and a judgment that was judicial in its comprehensiveness and wisdom. Not a great man, except morally; not an original or brilliant man, but sincere, thoughtful, deep, and gifted with courage that never faltered . . ." —Charles Dana, *Recollections*, p. 61

"Grant always seemed pretty certain to win when he went into a fight with anything like equal numbers. I believe the chief reason why he was more successful than others was that while they were thinking so much about what the enemy was going to do, Grant was thinking all the time about what he was going to do himself." —William T. Sherman, Porter, *Campaigning with Grant*, p. 70

"When he came to the Army of the Potomac . . . I never was more surprised in my life. I had expected to see quite another type of man . . . But behold, what did I see? A medium-sized, mild, unobtrusive, inconspicuously dressed, modest and naturally silent man. He had a low, gently vibrant voice and steady, thoughtful, softly blue eyes. Not a hint of self-consciousness, impatience, or restlessness . . . on the contrary, the centre of a pervasive quiet which seemed to be conveyed to everyone around him . . ." —Morris Schaff, *The Wilderness*, p. 47

"Grant is not a striking man, is very reticent, has never mixed with the world, and has but little manner, indeed is somewhat ill at ease in the presence of strangers; hence a first impression is never favorable. His early education was undoubtedly very slight; in fact, I fancy his West Point course was pretty much all the education he ever had ... At the same time, he has natural qualities of a high order, and is a man whom, the more you see and know him, the better you like him. He puts me in mind of old [General Zachary] Taylor, and sometimes I fancy he models himself on old Zac." —George G. Meade, *Life and Letters*, 2:191

"Grant in command was ... habitually reticent. Sherman was never so. Grant meditated on the situation, withholding his opinion until his plan was well matured. Sherman quickly, brilliantly gave you half a dozen ... Sherman had remarkable topographical ability. A country that he once saw he could not forget ... Grant appeared more inclined to systematize and simplify; bring up sufficient force to outnumber; do unexpected things; take promptly the offensive; follow up a victory ... It made Grant the man for campaign and battle. Sherman was always at his best in campaign—in general maneuvers— better than in actual battle. His great knowledge of history, his topographical scope, his intense suggestive faculties seemed often to be impaired by the actual conflict." —Oliver O. Howard, *Autobiography*, 1:474–475

"I was sorry to hear ... this evening that General Grant in Tennessee is not to be depended upon. He is a man of great energy and a laborious worker, but the general says that he cannot be depended upon. He is just as likely to be drunk in the gutter as to be sober. I am therefore sorry that he is to be made a major general. If it were not for Buell, the general says that he would be licked in Tennessee." —Stephen M. Weld, *War Diary*, p. 61

"Grant was always disposed to work with the tools he had, and through his whole military career showed himself averse to meddling much with the organization of his army. He had strong likes and dislikes, but was very reticent of his expression of them. He would quietly take advantage of vacancies or of circumstances to put men where he wanted them, but very rarely made sweeping reorganization. If anyone crossed him or became antagonistic without open insubordination, he would bear with it till an opportunity came to get rid of the offender. He hated verbal quarreling, never used violent language, but formed his judgments and bided his time for acting on them." —Jacob Cox, *Reminiscences*, 2:7

"The feeling about Grant is peculiar—a little jealousy, a little dislike, a little envy, a little want of confidence—all in many minds and now latent; but it is ready to crystallize at any moment and only brilliant success will dissipate the elements. All, however, are willing to give him a full chance and his own time for it. If he succeeds, the war is over." —Charles Francis Adams Jr., *A Cycle of Adams Letters*, 2:128

"I had no immense expectations about Grant, but I was never more disappointed in my life; a more ordinary, stupid, dirty looking man I never saw in a high position. He may be a second Napoleon but it doesn't 'stick out.'" —Charles J. Mills, *Through Blood and Fire*, p. 61

"Grant is certainly a very extraordinary man. He does not look it and might pass well enough for a dumpy and slouchy little subaltern, very fond of smoking. Neither do I know that he shews it in his conversation, for he never spoke to me and doesn't seem to be a very talkative man anyhow. They say his mouth shows character. It may, but it is so covered with a beard that no one can vouch for it. The truth is, he is in appearance a very ordinary looking man . . . it would require some study to find in his appearance material for hero worship . . . in figure Grant is comical. He sits a horse well, but in walking he leans forward and toddles . . . He handles those around him so quietly and well . . . he is cool and quiet, almost stolid and as if stupid, in danger, and in a crisis he is one whom all around . . . would instinctively lean." —Charles Francis Adams Jr., *A Cycle of Adams Letters*, 2:133–134

"I have unbounded confidence in Grant, but he puzzles me as much as he appears to the rebels. He fights when we expect him to march, waits when we look for motion, and moves when we expect him to fight . . . His tenacity and his strength, combined with his skill, must, on every general principle, prove too much for them in the end." —Charles Francis Adams Jr., *A Cycle of Adams Letters*, 2:148

"Grant evidently did not get enough of West Point into him to hurt him any; he was less like a West Point man than any officer I ever knew . . . ." —Ben Butler, *Butler's Book*, 2:867

"He wears his clothes very modestly, and smokes a cigar very awkwardly, and has the approbation of the entire army, because it is believed he knows and attends to his own business." —Alexander Hays, *Letters*, p. 591

"His manner of speech is Western and Yankee. His face indicates firmness and his manner is quiet and cool. His general appearance is most unsoldierly." —David Hunter Strother, *A Virginia Yankee*, p. 286

"He is as brave as any man should be, he has won several victories such as Donelson which ought to entitle him to universal praise, but his rivals have almost succeeded . . . in pulling him down . . . He is not a brilliant man and has . . . thoughtlessly used the press to give him éclat in Illinois, but he is a good and brave soldier . . . is sober, very industrious and as kind as a child." —William T. Sherman, *Home Letters*, p. 227, 228

"As for Grant, he was like Thor . . . striking blow after blow, intent on his purpose to beat his way through, somewhat reckless of the cost. Yet he was the first one of our commanders who dared to pursue his policy of delay without apology or fear of overruling . . . That gave him more freedom and 'discretion'

General Grant with staff officers Lt. Col. Bowers and General John A. Rawlins at Grant's headquarters, Cold Harbor, Virginia, June 11 or 12, 1864.

than any of his predecessors. He had somehow, with all his modesty, the rare faculty of controlling his superiors as well as his subordinates." —Joshua Lawrence Chamberlain, *Passing of the Armies*, p. 29

"Grant was a strategist; he was not an economist. He saw what was to be done, and he set himself to do it, without being much controlled by consideration of cost or probabilities. His mechanical calculations often failed to hold good— flank movements were often belated, and so anticipated and neutralized by the enemy's vigilance and celerity; direct front attacks often proved direful miscalculation and murderous waste . . . Though he studied lines of operations, foresight was not a characteristic of his; the resolve to do overbore all negations and obliterated the limits of the possible. He so bent his energies on the main object ahead that he did not consider the effect of subordinate movements. . . He seemed to rely on sheer force, rather than skillful maneuver." —Joshua Lawrence Chamberlain, *Passing of the Armies*, p. 381

"In October, 1861, General Grant was comparatively unknown. I recollect . . . two other things apropos his appearance . . . one, a uniform coat off-color and the worse for tarnished brass buttons; another, that there was nothing about him suggestive of greatness, nothing heroic." —*Lew Wallace: An Autobiography*, 1:352

"McClellan . . . is the only man on the Federal side who could have organized the army as it was. Grant had . . . more successes in the field . . . but Grant only came in to reap the benefits of McClellan's previous efforts . . . If Grant had commanded during the first years of the war, we would have gained our independence. Grant's policy of attacking would have been a blessing to us . . ." —John S. Mosby, *Memoirs*, p. xv

"Great confidence is felt in Grant, but the immense slaughter of our brave men chills and sickens us all . . . Grant has not great regard for human life." —Gideon Welles, *Diary*, 2:44, 45

"General Grant has not discriminating powers as regards men and fails in measuring their true character and adaptability to particular service. He has some weak and improper surroundings; does not appreciate the strong and particular points of character, but thinks what one man can do another can also achieve." —Gideon Welles, *Diary*, 2:222

"General Grant has proved himself a man of military talent. Those who have doubted and hesitated must concede him some capacity as a general. Though slow and utterly destitute of genius, his final demonstrations and movements have been masterly. The persistency which he has exhibited is as much to be admired as any quality in his character. He is, however, too regardless of the lives of his men." —Gideon Welles, *Diary*, 2:276

"Grant—incomparably the greatest. He possessed an individuality that impressed itself upon all that he did. [Major General George B.] McClellan was a skillful engineer, but never rose above the average conclusions of his

council. [Major General William T.] Sherman never fought a great battle, and displayed no ordinary power. But Grant was great. He understood the terrible power of concentration and persistency . . . He concentrated all his strength, trained his energies to a single purpose, and then delivered terrible sledge hammer blows against which strategy and tactics and valor could avail nothing. He knew that majorities properly handled must triumph in war as in politics, and he always gathered his resources together before striking."
—James Longstreet, *Battle and Leaders*, 5:692

"Grant appeared to be a pleasant looking man, with a brown beard covering his face; a man of determination, but a very quiet manner. As to his dress, I cannot say, except that it was inconspicuous." —Joseph Hayes, *Generals in Bronze*, p. 136

"There was absolutely nothing of the fuss-and-feathers style, nothing of the stage or picture general about him. His head was covered with the regulation black felt hat. He wore a major-general's coat, but it was unbuttoned and unbelted. He carried no sword. On his hands he had a pair of shining white cotton gloves, and on his feet low shoes which permitted a pair of white socks to be seen, all the more as his trousers had perceptibly slipped up. He smoked a large black cigar with great energy, and looked about him in a business-like way with an impassable face." —Carl Schurz, *Reminiscences*, 3:68–69

"Gen. Grant had an inordinate love for liquors. He was not an habitual drinker. He could not drink moderately. When at long intervals his appetite for strong drink caused him to accept the invitation of some old classmate . . . he invariably drank to excess unless someone was with him . . . to lead him away from temptation. Both extremes of public rumor rested on some foundation in fact." —Sylvanus Cadwallader, *Three Years with Grant*, p. 116

"He was always calm amid excitement, and patient under trials. He looked neither to the past with regret nor to the future with apprehension. When he could not control he endured, and in every great crisis he could 'convince when others could not advise.' His calmness of demeanor and unruffled temper were often a marvel even to those most familiar with him." —Horace Porter, *Campaigning with Grant*, p. 248

"He is a man of natural, severe simplicity, in all things—the very way he wears his high-crowned hat shows this; he neither puts it on behind his ears, nor draws it over his eyes; much less does he cock it on one side, but sets it straight and very hard on his head. His riding is the same; without the slightest 'airs,' and, *per contra*, without affectation of homeliness; he sits firmly in the saddle and looks straight ahead, as if only intent on getting to some particular point." —Theodore Lyman, *Meade's Headquarters*, p. 83

"He is rather under middle height, of a spare, strong build; light brown hair, and short light brown beard. His eyes of a clear blue; forehead high; nose aquiline; jaw squarely set, but not sensual. His face has three expressions; deep thought; extreme determination; and great simplicity and calmness."
—Theodore Lyman, *Meade's Army*, p. 107

"Grant was not exciting . . . I see a plainly uniformed general of common size and build, wearing his campaign hat set squarely on his head, and sitting his horse squarely and without distinction. The figure was not impressive, nor the face under the hat inspiring. It would be easy now to say that we all perceived in the square and bluntly bearded jaw the force of relentless persistence; but I doubt we more than glimpsed a quiet solidity." —Abner R. Small, *The Road to Richmond*, p. 130

"I do not see that Grant does anything but Sit quietly about, whittle, Smoke, and let Genl. [John A.] Rawlins talk Big . . ." —Marsena R. Patrick, *Inside Lincoln's Army*, p. 369

"The Union chief had . . . many excellent qualities for a soldier. He was taciturn, sturdy, plucky, not afraid of public responsibility or affected by public opinion. There was no ostentation in his position, and to an outsider he was not as showy as a corporal of the guard." —Fitzhugh Lee, *General Lee*, p. 327

"In the end his plans, quickly made and skillfully drawn, beat the South because he, flexible by nature, remained so despite everything against him and in the face of setback upon loss after defeat. Subordinates trusted him for being open and direct . . . Grant knew how to box the compass and set the course. With the energy that brought him fame he did things his way . . ." —Justus Scheibert, *A Prussian Observes the American Civil War*, p. 5–6

"I am a great deal smarter than Grant; I see things more quickly than he does. I know more about law, and history, and war, and nearly everything else than he does; but I'll tell you where he beats me and beats the world. He don't care a damn for what he can't see the enemy doing, and it scares me like hell!" —William T. Sherman, *Battles and Leaders*, 5:114

"Grant's temperament . . . made him modest, patient, and slow to anger . . . They kept him from putting on airs, assuming superiority, or otherwise offending the sensibilities and self-respect of either the officers or men who constituted the rank and file of the army, and while these were negative virtues, they were unfortunately not possessed by all the regular army officers who found themselves in command of volunteers . . ." —James Harrison Wilson, *Battles and Leaders*, 5:118–119

"I can't spare this man; he fights." —Abraham Lincoln, *Lincoln and Men of War Times*, p. 196

"I had heard so much about the general that I was very anxious to see him. I found him only a little taller than I, thin, and very pale. I had heard so much of his roughness, and seen so much in the papers concerning his drinking habits, that I had expected to witness a different sort of man altogether. As he looked up on my approach, the clearness of his complexion and the pleasant expression of his eyes told me at once a different story . . . There was no bluster about him. He was quiet, firm, quickly had in his own mind a well-settled plan of operation or of battle, and he proceeded to its execution without faltering." —Oliver O. Howard, *Battles and Leaders*, 6:375, 379

"Grant's manners are as unpretending as his person. He receives attentions with embarrassment, and is best pleased with simple ways and little ostentation. He would scarcely be held a good conversationalist . . . His friendships are strong; so also are his prejudices . . . He is . . . rarely willing to acknowledge that he has started on a wrong course; and he rarely forgives those who, in failing to execute impossible plans, have shown their impossibility. But he is singularly free from envy or jealousy . . . On political matters he is ignorant and careless." —Whitelaw Reid, *Ohio in the War*, 1:418

"Grant is not a mighty genius, but he is a good soldier, of great force of character, honest and upright, of pure purpose, I think, without political aspirations, certainly not influenced by them. His prominent quality is unflinching tenacity of purpose, which blinds him to opposition and obstacles—certainly a great quality in a commander, when controlled by judgment, but a dangerous one otherwise. Grant is not without his faults and weaknesses. Among these is a want of sensibility, an almost too confident and sanguine disposition, and particularly, a simple and guileless disposition . . ." —George G. Meade, *Life and Letters*, 2:246

"He was simple of habit and tastes, without influence, and unambitious. Having never been brought in contact with men of eminence, he had no personal knowledge of great affairs. He had never commanded more than a company of soldiers . . . He had never voted for a President but once; he knew no politicians . . ." —Adam Badeau, *Military History of Ulysses S. Grant*, 1:8–9

"If he possessed acquirements, he appeared unconscious of them; he made no allusion to the schools, and never hesitated to transgress their rules, when the occasion seemed to him to demand it. So, he neither won men's hearts by blandishments, nor affected their imaginations by brilliancy of behavior; nor did he seem profound, to those who are impressed only by a display of learning. All these things should be appreciated by those who seek to understand his character or career." —Adam Badeau, *Military History of Ulysses S. Grant*, 1:122

DAVID MCMURTRIE GREGG Brigadier general. West Point (1855). Cavalry brigade and division commander, Army of the Potomac.

"In General David McM. Gregg . . . the cavalry had one of its best officers. He had always belonged to that branch of the service, and was noted for sterling ability and great experience. Steady as a clock and as gallant as Murat, it has often been said that he was the best all-'round cavalry officer that ever commanded a division in either army." —James H. Wilson, *Under the Old Flag*, p. 364

"Gen. Gregg has a long, tawny beard & a clear, dark blue eye; he has less dash in his expression, but more of judgment & sense than the others." —Theodore Lyman, *Meade's Army*, p. 35

CHARLES GRIFFIN Major general. West Point (1847). Mexican War veteran. Brigade, division, and corps commander, Army of the Potomac.

"General Griffin is a well known officer of the old army . . . a young man and highly reputed . . . he never drinks . . . I found Griffin a young, rather handsome man, with a face expressive of a good deal of resolution and energy, pleasant manners and a good deal of conversation." —Charles Francis Adams Jr., *A Cycle of Adams Letters*, 1:269

"Griffin is alert and independent, sincere to the core, at his ease, ready for anything,—for a dash at the enemy with battery front, or his best friend with a bit of satire when his keen sense of the incongruous or pretentious is struck . . . He was a keen observer, a sharp critic, able and prompt to use a tactical advantage, but he was not the man to take pleasure which cost another's pain, or profit from another's loss." —Joshua Lawrence Chamberlain, *Passing of the Armies*, p. 121,148

CUVIER GROVER Major general. West Point (1850). Brigade commander, Army of the Potomac; division commander, Army of the Gulf.

"I like Grover very much. He stands well as an officer and a soldier . . . Grover is so pleasant and so kind. He is an excellent officer, brave, and he has distinguished himself." —Robert McAllister, *Civil War Letters*, p. 204, 211

HENRY W. HALLECK Major general. West Point (1839). Engineer. Lawyer and administrator. Commander, Department of the Mississippi, 1862; general in chief, 1862–1863; chief of staff, 1864–1865.

"General Halleck was a man of great capacity, of large acquirements, and at the time possessed the confidence of the country and of most of the army." —William T. Sherman, *Memoirs*, 1:396

"Halleck was a mistake in the field. Large and corpulent, he could not ride a horse out of a walk. He had a staff of old or middle aged men about him. General and staff rigged themselves out in soldier's blouses and great stiff hats . . . When this queer cavalcade came riding slowly, ponderously along our lines, it was hard to suppress the boisterous laughter of the soldiers." —David S. Stanley, *Memoirs*, p. 95

"[Secretary of War of Edwin] Stanton came to caution me against trusting Halleck, who was, he said, probably the greatest scoundrel and most barefaced villain in America; he said that he was totally destitute of principle. . . . When Halleck arrived, he came to caution me against Stanton, repeating almost the same words that Stanton had employed." —George B. McClellan, *McClellan's Own Story*, p. 137

"Of all men whom I have encountered in high positions Halleck was the most hopelessly stupid. It was more difficult to get an idea through his head than can be conceived by any one who never made the attempt. I do not think he ever had a correct military idea from beginning to end." —George B. McClellan, *McClellan's Own Story*, p. 137

"In this whole summer's campaign I have been unable to see, hear, or obtain evidence of power, or will, or talent, or originality on the part of General Halleck. He has suggested nothing, decided nothing, done nothing but scold and smoke and scratch his elbows." —Gideon Welles, *Diary*, 1:373

"He was a black-browed saturnine man, heavy of figure and of feature; suspicious of everybody and incapable of friendship. He seemed to proceed on the theory that everyone around him was seeking to get some advantage of him and he was continually taking precautions against his officers, which did not attract their regard to him . . . He had a large ability of a closet kind and was in no sense brilliant—with theories often sustained and put forth by the best authorities he was familiar; acts to illustrate these theories he was utterly incompetent to do . . . He was an office man altogether and in matters of administration he had both ability and industry." —John Pope, *Memoirs*, p. 13

"As to General Halleck and his advice . . . I would say every thing was bad and mischievous. He always looked wise, but never acted so, and it was a most unfortunate thing for the country he did not stick to the law and draw briefs in place of the . . . command." —William F. Smith, *Autobiography*, p. 51

"Halleck was, I believe, a man of great ability and of high military education, though with little practical experience in war; yet his peculiar views, and still more singular action, have seemed to me very remarkable . . . He probably knew that even his great ability and education did not suffice to qualify him for the command of an army in the field." —John M. Schofield, *Forty-Six Years in the Army*, p. 360

"Halleck was not thought to be a great man in the field, but he was nevertheless a man of military ability . . . and . . . was almost invaluable as an advisor to the civilians Lincoln and Stanton. He was an honest man, perhaps somewhat lacking in moral courage, yet earnest and energetic in his efforts to sustain the national government." —Charles A. Dana, *Recollections*, p. 187

"I am fully satisfied that Halleck is as competent a theorist as we have— naturally of good strong mind, a head as strongly marked as [Daniel] Webster's, and I have known him since 1836, a hard student . . . In such man the country must have confidence. I am willing to repose in his strategy all confidence, and I think the other generals, not politicians will do the same." —William T. Sherman, *Sherman at War*, p. 54

"Halleck is certainly 'a crusty cuss' ... in about one minute he signified an emphatic disapproval of me and of my plan ... yet I was by no means disgusted with old Halleck individually ... I do like to see a man who can say 'no' and say it with an emphasis, and for old Halleck's capacity in this respect I can vouch." —Charles Francis Adams Jr., *A Cycle of Adams Letters*, 2:186–187

"I formed a very high opinion of General Halleck's sound judgment, prudence and discretion, and was encouraged by him to express opinions and make suggestions on all matters pertaining to operations under my charge ... There is ... a widespread misapprehension in regard to the interference of general Halleck with the Generals in command of armies in the field ... this, I think, is an error, and does him great injustice." —Herman Haupt, *Reminiscences*, p. 302

"Gen. Halleck devotes all his time to work. He seems to know every thing here & yet I do not know whom he consults. He is an able man—perhaps the ablest in the Country—His management matters in this State, indicate the greatest ability." —Franklin Archibald Dick, *Troubled State*, p. 64

"The army has no head. Halleck is here in the Department, a military director, not a general, a man of some scholastic attainments, but without soldierly capacity. McClellan is an intelligent engineer and officer, but not a commander to head a great army in the field. To attack or advance with energy and power is not in him; to fight is not his forte. I sometimes fear his heart is not earnest in the cause, yet I do not entertain the thought that he is unfaithful." —Gideon Welles, *Diary*, 1:107

"General Halleck is nominally General-in-Chief ... He has a scholarly intellect and, I suppose, some military acquirements, but his mind is heavy and irresolute. It appears to me he does not possess originality and that he has little real talent. What he has is educational." —Gideon Welles, *Diary*, 1:119

"Halleck is heavy-headed; wants sagacity, readiness, courage, and heart. I am not an admirer of the man. He may have some talent as a writer and critic; in all military matters he seems destitute of resources, skill, or capacity. He is more tardy and irresolute than McClellan and is deficient in the higher qualities which the latter possessed." —Gideon Welles, *Diary*, 1:216

"Halleck ... lacks power, sagacity, ability, comprehension, and foresight to devise, propose, plan, and direct great operations ... Halleck originates nothing, anticipates nothing, to assist others; takes no responsibility, plans nothing, suggests nothing, is good for nothing. His being at Headquarters is a national misfortune." —Gideon Welles, *Diary*, 1:383–384

"Halleck lacked a general's virtues. I have described him as neither born with the energy to force a good result out of a bad plan nor granted the eyes to see an enemy's weakness. Initiative had not been thrust upon him, either. He wanted the energy, the determination, the enterprise to take obstacles in stride." —Justus Scheibert, *A Prussian Observes the American Civil War*, p. 186

"The President, on my asking if Halleck had any prejudices, rejoined 'No! Halleck is fully for the service. He does not care who succeeds or who fails so the service is benefitted.'" —John Hay, *Inside Lincoln's White House*, p. 37

"When it was proposed to station Halleck here in general command, he insisted . . . on the appt. of a General-in-Chief who shd. be held responsible for the results. We appointed him & all went well enough until after Pope's defeat when he broke down—nerve and pluck all gone—and has ever since evaded all possible responsibility—little more since that time than a first-rate clerk." —Abraham Lincoln, *Inside Lincoln's White House*, p. 191–192

"Halleck was a soldier purely, and had not a particle of sympathy with the personal or political schemes of the ambitious aspirants who swarmed into Washington from every quarter of the North; he was solely and sincerely anxious for military results . . ." —Adam Badeau, *Military History of Ulysses S. Grant*, 1:129

CHARLES S. HAMILTON   Major general. West Point (1843). Mexican War veteran. Brigade commander, Army of the Potomac; division commander, Army of the Mississippi.

"General Hamilton was the most disagreeable man I had served under. He lacked many things which I had been taught to believe were essential to a gentleman. He was tyrannical, dogmatic, and repulsive in his manner and seemed to arrogate to himself the assumption of being one of the great men of the age; was always dissatisfied with the commands assigned to him and had few friends among the officers of the army in the District of West Tennessee . . ." —Benjamin H. Grierson, *A Just and Righteous Cause*, p. 139

"General Hamilton is an old acquaintance, and I feel confident will make a good commander, as cool and imperturbable as marble." —Alexander Hays, *Letters*, p. 202

WINFIELD SCOTT HANCOCK
Major general. West Point (1844). Seminole and Mexican War veteran. Brigade, division, and corps command, Army of the Potomac; commander, Veteran Reserve Corps.

"Hancock . . . was . . . a very handsome, striking looking man . . . of the military type and looked and moved grandly. He was symmetrically large, with chestnut hair and rather low forehead, but authority was in his open face, which, when times were storming, became the mirror of his bold heart . . ." —Morris Schaff, *Wilderness*, p. 42

"He was a man of the most perfect bravery, and in battle, when shot and shell were flying about him, he would sit up erect in his saddle and give his orders, launch out his oaths, and fight his corps without apparently perceiving he was in danger . . . General Hancock was tremendous in making an attack, and no one could more gallantly resist one than he would when he could see his enemy . . ." —Thomas Livermore, *Days and Events*, p. 411–412

"He was a splendid fellow, a brilliant man, as brave as Julius Caesar, and always ready to obey orders, especially if they were fighting orders. He had more of the aggressive spirit than almost anybody else in the army." —Charles A. Dana, *Recollections*, p. 190

"Hancock was a brave and capable general, but he was demonstrably passionate, and vilely abusive with his tongue . . . he would get mad at his own brother . . . and blaspheme at him and call him the conventional name a man uses, when he wants to say a mean thing of the other fellow based on the alleged status of his mother." —Charles Augustus Fuller, *Recollections of the War of 1861*, p. 56

"While he was in my corps, Hancock's activity, gallantry, cheerfulness and freedom from spite and insubordination attracted me strongly. After he was transferred I was not near enough to him to note how great success and adulation in and after the war had affected his nature, and I know not his humor now that he has been jolted on the rough ways of politics . . . but it would be impossible to corrupt Hancock." —Erasmus Keyes, *Fifty Years' Observations*, p. 449

"Upon horseback . . . he was the most magnificent looking general in the whole Army of the Potomac . . . With a large, well-shaped person, always dressed with elegance . . . he would look as if he was '*monarch of all he surveyed*,' and few of his subjects would dare to question his right to command, or do aught else but obey. His quick eye, in a flash, saw what was to be done; and his voice and his royal right hand at once commenced to do it." —Frank Haskell, *Haskell of Gettysburg*, p. 101

"Hancock is the tallest, and most shapely, and in many respects is the best looking officer of them all. His hair is very light brown, straight and moist, and always looks, well—his beard is of the same color, of which he wears the moustache and a tuft upon the chin; complexion ruddy, features neither large nor small, but well cut, with full jaw and chin, compressed mouth, straight nose, full deep blue eyes, and a very mobile, emotional countenance. He always dresses remarkably well, and his manner is dignified, gentlemanly and commanding. I think if he were in citizen clothes, and should give commands in the army to those who did not know him, he would be likely to be obeyed at once, and without any question as to his right to command." —Frank Haskell, *Haskell of Gettysburg*, p. 133

"Hancock is not the soldier that some of them are. He is a good soldier but not a great one. He can command a corps but not fit for an independent command. He has fallen heir to more that belongs to other men than any other man except Sheridan. He had the luck of inheriting other men's deeds . . ." —John Newton, *Generals in Bronze*, p. 75

"The appearance of General Hancock at the front was a most fortunate event. It gave the troops a new inspiration. They all knew him by fame, and his

stalwart figure, his proud mien, and his superb soldierly bearing seemed to verify all the things that fame had told about him. His mere presence was a reinforcement, and everybody on the field felt stronger for his being there."
—Carl Schurz, *Reminiscences*, 3:14

"He was a man of the most chivalrous courage, and of a superb presence, especially in action; he had a wonderfully quick and correct eye for ground and for handling troops; his judgment was good, and it would be difficult to find a better corps commander." —George B. McClellan, *McClellan's Own Story*, p. 140

"He is a tall, soldierly man, with light-brown hair and a military heavy jaw; and has the massive features and the heavy folds round the eye that often mark a man of ability." —Theodore Lyman, *Meade's Headquarters*, p. 82

"Hancock stands the most conspicuous figure of all the general officers who did not exercise a separate command. He commanded a corps longer than any other one, and his name was never mentioned as having committed in battle a blunder for which he was responsible. He was a man of very conspicuous personal appearance. Tall, well-formed and, at the time ... young and fresh-looking, he presented an appearance that would attract the attention of an army as he passed. His genial disposition made him friends, and his personal courage and his presence with his command in the thickest of the fight won for him the confidence of troops serving under him." —Ulysses S. Grant, *Personal Memoirs*, 2:540

CHARLES G. HARKER Brigadier general. West Point (1858).
Brigade commander, Army of the Cumberland. Killed at Kennesaw Mountain.

"Harker was a most promising young general. He reminded me of [James B.] McPherson in his younger days. If he had lived, his career would have been upward and onward ... I think Harker was entitled to the first rank, and if he had lived he would have attained it by pure merit alone." —William P. Carlin, *Memoirs*, p. 128

WILLIAM S. HARNEY Major general. Creek, Seminole, and
Mexican War veteran. Commander, Department of the West, 1861.

"General Harney was for many years a noted character in the army ... He was much above six feet in height, perfectly formed in every respect, muscular and athletic, with all the grace of movement of the feline animals ... As a soldier he had a high reputation, and was often selected for important service on the frontier. He knew how to deal with the Indian, but with the politician and the schemer he was a child only." —John Pope, *Memoirs*, p. 6–7

"I had heard a great deal of General Harney, and of his extraordinary physical accomplishments and his prowess as an Indian fighter. I saw before me a man six feet two or three inches in height, faultless in proportion, complexion bordering on the sandy, head small, eyes and countenance ordinary. I felt at once that I was in the presence of a typical Southerner, and the coldness of his salutation inclined me to credit the reports or accusations I had heard that his official conduct towards Northern officers was often harsh." —Erasmus Keyes, *Fifty Years' Observations*, p. 287

"General Harney was a singular man; if he liked you, all that you did pleased him; if not, the reverse ... General Harney was the greatest swearer I ever heard; he used to say that there was but one man in the army that could beat him and that was his brother, the Doctor." —Henry Heth, *Memoirs*, p. 127

"Harney was very cordial ... He rose before me like a giant, six feet and a half, straight and well proportioned; said at one time to have been the handsomest man in the service. He was already gray, with just enough red in his whiskers to indicate what they had been in their best days. His characteristics were peculiar; always impatient when things went awry, his language was then rough in the extreme. I noticed, however, that occasionally a good-natured oath would escape him when he was pleased ... Harney's memory was not very good. He did not appear to reason at all, but jumped to his conclusions. Notwithstanding this weakness, everybody said, 'Harney has always been a good soldier.'" —Oliver O. Howard, *Autobiography*, 1:75–76

"General Harney, a native of Louisiana, was a very remarkable man. Of strong convictions and extraordinary physical powers, he made his presence felt by all sorts of people." —Dabney H. Maury, *Recollections of a Virginian*, p. 43

JOHN F. HARTRANFT Brevet major general. Civil engineer. Brigade and division commander, Army of the Potomac.

"I should imagine, from what I hear, that he is a very good man, and the little that I have seen of him, I like. He is a gentleman, at any rate ..." —Charles J. Wills, *Through Blood and Fire*, p. 127

GEORGE L. HARTSUFF Major general. West Point (1852). Seminole War veteran. Brigade commander, Army of the Potomac; and corps commander, Army of the James.

"He was a large man, of heavy frame; his face was broad, and his bald head, tapering high, gave a peculiar pyramidal appearance to his figure. He was systematic and accurate in administrative work, patient and insistent in bringing the young volunteer officers ... into habits of order and good military form." —Jacob Cox, *Reminiscences*, 1:112–113

MILO HASCALL   Major general. West Point (1852). Brigade and division commander, Army of the Ohio.

"Hascall was a brave and reliable Indiana officer, who had seen much active field service ... he was ardently loyal, but an excitable, matter-of-fact sort of person." —Jacob Cox, *Reminiscences*, 1:469

EDWARD HATCH   Brevet major general. Businessman. Cavalry brigade and division commander, western theater.

"I looked upon him as a brave, discreet, and capable officer; one whose whole heart was thoroughly aroused in the cause of his country." —Benjamin H. Grierson, *A Just and Righteous Cause*, p. 151

HERMAN HAUPT   Brigadier general. West Point (1835). Civil and railroad engineer. Chief of construction and transportation, United States Military Railroads.

"There is one man who seems thoroughly to reflect and satisfy him in everything he undertakes. This is Haupt the Rail Road man at Alexandria. He has ... a Major General's head on his shoulders. The President is particularly struck with the businesslike character of his dispatch, telling in the fewest words the information most sought for, which contrasted so strongly with the weak whining vague and incorrect despatches of the whilom General-in-chief. If heads of shoulder-straps could be exchanged, it would be a good thing, in either case, here. A good railroader would be spoiled but the General gained would compensate." —John Hay, *Inside Lincoln's White House*, p. 38

ALEXANDER HAYS   Brevet major general. West Point (1844). Mexican War veteran. Brigade and division commander, Army of the Potomac. Killed at the Wilderness.

"We served for a time in the same regiment in the Mexican War. He was a noble man and a gallant officer. I am not surprised that he met his death at the head of his troops; it was just like him. He was a man who would never follow, but would always lead in battle —Ulysses S. Grant, Porter, *Campaigning with Grant*, p.52

"He was a strong-built, rough sort of man, with red hair, and a tawny, full beard; a braver man never went into action, and the wonder is that he was not killed before, as he always rode at the very head of his men, shouting to them and waving his sword." —Theodore Lyman, *Meade's Headquarters*, p. 92–93

WILLIAM B. HAZEN Major general.
West Point (1855). Indian Wars veteran. Brigade and division commander, Army of the Cumberland.

"Hazen was an officer of real ability, of brilliant courage and splendid personal presence. His fault was that he was too keen in seeing flaws in other people's performance of duty, and apt to dilate upon them in his official reports when such officers were wholly independent of him. This made him a good many enemies notwithstanding his noble qualities and his genial kindliness to his friends." —Jacob Cox, *Reminiscences*, 2:114

"General Hazen is of medium height, and is Saxon in hair and complexion. He carries himself erect, with a dignified bearing, which is so well in keeping with his profession, and which so plainly stamps him a soldier. As a disciplinarian he was severe, but not harsh; and though never familiar with his men; yet, upon proper occasions and under proper circumstances, no man was more approachable . . . In the field his record is enviable. Others have risen more rapidly, but none more worthily. Others have achieved more brilliant successes, but none have made fewer mistakes. If . . . his advancement was slow, he remembered that he was educated a soldier, endured his disappointment without murmuring, and set to work with greater determination . . ." —Whitelaw Reid, *Ohio in the War*, 1:769

SAMUEL P. HEINTZELMAN
Major general. West Point (1826). Mexican War veteran. Brigade, division and corps commander, Army of the Potomac.

"I saw General Heintzelman . . . yesterday; ugly as his pictures are, they flatter him; a little man, almost black, with short, coarse grey hair and beard, his face one mass of wrinkles, he wears the most uncouth dress and gets into the most awkward positions possible. He talks way down in his throat too, having lost his palate, so that one can hardly understand him. I was much disappointed in him; could not see any signs of a great man." —Charles Wainwright, *A Diary of Battle*, p. 38

"He brought a good record from the Mexican War, and was in 1861 a hardy, fearless, energetic character, which our undisciplined levies then especially needed. He had a frank way of expressing the exact truth whether it hurt or not." —Oliver O. Howard, *Autobiography*, p. 1:142

"They have given a grade to Heintselman, whom they know has neither courage nor brains, to interfere with Hooker, nor myself during a Battle. To this day, he has never in Battle come near me, (being too near for him) nor given me an order. He knows that he has not the brains for it. Gen'l Keyes is promoted. And yet he was beaten disgracefully at Fair Oakes, and I was sent to help him ... So too noble old General Sumner. He was sent to the war in disgrace at Williamsburgh. He surrendered his position on the 29th of June, without reason. And had never done anything before that ... and yet he is promoted." —Phil Kearny, *Letters from the Peninsula*, p. 127

"Heintzelman is a knotty, hard-looking old customer with a grizzled beard and shambling one-sided gait. Evidently a man of energy and reliability, and esteemed a capital soldier." —David Hunter Strother, *A Virginia Yankee*, p. 89

FRANCIS JAY HERRON Major general. Banker. Brigade, division, and corps commander in Missouri.

"Herron is a driving, energetic sort of young fellow, not deficient in self-esteem or in common sense, and ... hardly destined to distinctions higher than those he has already acquired. ... He has not the first great requisite of a soldier, obedience to orders, and believes too much in doing things his own way ... Herron was a first-rate officer, and the only consummate dandy I ever saw in the army. He was always handsomely dressed; I believe he never went out without patent-leather boots on, and you would see him in the middle of a battle—well I can not say exactly that he went into battle with a pocket-handkerchief, but at all events he always displayed a clean white one. But these little vanities appeared not to detract from his usefulness." —Charles A. Dana, *Recollections*, p. 70, 87–88

ETHAN ALLEN HITCHCOCK Major general. West Point (1817). Seminole and Mexican War veteran. Advisor to the secretary of War.

"Major General Hitchcock ... a hale looking old gentleman, a little turned of sixty, with a broad round head of the J.Q. Adams type, with a monkish baldness, having only a fringe of thin hair perfectly white on the side and back portions. He has a fine blue eye, smooth-shaven face, and probably weighs 200 pounds. He is an old army man, but I don't know what he has done in this war." —James A. Garfield, *The Wild Life of the Army*, p. 187

JOSEPH HOOKER Major general.
**West Point (1837). Mexican War veteran.
Brigade, division, corps, and army command,
Army of the Potomac; corps command, Army
of the Tennessee.**

"Fightin' Joe ... was dressed in the full uniform
of a major general ... It was the first time I had
seen General Hooker to know him. His personal
appearance did not belie his reputation. He had a
singularly strong, handsome face, sat his superb
horse like a king, broad shouldered and elegantly
proportioned in form, with a large fine head, well
covered with rather long hair, now as white as
the driven snow and flowing in the wind as he
galloped down the line, chapeau in hand; he was a
striking and picturesque figure." —Frederick L.
Hitchcock, *War from the Inside*, p. 197

"In truth, the impetuous Joseph, surnamed Hooker, hates to be behind ... is
restless, prompt, sometimes impatient, and always 'Fighting Joe.' He is not so
reckless of his men as the world thinks but is exceedingly reckless of his own
safety. You will always find him in the front. He sometimes drags us division
commanders a little farther ... than we would think it judicious to go."
—Alpheus Williams, *From the Cannon's Mouth*, p. 334

"Hooker was a strange composition ... His apparently frank manner and
agreeable address attracted everybody who approached him and his coolness
and nerve ... gained him a great deal of additional renown. In private he was
in the habit of talking very freely and did not hesitate to criticize not only
his brother officers, but his commander ... I don't think Hooker ever liked
any man under whom he was serving ... he was essentially an intriguer. In
his intrigues, he sacrificed his soldierly principles whenever such sacrifice
could gain him political influence to further his own ends." —John Gibbon,
Personal Recollections of the Civil War, p. 107

"Hooker was a man of difficult character, and more dangerous ... He was
thoroughly unprincipled and began at once, in any position, to pull down
the man above him. With a superb confidence in himself, good looks, and

plausibility he finally pulled himself to the head of the army only to show that he had risen like other balloons to sink as the weight was put on which he was not fitted for carrying." —William F. Smith, *Autobiography*, p. 32

"General Hooker was then in the prime of manhood, with steel-blue eyes, sandy hair, and clear-cut features—well set-up, but not corpulent—about six feet high; soldierly in his bearing and movements, and the beau ideal of a division commander. His talk was brilliant and incisive, and instinctively he impressed all who came in contact with him as an officer who knew what to do and how to do it, and confident of accomplishing it." —James F. Rusling, *Men and Things I Saw*, p. 67

"Hooker in no way and in no degree represents the typical soldier of the Commonwealth. His record, either as an officer or as a man, was not creditable . . . He was in 1861 and from that time forward little better than a drunken, West Point military adventurer. A showy officer, and one capable of fairly good work in a limited command—he was altogether devoid of character; insubordinate and intriguing when at the head of a corps, as a commander he was in nearly every respect lacking . . . When Hooker was in command . . . the Headquarters of the Army of the Potomac was a place to which no self-respecting man liked to go, and no decent woman could go. It was a combination of barroom and brothel." —Charles Francis Adams Jr., *Autobiography*, p. 161

"General Hooker is decidedly a very handsome man, tall and portly, but very soldierly, with a florid complexion, bright blue eyes, and an expressive nervous mouth; I should think him about 47 years old; his hair is iron grey." —Charles S. Wainwright, *A Diary of Battle*, p. 12

"General Hooker was . . . as brave as brave could be beyond a doubt . . . But he seemed to know little of the ground where his infantry were fighting; and I must say did not impress me at all favourably as to his powers as a general. His great idea was to go ahead quick until you ran against the enemy, and then fight him." —Charles Wainwright, *Diary of Battle*, p. 56

"I wish I could tell when Hooker is really speaking the simple truth; but he so universally finds fault with everybody . . . that one can attach but little consequence to what he says." —Charles Wainwright, *Diary of Battle*, p. 103–104

"I do not think him much of a general in the higher branches of that position. His bravery is unquestioned, but he has not so far shown himself anything of a tactician . . . One great quality I think he has, a good judgment of men to serve under him. I am asked on all sides here if he drinks . . . I never saw him when I thought him the worse for liquor . . . I should say his failing was more in the way of women than whiskey." —Charles S. Wainwright, *A Diary of Battle*, p. 161–162

"It was really sad to see the ravages the demon, alcohol, has made in his noble countenance . . . General Hooker is almost a drunkard, and I believe that

herein lies the secret of the hesitancy to intrust him with a high command
... But still, he is unquestionably a superior Corps commander, his troops
have almost unbounded confidence in him and all are sorry to part with him."
—Harvey Reid, *The View from Headquarters*, p. 175–176

"In regard to his drinking ... I know of his having been tight twice since I
have been here ... He is, to tell the truth, a brave, dashing soldier, rather an
adventurer than anything else, and bound to win or lose everything. Too
much given to boasting and talking, he is nevertheless a man who will win the
love and admiration of soldiers, provided that he succeeds in his first fight."
—Stephen M. Weld, *War Diary*, p. 185

"Gen. Hooker has been beaten, because he did not know his mind ... he is an
ass. As to Heintselman [*sic*], he is an old fool, and I caution Genl. McClellan,
he commands a corps, never to trust him, without minute instructions."
—Phil Kearny, *Letters from the Peninsula*, p. 86

"The appointment of Gen. Hooker is more popular than I at first apprehended
it would be, and should he succeed he will knock the wind out of some peoples
sails that I could name. This is a possibility, for Hooker will fight '*to whip*'
when he makes a start, and you may look out either for a great victory, or a
corresponding defeat when he strikes." —John W. Geary, *A Politician Goes
to War*, p. 89

"I am confident that he is the least respectable and reliable and I fear the
least able commander we have had. I never saw him to speak to, but I think
him a noisy, low-toned intriguer, conceited, intellectually 'smart,' physically
brave. Morally, I fear, he is weak; his habits are bad and, as a general in high
command, I have lost all confidence in him." —Charles Francis Adams Jr.,
A Cycle of Adams Letters, 2:6

"Hooker today ... stands lower today in the estimation of the army than ever
did the redoubtable John Pope; but what can we do? Sickles, Butterfield, and
Hooker are the disgrace and bane of this army; they are our three humbugs,
intriguers and demagogues. Let them be disposed of and the army would be well
satisfied to be led by any of the corps commanders ... there are plenty to choose
from—Sedgwick, Meade, Reynolds, Slocum, and Stoneman, any of them would
satisfy." —Charles Francis Adams Jr., *A Cycle of Adams Letters*, 2:14–15

"I infer that Mr. Hooker had a narrower escape from being the greatest man
living than even General McClellan. If he had done anything on God's earth
except retreat; if in fact he had done anything at all, instead of folding his
hands after the first crossing of the river, he must have been successful. There
never were such chances and so many of them for a lucky man to play for,
but the audacious gentleman wanted precisely what we all thought he had too
much of, viz. audacity. And on the whole, much as I should be pleased with
victory, it would have been dearly bought by inflicting us with Joseph for our
model hero." —Charles Francis Adams Jr., *A Cycle of Adams Letters*, 2:33

"Lack of confidence has steadily grown upon us. In Hooker not one soul in the army that I meet puts the slightest . . . All whom I do see seem only to sadly enquire of themselves how much disaster and slaughter this poor army must go through before the Government will consider the public mind ripe for another change. Meade or Reynolds seems to be the favorite for the rising man and either is respectable and would be a great improvement on the drunk-murdering-arson dynasty now prevailing, of Hooker, Sickles, and Butterfield." —Charles Francis Adams Jr., *A Cycle of Adams Letters*, 2:38

"Hooker is a fighting man and intuitively a soldier, but he drinks very hard, was a great gambler, and in California was very low indeed. Those men leading a division are often very formidable, but he will be a child in Lee's hands in military science." —Samuel F. P. DuPont, *Civil War Letters*, 2:411–412

"Genl Hooker is in every respect a soldier and I know him well. Under him this army will succeed if under anyone. I know he appreciates his position with regard to the enemy, and I am devoted to aiding him all in my power. He will succeed if anyone can." —Gouverneur K. Warren, *Happiness is not My Companion*, p. 68

"Hooker I am afraid has been too wicked a man to succeed in a great and holy cause. In the hour of trial he lost that support which a good man would have felt even if he were not great." —Gouverneur K. Warren, *Happiness is not My Companion*, p. 81

"He was a dashing and brave leader of any army corps. His organization and discipline of the Army of the Potomac told at Gettysburg. He failed to command the army successfully because it was perhaps over his strength. He has lost caste with the army because he was treacherous with McClellan." —David Hunter Strother, *A Virginia Yankee*, p. 191

"I know Hooker well and tremble to think of his handling 100,000 men in the presence of Lee . . . he is envious, imperious and a braggart. Self prevailed with him . . ." —William T. Sherman, *Home Letters*, p. 250, 303

"What I had seen and observed of Hooker had impressed me favorably . . . there was a promptness, frankness, and intelligence about him that compared favorably with some others . . . From what I have since heard, I fear his habits are not such as to commend him, that at least he indulges in the free use of whiskey, gets excited, and is fond of play . . . aside from the infirmities alluded to, he doubtless has good points as an officer." —Gideon Welles, *Diary*, 1:229–230

"He had been one of the bitterest critics of McClellan and Burnside, and even the administration . . . But he had made his mark as a division and corps commander . . . The soldiers and also some . . . of the generals had confidence in him . . . Hooker was a strikingly handsome man—a clean-shaven, comely face, somewhat florid complexion, keen blue eyes, well-built, tall figure, and erect soldierly bearing. Anybody would feel like cheering when he rode by at the head of his staff. His organizing talent told at once." —Carl Schurz, *Reminiscences*, 2:403

"General Hooker proved himself a brilliant corps commander on many a battlefield ... His competency as a commander of a large army was very seriously put in doubt by his amazing failure at Chancellorsville. It was in a large measure the infirmities of his character that stood in his way, impeding, if not altogether preventing, hearty co-operation between him and his comrades. He had, deservedly, the reputation of an envious critic and backbiter, running down other persons' merit to extol his own. He did not spare the best." —Carl Schurz, *Reminiscences*, 3:93

"I am delighted with Genl. Hooker. He is a perfect model of a gentleman ... I don't wonder that Hooker is so much loved by all that know him. To know him is but to love him ..." —Robert McAllister, *Civil War Letters*, p. 238

"I was very much disappointed in his appearance: red-faced, very, with a lack-lustre eye and an uncertainty of gait and carriage that suggested a used-up man. His mouth is also wanting in character and firmness; though ... he must once have been a very handsome man." —Theodore Lyman, *Meade's Headquarters*, p. 230

"In person he was of large stature, with fine features, brilliant eye, his side whiskers and ruddy countenance giving a more youthful appearance than his light gray hair would indicate. His gleaming eye told of the spirit which animated the man, and his determined air betokened the persistent and fearless soldier. In battle or on review he rode a magnificent milk white steed, a powerful animal and of extraordinary fleetness. Mounted on this superb war horse, he was the most conspicuous, as he was always one of the handsomest men in the army." —George T. Stevens, *Three Years in the Sixth Corps*, p. 179

"Of Hooker I saw but little during the war. I had known him very well before, however ... I ... regarded him as a dangerous man. He was not subordinate to his superiors. He was ambitious to the extent of caring nothing for the rights of others. His disposition was, when engaged in battle, to get detached from the main body of the army and exercise a separate command, gathering to his standard all he could of his juniors." —Ulysses S. Grant, *Personal Memoirs*, 2:539

"General Hooker had come from the East with great fame as a 'fighter,' and at Chattanooga he was glorified by his 'battle above the clouds,' which I fear turned his head. He seemed jealous of all the army commanders, because in years, former rank, and experience, he thought he was our superior." —William T. Sherman, *Personal Memoirs*, 2:59

"Hooker, or 'Fighting Joe,' as he was sometimes called, had managed a corps well, possessed personal magnetism and a fine presence, but had not the ability to conduct great operations; and yet it must be admitted his preliminary steps toward reorganization and the promotion of the battle power of his army were well taken." —Fitzhugh Lee, *General Lee*, p. 239

"I had not seen Hooker for many years, and I remembered him as a very handsome young man, with florid complexion and fair hair, with a figure agile and graceful. As I saw him that afternoon on his white horse riding in rear of his line of battle, and close up to it, with the excitement of battle in his eyes, and that gallant and chivalric appearance which he always presented under fire, I was struck with admiration. As a corps commander, with his whole force operating under his own eye, it is much to be doubted whether Hooker had a superior in the army." —John Pope, *Battles and Leaders*, 2:465

"General Hooker had grand qualities. He was cool and brave in action, clearheaded in council, and of a popular turn with the troops, and probably as able in matters purely military—in forming and executing plans of campaign embracing tactics and strategy . . . His great fault was that he was unmerciful in his criticism of senior and rival commanders." —Oliver O. Howard, *Battles and Leaders*, 5:321

"Hooker drank very little . . . yet what little he drank made his cheek hot and red & his eye brighter. I can easily understand how the stories of his drunkenness have grown, if so little affects him as I have seen. He was looking very well . . . A tall and statuesque form—grand fighting head and grizzled russet hair—red florid cheeks and bright blue eyes, forming a fine contrast with Butterfield who sat opposite. A small stout compact man with a closely chiseled Greek face and heavy black mustache . . . Both very handsome and very different." —John Hay, *Inside Lincoln's White House*, p. 80–81

"When Hooker . . . was placed in command of the army, many of us were very much surprised; I think the superior officers did not regard him competent for the task. He had fine qualities as an officer, but not the weight of character to take charge of that army. Nevertheless, under his administration the army assumed wonderful vigor. I have never known men to change from a condition of the lowest depression to that of a healthy fighting state in so short a time." —Darius Couch, *Battles and Leaders*, 3:119

"Gen. Hooker now commands the Federal Army of the Potomac . . . Gen. R[ains], who knows Hooker well, says he is deficient in talent and character; and many years ago gentlemen refused to associate with him. He resigned from the army, in California, and worked a potatoe patch, Yankee like, on speculation—and failed." —John B. Jones, *A Rebel War Clerk's Diary*, 1:253

"Hooker is a very good soldier and a capital officer to command an army corps, but I should doubt his qualifications to command a large army. If fighting, however, is all that is necessary to make a general, he will certainly distinguish himself . . . I should fear his judgment and prudence, as he is apt to think the only thing to be done is to pitch in and fight . . . I fear he is open to temptation and liable to be seduced by flattery." —George G, Meade, *Life and Letters*, 1:318–319

"Happening to meet General [Joseph G.] Totten, Chief of Engineers . . . he told me that he had been depressed by the failure of so many enterprises of late, but Hooker's order had quite put him in heart again. I was a classmate of Hooker's, and knew him too well to participate in General Totten's hopefulness . . . I was afraid Hooker, though brave, and a good corps commander, had not the ready genius to be able to manage an army on the battle-field, against either Jackson, Longstreet, or Lee, and still less against all three together. Alas! so it happened." —Edward D. Townsend, *Anecdotes of the Civil War*, p. 87–88

ALVIN P. HOVEY   Brevet major general. Businessman and

lawyer. Mexican War veteran. Brigade and division commander, western theater. Commander, District of Indiana.

"He is a lawyer of Indiana, and from forty to forty-five years old. He is ambitious, active, nervous, irritable, energetic, clear-headed, quick-witted, and prompt-handed. He works with all his might and all his mind; and, unlike most volunteer officers, makes it his business to learn the military profession just as if he expected to spend his life in it." —Charles A. Dana, *Recollections*, p. 63–64

OLIVER O. HOWARD   Major general.

West Point (1854). Brigade, division, and corps commander, Army of the Potomac. Corps and army command, Army of the Tennessee.

"The General was the only Brigadier that I saw on the field who led his men into battle & handled them there— He acted with a bravery bordering on rashness & nobly sustained his reputation as a brave & efficient officer." —Edward E. Cross, *Stand Firm and Fire Low*, p. 35

"Howard is medium in size, has nothing marked about him—has lost an arm in the war—has straight brown hair and beard—shaves his short upper lip, over which his nose slants down, dim blue eyes, and on the whole appears a very pleasant, affable, well dressed little gentleman." —Frank Haskell, *Haskell of Gettysburg*, p. 133

"Howard . . . is a man of mind and intellect. He is very honest, sincere and moral even to piety, but brave, having lost an arm already." —William T. Sherman, *Home Letters*, p. 303

"Howard . . . is brave enough, and a most perfect gentleman. He is a Christian and an enthusiast, as well as a man of ability, but there is some doubt as to his having snap enough to manage the Germans, who require to be ruled with a rod of iron . . . He is the only religious man of high rank I know of in this army, and, in the little intercourse I have had with him, shewed himself the most polished gentleman I have met." —Charles S. Wainwright, *A Diary of Battle*, p. 183, 210

"He was a slender, dark-bearded young man of rather prepossessing appearance and manners; no doubt a brave soldier, having lost an arm in one of the Peninsular battles; a West Point graduate, but not a martinet, and free from professional loftiness. He did not impress me as an intellectually strong man. A certain looseness of mental operations, a marked uncertainty in forming definite conclusions became evident in his conversation. I thought, however, that he might appear better in action than in talk ... it soon became apparent that the regimental officers and the rank and file did not take to him ... And I do not know whether he liked the men he commanded better than they liked him." —Carl Schurz, *Reminiscences*, 2:405

"He would be a decidedly handsome man, were he a little taller, having a high, projecting forehead, with a comely beard and a very thick head of hair, just now turning gray. His eyes are large and of a mild but firm look ... This general has had much abuse ... which he takes with dignity & patience." —Theodore Lyman, *Meade's Army*, p. 28

"We saw a pale young man, taller than the governor, and slender, with earnest eyes, a high forehead, and a profusion of flowing moustache and beard. Howard talked down to us ... with the tone and manner of an itinerant preacher." —Abner R. Small, *The Road to Richmond*, p. 9

"Being ostentatiously and aggressively pious, his dislike of me was I suppose purely theological, since I had stiffly declined to encourage or take part in the public wrestlings in prayer with which he bedeviled his staff, and edified the admiring young newspaper reporters. By outliving his contemporaries, and cultivating an obsequious loyalty to the ruling party and its demagogues, he has, without winning a single professional success in his whole career, attained high parchment rank since the war." —Isaac Jones Wistar, *Autobiography*, p. 397

"If he [Howard] was not born in petticoats he ought to have been, and ought to wear them. He was always taken up with Sunday Schools and the temperance cause. Those things are all very good, you know, but have very little to do with commanding army corps. He would command a prayer meeting with a good deal more ability than he would an army." —Joseph Hooker, quoted in *The Battle Cry*, 9:1, Fall 2004

ALEXANDER A. HUMPHREYS   Major general.
West Point (1831). Topographical engineer. Brigade, division, and corps command, Army of the Potomac; chief of staff, Army of the Potomac.

"He was a small, bow-legged man, with chopped-off, iron gray moustache, and when he lifted his army hat you saw a rather low forehead, and a shock of iron gray hair. His blue-gray dauntless eyes threw into his stern face the coldness of hammered steel ... And yet off duty, by his simple manners, unfailing in their courtesy, and his clear, easy, and informing talk, he bound friends and strangers to him closely." —Morris Schaff, *Wilderness*, p. 44

"You never saw such an old bird as General Humphreys! I do like to see a brave man; but when a man goes out for the express purpose of getting shot at, he seems to me in the way of a maniac ..." —Theodore Lyman, *Meade's Headquarters*, p. 108

"General Humphreys . . . was a most determined fighter, a military savant, and as modest as, and more courteous, if possible, than a lady, He was short in stature, with gray hair, keen blue eyes which, protected by gold-bowed spectacles, beamed in a philosopher-like way on one, and a square lower jaw. One of the most unassuming and of the quietest men in the world, he was, I think, the best corps commander . . . in the army." —Thomas Livermore, *Days and Events*, p. 414

"The great soldier of the Army of the Potomac . . . was General Humphreys. He was . . . a strategist, a tactician, and an engineer. Humphreys was a fighter too . . . He was a very interesting figure. He used to ride about in a black felt hat, the brim of which was turned down all around, making him look like a Quaker. He was very pleasant to deal with, unless you were fighting against him, and then he was not so pleasant. He was one of the loudest swearers that I ever knew . . . Humphreys was a very charming man, quite destitute of vanity." —Charles A. Dana, *Recollections*, p. 192

"General Humphreys . . . impresses me as one of the few able men I have met in the Army, and he is somewhat notorious as a tough old fighter." —Charles Francis Adams Jr., *A Cycle of Adams Letters*, 2:252

"Genl Humphreys, a soldier by education by nature and by experience, who has proved his title to being a gentleman and soldier in every way, whose mind has made him an enduring ornament to society & science . . . commands only a small division . . . While Danl Sickles (a defeated democratic politician, tried for murder, morally debased, and of no military experience) is in command of an army corps. Simply because he is smart as a political maneuverer." —Gouverneur K. Warren, *Happiness is Not My Companion*, p. 68

"The Chief-of-Staff is General Humphreys, a very eminent engineer. He is an extremely neat man, and is continually washing himself and putting on paper dickeys. He has a great deal of knowledge, beyond his profession, and is an extremely gentlemanly man . . . He is most easy to get on with, for everybody; but, practically, he is just as hard as the Commander, for he has a tremendous temper, a great idea of military duty, and is very particular. When he does get wrathy, he sets his teeth and lets go a torrent of adjectives that must rather astonish those not used to little outbursts." —Theodore Lyman, *Meade's Headquarters*, p. 6–7, 73

HENRY J. HUNT Major general. West Point (1839). Artillerist. Mexican War veteran. Chief of Artillery, Washington defenses and chief of artillery, Army of the Potomac.

"Hunt . . . whose complexion was about the color of an old drum-head, had rather dull black eyes, separated by a thin nose. His West Point classmates loved him, and called him 'Cupid.' He was lion-hearted, and had won brevet on brevet for gallant conduct." —Morris Schaff, *Wilderness*, p. 45

"I regarded him as the best living commander of field-artillery. He was a man of the utmost coolness in danger, thoroughly versed in his profession, an admirable organizer, a soldier of a very high order ... a man whose service in any other army would have been rewarded by titles, high rank, and ample pension. He is one of the most marked instances ... of the highest merit and services passed over unacknowledged and unrewarded. Hunt's merits consisted not only in organizing his command to the utmost advantage, but in using it on the field of battle with the utmost skill and power." —George B. McClellan, *McClellan's Own Story*, p. 117

DAVID HUNTER   Major general. West Point (1822). Veteran of Seminole and Mexican War. Division commander, commander, Western Department, 1861; commander, Department of the South, 1862; commander, Army of the Shenandoah, 1864.

"He is a man of about sixty years of age, wears no other whiskers than a mustache which together with his somewhat thin hair is dyed black. He has keen gray eyes, a long nose, slightly aquiline, a large mouth with corners slightly depressed, and the whole shut with a sharp decisiveness. He has a habit of swaying his head from side to side when he speaks, and seems to sling his quick decisive words right and left. He is probably 5 feet 10 inches and weighs 175 pounds." —James A. Garfield, *The Wild Life of the Army*, p. 187

"Hunter ... was an old officer of the Regular Army, highly esteemed by everybody who knew him, whether in or out of the army and was altogether one of the most upright, earnest and honest men I ever knew. He was intensely patriotic and could find no excuse for anyone who was not zealous and pronounced on the Union side. He was a Virginian by birth, dark of visage, and healthy of complexion, with long black hair and piercing black eyes ... He was a thoroughly genuine and thoroughly trustworthy man and soldier." —John Pope, *Memoirs*, p. 12

"An effective campaign from our base was just as far from realization under Hunter as under [Thomas W.] Sherman. These two generals were equally brave, equally patriotic, and equally incompetent. They were lacking in aggressiveness and initiative ... Hunter ... was a fine, gallant, and manly old fellow, but for the time he was more interested in abolishing slavery than in putting down the rebellion." —James H. Wilson, *Under the Old Flag*, p. 91–92

"General Hunter is very unpopular—arbitrary and wholly taken up with his negro question. His one regiment is a failure ... and I have no faith in the experiment anyhow." —Charles Francis Adams Jr., *A Cycle of Adams Letters*, 1:171

"General Hunter is a man of the finest bearing, tone, and address; silent, but not like most silent men, he is uncommonly gracious and benign in his intercourse. He is easy in his private means, and very independent in thought and action, has no fear of responsibility, yet very devoid of pretension—I don't know what his military capacity is in the opinion of such as are capable of judging in such matters. To all who have approached him on the slavery question, he has been very frank." —Samuel F. DuPont, *Civil War Letters*, 2:45

"I like General Hunter. He is manly, frank, brave, cordial, and a Christian man to boot—makes it a point, like a military man, that his Bible and prayer book shall be on his table in his sitting room." —Samuel F. DuPont, *Civil War Letters*, 2:217

"Gen. Hunter is military in his bearing, systematic in his business affairs & fond of military display, rides a beautiful horse with elegance & admires the strong muscle of the hardy Western soldier, while he takes almost equal pride in the polished trappings of the soldiers of the Eastern Army. Nor does he despise the misfortune of the poor negro. He is sometimes called 'Black Dave' because of his efforts to ameliorate the condition of the poor blacks." —Alvin C. Voris, *A Citizen-Soldier's Civil War*, p. 115

"Major General David Hunter, of the United States Army, was a torch bearer if nothing else. He had no military distinction, but had served against the Indians . . . with the same cruelties it was now his delight to apply to non-combatant dwellers in southwest Virginia and the head of the Shenandoah Valley. No property within reach of his destroying hand seemed safe from him. His fame lay not in the soldier's hard-fought battles, but in burning farmers' houses and barns." —G. Moxley Sorrel, *Recollections of a Confederate Staff Officer*, p. 274–275

"I think him honest and patriotic, which are virtues in these days, but he has not that discretion and forbearance sufficient to comprehend rightly the position that was given him." —Gideon Welles, *Diary*, 2:97

"General Hunter must have possessed some high qualities, or he would not have been intrusted with the grave responsibilities which attach to the commander of a department; but it is hard to trace any evidences of knighthood in the wreck and ravage which marked the lines of his marches." —John B. Gordon, *Reminiscences of the Civil War*, p. 301–302

"If those old barbarians were savage and cruel, they at least had the manliness and daring of rude soldiers, with occasional traits of magnanimity. Hunter's deeds were those of a malignant and cowardly fanatic, who was better qualified to make war upon helpless women and children than upon armed soldiers." —Jubal A. Early, *Memoir of the Last Year of the War*, p. 48

"The memory of General Hunter will live and be handed down through the generations to come . . . in connection with deeds that illustrate how far the passions, fanaticism, and hate engendered by civil war can drag a man down, from the boasted civilization of our age and country, to the barbarism and implacable animosities of that long period of cruel persecution, oppression, and outrage which, by the common consent of mankind, we denominate 'The Dark Ages.'" —John D. Imboden, *The Annals of the Civil War*, p. 169–170

"Genl Hunter doesn't impress me as being a great man. There is some talk of his being relieved. If we could have Fremont in his place, wouldn't it be fine?" —Robert Gould Shaw, *Blue-eyed Child of Fortune*, p. 340

STEPHEN A. HURLBUT Major general. Lawyer, Seminole War veteran. Illinois politician. Division commander, Army of the Tennessee, commander 16th Corps at Memphis; commander, Department of the Gulf, 1864.

"Major General Hurlbut was a man of marked ability and generous impulses. The government had few more deserving officers, and no more earnest and devoted servant." —Benjamin Grierson, *A Just and Righteous Cause*, p. 234

"I had known Hurlbut as a young lawyer . . . at which time he took a special interest in military matters, and I found him far above average in the knowledge of regimental and brigade drill . . ." —William T. Sherman, *Personal Memoirs*, 1:247

RUFUS INGALLS Major general. West Point (1843). Quartermaster department service in ante bellum years. Chief quartermaster of U.S. armies during the Civil War.

"Ingalls, the chief quartermaster . . . [was] a chunky, oracular-looking man who carried sedulously a wisp of long hair over his otherwise balding pate, and who, besides being the best quartermaster the war produced, could hold his own very well with the best poker players in the army or Congress . . ." —Morris Schaff, *Wilderness*, p. 45

ANDREW JOHNSON Brigadier general. Politician. Military governor of Tennessee. Vice president and president of the United States.

"Andrew Johnson has been appointed & confirmed a Brigadier Genl.—*Military Governor of Tennessee* & goes out to start proper measures in the State, to enable the loyal people to take measures to constitute a loyal Civil Gov't. This is a most important thing & Johnson is the very man to lead & manage the reform." —Franklin Archibald Dick, *Troubled State*, p. 72

"The governor was fearfully drunk when he went on to Washington, and when he was sworn in as Vice President of the United States . . . From a bitter hater, he became the friend and servant of the Secessionists . . . Johnson sprang from the very lowest class of poor whites and naturally hated an aristocrat. But, when these same aristocrats became suppliants after the war, he took them to heart and made them confidants." —David S. Stanley, *Memoirs*, p. 225

"He had worked himself up from poverty and a low social position to political prominence by the energy of his character and a degree of ability which, if not brilliant, was at least higher than that of his political competitors in East Tennessee . . . His countenance was of a distinctly plebian cast . . . there was no genial sunlight in it; rather something sullen, something betokening a strong will inspired by bitter feelings . . . Johnson was by no means a man of culture." —Carl Schurz, *Reminiscences*, 3:95–96

RICHARD W. JOHNSON Brevet major general. West Point (1849). Frontier service. Brigade and division commander, Army of the Cumberland; chief of cavalry, Military Division of the Mississippi.

"General Johnson and General [Absolom] Baird were graduates of the military academy at West Point, and General [Jefferson C.] Davis was appointed from civil life . . . Johnson was a Kentuckian and not over fond of the anti-slavery policy of the government. He was, however, a patriotic man and was for the Union. Davis was an Indiana copperhead . . . but he was a soldier. He loved his country and honored its flag . . . He was one of the bravest of the brave. Baird . . . had belonged to the department of the adjutant-general before the war. He did not like my assignment to the corps, and I had much trouble with him; so that one day I called upon General [George H.] Thomas and asked him to relieve Baird . . . We entered upon the Atlanta campaign and fought several battles; Thomas said to me one day, 'how about relieving Baird?' I answered, 'No, Baird is a fighter—he devils the Rebs more than he ever did me.' General Baird is now retired, but I had no more gallant officer, and we became very warm friends." —John M. Palmer, *Personal Recollections*, p. 198–199

"Gen. Johnson, our division commander, was an accomplished soldier and a refined and genial gentleman, but . . . he was the politest when he was most dangerous." —Benjamin Scribner, *How Soldiers were Made*, p. 239

PHILIP KEARNY Major general. Adventurer. Graduate of French Cavalry School at Saumur (1839). Mexican War veteran. Brigade and division commander, Army of the Potomac. Killed at Chantilly, September 1, 1862.

"Kearny was tall—nearly 5 foot 10 or 11; Moderate prominent cheekbones; well developed jaws marking decision in every lineament; his forehead was very full over the brows; his eyes were light, mixed between blue and gray; sharp angular features with the old French style of mustache and goatee . . . Kearny gave great personal attention to his mustache and goatee, having a barber every morning . . . Every muscle of his face bristled with the military spirit of the man, and so powerful was the expression of his countenance . . . that he seemed to spread a very contagion of courage and enthusiasm among those about him . . ." —James Rowan O'Beirne, *Generals in Bronze*, p. 293

"I called on and saw for the first time Gen. Phil Kearney, the one-armed hero of the Mexican War. Kearny without being a handsome man was one calculated to attract attention anywhere. He was all soldier, but his soldierly bearing was not seen to perfection until mounted on his spirited, well-broken horse he passed in review at the head of his troops, and gracefully dropping his rein from his single hand, saluted with his sword." —John Gibbon, *Recollections of the Civil War*, p. 20–21

"Although he stood high as a remarkably daring man and good cavalry captain in the Mexican war, I had not sufficient confidence in his brains to give him one of the first divisions. I have . . . sometimes thought that I would have done well had I given him command of the cavalry." —George B. McClellan, *McClellan's Own Story*, p. 138

"General Phil Kearny [was] always irritable, and ungovernable—his disposition had been additionally soured by his domestic and social cares, and like most of the old officers he could not conform himself to the new regime . . ." —William F. Smith, *Autobiography*, p. 32

"There have been few such officers as Kearny in our own or any other army. In war he was an enthusiast, and he never seemed so much at home and so cheerful and confident as in battle. Tall and lithe in figure, with a most expressive and mobile countenance, and a manner which inspired confidence and zeal in all under his command, no one could fail to admire his chivalric bearing and his supreme courage . . . He was a great and most accomplished soldier, and died as he would himself have wished to die . . . at the head of his troops and in the front of the battle." —John Pope, *Battles and Leaders*, 2:492

"Kearny . . . was calm and deliberate, and would not put a man into position until he had examined his ground, and knew what he had to do." —Charles Wainwright, *Diary of Battle*, p. 56

"One who saw Philip Kearny recognized in him the typical soldier . . . A head, the picture of energy . . . a strongly marked nose, and a piercing eye, gave him the look of an eagle. His abrupt speech and his imperious manner denoted a proud disposition, and a character incapable of flattery or of dissimulation. But though at first his manner was not always fitted to attract, one soon learned to appreciate the noble qualities of his heart . . . This man . . . was calmness itself in the presence of the enemy. His unerring eye, his prompt decision, his clear and concise orders, at once revealed in him the warrior." —Comte de Paris, *Letters from the Peninsula*, p. 25

"His bravery and dash were proverbial, and never questioned by any one. He was rich by inheritance, profuse in his generosity, and polite in society. His occasional rashness in the pursuit of fame, and his lack of reserve when opposed or thwarted in his ambition, were also well understood." —Erasmus Keyes, *Fifty Years' Observations*, p. 470

"Kearny had been a conspicuous young officer in the Mexican War, where he lost his arm . . . he was a small, dashing-looking man, possessed, it was thought, of considerable military ability." —G. Moxley Sorrel, *Recollections of a Confederate Staff Officer*, p. 98

"I find him . . . a strikingly fine, soldierly figure, one-armed, thin face, pointed beard, fiery eyes, his cap somewhat jauntily tipped on the left side of his head, looking much as we might expect a French general to look." —Carl Schurz, *Reminiscences*, 2:365

"General Phil Kearny [was] always irritable, and ungovernable—his disposition had been additionally soured by his domestic and social cares, and like most of the old officers he could not conform himself to the new regime of a general-in-chief of McClellan's role in the army." —William F. Smith, *Autobiography*, p. 32

"He was known as the 'one-armed Devil,' and was, by odds, the best educated of all the Federal military chiefs. But, singularly enough, he departed from all tactics, when hotly afield. His personal energy and courage have given him renown, and he loved to lead forlorn hopes, or head storming-parties, or ride upon desperate adventures." —George A. Townsend, *Campaigns of a Non-Combatant*, p. 176

ERASMUS D. KEYES Major general.
West Point (1832). West Point instructor. Brigade, division and corps commander, Army of the Potomac.

"It was in November 1861, that I reported to General Keyes for duty as aide de camp; and very early in my career on his staff I learned to appreciate his worth as a man and soldier. To a constitution of iron, and an untiring industry . . . with all the duties appertaining to his profession, and a finished ability in the performance of those duties, he added, in a marked degree, an intense earnestness and honesty of purpose. To him the war meant something more than the mere gaining of battles, something far higher and nobler than the personal rewards of success. His whole heart was in the cause of suppressing the Rebellion and maintaining the dignity of the Government, and he was outspoken in expressing his convictions." —Colonel C. C. Suydam, *Fifty Years' Observations*, p. 491

HUGH JUDSON KILPATRICK

Major general. West Point (1861). Cavalry brigade and division commander, Army of the Potomac; chief of cavalry with William T. Sherman 1864–1865.

"Gen. Kilpatrick is a spare, nervous, jerky man, with a long, thin, aquiline nose, no upper lip to speak of and light hair." —Theodore Lyman, *Meade's Army*, p. 35

"I know that Kilpatrick is a hell of a damned fool . . . but I want just that sort of man to command my cavalry on this expedition." —William T. Sherman in Wilson, *Under the Old Flag*, 1:372

NATHAN KIMBALL   Brevet major general. Teacher and doctor.

Mexican War veteran. Brigade and division commander, Army of the Potomac; division commander in western theater.

"Gen. Kimball was cool, brave and popular. His men would fight at anytime, and win, too. He was emphatically a fighting man & thoroughly believed in the philosophy of hard knocks. We won with him." —Alvin C. Voris, *A Citizen Soldier's Civil War*, p. 115

"He is not so bad a commander as [Jacob G.] Lauman, but he is bad enough; brave, of course, but lacking the military instinct and the genius of generalship." —Charles A. Dana, *Recollections*, p. 67

"General Nathan Kimball [was] a swarthy, grizzly-bearded old gentleman, with lots of fire and energy in his eyes . . . General Kimball was a rigid disciplinarian, but withal a very kind-hearted man." —Frederick L. Hitchcock, *War from the Inside*, p. 20, 26

RUFUS KING   Brigadier general. West Point (1833). Civil engineer.

Brigade and division commander, Army of the Potomac.

"Brigadier General King . . . a man of about 40 years, rather spare built, with shaggy black hair and full whiskers of the same color, with a rugged, strongly-marked face enlightened by a steel-gray eye and surmounted by a knotty Roman nose of the Bascom sort. He has a weather-beaten, powder-blackened look which reminds us for [of] the rugged fighting he has done and the sturdy blows he has struck . . . Three deep, permanent, vertical wrinkles in the forehead where brow and nose join set off the expression and complete the picture of the man who has evidently got him a large fund of hard sense and hard work." —James A. Garfield, *The Wild Life of the Army*, p. 187

EDWARD N. KIRK Brigadier general. Lawyer. Brigade
commander, Army of the Cumberland. Mortally wounded at Stones River.

"Kirk was a gallant man, a good soldier, and a careful commander . . . A braver man never went into battle than E.N. Kirk, and the members of his family have every reason to be proud of the splendid record, for courage and devotion to duty, which he has left them." —Richard W. Johnson, *Battles and Leaders*, 5:300

FREDERICK W. LANDER Brigadier general. Engineer.
Brigade and division commander in eastern theater. Died suddenly in Shenandoah Valley.

"He was of reckless daring, of rough manners, but a kind & generous heart, perhaps not a great General but was a noble soldier. It is feared that intemperance had much to do in taking him thus untimely from the field." —Alvin C. Voris, *A Citizen Soldier's Civil War*, p. 33

JACOB GARTNER LAUMAN Brevet major general.
Businessman. Brigade and division commander, Army of the Tennessee.

"This general got his promotion by bravery on the field and Iowa political influence. He is totally unfit to command—a very good man but a very poor general." —Charles A. Dana, *Recollections*, p. 67

MICHAEL K. LAWLER Brigadier general. Farmer and
Mexican War veteran. Brigade and division command in Army of the Tennessee and other assignments in western theater.

"General Lawler was a large and excessively fat man—a fine type of the generous, rollicking, fighting Irishman. His cherished maxim was the Tipperary one: 'If you see a head, hit it.' He was precisely the kind of officer to make an assault, and ask permission to do so afterwards." —Sylvanus Cadwallader, *Three Years with Grant*, p. 83–84

"When it comes to just plain hard fighting, I would rather trust Old Mike Lawler than any of them . . ." —Ulysses S. Grant in Wilson, *Under the Old Flag*, 1:178

"That officer was a very remarkable volunteer tactician, an ex-captain of the Mexican War, a plain Illinois farmer all his life, with a fine literary taste, and a most gallant bearing . . . he was a man of no pretensions either in manners or dress. His favorite uniform was a blue flannel shirt, on which he tacked his shoulder straps, and he was of such ample proportions that he always wore his sword hung by a strap over his shoulder . . . Lawler . . . was a strictly temperate man, a devout Catholic, and as imperturbable under fire as any 'Ironsides.'" —James H. Wilson, *Under the Old Flag*, p. 177–178

"Lawler weighs two hundred and fifty pounds, is a Roman Catholic . . . and served in the Mexican War. He is as brave as a lion, and has about as much brains; but his purpose is always honest, and his sense is always good. He is a good disciplinarian and a first-rate soldier." —Charles A. Dana, *Recollections*, p. 65

JAMES H. LEDLIE   Brigadier general. Civil and railroad engineer. Brigade and division commander, Army of the Potomac.

"General Ledlie was drunk on May 24, at the North Anna. There were several times that he had had too much to drink during the campaign. I think the poor man was a coward and took the liquor to try and fortify himself for the fight." —Stephen M. Weld, *War Diary*, p. 311

"He is about thirty, very talkative, and 'blows' a good deal, and fusses, though at the same time he has considerable ability . . . He is brave to rashness in a fight, but apt to lose his head, and on the whole I shouldn't have much confidence in him. He is rather a 'rough,' but at the same time can be gentlemanly and pleasant, and is always very kind and considerate . . . On the whole, we might do much worse, but he is by no means my ideal of a General." —Charles J. Mills, *Through Blood and Fire*, p. 101–02

MORTIMER D. LEGGETT   Major general. Lawyer and school superintendent. Brigade and division commander, Army of the Tennessee.

"He possesses a clear head, and equable temper, and a great propulsive power over his men. He is also a hard worker, and whatever he touches goes easily." —Charles A. Dana, *Recollections*, p. 68

"He is a strictly moral man, never drinks anything that will intoxicate, never smokes cigars, never chews tobacco, never uses profane language, and never plays cards; and drinking and card-playing were always prohibited at his head-quarters. His services lasted from the beginning to the close of the war; they were always honorable, often arduous, and sometimes distinguished, so that in the end he came to command the trust of his superiors, the admiration of his soldiers, and that gratitude from the country which all deserve who add capacity and skill to their personal devotion." —Whitelaw Reid, *Ohio in the War*, 1:810

JOSEPH ANDREW JACKSON LIGHTBURN
Brigadier general. Regular army service as enlisted man. Brigade commander, Army of the Tennessee.

"Lightburn was one of the loyal West Virginians whose standing and intelligence made him naturally prominent among his people. He was a worthy man and an honorable officer, whose knowledge of the country and of the people made him a fit selection to preserve the peace and protect our communications..." —Jacob Cox, *Reminiscences*, 1:206

JOHN A. LOGAN   Major general. Mexican
War veteran. Lawyer and Congressman from Illinois. Brigade, division, and corps command, Army of the Tennessee.

"Logan was very successful in civil life and made his mark upon the history of the country as a statesman, yet he was first and pre-eminently a soldier in instinct, in capacity and in inclination ... His swarthy countenance, his fierce black eyes and long black hair, his erect martial figure and impetuous mien were known to all the armies with which he served..." —John Pope, *Memoirs*, p. 99

"Logan ... was an officer of volunteers. Although he had gained his knowledge of the art of war in the face of the enemy—was capable, worthy, and efficient, and always successful wherever placed ... yet he was passed over, or pushed aside, [so] that an officer of another army ... might be given the place." —Benjamin Grierson, *A Just and Righteous Cause*, p. 281

"We must deal with men as we find them and it is not Logan's fault that he was a citizen only three years ago, and looks at all questions from another view than a professional soldier ... I was not sorry to hear him say that on the whole he would content himself with his present command, though it is an inferior one." —William T. Sherman, *Sherman at War*, p. 126

"Logan had won his military promotion by brave and valuable service, and could show honorable scars for each of his grades. The trait in him most criticised by his companions in arms was his querulousness and disposition to find fault with commands given him. He could see fifty reasons why a different order should have been issued; but when once in battle his conduct was brilliant as well as judicious, and his personal gallantry was proverbial." —Jacob Cox, *Atlanta*, p. 178

"A great change came over him in after life, when I think he renounced his earlier political habits of drinking and swearing. He was developed and broadened by the times, and grew up to requirements of the eminent military and civil positions he afterwards held . . . I saw him on one occasion . . . with nothing on him in the way of clothing but his hat, shirt and boots, sitting at a table on which stood a bottle of whiskey and a tin cup, and playing on a violin for a lot of darky roustabouts to dance . . . Yet he was never accused of drunkenness . . ." —Sylvanus Cadwallader, *Three Years with Grant*, p. 67

"In the beginning of a fight he was one of the bravest men that could be, saw no danger, went right on fighting until the battle was over. Then, after the battle was won, his mind gained an immovable conviction that it was lost. Where we were victorious, he thought that we were defeated . . . It was merely an intellectual peculiarity. It did not in the least impair his value as a soldier or commanding officer. He never made any mistake on account of it." —Charles A. Dana, *Recollections*, p. 54

"This is a man of remarkable qualities and peculiar character. Heroic and brilliant, he is sometimes unsteady . . . A man of instinct and not of reflection, his judgments are often absurd, but his extemporaneous opinions are very apt to be right. Deficient in education, he is full of generous attachments and sincere animosities. On the whole, few can serve the cause of the country more effectively than he, and none serve it more faithfully." —Charles A. Dana, *Recollections*, p. 68

NATHANIEL LYON Brigadier
general. West Point (1841). Seminole and Mexican War veteran. Commander of St. Louis Arsenal. Killed at Wilson's Creek, August 10, 1861.

"I think Lyon could never have been a great commander. He had been an infantryman too long and was always absorbed in details. He wanted to do everything himself, instead of dividing up his work among others. He was a quartermaster, commissary and ordnance officer . . . and hard work was breaking him down rapidly. In appearance he was singular—of delicate, slim figure, his heavy hair was auburn, his whiskers red and his eyes blue. A man of great resolution, he had traits that made him unpopular. He was a radical abolitionist and an aggressive atheist. He continuously thrust his doctrines

upon people who despised them. Lyon liked to argue, especially with women, and he would insist that religion was only superstition. Of course such a man could not be popular . . . Lyon's was a great loss to the Union cause, but I doubt if he could ever have become a great general."
—David S. Stanley, *Memoirs*, p. 74

"Rarely have I met so extraordinary a man as Lyon, or one that has interested me so deeply . . . this mere captain of infantry, this little, rough-visaged, red-bearded, weather-beaten Connecticut captain, by his intelligence, his ability, his energy, and his zeal, had at once acquired the confidence of all the Union men of Missouri, and had made himself respected, if not feared, by his enemies." —Col. Thomas L. Snead, *Battles and Leaders*, 1:273

"Lyon was a Yankee of Yankees, with all the forbidding manners and stern look of the Covenanters of old, but with none of their piety. He believed in the government and the flag with the fury of the wildest fanatic and could scarce hold conference with those who were disloyal to either. To the Secessionist and the schemer in Missouri there could not have been found a more formidable and dangerous opponent than General Lyon."
—John Pope, *Memoirs*, p. 8

"Nathaniel Lyon, of the regular army . . . was . . . a man of as much capacity as (Francis P.) Blair, fully as energetic, and as quick to decide and execute, with a will as strong but even more relentless; and absolutely fanatical and indifferent concerning the means he employed to accomplish what he deemed a proper end." —Basil Duke, *Reminiscences*, p. 35

"Lyon was a man whose appearance made a false report of his qualities. He was plain in person, and his countenance was not expressive. Nevertheless, he possessed decided ability, and his temperament was of the most ardent . . . he avowed his Northern sentiments in all situations with a fearlessness which had few examples in the army under the old regime." —Erasmus Keyes, *Fifty Years' Observations*, p. 359

"He was a small man, about 5 ft 5, sandy hair, & beard & mustache—wore a black slouched hat & his captain's uniform—not very neat—& carried a hooked old hickory cane all the time. I . . . found him well informed in the latest occurrences & possessed of congeniality . . . He was a great strength to the cause in Missouri." —Franklin Archibald Dick, *Troubled State*, p. 7, 11

"Lyon was one of the most valuable of their Generals, being a man of more than average ability, and of unswerving purpose. He would have been the general of the abolition school. He was a man of cruel disposition—who would never forego an advantage over an enemy . . . His ability was shown at West Point, chiefly in mathematics. He could not acquire languages, chemistry, or anything in which memory played a part." —Josiah Gorgas, *The Journals of Josiah Gorgas*, p. 42

WILLIAM H. LYTLE
Brigadier general. Lawyer. Mexican War veteran. Brigade commander, Army of the Cumberland. Killed at Chickamauga, September 20, 1863.

"In figure General Lytle was graceful and well-developed. His head was well-proportioned, and was covered with masses of long silken brown hair. His complexion was so fair as to be almost effeminate; but it was relieved by a flowing beard. A high, intellectual brow, expressive gray eyes, delicately curved nostrils, and a resolute mouth, made up an agreeable face, illuminated with the light of genius, and toned down by that unaffected modesty which ever distinguished him. Till the outbreak of the war poetry was to him a frequent occupation and amusement . . ." —Whitelaw Reid, *Ohio in the War*, p. 883

JOSEPH K. MANSFIELD
Major general. West Point (1822). Engineer. Mexican War veteran. Brigade, division, and corps commander, Army of the Potomac. Killed at Antietam, September 17, 1862.

"General Mansfield . . . was a peculiar man, combining in his own person two quite distinct characters, almost the precise opposite of each other. In ordinary times . . . he was a sort of fussy, particular man, very much given to pry into all manner of details and to meddle with other peoples' work . . . His manner, too, was querulous and fault-finding . . . Place this same man on a field of battle . . . and a transformation . . . at once appeared. It was magnificent to see General Mansfield in battle. He visibly swelled before your eyes; his face flamed out with fiery ardor and his whole figure and his every movement seemed filled with a sort of terrible passion. He was like a lion . . . Mansfield had a keen military eye and most excellent military judgment . . . General Mansfield was of middle height and robust figure. He had a broad and rather ruddy face, with a thick shock of white hair and beard. He was a man of kindly disposition and very just; but . . . he was rather fussy and fond of meddling with his subordinates . . ." —John Pope, *Memoirs*, p. 199

"He was already frosted with age and long service. Probably from his own Christian character no officer of the army then could have inspired me with more reverence than he." —Oliver O. Howard, *Autobiography*, p. 132

"Lamon says Gen. Mansfield is a good enough old man but he never had an idea till the next day." —John Hay, *Inside Lincoln's White House*, p. 77

JOHN HENRY MARTINDALE
Brevet major general. West Point (1835). Lawyer. Brigade and division commander, Army of the Potomac.

"He is full of business, as usual, spread Eagle, but withal, very able & devoted to his profession." —Marsena R. Patrick, *Inside Lincoln's Army*, p. 31

ROBERT McALLISTER
Brevet major general. Farmer and railroad executive. Brigade commander, Army of the Potomac.

"McAllister—a middle-aged, dried up, Puritanical man, not brilliant of intellect, but an indomitable fighter." —Theodore Lyman, *Meade's Army*, p. 258

JOHN A. McARTHUR
Brevet major general. Iron manufacturer. Brigade and division commander, Army of the Tennessee.

"He is a shrewd, steady Scotchman, trustworthy rather than brilliant, good at hard knocks, but not a great commander." —Charles A. Dana, *Recollections*, p. 68

GEORGE A. McCALL
Brigadier general. West Point (1822). Seminole and Mexican War veteran. Commanded Pennsylvania Reserves, Army of the Potomac.

"He was more tenacious of his battle than any one who came within my experience during the war, if I except D.H. Hill at Sharpsburg." —James Longstreet, *From Manassas to Appomattox*, p. 139

GEORGE B. McCLELLAN
Major general. West Point (1846). Engineer. Mexican War veteran. Railroad executive. Commanded Army of the Potomac, 1861–1862.

"We must encounter risks if we fight, and we cannot carry on war without fighting. That was McClellan's vice. He was always waiting to have everything just as he wanted before he would attack, and before he could get things arranged as he wanted them, the enemy pounced on him and thwarted all his plans. There is now no doubt he allowed three distinct occasions to take Richmond slip through his hands, for want of nerve to run what he considered risks. Such a general will never command success, though he may avoid disaster." —George G. Meade, *Life and Letters*, 1:345

"Gen. McClellan is an indefatigable officer in organization. Nothing seems to escape his attention or his anticipation. Every endeavor is made, and constantly kept up, to enforce drill and discipline and to create an esprit de corps and confidence. I have met no officer at all his equal in this respect. But he keeps everybody hard at work." —Alpheus Williams, *From the Cannon's Mouth*, p. 136

"I have more confidence in General McClellan than in any man living. I would forsake everything and follow him to the ends of the earth. I would lay down my life for him." —George A. Custer, *The Custer Reader*, p. 11

"McClellan was thoroughly posted in the details of the service . . . he was an excellent organizer of troops, a good engineer and not without the talent of handling an army . . . but he was too systematic, too slow and even timid . . . his battle array and attack were wanting in energy, dash and simultaneous concentration and development of his disposable forces." —Franz Sigel, quoted in Engle, *Yankee Dutchman*, p. 141

"McClellan . . . seemed pointed out by Providence as the ideal chieftain . . . His personal intercourse with those about him was so kindly, and his bearing so modest, that his dispatches, proclamations and correspondence are a psychological study, more puzzling to those who knew him well than to strangers. Their turgid rhetoric and exaggerated pretense did not seem natural to him . . . he seemed to be composing for stage effect, something to be spoken in character by a quite different person from the sensible and genial man we knew in daily life and conversation." —Jacob Cox, *Battles and Leaders*, 1:135

"McClellan is an intelligent engineer and officer, but not a commander to head a great army in the field. To attack or advance with energy and power is not in him; to fight is not his forte . . . The study of military operations interests and amuses him. It flatters him to have on his staff French princes and men of wealth and position; he likes show, parade, and power. Wishes to out general the Rebels, but not to kill and destroy them." —Gideon Welles, *Diary*, 1:107

"Surrounded for the most part by young officers, he was himself the most youthful of us all, not only by reason of his physical vigor, the vivacity of his impressions, the noble candor of his character, and his glowing patriotism, but also . . . by his inexperience of men. His military bearing breathed a spirit of frankness, benevolence and firmness. His look was piercing, his voice gentle, his temper equable, his word of command clear and definite. His encouragement was most affectionate, his reprimand couched in terms of perfect politeness. Discreet as a military or political chief should be, he was slow in bestowing his confidence; but, once given, it was never withdrawn. Himself perfectly loyal to his friends, he knew how to inspire others with an absolute devotion." —Philippe Comte de Paris, *Battles and Leaders*, 2:112–113

"I feel for Gen. McClellan. He was a safe man; and if he got into difficulties, he could get us out. He knew that; Pope did not. Burnside is a good man, but he is to be tried on a large scale. If he fails, the results will be disastrous . . ." —Robert McAllister, *Civil War Letters*, p. 219

"General McClellan was a very accomplished soldier and a very able engineer, but hardly equal to the position of a field marshal as a military chieftain. He organized the Army of the Potomac cleverly, but did not handle it skillfully when in actual battle." —James Longstreet, *Battles and Leaders*, 2:404

"General McClellan was no judge of character—a very important weakness in a public man, and an especial failing in a commanding general . . . McClellan was too cautious from an undue sense of responsibility resting on him as

General-in-Chief and general commander of the Army of the Potomac ...
he never could make up his mind to bring on a decisive engagement, and
allowed the enemy to concentrate and assail him ... a thorough engineer
and an extremely well read military man, he could not put his reading to use
in the field." —William F. Smith, *Autobiography*, p. 33

"McClellan was popular with the army ... down to the very last. His
manners were simple and unaffected. He was always in uniform, but readily
approachable. His personal life and character were beyond reproach. He read
Latin and Greek ... and spoke both French and Spanish ... He knew all West
Point could teach him, and indeed was an adept in all branches of the military
profession, except the last and most important one of all, and that is, how to
fight and conquer. As an organizer, and drillmaster, and disciplinarian, we did
not produce McClellan's equal during the war ... But there he seems to have
ended ... He never knew when to take the initiative, and lacked aggressiveness
and fighting energy ..." —James F. Rusling, *Men and Things I Saw*, p. 36

"It is considered generally that McClellan has been completely outwitted &
that our present safety is owing more to the severe fighting of some of our
divisions than to any skill of our generals." —Francis C. Barlow, *Letters*, p. 91

"I think McClellan & many more of our generals are damned miserable
creatures & that unless there is a radical change in the leaders, the enemy will
whip us again & again. I think officers & men are disgusted with & have lost
all confidence in McClellan & are disgusted with the attempts of the papers to
make him out a victorious hero." —Francis C. Barlow, *Letters*, p. 99

"It was the first time I had seen McClellan near enough to know what he looks
like ... He has a good face, open and manly, set on a very thick, short neck,
and is what may be called thick-set altogether. I should not, from his looks, set
him down as a great man by any means." —Charles S. Wainwright, *A Diary
of Battle*, p. 109

"As he rode past me that day with his proud staff ... his person and bearing
made an indelible impression upon my memory. I saw a man five feet eight in
height, with a good figure, muscular and closely knit, square shoulders, shapely
head, and fine face ruddy with health; he had withal a quiet and reserved
manner and showed vigor in his motions ... Though McClellan never drew
me to him ... I have uniformly cherished the belief that he was a pure man,
loyal to truth, to honor, and to his country ... His popularity ... was ... made
permanent throughout the army by his showing on all occasions a marked
courtesy." —Oliver O. Howard, *Autobiography*, 1:167

"McClellan is no General, but a very weak, paltry individual, surrounded, and
flattered and cajoled by hypocrites, who are only waiting to rise by him,
and then machinate against him ... McClellan is an ass, and has foolishly
placed in high trusts near him persons, who cannot from ignorance aid or
serve him." —Philip Kearny, *Letters from the Peninsula*, p. 37, 45

"McClellan was an engineer rather than a leader of armies ... McClellan's entire merit consisted in organizing the freshly raised troops as they arrived here in the beginning of the war. The moment he attempted to handle the troops he proved himself entirely unequal to the task." —Ethan Allen Hitchcock, *Fifty Years in Camp and Field*, p. 461

"Believe me, that McClellan is a dirty sneaking traitor. Many of his acts look like complicity with the enemy. He has twice allowed them to escape, once at Manassas, and now again at Williamsburgh ... It has always occurred to me, that he was in secret negotiation with the South for their votes, as president, or to adopt some new Constitution for the Country. Because McClellan's mathematical talents have never fitted him to comprehend, nor appreciate neither things, nor men, he is the very one to commit a treasonable blunder. He was a fair young soldier of no great mark in Mexico." —Phil Kearny, *Letters from the Peninsula*, p. 87–88

"McClellan ... is timid, ignorant of the nature of soldiers, and utterly incapable. He surrounds himself with weak favorites, and is fearful of noticing the truly distinguished officers for fear of being subjected to comparisons. And most feeble thinks, that by raising small men, and dwelling on small successes, that he can keep down the true soldier." —Phil Kearny, *Letters from the Peninsula*, p. 101

"Few men could excel him in strictly defensive operations. He did not lack personal courage, nor did his intellectual powers become obscured in the excitement of actual war. He showed the ordinary evidences of presence of mind and coolness of judgment under fire. His tendency to see his enemy doubled in force, was however, a constitutional one, and no amount of experience seemed to cure it." —Jacob Cox, *Reminiscences*, 1:368

"The downfall of McClellan was a heavy blow to all below the rank of a General. The army believed in McClellan, but the Generals are jealous and ambitious and little, and want to get a step themselves, so they are willing to see him pulled down. We believed in him, not as a brilliant commander, but as a prudent one and one who was gradually learning how to handle our immense army ..." —Charles Francis Adams Jr., *A Cycle of Adams Letters*, 1:197

"I esteemed General McClellan highly, but as a commander he was too slow and his caution excessive. He did not wish to move until he could strike with positive certainty. When all the reinforcements and supplies he invariably asked for had been furnished, he would continue to ask for something more, something else, until the patience of the President, following that of Secretary Stanton, became completely exhausted ... He possessed personal magnetism, was affable and courteous, treated newspaper reporters with the greatest consideration, and they in return wrote him up as a hero ... My observations of McClellan would lead me to characterize him as The Unready." —Herman Haupt, *Reminiscences*, p. 157, 305, 306

"McClellan was a lovable man, an admirable organizer, but with little taste for battle unless largely outnumbering his opponent." —G. Moxley Sorrel, *Recollections of a Confederate Staff Officer*, p. 57

"McClellan was of decided ability in many respects; timorous, but safe; and there was no better organizer. He seemed to hate battle, and it is surprising that with such a record he should have secured and retained the devotion and confidence of his men to the very end. There was no lack of physical courage; it was a mental doubt with him." —G. Moxley Sorrel, *Recollections of a Confederate Staff Officer*, p. 122

"My opinion of McClellan is that he is the most capable man we have in military affairs. His head is clear and his knowledge complete. He wants force of character and is swayed by those around him. Fitz-John Porter with his elegant address and insinuating plausibility, technical power, and total want of judgment has been the evil genius, and ruined him as he did [Robert] Patterson. The people about McClellan . . . were the most ungallant, good-for-nothing set of martinets that I have yet met with . . . A self-indulgent and timorous policy seemed to pervade the whole surrounding and the General. His very mildness of manner, voice, and deportment show him unfitted by character to wield successfully a great power . . ." —David Hunter Strother, *A Virginia Yankee*, p. 129

"I have often said that McClellan's reputation as a scholar and soldier was second to none after Mexico. I heard Gen. Persifor F. Smith in 1849 pronounce him better qualified to command than any of our then generals . . ." —William T. Sherman, *Home Letters*, p. 249–250

"Something in the nature of the man and something in his environment caused his failure. With great organizational power, he failed in practical application. He lacked dash, resolution; he hesitated to seize the golden moment, to profit by his own openings, to press his advantage, to solve doubt by daring. With all that marvelous magnetism which won the love and enthusiasm of his subordinates, he lacked the skill, or the will, to gain the sympathy of his superiors." —Joshua Lawrence Chamberlain, *Passing of the Armies*, p. 27–28

"To me it seemed he had no plan or policy of his own, or any realizing sense of the true condition of affairs . . . He was occupied with reviews and dress-parades, perhaps with drills and discipline, but was regardless of the necessities of the case—the political aspect of the question . . . I do not think . . . that he was imbecile, a coward, a traitor; but it was notorious that he hesitated, doubted, had not self-reliance, any definite and determined plan, or audacity to act. He was wanting, in my opinion, in several of the essential requisites of a general in chief command; in short, he was not a fighting general." —Gideon Welles, *Diary*, 1:103

"Gen. George B. McClellan was a graduate of West Point and stood high in the old army. He was a good general, a splendid organizer and disciplinarian, rather slow and cautious in his movements, but when engaged a hard fighter.

President Abraham Lincoln and General George B. McClellan at McClellan's headquarters at Antietam, October 1862.

McClellan was a high-toned gentleman and observed strictly the rules of civilized and honorable warfare, and advised against the policy of the Administration of practicing emancipation of slaves wherever they came within the lines of the Union army." —William C. Oates, *The War Between the Union and the Confederacy,* p. 108–109

"General McClellan was of short, stout figure, but was of soldierly presence, graceful, and handsome-featured . . . With McClellan it was more difficult to strike than to march for the enemy." —James Longstreet, *From Manassas to Appomattox,* p. 288

"McClellan was a man of handsome appearance, winning manners, and fine, soldierly bearing. The government gave him its full confidence, and freedom of action . . . He was the 'young Napoleon,' the pet of the nation. The soldiers adored him, and the commanding officers were attached to him with warm personal devotion. The army under McClellan's command was by far the strongest and finest that had ever been assembled on this continent . . . McClellan was a splendid organizer and administrator. He knew perfectly well how to construct the engine of war. But when that engine was constructed, he hesitated to set it in motion." —Carl Schurz, *Reminiscences,* 2:333, 334

"He bore every evidence of gentle nature and high culture, and his countenance was as charming as his demeanor was modest and winning . . . A brighter, kindlier, more genial gentleman did not live than he. Sharing freely in all the convivial hospitality of the mess, he was a constant student of his profession . . . He was an excellent horseman, and one of our most athletic and best swordsmen." —Dabney H. Maury, *Recollections of a Virginian*, p. 59–60

"He was rather under the medium height, but muscularly formed, with broad shoulders and a well-poised head, active and graceful in motion. His whole appearance was quiet and modest, but when drawn out he showed no lack of confidence in himself. He was dressed in a plain travelling dress and wore a narrow-rimmed soft felt hat. In short, he seemed what he was, a railway superintendant in his business clothes." —Jacob Cox, *Battles and Leaders*, 1:89–90

"The attitude of our officers and men toward McClellan . . . was peculiar. We seemed to understand his limitations and defects of military character, and yet we were invariably relieved when he was relieved, for we unquestionably always believed him to be a stronger and more dangerous man than anyone who might be his successor. His great professional ability was never questioned." —Henry Kyd Douglas, *I Rode with Stonewall*, p. 202

"I liked McClellan, but was not 'daft' about him; and was indeed somewhat shaken by the great cry and stories against him . . . But . . . I wish to say, in all coolness, that I believe he was, both as a military man and as a manager of a country under military occupation, the greatest general this war has produced." —Theodore Lyman, *Meade's Headquarters*, p. 141

"He was dressed in the full uniform of a major-general and rode a superb horse, upon which he sat faultlessly. He was certainly a fine-looking officer and a very striking figure. But whether all this 'fuss and feathers' was designed to impress the men, or was a freak of personal vanity, it did not favorably impress our men." —Frederick L. Hitchcock, *War from the Inside*, p. 40

"He is a very squarely-built, thick-throated, broad-chested man, under the middle height, with slightly-bowed legs, a tendency to *embonpoint*. His head, covered with a closely-cut crop of dark auburn hair, is well set on his shoulders. His features are regular and prepossessing—the brow small, contracted, and furrowed; the eyes deep and anxious-looking. A short thick reddish moustache conceals his mouth; the rest of his face is clean shaven . . . He looks like a stout little captain of dragoons, but for his American seat and saddle . . . I confess that General McClellan does not appear to me a man of action, or, at least, a man who intends to act as speedily as the crisis demands." —William Howard Russell, *My Diary North & South*, p. 240, 250

"General McClellan, who was bent on taking his own time to make an army that would be sure of success and who had determined to 'carry this thing on en grand and crush the rebels in one campaign,' anticipated and ignored the popular and official clamor . . . With an unusual knowledge of the mechanics of war and with a strategic mind of high order, he felt confident that if he were

President Lincoln and General McClellan in the general's tent at Antietam, October, 1862.

allowed to perfect his field strength and plan his own campaigns, he could end the war in a short time." —D. H. Hill, *Bethel to Sharpsburg*, 1:142

"McClellan, though unfit to command in battle, had no superior in organizing an army to take the field as a thoroughly fit machine, able to concentrate its energies wherever needed." —E. P. Alexander, *Military Memoirs of a Confederate*, p. 56

"McClellan was always and everywhere a gentleman, who believed in fighting war in a Christian and humane manner. He had strategic, but no tactical ability. Risks have to be taken when battle is joined, but he never took them . . . He had none of the inspiration of war . . . The Federal general could organize with great ability and inspire confidence in his troops, and would have been a great commander had he been more rapid in his movements and adventurous in his plans." —Fitzhugh Lee, *General Lee*, p. 220–221

"McClellan's extreme caution, or tardiness, or something, is utterly exhaustive of all hope and patience, and leaves one in that feverish apprehension that as something *may* go wrong, something most likely *will* go wrong. Risks of battle are proverbially uncertain; but I am beginning to feel that the apprehension of defeat is worse than defeat itself." —John G. Nicolay, *With Lincoln in the White House*, p. 80

"The President seemed to think him a little crazy. Envy jealousy and spite are probably a better explanation of his present conduct. He is constantly sending despatches to the President and Halleck asking what is his real position and command. He acts as chief alarmist and grand marplot of the Army." —John Hay, *Inside Lincoln's White House*, p. 37

"He seems to have been troubled all the time with the spectre of 'overwhelming numbers' opposed to him, and that he should have believed so when he had 'Professor [Thaddeus] Lowe' with his balloons to make reports from the clouds, and his 'Chief of the Secret Service' and 'intelligent contrabands,' to fool him with their inventions, may perhaps be conceded by some charitable persons, but that he should have written such nonsense as the above in 1863, and published it in 1864, is perfectly ridiculous." —Jubal A. Early, *Narrative of the War Between the States*, p. 89

"In the field his professional and technical knowledge overburdened him till he was incapable of skillfully using it; in the solitude of his head-quarters, and freed from his absorbing attention to personal considerations, it made him an excellent strategist. It was his misfortune that he overrated his own capacity, and set himself tasks to which he was unequal. But he was always able to oppose a front of opposition to the enemy, and to maintain the *morale* of his army . . . In person General McClellan is below the middle height, with unusually large chest, and well-shaped head. His features are regular, and, in conversation, light up with a pleasing smile. His manners are singularly charming and graceful; and the magnetism of his personal presence and his gracious ways is always sure to fill his private life with friends, as it bound him to the officers and soldiers of the Army of the Potomac . . ." —Whitelaw Reid, *Ohio in the War*, 1:308, 309

"McClellan is not the man to make himself popular with the masses. His manners are reserved and retiring. He was not popular either in Chicago or Cincinnati, when at the head of large railroad interests. He has never studied or practiced the art of pleasing, and indeed has not paid attention to it which every man whose position is dependent on popular favor must pay, if he expects to retain his position." —George G. Meade, *Life and Letters*, 1:253

"Before this reaches you, you will have read of the removal of McClellan. God be praised that this act of justice to the army and the country, so long delayed, has been consummated at last. It is better to the country than a decisive victory over the enemy. Indeed, I am not sure that it is in itself a decisive victory over rebels at home." —James A. Garfield, *The Wild Life of the Army*, p. 176

"I consider him one of the weakest and most timid generals that ever led an army. This opinion is held by General Hooker and nearly every prominent one of his field marshals . . . He is constantly scheming in politics, and I think the Government would at once remove him but for the fear that it would strengthen the Democratic party too much in the coming election . . . I have no hope for the success of our arms in the East till McClellan is removed entirely from active command." —James A. Garfield, *The Wild Life of the Army*, p. 315

JOHN A. McCLERNAND   Major general.
Illinois Congressman. Veteran of Black Hawk War.
Division and corps commander, Army of the Tennessee.

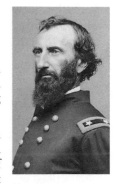

"John A. McClernand . . . By profession a lawyer, he was in his first of military service. Brave, industrious, methodical, and of unquestioned cleverness, he was rapidly acquiring the art of war." —Lew Wallace, *Battles and Leaders*, 1:405

"He was not a military man; he was a politician and a member of Congress. He was a man of a good deal of a certain kind of talent, not of a high order, but not one of intellectual accomplishments. His education was that which a man gets who is in congress five or six years. In short, McClernand was merely a smart man, quick, very active-minded, but his judgment was not solid, and he looked after himself a great deal." —Charles Dana, *Recollections*, p. 59

"He is entirely unfit for the position of corps commander, both on the march and on the battle-field. Looking after his corps gives me more labor and infinitely more uneasiness than all the remainder of my department." —Ulysses S. Grant, in Badeau, *Military History of Ulysses S. Grant*, 1:655

"McClernand . . . regarded himself in a measure, if not entirely, independent of the army commander and acted . . . as though Grant's presence and exercise of authority on the battlefield were in violation of his own privileges and rights. He was naturally a proud, austere, and imperious man, who took but little pains to conceal his feelings and acted always with noticeable reserve and hauteur toward Grant." —James H. Wilson, *Under the Old Flag*, p. 175

"I avoid McClernand because I know he is envious and jealous of everybody who stands in his way . . . I will not serve under McClernand . . . With an intense selfishness and lust of notoriety he could not let his mind get beyond the limits of his vision, and therefore all was brilliant about him and dark and suspicious beyond." —William T. Sherman, *Home Letters*, p. 256, 257, 272

"I had known General McClernand by reputation as a Democratic politician . . . His face was agreeable, though weatherbeaten and unshaven . . . His head was covered with one of the abominable regulation wool hats hooked up on one side. Besides being thin and slightly under average height, he was at further disadvantage by sitting too far back in his saddle and stooping." —*Lew Wallace: An Autobiography*, 1:411

"Gen. John A. McClernand belonged to that class of officers who were taken from civil life at the beginning of the war and made full Major Generals without any previous military training or experience, because of their supposed political influence in their respective states . . . Every such major general proved a signal failure." —Sylvanus Cadwallader, *Three Years with Grant*, p. 92–93

"He had been a politician, and a member of Congress from Illinois, as well as an old acquaintance and legal associate of the President; he was a man of moderate ability, of energy and courage, but ignorant of the meaning of military subordination. Ambitious and vain, he expected to step at once to the highest positions in the army, without the knowledge or experience which alone could fit him for important command. He had political and personal influence, however, and made ample use of it." —Adam Badeau, *Military History of Ulysses S. Grant*, 1:128

ALEXANDER McDOWELL McCOOK
Major general. West Point (1852). Brigade and division commander, Army of the Ohio; corps commander, Army of the Cumberland.

"McCook . . . called while we were at (General) Negley's; he looks, if possible, more like a blockhead than ever, and it is astonishing that he should be permitted to retain command of a corps for a single hour." —John Beatty, *The Citizen Soldier*, p. 295

"McCook . . . seemed . . . pursued by a strange fatality. He assumed a kind of boastful overconfidence that in war always presages failure, because it takes the place of the careful preparation that secures success . . . McCook possessed a peculiar open frankness of manner and bonhomie that made him many friends, and he had many admirable traits of character . . ." —William B. Hazen, *Narrative*, p. 152–153

"It was the misfortune of General McCook, that in the universal rawness at the outset of the war, his familiarity with the subject of tactics, which he had been engaged in teaching at West Point, was mistaken for military genius. His promotions naturally ensued long before he had any opportunity to grow, practically, up to them, and as naturally the repeated disappointments in his performance led to a revulsion which went, perhaps, as far to the other extreme." —Whitelaw Reid, *Ohio in the War*, 1:809

DANIEL McCOOK   Brigadier general. Lawyer. Brigade
commander, Army of the Tennessee. Mortally wounded at Kennesaw
Mountain, June 27, 1864.

"Daniel McCook was a brave soldier and a sensible man, his loss was indeed
a very severe one. Of the many McCooks who held high positions in the
Union army, Daniel and his cousin, Anson G., were by no means the least
meritorious." —William P. Carlin, *Memoirs*, p. 128

ROBERT L. McCOOK   Brigadier general. Lawyer. Brigade
commander, Army of the Ohio. Mortally wounded August 5, 1862.

"I found a hearty and loyal character under his bluff exterior and rough
speech, with real courage, a quick eye for topography, and no lack of earnest
subordination when work was to be done . . . I learned to have real respect for
him . . ." —Jacob Cox, *Reminiscences*, 1:110

"General McCook was personally a man of warm disposition and hearty
attachments. No man was more beloved by his soldiers or deplored by his
State. His abilities were fine, his standing among his brother officers and in
the esteem of his commanders was of the best, and there was every reason to
predict for him a brilliant future." —Whitelaw Reid, *Ohio in the War*, 1:879

IRVIN McDOWELL   Major general.
West Point (1838). Mexican War veteran. West
Point instructor (tactics). Army and corps
commander, Army of the Potomac.

"I had heard and seen his name connected
with the orders from General Scott, and
was surprised to find him so tall and of
such full build. His habitual demeanor now
was that of one self-absorbed and distant.
He was the subject at that time of constant
observation and remark, for it was believed
that he would soon command all our movable
forces on the Potomac." —Oliver O. Howard,
Autobiography, 1:139

"The jealousies among the Commanders of
Divisions and Corps d'Armee is making bad
work—McDowell appears to be insatiable in his Ambition & now that he is
a Major General he is taking airs upon himself—but for McClellan he would
never have been confirmed." —Marsena Patrick, *Inside Lincoln's Army*, p. 53

"At this period I committed one of my greatest errors—that was in retaining
Gen. McDowell on duty with the troops under my command. I knew that
he had been a close student of military affairs and . . . he possessed sufficient

ability to be useful in subordinate capacity ... I pitied him extremely and thought that circumstances had as much to do with his failure at Bull Run as any want of ability and energy on his part ... subsequent events proved that ... he lacked the qualities necessary for a commander in the field."
—George B. McClellan, *McClellan's Own Story*, p. 70–71

"He was forty-three years of age, of unexceptionable habits and great physical powers ... Always a close student, he was well informed outside as well as inside his profession. Distinguished in the Mexican War, intensely Union in his sentiments, full of energy and patriotism, outspoken in his opinions ... Without political antecedents or acquaintances, he was chosen for advancement on account of his record, his ability, and his vigor." —James B. Fry, *Battles and Leaders*, 1:171

"He was ... fully six feet tall, deep-chested, strong-limbed, clear-eyed, and in every respect a fine and impressive soldier, but at dinner he was such a Gargantuan feeder and so absorbed in the dishes before him that he had but little time for conversation. While he drank neither wine nor spirits, he fairly gobbled the larger part of every dish within reach, and wound up with an entire watermelon, which he said was 'monstrous fine!' That he was in every way a true patriot and an accomplished soldier there is no room to doubt."
—James H. Wilson, *Under the Old Flag*, p. 66

"Of all the commanders of the Armies of the East ... I considered General McDowell the most able, but at the same time the most unfortunate and the most unpopular ... I was a member of his staff, enjoyed his confidence and was authorized by him to attach orders in his name ... He was a man of fine education, with superior conversational powers, but a very strict disciplinarian ... He had no use for regimental bands, and objected to the barrels of lager and the cases of wines and liquors which increased the wagon trains and delayed movements ... he regarded newspaper reporters as a nuisance ... he was thoroughly systematic, and when sending an order always sent a duplicate ..."
—Herman Haupt, *Reminiscences*, p. 303–304

"When McDowell was made a brigadier general and placed in command ... he was about forty-three years of age, tall and stalwart, with short hair and full face, inclining to redness ... His eyes were very bright, his tones of voice rough and metallic, his manner arbitrary and at times irritating. He was an accomplished soldier, full of the book knowledge of the science of war and full of energy and zeal. It may be said of him ... that he was an intensely loyal man, not alone to his country, but to his duty." —John Pope, *Memoirs*, p. 214

"He was ... a gentleman of high character, and a learned, and able, and thoroughly loyal soldier. He was a fluent conversationalist, and somewhat given to impulsive and sharp sayings, the effect of which he probably did not always foresee. His figure was of portly proportions, and his countenance not impressive —somewhat pudgy and puffy." —Carl Schurz, *Reminiscences*, 2:383

"General McDowell was a vain, arrogant man hounded by the defeat at Bull Run, which had caused McClellan to supersede him. Who never accepted the situation his defeat at Bull Run naturally brought him to and began at once . . . to work for an independent command." —William F. Smith, *Autobiography*, p. 32

"I have never injured McD . . . I bear no hatred to the man—I simply regard him as a scoundrel a liar & a fool who in seeking to injure me has killed himself— I have the most thorough contempt for him—nothing more. All I ask is that I may never set eyes on him again—as for ever having any friendly relations with him it is simply absurd . . ." —George B. McClellan, *Civil War Letters*, p. 449

"He was a big, muscular man, with a look of solid strength about him, but his chunky face was half tired, half worried." —Abner R. Small, *The Road to Richmond*, p. 20

"He is a man about forty years of age, square and powerfully built, but with a rather stout and clumsy figure and limbs, a good head covered with close-cut thick dark hair, small light-blue eyes, short nose, large cheeks and jaws, relieved by an iron-grey tuft somewhat of the French type, and affecting in dress the style of our gallant allies. His manner is frank, simple, and agreeable . . . As an officer of the regular army he has a thorough contempt for what he calls 'political generals' . . . Nor is General McDowell enamoured of the volunteers, for he served in Mexico, and has from what he saw there formed rather an unfavourable opinion of their capabilities in the field." —William Howard Russell, *My Diary North & South*, p. 192–193

"Faults inherent in the character of the man helped to swell the bias against him. His aristocratic ideas led to an imprudent scorn of public opinion. His dislike for adventurers led to an ill-concealed contempt for the suddenly-advanced officers of foreign services. His prejudices against the unquestioned irregularities of volunteers led to an unwise harshness of bearing and of discipline . . . His intellectual conservatism led to a revulsion against the abolition current which was the lifeblood of the war. His somewhat torpid habit of perceptions caused him sometimes to persist in a wrong course . . . to be blind to the injurious workings of his discipline, to be incredulous of evil reports. His pride was so great that, knowing himself odious, he would resort to none of the common modes for acquiring or regaining popularity." —Whitelaw Reid, *Ohio in the War*, 1:693

"I have never believed the absurd stories about McDowell's being disloyal, or anything of that sort, but I was not prepared to find a man of such perfect, open, frank, manly sincerity. I believe he is the victim of jealousy, envy, and most marvelous bad luck . . . On the whole I have a higher opinion of McDowell's talents than of any other man's in the army, and if he is again assigned a command I would prefer to go under him than any other." —James A. Garfield, *The Wild Life of the Army*, p. 155, 195

"General McDowell is a man of far more than ordinary ability and culture. He is frank, open, manly, severe and sincere. He is truly patriotic, but is not a politician. He does not deem it a discredit to be a *mere soldier*. His military education has led him to obey, without question . . . If he had asserted himself more, it would have been better for him and for the country.

Whether he has the dash and audacity to make a good general I do not know. That he is a true brave man I have no doubt. *I like General Irvin McDowell.*" —James A. Garfield, *The Wild Life of the Army*, p. 313–314

GEORGE FRANCIS McGINNIS Brigadier general. Mexican War veteran. Manufacturer. Brigade commander, Army of the Tennessee.

"McGinnis is brave enough, but too excitable. He lost his balance at Champion's Hill. He is not likely ever to be more than a brigadier." —Charles A. Dana, *Recollections*, p. 640

THOMAS JEFFERSON McKEAN Brevet major general. West Point (1831). Seminole and Mexican War veteran. Administrative and district command. Chief of cavalry, Department of the Gulf.

"McKean, an old graduate of West Point . . . was now sixty years old, had failed in all civil pursuits, had enlisted in the ranks to make a living, and now, as a brigadier commanding a division was a failure." —David S. Stanley, *Memoirs*, p. 115

JAMES B. McPHERSON Major general. West Point (1853). Engineer. Aide-de-camp. Corps command and army command, Army of the Tennessee. Killed at Atlanta, July 22, 1864.

"McPherson, who graduated at the head of the class, was a brilliant student, an admirable engineer, but never a great leader. The student predominated in his organization and he lacked in decision and nerve. He rose very high in rank in the regular army, but it was owing less to his available talents and practicability than to the care of Grant and Sherman, with whom he was a favorite." —William F. Shanks, *Personal Recollections of Distinguished Generals*, p. 136–137

"He was as affectionate and gentle as a woman, but a man amongst men. Not only was his physique perfect, but he had intellect of the highest order . . . he served with the highest distinction in [the] army . . . He grew so rapidly in reputation and in personal popularity that he soon became the favorite general in the Northern armies." —John Pope, *Memoirs*, p. 95

"He was one of the best officers we had. He was but thirty-two years old . . . and a very handsome, gallant-looking man, with a rather dark complexion, dark eyes and a most cordial manner. McPherson was an engineer officer of fine natural ability and extraordinary acquirements . . . He was a man without any pretensions, and always had a pleasant hand-shake for you." —Charles Dana, *Recollections*, p. 58

"McPherson, among other qualities, was one of the most generous men I ever knew. He was remarkably skilful in topographical drawing, etching, lettering, and all other uses of the pen ... he would spend a very large part of that precious time in 'lettering' problems for classmates who needed such help." —John M. Schofield, *Forty-Six Years in the Army*, p. 137–138

"His affability and cordial good-will struck one at once. His graceful bearing and refined, intelligent face heightened the impression, and one could not be with him many minutes without seeing that he was a lovable person. An evenly balanced mind and character had given him a high grade as cadet, and at the beginning of the war he was serving as a captain of engineers." —Jacob Cox, *Reminiscences*, 2:308

"General McPherson ... rose very rapidly in rank and command. He was a man of great talent combined with truthfulness—a quality not always present with the rising generals of that date." —David S. Stanley, *Memoirs*, p. 105

"McPherson was then in his prime (about thirty-four years old), over six feet high, and a very handsome man in every way, was universally liked, and had many noble qualities. He had on boots outside his pantaloons, gauntlets on his hands, had on his major-general's uniform, and wore a sword-belt but no sword." —William T. Sherman, *Personal Memoirs*, 2:76

"He was one of the most attractive & universally popular men whom I ever met. There was a gentleness & refinement about him which was almost feminine. He was one of those whom a man might love almost like a woman. Physically too he was a rarely fine specimen ... he had been Grant's right hand man at Vicksburg & Sherman's in his Georgia campaign. And he had been noted among Confederates everywhere for his kind & considerate treatment of the non combatants with whom he came in contact. No finer specimen of soldier or gentleman ever lived ..." —E. P. Alexander, *Fighting for the Confederacy*, p. 24–25

"McPherson ... was also an officer of rare merit ... and was justly noted for the brilliancy of his intellect and his high standing and attainments in the military profession ... He was cheerful, modest and unassuming, but vigorous and active in the performance of every duty ... He neither furnished brains nor plans ... but confined himself to the duty of commanding his corps, and doing cheerfully and ably whatever he was ordered to do ... He was an ideal subordinate, with a commanding figure and a lofty and patriotic character ..." —James Harrison Wilson, *Battles and Leaders*, 5:125

"He was not conspicuous as a director of campaigns. He was not recognized as the author of any great victory. He was not ranked among the foremost of the country's generals. He was great in his possibilities rather than in his actual achievements. He was young and scarcely known in person to the public. But his soldiers knew him to be superbly gallant; and his commanders knew him to be eminently able, prudent, and skillful ... So loveable was the nature of the man, so simple, so sincere, so manly, that the admiration of the public was heightened in his army into love." —Whitelaw Reid, *Ohio in the War*, 1:561

"He was not only brilliant in achievement and gallant to a fault, clear in conception and admirable in all professional knowledge, but endowed with personal characteristics which endeared him in an unusual degree to all his associates." —Adam Badeau, *Military History of Ulysses S. Grant,* 2:462

GEORGE G. MEADE Major general. West

Point (1835). Civil engineer. Army topographical engineer. Mexican War veteran. Brigade, division, corps, and army command, Army of the Potomac.

"My chief . . . is a thorough soldier, and a mighty clear-headed man; and one who does not move unless he knows where and how many his men are; where and how many his enemy's men are; and what sort of country he has to go through. I never saw a man in my life who was so characterized by straightforward truthfulness as he is. He will pitch into himself in a moment, if he thinks he has done wrong; and woe to those, no matter who they are, who do not do right!" —Theodore Lyman, *Meade's Headquarters,* p. 25

"General Meade was then forty-nine years of age, of rather spare figure, and graceful in his movements. He had a full beard, which like his hair was brown, slightly tinged with gray. He wore a slouched felt hat with a conical crown, and a turned down rim, which gave him a sort of Tyrolese appearance." —Horace Porter, *Campaigning with Grant,* p. 28

"Meade was tall, spare, nervous and excitable; with elegant manners and a patrician aspect; large, bulging, brilliant eyes and a hawk nose. I remember him in action, when he turned his hat around, with the acorns and scrolls behind—we knew there was hot work before us . . . He was a dasher—a fiery fellow . . ." —Joseph Hayes, *Generals in Bronze,* p. 136

"Meade is proved—a plain soldier fit to lead a corps but without power or ambition and utterly incompetent at the head of a hundred thousand men . . ." —David Hunter Strother, *A Virginia Yankee,* p. 192

"Meade was an excellent officer of long service, who had always proved equal to his position, whether as a specialist or a commander of troops. Many welcomed his advent—some regretted Hooker's departure." —Henry J. Hunt, *Battles and Leaders,* 3:270

"He seemed at times perfectly beside himself with passion at some real or imaginary slight he considered had been put upon him in connection with the construction of some subsidiary line of works ordered to be put up, in regard to which he appeared to think sufficient importance had not been given to his opinion. . . . Gen. Meade was a man of peculiarly excitable disposition and his sensibility was such that he very quickly felt any lack of deference to himself or respect for his position." —John Gibbon, *Personal Recollections of the Civil War,* p. 239, 240

"I found him to be a conscientious and hard worker; as a rule, rising early and retiring late . . . He was not social . . . was habitually grave and reticent . . . As a rule, he was a better listener than talker . . . Meade's sense of humor was not large, but he was keen and intelligent, his mind worked broadly and comprehensively; his patriotism was perfect, his sense of duty intense; and he would willingly have laid down his life at any time had our cause required it. In manner he was often sharp and peremptory, but this was because of his utter absorption in great affairs." —James F. Rusling, *Men and Things I Saw*, p. 73

"He showed himself the personification of earnest, vigorous action in rousing his subordinate commanders to superior exertions. Even his fits of anger and his resort to intemperate language stood him at times in good stead in spurring on every one upon that active filed . . . His aquiline nose and piercing eyes gave him something of the eagle's look, and added to the interest of his personality." —Horace Porter, *Campaigning with Grant*, p. 209

"His manners were native and high-bred, but, alas! They reared a barrier around him which cut him off from the love of his army . . . He had, too . . . a rich, cultivated voice. But nature had not been altogether partial: she had given him a most irritable temper. I have seen him so cross and ugly that no one dared to speak to him,—in fact, at such times his staff and everybody else at headquarters kept as clear of him as possible." —Morris Schaff, *Wilderness*, p. 41

"General Meade was a gentleman and a man of high character; but he was irritable, petulant and dyspeptic. He did not give the idea of calm reserved force. Grant did; but Grant was a man of coarse fibre, and did not impress with a sense of character. Hancock was a dashing field-marshal; a handsome, superb commander of a corps. Warren left on me a sense of lightness. Humphreys and Sedgwick were the only two generals I ever met who inspired me with an adequate sense of force and reliability. Officers, they were also quiet, unassuming gentlemen. About them there was no pretence, no posing for effect, no stage tricks. I felt for them a profound respect . . ." —Charles Francis Adams, *Autobiography*, p. 157–158

"In command of the army was Major-General George G. Meade. He was a tall, thin man, rather dyspeptic, I should suppose from the fits of nervous irritation to which he was subject. He was totally lacking in cordiality toward those with whom he had business, and in consequence was generally disliked by his subordinates . . . He was an intellectual man, and agreeable to talk with when his mind was free, but silent and indifferent to everybody when he was occupied with that which interested him . . . Meade seemed . . . to lack the boldness that was necessary to bring the war to a close. He lacked self-confidence and tenacity of purpose, and he had not the moral authority that Grant had attained from his grand successes in other fields." —Charles A. Dana, *Recollections*, p. 189

"He looked tall and spare, weary, and a little flushed, But I knew him to be a good, honest soldier . . . He had served in the artillery among the Indiana . . . in the Topographical Engineers . . . in Mexico, where he was brevetted for his gallantry and had become favorably known at Washington . . . He won me more by his thoroughness and fidelity than by any show of sympathy or companionship. To me . . . he stood in the light of an esteemed, experienced regular officer, old enough to be my father, but like a father that one can trust without his showing him any special regard. So we respected and trusted Meade from the beginning." —Oliver O. Howard, *Autobiography*, 1:395–396

"General Meade is of a perverse nature; when he gets in a disagreeable place, he is apt to stay there. I think he likes to have officers who are prone to comfort feel decidedly *un*-comfortable." —Theodore Lyman, *Meade's Headquarters*, p. 123

"I had long known Meade to be a man of the worst possible temper, especially toward his subordinates. I think he had not a friend in the whole army. No man, no matter what his business or his service, approached him without being insulted in one way or another, and his own staff officers did not dare to speak to him unless first spoken to, for fear of either sneers or curses." —Charles A. Dana, *Recollections*, p. 227

"I for one have faith in Meade; a little time works wonders . . . We know him to be honest and thoroughly brave and reliable, and he is a good judge of men, having collected round him young men like Humphreys and Warren—the very best of our army." —Charles Francis Adams Jr., *A Cycle of Adams Letters*, 2:72

"Some talk about Meade's quarreling with all his subordinates & [John A.] Rawlins talks wildly. The truth is Meade is a bear to his subordinates. I have heard him abuse Burnside, Hancock & Warren to their faces. [Rufus] Ingalls is glad to get away from him . . . Have talked with very different persons—all snubbed by Meade & think that while they all have private grievances, that he would be first-choice for Cmdg Genl. both among his staff officers & the Maj. Gen's." —Cyrus B. Comstock, *Diary*, p. 279

"Tall, restless, angular, with piercing eye, aquiline nose, rapid gait, and nervous manner—he looked every inch a soldier. He was ill-tempered, and impatient, but his ill-temper often made him say good things; and his very impatience and testiness, disagreeable though they were, contributed to his talent . . ." —Adam Badeau, *Military History of Ulysses S. Grant*, 2:369–370

"As to Meade, be assured he has the confidence of this army. He is a brave, reliable, conscientious soldier and under him we need fear no heavy disaster, and may hope for all reasonable success. He is not Grant or Rosecrans, but he is ten times Hooker and twice McClellan. He is an able and formidable General of the Fabian school, more of Marshal Daun than Frederick the Great." —Charles Francis Adams Jr., *A Cycle of Adams Letters*, 2:111

"Meade is a tall, spare man, with full beard, which with his hair, originally brown, is quite thickly sprinkled with gray—has a Romanish face, very large nose, and a white large forehead, prominent and wide over the eyes, which are full and large, and quick in their movements, and he wears spectacles. His fibres are all of the long and sinewy kind. His habitual personal appearance is quite careless, and it would be rather difficult to make him look well dressed." —Frank Haskell, *Haskell of Gettysburg*, p. 132

"General Meade is now the ranking officer of the corps . . . He is a West Pointer and major of Engineers; a fine, soldierly, somewhat stiff-looking man, and the most thoroughbred gentleman in his manners I have yet met within the army." —Charles S. Wainwright, *A Diary of Battle*, p. 105

"Of Meade I know very little. He is not great. His brother officers speak well of him, but he is considered rather a 'smooth bore' than a rifle . . . He has a sharp visage and a narrow head. Would do better as second in command than as General-in-Chief. Is doubtless a good officer, but not a great and capable commander . . . Shows intelligence and activity, and on the whole I was as well or better pleased with him than I expected I should be . . ." —Gideon Welles, *Diary*, 1:349, 404

"Meade enjoyed generally the repute, not of a very brilliant, but of a brave, able and reliable officer. Everybody respected him. It was at once felt that he had grasped the reins with a firm hand . . . There was nothing in his appearance or bearing—not a smile nor a sympathetic word addressed to those around him—that might have made the hearts of the soldiers warm up to him, or that called forth a cheer. There was nothing of pose, nothing stagey, about him. His mind was evidently absorbed by a hard problem. But this simple, cold, serious soldier with his business-like air did inspire confidence." —Carl Schurz, *Reminiscences*, 3:4, 21

"Gen. Meade's military and classical education was at least equal to that of any officer in the Union army. His integrity was never questioned. His capacity to command great armies is no longer disputed. His tactics were those of the best schools, broadened by experience in the field, and modified by the ever-changing conditions constantly confronting him . . . He was uniformly dignified, polite, attentive and generally quite affable in demeanor." —Sylvanus Cadwallader, *Three Years with Grant*, p. 342–343

"I do not feel right towards Meade, for his entire want of management, as to the interior discipline & economy of his Army—He makes no arrangements to meet their wants in a reasonable and business like manner, and the consequence is, a bad state of affairs generally—I am greatly disgusted at it . . . He knows little of his Army, excepting so far as the fighting material is concerned & it is difficult to do business with him . . ." —Marsena R. Patrick, *Inside Lincoln's Army*, p. 321, 325

"He was an excellent officer; cool, brave, and intelligent; he always did his duty admirably, and was an honest man. As commander of an army he was far superior to either Hooker or Burnside." —George B. McClellan, *McClellan's Own Story*, p. 140

"General Meade was a most accomplished officer. He had been thoroughly educated in his profession, and had a complete knowledge of both the science and the art of war in all its branches. He was well read, possessed of a vast amount of interesting information, had cultivated his mind as a linguist, and spoke French with fluency . . . He was a disciplinarian to the point of severity, was entirely subordinate to his superiors, and no one was more prompt than he to obey orders to the letter. In his intercourse with his officers the bluntness of the soldier was always conspicuous, and he never took pains to smooth any one's ruffled feelings." —Horace Porter, *Campaigning with Grant*, p. 247

"He has done better with the Army of the Potomac than McClellan, Pope, Burnside or Hooker: and—I will add boldly without disparagement to the

Lieutenant-General—better than Grant! . . . Meade's great virtue is, that he knows when to fight, and when *not* to fight." —Theodore Lyman, *Meade's Headquarters*, p. 272

"He is a slasher, is the General, and cuts up people without much mercy. His family is celebrated for fierceness of temper and a sardonic sort of way that makes them uncomfortable people; but the General is the best of them, and exhausts his temper in saying sharp things. When it comes to practice he is full of kindness and often lets off men that should be summarily dealt with." —Theodore Lyman, *Meade's Army*, p. 118

"The army was not dissatisfied with the appointment of General Meade . . . General Meade was well known to the army as a good soldier, the brave soldier who had, with his single division, dashed upon the rebels at the first Fredericksburgh, and as the leader of a corps which behaved gallantly at Chancellorsville. All were willing to try him, and hoped for the best." —George T. Stevens, *Three Years in the Sixth Corps*, p. 238

"Meade's head is tolerably clear, generally, but when he gets 'Lee on the Brain' he errs thro' timidity, based on obstinacy . . . He has never been in command of men, immediately, knows nothing of the wants of an Army so far as the rank and file are concerned & does not seem to care much about them if he can avoid the trouble." —Marsena R. Patrick, *Inside Lincoln's Army*, p. 298, 302

"Meade in his well-worn uniform, splashed with mud, with his glasses, and his nervous and earnest air, looked more like a learned pundit than a soldier, but he at once informed himself of the position of the army and took the reins in that businesslike fashion he so well maintained till the end." —Thomas W. Hyde, *Following the Greek Cross*, p. 140

"General Meade was an officer of great merit, with drawbacks to his usefulness that were beyond his control . . . He saw clearly and distinctly the position of the enemy, and the topography of the country in front of his own position. His first idea was to take advantage of the lay of the ground, sometimes without reference to the direction we wanted to move afterwards . . . He was brave and conscientious, and commanded the respect of all who knew him. He was unfortunately of a temper that would get beyond his control . . . and make him speak to officers of high rank in the most offensive manner. No one saw this fault more plainly than he himself, and no one regretted it more." —Ulysses S. Grant, *Personal Memoirs*, 2:538

"He was an excellent fighter, but too lacking in audacity for a good commanding general. He was also of cross and quarrelsome disposition, and unpopular with his leading officers." —E. P. Alexander, *Military Memoirs of a Confederate*, p. 377–378

"Personally very brave, an excellent corps commander, General Meade had not that grasp of mind, when thrown into a new and responsible position, to quickly comprehend and decide upon important events as they occurred. He required time to come to a decision." —Alfred Pleasonton, *Annals of the Civil War*, p. 455

THOMAS FRANCIS MEAGHER   Brigadier general. Irish revolutionary. Commander of the Irish Brigade, Army of the Potomac.

"And here let me record the opinion formed after more than one year's observation in the field—that there is not in the United States, certainly not in the Army of the Potomac, another such consummate humbug, charlatan, imposter pretending to be a soldier as Thos Francis Meagher! Nor do I believe him to be a *brave* man, since in every battle field he has been *drunk* and not with his Brigade." —Edward Cross, *Stand Firm and Fire Low*, p. 57

"Large, corpulent, and powerful of body; plump and ruddy—or as some would say, bloated—of face; with resolute mouth and heavy animal jaws; expressive nose, and piercing blue eyes; brown hair, mustache, and eyebrows; a fair forehead, and short sinewy neck, a man of apparently thirty years of age . . . He wore the regulation blue cap, but trimmed plentifully with gold lace, and his sleeves were slashed in the same manner. A star glistened in his oblong shoulder-bar; a delicate gold cord seamed his breeches from his Hessian boots to his red-tasseled sword-sash; a seal-ring shone from the hand with which he grasped his gauntlets, and his spurs were set upon small aristocratic feet . . . He was fitfully impulsive, as all his movements attested, and liable to fluctuations of peevishness, melancholy, and enthusiasm. This was 'Meagher of the Sword.'" —George A. Townsend, *Campaigns of a Non-Combatant*, p. 129

WESLEY MERRITT   Major general. West Point (1860). Cavalry brigade and division commander, Army of the Potomac.

"He has an army reputation as a cavalry officer second to none, and is admired by his fellow-soldiers for his gallantry under fire, and for the rare good judgment shown in the splendid manner in which he handles his troops on all occasions." —Charles A. Page, *Letters*, p. 293–294

ROBERT H. MILROY   Major general. Graduate of Captain Partridge's Academy, in Norwich, Vermont. Mexican War veteran. Lawyer. Commander, Cheat Mountain District. Commander of independent brigade in Shenandoah Valley.

"Milroy is a man of fifty, tall and well made, florid complexion with red beard, sharp features crowned with stiff, grey hair which rose from his forehead like a porcupine's quills." —David Hunter Strother, *A Virginia Yankee*, p. 194–195

"His course in shamelessly abandoning his men in time of danger, after getting them into the trap, is in keeping with his cruel oppression to the helpless and unprotected people of the lower valley. He seems to be brave only when his opponents are women and children. He flies when armed men approach." —W. W. Blackford, *Letters from Lee's Army*, p. 178

"Milroy was a picturesque character, with some excellent qualities. A tall man, with trenchant features, bright eyes, a great shock of gray hair standing out from his head, he was a marked personal figure. He was brave, but his bravery was of the excitable kind that made him unbalanced and nearly wild on the battlefield. His impulsiveness made him erratic in all performances of duty, and negligent of the system without which the business of an army cannot go on . . . Under the immediate control of a firm and steady hand he could do good service, but was wholly unfit for independent responsibility." —Jacob Cox, *Reminiscences*, 1:405–406

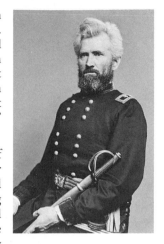

"General Milroy was . . . an Indianian, gaunt of appearance and strikingly Western in character and manners. When he met the enemy he would gallop up and down his front, fiercely shaking his fist at the 'rebel scoundrels over there,' and calling them all sorts of outrageous names . . . he would 'pitch in' at the head of his men, exposing himself with the utmost recklessness. He was a man of intense patriotism. He did not fight as one who merely likes fighting. The cause for which he was fighting—his country . . . was constantly present to his mind . . . he did good service, was respected and liked by all, and we saw him part with great regret." —Carl Schurz, *Reminiscences*, 2:387–388

ORMSBY M. MITCHEL Major general. West Point (1829). Astronomer. Commander, Department of the Ohio. Brigade and division commander, army of the Ohio. Commander 10th Corps, Department of the South.

"General Mitchel was a valuable officer. He was a graduate of West Point, about fifty-five years of age, a man of good bearing and pure morals, of considerable culture, and some reputation in science . . . he was energetic in a certain way, and had some qualifications from practical experience . . . in railroad construction and management . . . He was not insubordinate, but was restless in ordinary service, ambitious in an ostentatious way, and by temperament unsuited to an important independent command." —Don Carlos Buell, *Battles and Leaders*, 2:707

"General Mitchell [*sic*] never drinks and never swears. Occasionally he uses the words 'confound it' in rather savage style; but further than this I have never heard him go. Mitchell is military; [Ebenezer] Dumont is militia. The latter winks at the shortcomings of the soldier; the former does not." —John Beatty, *The Citizen Soldier*, p. 96–97

"He had genius rather than talent. He was bold, adventurous, wonderfully energetic, fertile in resources. He had a keen eye for strategic advantages. He managed the executive business of war with skill. He was penetrated with a fervid enthusiasm, which communicated itself to his soldiers . . . This enthusiasm led to an appearance of eccentricity and nervous excitability that . . . engendered a distrust of his stability and judgment." —Whitelaw Reid, *Ohio in the War*, 1:615–616

EDWARD L. MOLINEAUX Brevet major general. New York National Guard service. Brigade commander, Army of the Shenandoah; district commander, Lafourche, Louisiana.

"A little, fussy martinet, disliked cordially by the prisoners and hated, apparently, still more by the Federal soldiers of his command, who did not scruple to speak of him as a coward." —Henry E. Handerson, *Yankee in Gray*, p. 82

GEORGE W. MORELL Major general. West Point (1835). Railroad engineer and lawyer. Mexican War veteran. Brigade and division command, Army of the Potomac.

"General Morell has been transferred to the command of the Upper Potomac, and General Butterfield now commands Morell's division. The change is a very beneficial one, and will greatly improve the command. Morell is an awfully slow man, and would never take any responsibility upon himself. His whole division is heartily glad to have this change made." —Stephen M. Weld, *War Diary*, p. 146

WILLIAM H. MORRIS Brevet major general. West Point (1851). Brigade commander, Army of the Potomac.

"The general is a stout, easy-mannered man of thirty-four or thirty-five, not much of a soldier in appearance. He seemed to get all his orders from General [Robert] Schenck and declined doing anything on his own responsibility." —David Hunter Strother, *A Virginia Yankee*, p. 182

GERSHOM MOTT Brevet major general. Mexican War veteran. Brigade and division commander, Army of the Potomac. Corps commander, Army of the James.

"Though Genl. Mott is in command of the Brigade, I am always on the front line and in command. They all say that I am the 'fighting commander' of the Brigade. The General is in command when all is quiet. His Headquarters are well to the rear, and he don't seem to be anxious to get to the front . . . It seems a strange way to do business, but it is." —Robert McAllister, *Civil War Letters*, p. 427

"Gersham Mott . . . is a fine soldierly-looking man; was . . . in the Mexican war; says little, but seems very sound in his military ideas." —Charles S. Wainwright, *A Diary of Battle*, p. 31

JAMES S. NEGLEY Major general. Mexican War veteran. Gardener. Brigade and division command, Army of the Cumberland.

"He is a large, rosy-cheeked, handsome, affable man, and a good disciplinarian." —John Beatty, *The Citizen Soldier*, p. 268

THOMAS H. NEILL Brevet major general. West Point (1847). Frontier duty. Brigade and division command, Army of the Potomac.

"The general was a portly gentleman with light red hair and whiskers, and a small blue eye, ceremonious in his style and a perfect pattern of courtliness. He had at West Point, won the appellation of 'Beau Neill,' a title which never left him. He was a good commander in camp. He originated the brigade dress parade . . . substituting the brigade for the regimental parade." —George T. Stevens, *Three Years in the Sixth Corps*, p. 177

WILLIAM B. NELSON Major general. Naval lieutenant. Mexican War veteran. Division command, Army of the Ohio.

"He was killed by a pistol-shot fired by Gen. Jeff C. Davis, of his own command . . . The only surprise felt by those who knew him was that some such fate had not befallen him before. He was the most tyrannical, arrogant and abusive officer to those junior to him in rank that I ever saw and would use toward any of them on the smallest provocation the most outrageous and insulting language. Indeed, he did not appear to make any effort to control his violent temper . . . it was impossible that he could have long avoided a violent end at the hands of some of the victims of his wrath." —John Pope, *Memoirs*, p. 101–102

"He was a man of heroic build, six feet four inches high, and carrying lightly his weight of three hundred pounds; he had many accomplishments, spoke several languages, and was endowed with a strong intellect and a memory which enabled him to repeat, verbatim, page after page of his favorite authors. A fluent and captivating talker, when he wished to please, no man could be more genial and companionable, but he had a quick and impetuous temper and an overbearing disposition, and when irritated or opposed was offensively dictatorial and dogmatic." —R. M. Kelly, *Battles and Leaders*, 1:375

"I knew him only as a kind and genial gentleman. As a soldier he was vigilant and painstaking to the last degree. In quick perception and industry . . . he was unsurpassed. No man could be braver, more just to those he thought meritorious, or more severe with every manner of dereliction; but at times he was very harsh and petulant." —William B. Hazen, *Narrative*, p. 55

"You can hardly say too much in commendation of him as a soldier. He was watchful about the well-being and efficient condition of his troops, exacting about the duty of his inferiors, habitually alert to the extreme of prudence, and yet bold and impetuous in action. He never hesitated about obeying orders, and threw into his obedience the force of a conspicuously strong physical and mental organization." —Don Carlos Buell in William B. Hazen, *Narrative*, p. 56

"He was a man of great power over men, active, aggressive, and intelligent. He had the reputation of being overbearing and rough in his treatment towards subordinates, except in battle, when he was amiable and kind towards all. His death was a positive loss to the Union cause and to Kentucky." —William P. Carlin, *Memoirs*, p. 58

"Nelson, though often rough in command, was always solicitous about the well-being of his troops, and was held in high esteem for his conspicuous services, gallantry in battle, and great energy; and his death caused much indignation among the troops that knew him best." —Don Carlos Buell, *Battles and Leaders*, 3:43

JOHN NEWTON Major general. West Point (1842). Brigade, division, and corps commander, Army of the Potomac; division command, Army of the Tennessee.

"I ... met General John Newton, commanding a division. This was another gallant Virginian who remained true to the Union, like Thomas." —William P. Carlin, *Memoirs*, p. 127

"He was a bright man with a bad temper and disgruntled. He had been sent away from the Army of the Potomac for criticizing his commanding officers and for general bad temper." —David S. Stanley, *Memoirs*, p. 185

"Newton is a well-sized, shapely, muscular, well dressed man, with brown hair, with a very ruddy, clean-shaved, full face, blue eyes, blunt, round features, walks very erect, curbs in his chin, and has somewhat of that smart sort of swagger, that people are apt to suppose characterizes soldiers." —Frank Haskell, *Haskell of Gettysburg*, p. 133

"Newton has an intelligent face and is a somewhat tall, strongly built man, with a good deal of light hair, and a gentle way of talking, somewhat like Gen. Humphreys ... Newton is said to be an excellent subordinate and fine engineer; but as a commander he loses all aplomb and is a regular stampeder." —Theodore Lyman, *Meade's Army*, p. 28, 116–117

"General Newton is another undersize, smooth face, and light hair; he seems a gentlemanly man, and quite affable ... General Newton differs very much from [John F.] Reynolds in his love for the comforts of life, and for good eating ... He knows enough theoretically at any rate, but is intensely lazy ... being only too glad to leave matters in the hands of anyone who would take all the trouble off of his shoulders ... General Newton ... likes to lounge in the house, and be entertained ... He is very fond of music ..." —Charles S. Wainwright, *A Diary of Battle*, p. 256, 268–269, 279

EMERSON OPDYKE Brevet major general. Businessman. Brigade command, Army of the Cumberland.

"Opdyke was a very singular man; he had unusual bravery—I never saw a more daring man; but he had an ugly disposition that repelled all friendship and he was full of envy and utterly untruthful . . . His own unhappy nature with his envious exercise of mind led to his self destruction." —David S. Stanley, *Memoirs*, p. 213

EDWARD OLIVER CRESAP ORD Major general. West
Point (1839). Seminole and Mexican War veteran. Brigade and corps commander, Army of the Tennessee; commander, Army of the James and Department of North Carolina.

"There appeared a tall man, with bushy eyebrows and a nervous manner, who looked like an eccentric Irishman who was about to tell a funny story. This was Gen. Ord . . ." —Theodore Lyman, *Meade's Army*, p. 230

PETER J. OSTERHAUS Major general. German revolutionary.
Brigade, division, and corps commander, Army of the Tennessee.

"This general is universally well spoken of. He is a pleasant, genial fellow, brave and quick, and makes a first-rate report of a reconnaissance. There is not another general in this army who keeps the commander in chief so well informed concerning whatever happens at his outposts. As a disciplinarian he is not equal to Hovey, but is much better than some others. On the battlefield he lacks energy and concentrativeness." —Charles A. Dana, *Recollections*, p. 640

JOHN M. PALMER Major general. Illinois Senator and
governor. Brigade, division, and corps commander, Army of the Mississippi and Army of the Tennessee.

"[Palmer] was a brave and efficient commander of volunteers in the civil war. His clear and strong intellect made his practical methods in the war valuable to the army and the country." —Augustus Chetlain, *Recollections of Seventy Years*, p. 231

"I had always regarded General Palmer as a strong man, brave and resolute and of good judgment." —Oliver O. Howard, *Autobiography*, 2:30

JOHN GRUBB PARKE Major general. West Point (1849).
Engineer. Brigade, division, and corps command, Army of the Potomac.

"He is a perfect gentleman, and an excellent soldier in every respect. His only fault is that he is too modest, and has not quite enough self-assertion or ambition for a very brilliant soldier." —Major Charles Mills, *Through Blood and Fire*, p. 173

"He is a very pleasant-looking man and liked apparently by everyone. He has been obliged twice to return to the North by reason of malarial attacks, which is a pity, as he acted usually as adviser to General Burnside and had an excellent effect on him. He cured himself twice of malarial fever by accidentally taking an overdose of medicine." —Theodore Lyman, *Meade's Headquarters*, p. 213

MARSENA PATRICK Brigadier general. West Point (1835). Mexican War veteran. Brigade commander and provost marshal general, Army of the Potomac.

"Patrick was a man of vigor, of conscience, and of system, and though he was greatly desirous of keeping a field command, proved so useful, indeed so necessary a part of the organization, that he was retained in it against his wishes, to the end of the war, each commander of the Army of the Potomac in turn finding that he was indispensable."
—Jacob Cox, *Reminiscences*, 1:266

"Gen. Marcellus [Marsena] Patrick was Provost Marshall General of the Army of the Potomac. He was then (and so remained until the day of his death) in my opinion, the finest existing fossil of the Cenozoic age."
—Sylvanus Cadwallader, *Three Years with Grant*, p. 180

ROBERT PATTERSON Major general. Veteran of War of 1812 and Mexican War. Major general of Pennsylvania volunteers, 1861.

"Opposing [Joseph E.] Johnston in the Valley was General Robert Patterson, of Philadelphia, a veteran of the war of 1812, and of the Mexican War, especially distinguished in the latter by the prestige of the former service. Johnston was a veteran of the Mexican War, who had won distinction by progressive service and was well equipped in the science of war. [Pierre G. T.] Beauregard and [Irvin] McDowell were also veterans of the Mexican War, of staff service, and distinguished for intelligent action and attainments, both remarkable for physical as well as mental power." —James Longstreet, *From Manassas to Appomattox*, p. 42

"Patterson . . . was a political general, only remembered for having allowed the force he commanded in the Shenandoah Valley to render no service at a critical time . . . It was evident that his prime object had been not to divert Johnston's army but to avoid a collision. Patterson no doubt thought that he had effected his purpose and was content to rest where he was." —John S. Mosby, *Memoirs*, p. 40, 47

JOHN J. PECK Major general. West Point (1843). Division commander, Army of the Potomac. District commander at Suffolk; commander, Department of the East.

"General Peck forbids us to shoot, unless we are attacked. We were biting our fists with anger, but we must obey ... Peck ... is too careful with his and our safety, and ... likes bombs and bullets very little. We almost never see him in our lines where our soldiers openly say that it is too hot for him."
—Regis de Trobriand, *Our Noble Blood*, p. 49

"Gen. Peck was a nervous, dyspeptic gentleman who would fret himself to exhaustion for fear that he might be caught napping." —Alvin C. Voris, *A Citizen Soldier's Civil War*, p. 115

JOHN W. PHELPS   Brigadier general. West Point (1836). Seminole and Mexican War veteran. Commanded defenses of Newport News and Ship Island.

"Brave, cool, and capable, he was thoroughly liked by his men and by his superior officers. He spoke with a long, drawling 'Yankee' accent, and his piquant sayings were very entertaining. Hating display and egotism, he invariably showed his displeasure when in the presence of men who were guilty of either." —Joseph B. Carr, *Battles and Leaders*, 2:147

"He is a swarthy, grizzled six-footer, who looks all the more giant-like because of a loose build and a shambling carriage, and says unexpected things in a slow, solemn humoristic way . . . He hates the Rebels bitterly, not so much because they are rebellious as because they are slaveholders, for he is a fervid abolitionist . . . On the drill ground the general is instructive and amusing. He gives his orders in a high-keyed, penetrating, tranquil drawl which makes the men titter, partly because the tone is funny in itself, and partly because the commands follow each other so closely . . . If things go wrong . . . the general tumbles all to pieces with distress. His body jerks forward; his elbows flap up and down like wings; he seems to trot several feet ahead of his horse; he arrives at the scene of confusion with a face of anguish. Sometimes he instructs; sometimes he scoffs; sometimes he swears." —John William De Forest, *A Volunteer's Adventures*, p. 9–10

"I had no better soldier or officer, none in whose care I felt any more safe to leave everything in possession, than General Phelps . . . He had but one fault: he was an anti-slavery man to a degree that utterly unbalanced his judgment . . . He disciplined his troops very admirably . . ." —Ben Butler, *Butler's Book*, 2:896–897

ALFRED PLEASONTON   Major general. West Point (1844). Seminole and Mexican War veteran. Cavalry brigade, division, and corps commander, Army of the Potomac.

"Pleasonton is the bête noire of all cavalry officers. Stoneman we believe in. We believe in his judgment, his courage and determination. We know he is ready to shoulder responsibility, that he will take good care of us and won't get us into places from which he can't get us out. Pleasonton also we have served under. He is pure and simple a newspaper humbug. You always see his name in the papers, but to us who have served under him and seen him under fire he is notorious as a bully and toady. He does nothing save with a view to a newspaper paragraph . . . Yet

mean and contemptible as Pleasonton is, he is always *in* at Head Quarters . . ."
—Charles Francis Adams Jr., *A Cycle of Adams Letters*, 2:8

"Pleasonton is, next to Hooker, the greatest humbug of the war, and Kilpatrick
is a brave injudicious boy, much given to blowing and who will surely come to
grief." —Charles Francis Adams Jr., *A Cycle of Adams Letters*, 2:44–45

"Pleasonton is quite a nice little dandy, with brown hair and beard,—a straw
hat with a little jockey rim, which he cocks upon one side of his head, with
an unsteady eye, that looks slily at you, and then dodges." —Frank Haskell,
Haskell of Gettysburg, p. 134

"General Pleasonton was always a gentleman whenever you found him,
always and at all times. He was not assertive . . . but he always seemed to
keep to himself. He was like the captain of a ship. He always messed alone
. . . I never saw him intimate with any body . . . He never swore like others . . ."
—James Franklin Wade, *Generals in Bronze*, p. 131

"He is a singular man, cold-blooded yet kindly; ambitious but not soaring; of
a quick, ready brain, though not capable of judging things *en grand*. He has a
good mind to command a division of cavalry." —Theodore Lyman, *Meade's
Army*, p. 116

ORLANDO M. POE Major general. West Point (1856). Engineer.
Brigade commander, Army of the Potomac; chief engineer, Army of the
Ohio and Military Division of the Mississippi.

"He was in person the model for a young athlete, tall, dark, and strong, with
frank, open countenance . . . He was indefatigable in his labors, assisting the
governor in organizing the regiments, smoothing the difficulties constantly
arising . . . with the details of the administrative service of the army, and giving
wise advice to the volunteer officers . . ." —Jacob Cox, *Reminiscences of the
Civil War*, 1:20

JOHN POPE Major general. West Point
(1842). Topographical engineer. Mexican War veteran.
Commander, Army of the Mississippi, Army of
Virginia, Department of the Northwest.

"He is a stout man of medium height, prepossessing
manners and appearance. He is young and alert . . . Pope
is a bright, dashing man, self-confident and clearheaded.
He has a good memory and has been a topographical
engineer. I observe that he is wonderfully quick to seize
all information on this subject. He remembers it all if once told and wants new
details. Whether his mind grasps general subjects with capacity and clearness
I have not had an opportunity to judge. He is irascible and impulsive in his
judgments of men, but in his pleasant moods, jolly, humorous and clever in
conversation." —David Hunter Strother, *A Virginia Yankee*, p. 64, 74–75

"Briefly it may be said that Pope's general reputation in army circles . . . was that of a blatherskite . . ." —Edward P. Alexander, *Fighting for the Confederacy*, p. 123

"Of General Pope's character and history everything was known to all the old officers in the army who had graduated at West Point. I knew him to be a man of ability in certain directions but did not know how he would develop as a general, and though I did not think he was the stuff from which a leader could be made I joined him in the sincere hope that he would be what I felt we needed . . ." —William F. Smith, *Autobiography*, p. 51

"Poor Pope . . . was indeed an object of pity. He had gone up like a rocket & had put on airs & boasted what he would do. Now he came down like a stick, & his rival took his command from him on the road . . . But there is one thing which may be said in Pope's favor. He was not afraid to fight his men, & when he did fight them he did his best apparently to get in all he had at the same time. And that is what McClellan never learned to do." —E. P. Alexander, *Fighting for the Confederacy*, p. 139

"Lee had not known Pope . . . but accepted the popular opinion of him as a boastful man, quite ambitious to accomplish great results, but unwilling to study closely and properly the means necessary to gratify his desires in that direction . . . I was graduated with Pope at West Point. He was a handsome, dashing fellow, and a splendid cavalryman . . . He did not apply himself to his books very closely. He studied about as much as I did, but knew his lessons better . . . Pope saw little of active of service till the opening of the Civil War." —William B. Taliaferro, *Battles and Leaders*, 2:513, 524

"General Pope was lacking in that sort of independence of character which not only prompts but enables an army commander to do on the spot that which he knows the exigencies require, independent of orders received from superiors at a distance and ignorant of the situation." —John Gibbon, *Personal Recollections of the Civil War*, p. 47

"His reputation in 1861 was that of an able and energetic man, vehement and positive in character, apt to be choleric and even violent toward those who displeased him. I remember well that I shrunk a little from coming under his immediate orders through fear of some chafing, though I learned in the army that choleric commanders, if they have ability, are often warmly appreciative of those who serve them with soldierly spirit and faithfulness. No one who had any right to judge questioned Pope's ability or his zeal in the National cause." —Jacob Cox, *Reminiscences*, 1:247

"I had known General Pope pretty well, almost from his boyhood. Whatever his military ability might have been, he was very much disliked by his comrades of the regular army, and while commanding a division in North Missouri . . . he managed to make himself very unpopular with the officers and men under him. I thought at the time his appointment to the newly formed Army of Virginia very injudicious, and his very first address to his army on taking command was so pompous and so insulting to the army . . . that many people doubted his common sense." —Gustave Koerner, *Memoirs*, 2:235

"Shall I go onto Pope's staff? I think not ... Do you know that Pope is a humbug and known to be so by those who put him in his present place? Do you know that today he is so completely outgeneraled as to be cut off from Washington? Yet these are not rumors, but facts, doled out to me by members of McClellan's and Halleck's staffs ... I am ashamed at what I hear of Pope. All army officers say that he is a humbug and is sure to come to grief; 'as big a liar as John Pope' is an old army expression; he has already played himself out in the army of Virginia ... he may come out with colors flying, for he is a lucky man; but if he does, he is a dangerous one, and I am advised not to connect my fortunes with his ..." —Charles Francis Adams Jr., *A Cycle of Adams Letters*, 1:178, 181

"'Damn John Pope,' is the motto here, which I am quite disposed to indorse." —Charles J. Mills, *Through Blood and Fire*, p. 8

"He was a man of some ability, but did not have a reputation for high character in the old Army; and now with high rank and command thrust upon him, he turned into abuse of his enemy, explained how he meant to whip him, and filled the air with bombast and threatening." —G. Moxley Sorrel, *Recollections of a Confederate Staff Officer*, p. 87

"A more utterly unfit man than Pope was never seen. Every dispatch he sent to the Department was, as published, a gross lie." —Gouverneur K. Warren, *Happiness is not My Companion*, p. 57

"Pope was entirely deceived and outgeneraled. His own conceit and pride of opinion led him into these mistakes. On the field his conduct was cool, gallant, and prompt. When the facts of the case were forced upon him, he met them with soldierly coolness and energy, but he was in the general planning of the campaign unable to cope with his opponents ... In war men should not maneuver but should fight. I like Pope's pluck in fighting." —David Hunter Strother, *A Virginia Yankee*, p. 97, 99

"Those who have favored Pope are disturbed and disappointed. Blair, who has known him intimately, says he is a braggart and a liar, with some courage, perhaps, but not much capacity. The general conviction is that he is a failure here, and there is a belief and admission on all hands that he has not been seconded and sustained as he should have been by McClellan, Franklin, Fitz John Porter, and perhaps some others." —Gideon Welles, *Diary*, 1:104

"Had Pope been an able, enterprising general, like [French general Louis Lazare] Hoche or Napoleon, or like Jackson or Lee, he would have beaten the Confederates in detail ... but he was a common-place general, a braggart and a failure, like Lachelle, whose only order was to 'march majestically and en masse.'" —William C. Oates, *The War Between the Union and the Confederacy*, p. 136

"General John Pope is the only warrior of modern times who can find a battle whenever he wants to, and take any number of prisoners his heart desires. Even his brilliant achievements, however, afford the people but temporary satisfaction, for, upon investigation, they are unable to find either the captives or the discomfited hosts." —John Beatty, *The Citizen Soldier*, p. 189

"I have a strong idea that Pope will be thrashed during the coming week—& very badly whipped he will be & ought to be—such a villain as he is ought to bring defeat upon any cause that employs him . . ." —George B. McClellan, *Civil War Papers*, p. 389

"Pope was a favorite of his Government, and the Honorable Secretary of War was 'yours truly' to all his demands . . . He was to be the Wellington of the war; but he was not made of the right material. He had none of the metal of the Iron Duke in his composition. He had none of the excellencies of Sheridan, but he was the supreme possessor of his faults. Indeed, he bore a striking family likeness to the great Cavalryman in the Plenitude of his villainy. Together they formed a pair of loyal freebooters who cared nothing for the honor of man, the purity of woman or the sanctity of religion." —Cullen Andrews Battle, *Third Alabama*, p. 41

"In person he was dark, martial, and handsome—inclined to obesity, richly garbed in civil cloth, and possessing a fiery black eye, with luxurious beard and hair. He smoked incessantly, and talked imprudently . . . his vanity was apparent to the most shallow observer, and although he was brave, clever, and educated, he inspired distrust by his much promising and general love of gossip and story-telling. He had all of Mr. Lincoln's garrulity . . . and none of that good old man's unassuming common sense." —George A. Townsend, *Campaigns of a Non-Combatant*, p. 221

"I want Pope to be suppressed. The course indicated in his orders if the newspapers report them correctly cannot be permitted and will lead to retaliation on our part."Robert E. Lee, *Wartime Papers*, p. 239

"Pope had met with some success in the campaigns in the West, and was looked upon as a rising officer whose military capacity would be productive of great results, and ultimately seat him in McClellan's saddle . . . He was evidently deeply impressed with the idea that the war in Virginia had not been conducted properly . . . There was a striking contrast between McClellan and Pope." —Fitzhugh Lee, *General Lee*, p. 173–174

"We have some of Gen. Pope's proclamations and orders. He is simply a braggart, and will meet a braggart's fate . . . we shall see how he will face a Stonewall!" —John B. Jones, *A Rebel War Clerk's Diary*, 1:143

"Pope criticizes and abuses McClellan with a will, showing in a man in his position no better taste than appeared in his proclamation and some of his orders. His personal appearance is certainly not calculated to inspire confidence or liking. He looks just what we have always understood he was—a great *blow-hard*, with no lack of confidence in his own powers." —Robert Gould Shaw, *Blue-eyed Child of Fortune*, p. 225

"Pope was successful in the purpose for which he went out, but his general orders were full of claptrap and braggadocio and his return seemed to be much more of a failure than he was . . . Pope has been greatly wronged, is a man of some . . . [considerable] ability and vigor, but given to fanfaronade and on the whole I don't admire him very much." —James A. Garfield, *The Wild Life of the Army*, p. 314

DAVID DIXON PORTER, USN   Rear admiral. Mexican War veteran. Commander, Mississippi River Squadron.

"He has ... stirring and positive qualities, is fertile in resources, has great energy, excessive and sometimes not over-scrupulous ambition, is impressed with and boastful of his own powers, given to exaggeration in relation to himself—a Porter infirmity—is not generous to older and superior living officers, whom he is too ready to traduce, but is kind and patronizing to favorites who are juniors, and generally to official inferiors. Is given to cliquism but is brave and daring like all his family." —Gideon Welles, *Diary*, 1:157

"I pronounce him by all odds the greatest humbug of the war. He never accomplished anything if unaided ... The Confederates laughed at him ... Add to this that Porter was vain, arrogant and egotistical to an extent that can neither be described nor exaggerated and you have his calibre completely. He possessed many polite accomplishments; but very few qualities of a great naval commander." —Sylvanus Cadwallader, *Three Years with Grant*, p. 53

FITZ JOHN PORTER   Major general. West Point (1845). Mexican War veteran. Division and corps commander, Army of the Potomac.

"I have never thought much of him. I have never doubted he was unnecessarily slow and cautious in his conduct. ... I have always regarded the excuse that it was 'too late' when he received Pope's orders to attack, as frivolous and absurd ... I have always believed that Porter was naturally and professionally one of our ablest generals ... he became obsessed with the idea that McClellan was a great man and Pope a fool. In short, ... he submerged his own personality and sense of soldierly duty, in those of McClellan ... if this was not false to the country and its cause it was at least false to himself and his duty as a soldier." —James H. Wilson, *Generals in Bronze*, p. 280

"Porter was the most skillful tactician and strongest fighter in the Federal army, thoroughly trained in his profession from boyhood, and of some experience in field work." —James Longstreet, *From Manassas to Appomattox*, p. 84

"He had so high a reputation in the army and for services since the outbreak of the war, that I was not only curious to see him, but was exceedingly glad that he had joined the army under my command ... He appeared to me a most gentlemanlike man, of a soldierly and striking appearance ..." —John Pope, *Battles and Leaders*, 2: 462

"He is not a man who talks much ... One can rely on what General Porter says. He is very kind and pleasant to me and every one, but I should not like to do anything he did not like, for I guess any one who did so would catch a blessing.

He is not quick-tempered or anything of that kind, but he has an eye that shows some determination. He is a very handsome man . . . with dark colored beard and whiskers pretty closely cut . . ." —Stephen M. Weld, *War Diary*, p. 54

"I look on McClellan with horror . . . I regard him as in the past, a traitor . . . I understand, that they speak of a successor from the Corps Commanders, as Fitz John Porter, or [Edwin V.] Sumner. As to Porter, he is not of the calibre. He would make bad worse. As to Sumner, he would be even worse. He has neither capacity, nor sane judgment. He is a proverbial blunderer. If it were [Erasmus D.] Keyes, it would be no better . . . As to [Samuel P.] Heintzelman, he is almost worse . . . his small quanteen of brains have been fossilized by near 40 years of small garrison routine at the head of 100 foot . . . As to [William B.] Franklin, he had talents. It may hold good as to engineering. He may have judgement, in ordinary matters . . . under an air of frankness . . . he is most astute as to his own advancement. He played double with McDowell and McClellan. He is now in Washington cultivating Halleck." —Phil Kearny, *Letters from the Peninsula*, p. 146

"General Porter . . . I found to be a man of rather above the middle height, with a frank and agreeable face, the lower part of which was covered with a luxuriant black beard, and in his whole bearing and appearance the soldier . . . General Fitzjohn Porter proved to be too much of the gentleman for the Northern Government . . . but I have pleasure in bearing my testimony (that of an enemy) to his qualities as a gallant soldier and an excellent fighter." —Heros Von Borcke, *Memoirs*, 1:282, 284

"I remember him as carefully attired, reserved in manner, quick in observation, graceful in person; in other words, looking the fine soldier." —*Lew Wallace: An Autobiography*, 1:311

"Fitz John Porter was the best corps commander in the Federal Army. He was a strong friend and admirer of McClellan and had no respect for Pope nor confidence in his ability as a general, hence he doubted and hesitated to obey his order with reference to attacking Jackson's right on Friday evening, the 29th of August . . . the responsibility had to be fixed on some one for the loss of the battle. Porter being a McClellan man and a Democrat . . . was selected for the sacrifice." —William C. Oates, *The War Between the Union and the Confederacy*, p. 147

"Take him for all in all, he was probably the best general officer I had under me. He had excellent ability, sound judgment, and all the instincts of a soldier. He was perfectly familiar with all the details of his duty, an excellent organizer and administrative officer, and one of the most conscientious laborious men I ever knew . . . I always knew that an order given to him would be fully carried out, were it morally and physically possible. He was one of the coolest and most imperturbable men in danger whom I ever knew . . ." —George B. McClellan, *McClellan's Own Story*, p. 139

"Porter was a polite, soldierly gentleman . . . who had been in the regular army since early manhood. He fought gallantly in the Mexican war . . . and he was now forty years of age—handsome, enthusiastic, ambitious, and popular." —George A. Townsend, *Campaigns of a Non-Combatant*, p. 115

WILLIAM D. PORTER, USN   Commodore. Commanded
USS *St. Mary's* and USS *Essex*

"Porter is a bold, brave man, but reckless in many respects, and unpopular, perhaps not without reason, in the service. He has been earnest and vigorous on the Mississippi, and made himself." —Gideon Welles, *Diary*, 1:88

ROBERT B. POTTER   Major general. Lawyer. Brigade and
division command, Army of the Potomac.

"Potter is tall, with a full, phlegmatic black eye. He is particular about his dress, of few words, and reputed an excellent division commander." —Theodore Lyman, *Meade's Army*, p. 162

BENJAMIN M. PRENTISS   Major general. Mexican War
veteran. Lawyer. Brigade and division commander, Army of the Tennessee. Commander, District of Eastern Arkansas.

"I was introduced the General Prentiss, an agreeable person, without anything about him to indicate the soldier." —William Howard Russell, *My Diary North & South*, p. 174

"He was a brave and very earnest soldier. No man in the service was more sincere in his devotion to the cause for which we were battling; none more ready to make sacrifices or risk life in it."Ulysses S. Grant, *Personal Memoirs,* 1:264

"Brigadier General Prentiss, a man strongly resembling Esquire Williams, constable of Chagrin Falls, or perhaps a cross between him and the Honorable Blakessee . . . of the same place. His face is not sufficiently marked to lead me to take his picture *in extenso* . . . He is a pleasant little man, on the whole rather sensible, but will never be considered the avatar of intellect." —James A. Garfield, *The Wild Life of the Army*, p. 187

ISAAC F. QUINBY   Brigadier general. West Point (1843).
Garrison duty. Commander, District of Mississippi. Division command, Army of the Tennessee.

"A good commander of a division he is not, though he is a most excellent and estimable man, and seemed to be regarded by the soldiers with much affection. But he lacks order, system, command, and is the very opposite of his successor . . ." —Charles A. Dana, *Recollections*, p. 69

JOHN RAMSEY   Brevet major general. Brigade command, Army
of the Potomac.

"Genl. Ramsey was not at all popular with either officers or men . . . He has, however, been assigned to the 4th Brigade, 2nd Division of this Corps and has left to take command. I am glad of it, for he is a snake in the grass. There is a great deal of low cunning about him." —Robert McAllister, *Civil War Letters*, p. 563

THOMAS E. G. RANSOM
Brevet major general. Civil Engineer and realtor. Brigade, division, and corps commander in western theater. Died at Rome, Georgia, 1864.

"Ransom ... has exceeded every other brigadier in the zeal, intelligence, and efficiency with which his siege works were constructed and pushed forward ... No young man in all this army has more future than he." —Charles A. Dana, *Recollections*, p. 69

"Ransom was one of the daring and dashing young generals who, if he had lived and the war had continued, would have reached higher rank at no distant day. His father was a distinguished officer of the Army of the United States during the war with Mexico, and was killed in leading the assault on the Castle of Chapultepec. It was a family of military instincts, and young T.E.G. Ransom was certainly a brilliant and promising son of so gallant a father." —William P. Carlin, *Memoirs*, p. 142

"He was a brave gallant officer and most agreeable gentleman ... Had he lived longer, no doubt he would have risen to higher rank and command." —Benjamin Grierson, *A Just and Righteous Cause*, p. 199

JOHN A. RAWLINS
Brigadier general. Lawyer. Chief of staff to Ulysses S. Grant.

"He was always most loyal and devoted to his chief, an enthusiastic patriot, and of real ability ... a lawyer in good practice, an intense thinker, and a man of vehement expression; a soldier by force of circumstances rather than of education or practice, yet of infinite use to his chief ..." —William T. Sherman, *Battles and Leaders*, 4:257

"He was above medium size, wore a long black beard, and talked in a loud, emphatic voice. Sincerity and earnestness was the look of his face." —Morris Schaff, *Wilderness*, p. 49

"Rawlins was one of the most valuable men in the army, in my judgment. He had but limited education ... but he had a very able mind, clear, strong, and not subject to hysterics. He bossed everything at Grant's headquarters. He had very little respect for persons, and a rough style of conversation ... but he was entirely devoted to his duty, with the clearest judgment, and perfectly fearless." —Charles A. Dana, *Recollections*, p. 62

"General Rawlins, though he had not the advantage of an early military education, was a man of great natural ability, and had learned much from more than three years' experience in war . . ." —John M. Schofield, *Forty-Six Years in the Army*, p. 323

"He interested me from the first by his steady gaze, his strong voice, and his direct and emphatic speech . . . He was then about thirty-two years old, five feet seven inches tall, broad-shouldered, stout-limbed, and of strong and vigorous health. With jet black hair and brown steady eyes, swarthy complexion, fine teeth, a firm mouth, and a clear resonant voice, he impressed me as a very earnest, able man . . ." —James H. Wilson, *Under the Old Flag*, p. 133

"Rawlins . . . was clear-headed, energetic, fearless and conscientious in the discharge of duty, and endowed with unusual administrative ability." —Augustus L. Chetlain, *Recollections of Seventy Years*, p. 93–94

"Rawlins was a man of strong likes and dislikes, and positive always both in speech and action, exhibiting marked feelings when greeting any one . . ." —Philip H. Sheridan, *Memoirs*, 2:126

"He arrived yesterday . . . Was much pleased with him, his frank, intelligent, and interesting descriptions of men and account of army operations . . . His honest, unpretending, and unassuming manners pleased me; the absence of pretension, and I may say the unpolished and unrefined deportment, of this earnest and sincere man, patriot, and soldier pleased me more than that of almost any officer whom I have met. He was never at West Point . . . yet he is a soldier, and has a mind which has served his general and his country well." —Gideon Welles, *Diary* 1:386

"Rawlins quietly but relentlessly exercised his personal and official influence and authority . . . His authority was unquestioned. His control over Grant was fully recognized. More than one staff officer was barely given the option of resigning, or of being crushed by the iron hand of the great Chief of Staff." —Sylvanus Cadwallader, *Three Years with Grant*, p. 118

"He was frank, honest, and resolute, and loyally devoted to his chief. He always had the courage of his convictions, and was capable of stating them with great force. He was plain and simple in manner, of a genial disposition, and popular with all the other members of the staff. He had never served in a military organization, nor made a study of the art of war; but he possessed natural executive ability of a high order, and developed qualities which made him exceedingly useful to his chief and to the service." —Horace Porter, *Campaigning with Grant*, p. 32

"He was an able man, possessed of great firmness, and could say 'no' so emphatically to a request which he thought should not be granted that the person he was addressing would understand at once that there was no use of pressing the matter. General Rawlins was a very useful officer in other ways than this. I became very much attached to him." —Ulysses S. Grant, *Personal Memoirs*, 1:256

"General Rawlins . . . never commanded troops, and gained all his military knowledge and experience as a staff officer taken from civil life. He was a man of undoubted ability, of instinctive sympathy with popular feeling, whether in the army or out of it, and of prodigious energy in manner and language. He was passionately patriotic, and would have died for Grant. His intellect, however, was entirely undisciplined, and his genius was quick, rather than original, or profound." —Adam Badeau, *Military History of Ulysses S. Grant*, 2:191

JESSE L. RENO   Major general. West Point (1846). Mexican War veteran. Brigade and division commander, army of the Potomac. Mortally wounded at Fox's Gap, September 14, 1862.

"I shall not soon forget the bright and confident face and the alert and hearty manner of that most accomplished and loyal soldier . . . from first to last . . . he was always cheerful and ready; anxious to anticipate if possible, and prompt to execute with all his might, the orders he received. He was short in stature and upright in person, and with a face and manner so bright and engaging at all times, but most especially noticeable in the fury of battle . . ." —John Pope, *Battles and Leaders*, 2:474

"Reno was one of our ablest and most promising commanders. D.H. Hill's comment, considering his passion, was a compliment, when he said: 'The Yankees lost . . . General Reno, a renegade Virginian, who was killed by a happy shot from the Twenty-third North Carolina.' As Reno was never a secessionist, and as he was always true to the flag of his country . . . no stretch of language could truthfully brand him a deserter. He was a true man . . ." —Oliver O. Howard, *Autobiography*, 1:281

JOHN F. REYNOLDS   Major general. West Point (1841). Mexican War veteran. Brigade, division, and corps command, Army of the Potomac. Killed at Gettysburg, July 1, 1863.

"Reynolds . . . has the perfect confidence of his troops & of the Army . . . but [John] Newton . . . does not, I think, amount to very much. [John] Sedgwick, I fear, is not enough of a general for that position—He is a good honest fellow & that is all. I do not think his officers have very much confidence in him—[Daniel] Sickles & the most of his crew, are poor—very poor concerns, in my opinion . . ." —Marsena Patrick, *Inside Lincoln's Army*, p. 237

"From soldiers, cadets, and officers, junior and senior, he always secured reverence for his serious character, respect for his ability, care for his uniform discipline, admiration for his fearlessness, and love for his unfailing generosity." —Oliver O. Howard, *Autobiography*, 1:402

"I felt very badly indeed about his death, because he had always treated me very kindly, and because he was the best general we had in our army. Brave, kind-hearted, modest, somewhat rough and wanting polish, he was a type of the true soldier." —Stephen M. Weld, *War Diary*, p. 230

"He was known as an officer of superior merit, and in the opinion of many it was he that ought to have been put at the head of the Army of the Potomac." —Carl Schurz, *Reminiscences*, 3:6

"He was a splendid soldier and performed admirably every duty assigned to him . . . he was remarkably brave and intelligent, an honest, true gentleman." —George B. McClellan, *McClellan's Own Story*, p. 140

"He was a superb-looking man, dark complexioned, wearing full black whiskers, and sat his fine horse like a Centaur, tall, straight, and graceful, the ideal soldier . . . he was one of the few great commanders developed by the war. A quiet, modest man, he yet possessed a very decisive element of character . . ." —Frederick L. Hitchcock, *War from the Inside*, p. 101–102

JOSEPH J. REYNOLDS   Major general. West Point (1843). Frontier duty. Brigade and division command in Army of the Cumberland. Chief of staff to George H. Thomas.

"General Reynolds is a graduate of West Point, and has the theory of war completely; but whether he has the broad, practical common sense, more important than book knowledge, time will determine. As yet, he is an untried quantity, and, therefore, unknown." —John Beatty, *The Citizen Soldier*, p. 36–37

JAMES C. RICE   Brigadier general. Teacher and lawyer. Brigade command, Army of the Potomac. Killed at Spotsylvania, May 10, 1864.

"He had been a faithful officer since the opening of the struggle, brave to rashness, generous to a fault, kind and even fatherly to his men." —Oliver P. Norton, *Army Letters*, p. 280

ISRAEL B. RICHARDSON   Major general. West Point (1841). Seminole and Mexican War veteran. Brigade, and division command, Army of the Potomac. Mortally wounded at Antietam, September 17, 1862.

"'Old Dick' Richardson was our brigade commander. We remember him as a man who understood volunteers and appreciated the difference between them and regulars. He generally went around camp wearing an old straw hat and citizen's coat, his slouchy appearance anything but military, but he would stay in a fight as long as any one, and looked after the comfort of his men with a fatherly solicitude." —*Natl Tribune*, July 7, 1887

"I must chronicle my opinion of some of the chief actors in the eventful scene [Antietam]. General Richardson behaved gallantly—leading & ordering his men until he was struck by a piece of shell in the breast. Gen. [Thomas F.] Meagher was drunk as usual. Gen. [George] Caldwell did not show himself either brave or skillful; & he lost the confidence of his soldiers . . ." —Edward Cross, *Stand Firm and Fire Low*, p. 51

"Richardson is a dark, slim man, with stooping shoulders, and a pronounced nasal voice. He looks like a farmer more than a soldier, and is utterly devoid of style; but has good common sense, a rare commodity apparently, and is very popular with his command . . . He made me think he smelt something disagreeable all the time, by the way he moved the muscles of his face. He is a typical Yankee." —Josiah Favill, *Diary of a Young Officer*, p. 103

"General Richardson[was] a veteran of the Mexican War, a most sterling character, a good organizer and persistent fighter, a man who was regardless of his own appearance or safety, yet ever thoughtful of his command and duties . . ." —Nelson A. Miles, *Serving the Republic*, p. 46

"He was a large, heavy, powerful man, a West Pointer . . . He put on no military style; generally he was clothed in a private's blouse . . . His speech, when not aroused, was slow and drawling; he did not appear to care for salutes and the men began to regard him as one of them; he had their confidence and affection, and they willingly followed him." —Charles Augustus Fuller, *Recollections of the War of 1861*, p. 10

"He was an officer of the old army, 'bull-headed,' brave, a good disciplinarian." —George B. McClellan, *McClellan's Own Story*, p. 139

"General Richardson impressed me as a man of great determination and courage. He was a large, heavy man, dressed roughly and spoke and acted very brusquely." —Frederick L. Hitchcock, *War from the Inside*, p. 39

JAMES B. RICKETTS Brevet major general. West Point (1839). Artillerist. Mexican War veteran. Division command, Army of the Potomac.

"Gen. Ricketts is a man of gentlemanly manners, stoutly built and with a John Bunyan sort of head. He looks to me like a person of very small ability, but is known as a brave officer." —Theodore Lyman, *Meade's Army*, p. 118

"Brigadier General Ricketts of New York, about 35 years of age, of fresh complexion, rather of the precise, clerkly sort, pointed chin, tipped with light . . . whiskers which mingle with a curling mustache, pale blue eyes and a smooth, fresh-looking forehead slightly marred by a scar which resembles a saber cut." —James A. Garfield, *The Wild Life of the Army*, p. 188

JOHN C. ROBINSON Brigadier general. Dismissed from West Point in 1837. Mexican War veteran. Brigade and division commander, Army of the Potomac.

"General Robinson was an officer of long experience in the regular service, and was rather fierce in appearance and manner. In a much bearded army he was the hairiest general I ever saw." —Abner R. Small, *The Road to Richmond*, p. 80

WILLIAM S. ROSECRANS   Major general.

West Point (1842). Engineer. Wing commander in
Halleck's army group, 1862. Commander, Army of the
Cumberland, 1862–1863. Commander, Department of
Missouri, 1864–1865.

"He seemed to be a great enthusiast in regard to
the Catholic Church; seemed to think of nothing else,
talk of nothing else, and in fact do nothing else, except to
proselyte for it . . . and no occasion, however inappropriate, was ever lost sight
of to advocate its cause; in fact, he . . . might not inappropriately be considered
a one-ideaed man lacking in breadth and poise, so necessary to success in the
commander of an army in the field . . . His head seemed to have been completely
turned by the greatness of his promotion. Instead of quiet dignity, orderly and
business methods that had formerly obtained at headquarters of the Army,
the very reverse seemed to be the rule . . . The Commanding General was such
a narrow-minded bigot in regard to Catholicism, that it was impossible for
him not to allow considerations of this kind to control his estimate of men."
—Milo S. Hascall, *Personal Recollections of Stone River*, p. 4–5

"Rosecrans was . . . a very busy man . . . very accomplished and able officer
with a wonderful working capacity that knew no limit . . . [he was] the picture
of robust health and vigor, and was full of energy and active enterprise. By
his amiability and social good nature he soon became a favorite and was for
several years the idol of those he commanded. That he had courage and even
genius to become a great general there is no doubt. His weakness was gullibility
and he often did foolish things, being cajoled into them by humbugs and
frauds. His temper was also bad, and when provoked he showed no patience."
—David S. Stanley, *Memoirs*, p. 101

"He certainly enters into his work with his whole soul . . . and he will soon
be recognized as the first general of the Union. I account for his success thus
far, in part at least, by the fact that he has been long enough away from West
Point, mixing with the people, to get a little common sense rubbed into him."
—John Beatty, *The Citizen Soldier*, p. 229–230

"I regard Rosecrans as of the first order of military mind. He was both brave
and generous, impulsively so; in fact, in his impulsiveness lay a military
defect, which was to issue too many orders while his men were fighting."
—Thomas L. Crittenden, *Battles and Leaders*, 3:633

"Grant don't like Rosecrans . . . Rosecrans may be Grant's superior in intellect,
but not in sagacity, purity of character and singleness of purpose. Rosecrans
is selfish and vainglorious. Grant not a bit so. He would never appropriate the
just fame of another. He and I have been always perfect friends . . . Grant would
stand by his friend, but Rosecrans would sacrifice his brother if he stood in the
way of his popular renown."   —William T. Sherman, *Sherman at War*, p. 123

"General Rosecrans was then but little over forty years of age and was the picture
of health. His general and amiable manners had won the love of the soldiers,

and certainly no one had a higher appreciation of him as a man and officer than myself. Whatever misfortunes or errors may have attended his efforts at a later day, no general who ever commanded the Army of the Cumberland was so well loved as Rosecrans." —William P. Carlin, *Memoirs*, p. 91

"While few persons exhibited more estimable social qualities, I have never seen a public man possessing talent with less administrative power, less clearness and steadiness in difficulty, and greater practical incapacity than General Rosecrans. He had inventive fertility and knowledge, but he had no strength of will and no concentration of purpose. His mind scattered; there was no system in the use of his busy days and nights, no courage against individuals in his composition, and, with great love of command, he was a feeble commander. He was conscientious and honest, just as he was imperious and disputatious; always with a stray vein of caprice and an overweening passion for the approbation of his personal friends and the public outside." —Charles A. Dana, *Recollections*, p. 128

"Grant's intimates knew that he regarded Rosecrans as an able man, but as Jesuitical, insincere, and pretentious and that Rosecrans on the other hand thought Grant rather 'a fool for luck' than a great commander." —James H. Wilson, *Under the Old Flag*, p. 265

"General Rosecrans has the utmost confidence and affection of every soldier in this army and the news that he was going to leave us was received with the deepest regret and even rage . . ." —Harvey Reid, *The View from Headquarters*, p. 100

"His standard of soldierly excellence was high, and he was earnest in insisting that his brigadiers and his staff officers should cooperate vigorously in trying to attain it. His impulsiveness, however, led him sometimes into personal efforts at discipline where the results were at least doubtful." —Jacob Cox, *Reminiscences*, 1:127

"Rosecrans's perceptions were acute and often intuitively clear. His fertility was great. He lacked poise, however, and the steadiness of will necessary to handle great affairs successfully. Then there was the fatal defect of the liability to be swept away by excitement and to lose all efficient control of himself and of others in the very crisis when complete self-possession is the essential quality of a great general." —Jacob Cox, *Reminiscences*, 2:10

"He is a fine hearty abrupt sort of talker, heavy-whiskered blond, keen eyes, with light brows and lashes, head shunted forward a little: legs a little unsteady in walk." —John Hay, *Inside Lincoln's White House*, p. 204

"He can not be placed in that small category of commanders who were always successful . . . Few of his battles or campaigns are entirely free of criticism . . . But as a strategist he stands among the foremost . . . of all our Generals . . . When he did move his tactical ability shone as conspicuously as his strategy. He handled troops with rare facility and judgment under the stress of battle. More than all, there came upon him in the hour of conflict the inspiration of war, so that men were magnetized by his presence into heroes . . . He was singularly nervous, but in battle this quality was generally developed in a nervous exaltation, which seemed to clear his faculties and intensify his vigor . . . His fatal defect as a General was his lack of knowledge of human nature. Whatever he did himself was well done. When he came to intrust work to others he had no faculty of seeing . . . whom to trust and whom to avoid." —Whitelaw Reid, *Ohio in the War*, 1:346–348

"Old Rosecranse [*sic*] can, and will whip them every time. He will be the great man in this war yet. I think he is the best, bravest and biggest general we have got." —Hans C. Heg, *Civil War Letters*, p. 171

"I am . . . greatly pleased with some features of General Rosecrans' character. He has that fine quality of having his mind made up on all the great questions which concern his work. In a military man this is a cardinal virtue . . . a man who does not think decisively and place full and implicit reliance upon his own judgments cannot act with confidence. General Rosecrans thinks rapidly and strikes forward into action with the utmost confidence in his own judgment. In this he is perfectly unlike McClellan, who rarely has a clear-cut, decisive opinion and dare[s] not trust it when he has." —James A. Garfield, *The Wild Life of the Army*, p. 225

LOVELL H. ROUSSEAU Major general. Lawyer and politician. Mexican war veteran. Brigade and division command, Army of the Cumberland.

"This dashing and in every way gallant officer had taken the precaution that the world, and especially that part of the planet known as 'the dark and bloody ground,' should not be kept in ignorance of his achievements. He took his fair historian along with him . . . Her panegyrics were so glowing . . . that a disinterested reader would naturally have inferred that all the valor, all the military genius, and all the masculine beauty in the Army of the Ohio was monopolized by General Rousseau. And it was generally admitted that Rousseau was active and efficient . . . and did good fighting." —William P. Carlin, *Memoirs*, p. 69

"General Rousseau has been assigned to the command of our division. I am glad to hear that he discards the rose-water policy of General Buell under his nose, and is a great deal more thorough and severe in his treatment of rebels than General [Ormsby] Mitchell. . . . He damns the rebel sympathizers, and says if the negro stands in the way of the Union he must get out. Rousseau is a Kentuckian, and it is very encouraging to learn that he talks as he does." —John Beatty, *The Citizen Soldier*, p. 155

"Rousseau was deficient in technical knowledge on military subjects, and if by reading the tactics and army regulations once over he could have been assured that ever afterward he would know their contents, it is very doubtful whether he would have taken so much pains. But the men thought he knew it all. He would not even study his maps, and often turned them over to me unopened. And yet when Rousseau came upon the battle-field, he had that coup d'oeil, that intuitive comprehension, that broad and far-reaching common sense, that boldness and determination, which carried every one away with him and secured success." —Benjamin Scribner, *How Soldiers were Made*, p. 277

DAVID A. RUSSELL   Brigadier general. West Point (1845).
Mexican War veteran. Brigade and division commander, Army of the Potomac. Killed at Winchester, September 19, 1864.

"Russell was a man of extraordinary personal courage and, at the same time, a very plain and retiring man; one of his peculiarities was, that, when wounded, he never would make it public, but sought to conceal it." —Theodore Lyman, *Meade's Army*, p. 268

ELIAKIM PARKER SCAMMON   Brigadier general. West
Point (1837). Topographical engineer. Seminole and Mexican War veteran. Brigade commander. Commander, Department of the Kanawha.

"Scammon was well instructed in his profession. He was perhaps too much wedded to the routine of the service, and was looked upon by his subordinates as a martinet who had not patience enough with the inexperience of volunteer soldiers. He was one of the older men of our army, somewhat under the average height and weight, with a precise politeness of manner which reminded one of a Frenchman . . . His nervous irritability was the cause of considerable chafing in his command, but this left him under fire, and those who had been with him in action learned to admire his courage and conduct." —Jacob Cox, *Reminiscences*, 1:111

"From the beginning of the war General Scammon held radical views on the subject of slavery, believing that it was the cause of the war, and that it was doomed to perish with it. He is a person of affable and winning manners; to his equals just and kind, but not familiar, and to his inferiors a rigid disciplinarian. In religion he is a sincere and earnest Roman Catholic." —Whitelaw Reid, *Ohio in the War*, 1:916

ROBERT C. SCHENCK   Major general.
Lawyer, politician, and Congressman. Brigade and division commander in Virginia, 1861–1862.

"I have only to say that a more gallant and devoted soldier never lived . . ." —John Pope, *Battles and Leaders*, 2:487

"In military and civil life he has been the same bold, bitter, fearless fighter. He practices no concealments, displays little strategy, never shrinks from a course because it will increase the number of his enemies, strikes

with a broadsword rather than thrust with a rapier, hews his way through difficulties, rather than take the trouble to turn into an equally good path that may carry him around them. He has all the combative energy of his American birth, and all the tenacity of his Dutch ancestry. When he has friends, they are warm friends; when he has enemies, they never forgive him ... General Schenck is of about the middle height, square, compact, and broad-chested. His rugged features fairly indicate his strong passions and inflexible will."
—Whitelaw Reid, *Ohio in the War*, 1:737–738

NEWTON SCHLEICH Brigadier general. Lawyer and politician. Three months' service.

"He is a three months brigadier and a rampant demagogue ... Schleich was a state senator when the war began. He is what might be called a tremendous little man, swears terribly and imagines that he thereby shows his snap. Snap, in his opinion, is indispensable to a military man. If snap is the only thing a soldier needs, and profanity is snap, Schleich is a second Napoleon."
—John Beatty, *The Citizen Soldier*, p. 35

JOHN M. SCHOFIELD Major general. West Point (1853). Commander, Army of the Frontier, 1862–1863. Division command, 14th Corps. Commander, Department of the Missouri, 1863. Commander, Army of the Ohio, 1864.

"Schofield, who was ambitious and who always sought favor from a politician ... never profited at all by carrying water on both shoulders ... Whilst Schofield is a pretty fair man, his fear of politicians has made him play a very low, mean part in many things. Pope said of him that he could stand steadier on the bulge of a barrel than any man who ever wore shoulder straps ... But he assumes a grand superiority and wisdom, in each case entirely at variance with the facts, and appropriates circumstances entirely accidental ... as a result of his wise foresight."
—David S. Stanley, *Memoirs*, p. 214

"I think of all the generals I met during the war Schofield was the coolest and most self-possessed. I never saw him excited; he was always ready for any emergency ..." —Richard Johnson, *Soldier's Reminiscences*, p. 286

"In person he was a solid, rather stout man, of medium height, with a round bald head and long black beard coming down on his breast. He had a reputation for scientific tastes, and had, after his graduation at West Point, been instructor in astronomy there." —Jacob Cox, *Reminiscences*, 2:140

CARL SCHURZ   Major general. Revolutionary, politician. Brigade and division commander, Army of the Potomac.

"General Schurz ... was not a military man by profession ... but ... had participated in the revolution of 1848 ... tall, slender, and professor-like in appearance ... He had already become famed as an orator ... but never rose to any great distinction as a commander of troops. While he was zealous and courageous, he probably adopted the military calling too late in life and entered it with too much rank to ever become highly proficient in it." —James H. Wilson, *Under the Old Flag*, p. 313

"Presently General Carl Schurz came in, a pale, wide-foreheaded, red-mustached, spectacled, effeminate-looking German. He had sharp, hazel eyes, was thin and tall, the very pattern of a visionary, itching philanthropist and philosopher such as disturb society everywhere with their restless conceits and babblings ..." —David Hunter Strother, *A Virginia Yankee*, p. 74

"He has great confidence in his military powers, and his capability of arousing the enthusiasm of the young. He contemplates the career of a great guerrilla chief with ardent longing ... He will make a wonderful land pirate, bold, quick brilliant and reckless. He will be a hard man to control and difficult to direct. Still, we shall see. He is a wonderful man." —John Hay, *Inside Lincoln's White House*, p. 12, 13–14

WINFIELD SCOTT   Brevet lieutenant general. General in chief, 1861. Veteran of the War of 1812, Seminole War and Mexican War.

"He was an immense man, both in height and breadth, and ... was so unwieldy that he moved about with difficulty, but his mind was as clear and as active as it ever was and I think I never before or since looked into such bright and piercing blue eyes. I carried away with me a feeling of admiration and reverence for him which I have maintained." —John Pope, *Memoirs*, p. 206

"General Scott is the great obstacle. He will not comprehend the danger. I have to fight my way against him ... I suppose it will result in enmity on his part against me; but I have no choice. The people call upon me to save the country. I must save it, and cannot respect anything that is in the way." —George B. McClellan, *McClellan's Own Story*, p. 85

"How does he think I can save this country when stopped by Gen. Scott—I do not know whether he is a dotard or a traitor! I can't tell which. He *cannot* or *will* not comprehend the condition in which we are placed & is entirely unequal to the emergency ... Every day strengthens me ... but that confounded old general always comes in the way—he is a perfect imbecile ... He understands nothing, appreciates nothing and is ever in my way." —George B. McClellan, *Civil War Papers*, p. 81

"Of great stature and of a martial figure, General Scott joined to his physical advantages rare military and diplomatic attainments . . . But age had attacked him physically and mentally. Obese and impotent, the brilliant Scott was in 1861 but the shadow of his former self . . . the young generals reproached him with paralyzing their ardor and interfering with their projects." — Philippe, Comte de Paris, *Battles and Leaders*, 2:114

"He was the largest man I ever saw in uniform and very majestic in appearance. Six feet seven in height and large in proportion, with a very manly face—he was, indeed, the model for a great hero." —David S. Stanley, *Memoirs*, p. 19

"Although a Virginian, no shadow of suspicion had ever been cast upon his loyalty. I found him still grand and majestic, but borne down by the weight of his laurels and of his public services . . . Although clad yet with the power and responsibility, he was the setting sun . . . a herculean figure like a mighty ruin . . ." —James H. Wilson, *Under the Old Flag*, p. 59

"Under Scott, the army at Washington was a heterogeneous mass, undisciplined and inefficient. Old Scott was utterly deficient to perform his duties. He knew nothing of the state of the army, and seemed to be blind to the condition of things." —Franklin Archibald Dick, *Troubled State*, p. 13

"He was great in stature, and had great qualities with some singular weaknesses or defects. Vanity was his great infirmity . . . Courteous, deferential, and respectful to his superior always, he expected and required the same from others. Though something of a politician, I do not think his judgment and opinion in regard to public affairs were always correct or reliable." —Gideon Welles, *Diary*, 2:514–515

"Scott was big and puffy. He used to get drunk on champagne and was a great eater . . . I never saw a man who could drink so much. He used to get a punch-bowl which would hold about two quarts; he would give an officer a glass—never more— and finish the rest himself. He was very inert and used to ride in an ambulance drawn by four horses . . ." —Alfred Pleasonton, *Generals in Bronze*, p. 130

"This eminent commander represented that element of the South which remained loyal to the government . . . The infirmities of age had rendered him . . . unavailable for field service, but his executive ability and wise counsel were invaluable to the nation, and his firm loyalty inspired confidence and brought tens of thousands of young men to the national standard." —Nelson A. Miles, *Serving the Republic*, p. 21

"He was a great shot. He could throw up two potatoes, and as they crossed, he could put a hole through both. But some used to say that he had a fellow put a hole through one before it was thrown up." —David S. Stanley, *Generals in Bronze*, p. 131

"General Scott was no longer himself when the war broke out. The weight of years and great bodily suffering pressed heavily upon him, and really rendered him incapable of performing the duties of his station. For some time before he retired he was simply an obstacle, and a very serious one, in the way of active work." —George B. McClellan, *McClellan's Own Story*, p. 136–137

"He was a grim old giant, gorgeously appareled, surrounded by a glittering staff . . . It was plain that this infirm old man, riding on a softly cushioned carriage seat, couldn't be in the fighting; yet the mere living presence of the ancient hero seemed to foretoken victory." —Abner R. Small, *The Road to Richmond*, p. 17

"With his commanding figure, his quite colossal size and showy uniform, I thought him the finest specimen of manhood my eyes had ever beheld, and the most to be envied." —Ulysses S. Grant, *Personal Memoirs*, 1:41

"The renown of a long lifetime gallantly spent in his country's service had gradually but justly placed General Scott far above all contemporary chieftains in the admiration and hero worship of his fellow countrymen; and in the youthful minds of the West Point cadets of those days Scott was looked up to as a leader whose military abilities were scarcely second to those of a Napoleon, and whose patriotism rivaled that of Washington." —George A. Custer, *Battles and Leaders*, 6:15

"During his long life, the nation has not been unmindful of his merit; yet, on calling to mind how faithfully, ably and brilliantly he has served the country, from a time far back in our history . . . and thenceforward continually, I cannot but think we are still his debtors." —Abraham Lincoln, *Abraham Lincoln, Speeches and Writings*, p. 294

General Winfield Scott and staff in 1861, photographed by Mathew Brady.

JOHN SEDGWICK
Major general. West Point (1837). Seminole and Mexican War veteran. Brigade, division, and corps commander, Army of the Potomac. Killed at Spotsylvania, May 9, 1864.

"General John Sedgwick, then well known as one of our best division commanders, and one of the sternest soldiers in the Army of the Potomac. Bred as a soldier, he had served with great distinction in Mexico . . . Modest and retiring in his ordinary intercourse with his fellows, he exhibited the most brilliant qualities in time of battle. The dignity of his bearing fitted him to command and he needed not the insignia of rank to command the deference of those about him . . . No soldier was more beloved by the army or honored by the country than this noble general. His corps regarded him as a father, and his great military abilities made his judgment, in all critical emergencies, sought after by his superior as well as his fellows." —George T. Stevens, *Three Years in the Sixth Corps*, p. 186, 328

"Our first impressions of Sedgwick were not happy. I have heard that a smile occasionally invaded his scrubby beard, but I never saw one there. His official manner sent chills down the backs of the rank and file. He was an old bachelor with oddities; addicted to practical jokes and endless games of solitaire, rather careless of his personal appearance, and habitually crowning his rough head, when not on parade, with a hat that looked like a small beehive of straw." —Abner Small, *The Road to Richmond*, p. 30–31

"Sedgwick was a fine man, a man you could be fond of. He was a good soldier, but not a great soldier, such as some of his friends would like to make you believe. He could never tell about location. In the Wilderness he told me where he wanted to move, and asked me if I could do it. . . . I got the maps and found out where we were . . . and taking my bearings . . . came out about 50 yards from where I started for . . . He wondered how I did it . . ." —Horatio Wright, *Generals in Bronze*, p. 210

"He was a very solid man; no flummery about him. You could always tell where Sedgwick was to be found, and in a battle he was apt to be found where the hardest fighting was. He was not an ardent impetuous solider like Hancock, but was steady and sure." —Charles A. Dana, *Recollections*, p. 190–191

"Sedgwick was essentially a soldier. He had never married; the camp was his home, and the members of his staff were his family. He was always spoken of familiarly as "Uncle John," and the news of his death fell upon his comrades with a sense of grief akin to the sorrow of a personal bereavement." —Horace Porter, *Campaigning with Grant*, p. 90

"Sedgwick . . . was stocky, had short, curling chestnut hair, was a bachelor and spent lots of time playing solitaire. His whole manner breathed of gentleness and sweetness, his soldiers called him Uncle John, and in his broad breast was a boy's heart." —Morris Schaff, *Wilderness*, p. 43

"Sedgwick is quite a heavy man,—short, thick-set, and muscular, with florid complexion, dark, calm, straight looking eyes, with full, heavyish features, which with his eyes, have plenty of animation when he is aroused,—he has a magnificent profile,—well cut, with the nose and forehead forming almost a straight line, curly short chestnut hair and full beard, cut short, with a little gray in it. He dresses carelessly, but can look magnificently when he is well dressed. Like Meade, he looks, and is, honest and modest,—You might see at once, why his men, because they love him, call him 'Uncle John' . . ." —Frank Haskell, *Haskell of Gettysburg*, p. 132–133

"He was tall; ruddy complexion; a very smooth silky voice; his hair growing rather long on his forehead, with a large mustache and side whiskers. He always wore his boots under his pants. He wore an old fashioned pair of brass spurs— never taking them off; he fairly used to sleep in them. His coat he kept open with his swordbelt underneath; no vest; a gray flannel shirt; black cravat tied under the collar. He wore a little round hat . . ." —Martin Thomas McMahon, *Generals in Bronze*, p. 85

"He was among the good and brave generals, though not of the class of dashing officers, and was ever reliable and persistent." —Gideon Welles, *Diary*, 2:27

"I did not at first appreciate his high qualities, but soon discovered them . . . he was one of the best and most modest soldiers we had. Possessing excellent ability and judgment, the highest bravery, great skill in handling troops, wonderful powers in instructing and disciplining men, as well as in gaining their love, respect, and confidence, he was withal so modest and unobtrusive that it was necessary to be thrown closely in contact with him to appreciate him. He was thoroughly unselfish, honest, and true as steel." —George B. McClellan, *McClellan's Own Story*, p. 140

"He stood very high in the army . . . as an officer and a man. He was brave and conscientious. His ambition was not great, and he seemed to dread responsibility. He was willing to do any amount of battling, but always wanted some one else to direct. He declined the command of the Army of the Potomac once, if not oftener." —Ulysses S. Grant, *Personal Memoirs*, 2:540

TRUMAN SEYMOUR Brevet major general. West Point

(1846). Mexican War veteran. Brigade and division commander, Army of the Potomac.

"Seymour has been relieved from duty . . . at his own request . . . Seymour was an excellent soldier, of good judgment, cool courage, and in time of action of great and valuable assistance . . . As these are considerations of the utmost importance, his loss will be seriously felt by me." —George G. Meade, *Life and Letters*, 1:328–329

GEORGE F. SHEPLEY: Brigadier general. Lawyer. Military

governor of Louisiana, 1862; commander, District of Eastern Virginia, 1864.

"General Shepley, so ably and successfully Military Governor of Louisiana, and now of Norfolk and vicinity, [is] evidently an able, scholarly, yet executive man, judging by his dignified, manly bearing." —Charles A. Page, *Letters*, p. 58

PHILIP H. SHERIDAN   Major general.
West Point (1853). Frontier service. Brigade and division command, Army of the Cumberland; Cavalry Corps command, Army of the Potomac. Commander, Army of the Shenandoah.

"[Sheridan is a] brown chunky little chap, not enough neck to hang him and such long arms that if his ankles itch he can scratch them without stooping." —Abraham Lincoln, in Morris, *The Life and Wars of General Phil Sheridan*, p. 1

"He weighed only a hundred and fifteen pounds, and his height was but five feet six inches, he looked anything but formidable as a candidate for a cavalry leader." —Horace Porter, *Campaigning with Grant*, p. 24

"Sheridan . . . would certainly not impress one by his looks . . . He is short, thickset, and common-Irish looking. Met in the Bowery, one would certainly set him down as a 'b'hoy'; and his dress is in perfect keeping with that character . . ." —Charles Wainwright, *A Diary of Battle*, p. 517

"The general was short in stature—below the medium—square shouldered, muscular, wiry to the last degree . . . He had a strangely shaped head with a large bump of something or other—behind the ears . . . His face was very much tanned by exposure, but was lighted up by uncommonly keen eyes, which stamped him anywhere as a man of quickness and force . . . He was exacting on duty and hard on delinquents and his ideas of duty were peculiar . . ." —Frederick Newhall, *With Sheridan in the Final Campaign*, p. 3

"His determination to absorb the credit of everything done is so manifest as to have attracted the attention of the whole army." —George G. Meade, *Life and Letters*, 2:271

"Truth demands that I say of General Sheridan that his style of conversation and general bearing, while never discourteous, were far less agreeable and pleasing than those of any other officer of the Union army whom it was my fortune to meet." —John B. Gordon, *Reminiscences of the Civil War*, p. 441–442

"He was not of delicate fibre. His pictures are excellent, preserving faithfully the animation of his ruddy, square face and large, glowing dark eyes. With his close army associates he threw off rank and fame and made many a night memorable and loud . . . he had a genius for war." —Morris Schaff, *The Wilderness*, p. 43

"Sheridan . . . was essentially an Irish adventurer . . . with a well developed natural aptitude for military life, he was not conspicuous for character." —Charles Francis Adams, *Autobiography*, p. 158

"General Sheridan has the appearance of great nerve, and hitherto has been quite successful . . . I am better pleased with his appearance than that of any other commander under whom I have served." —Emory Upton, *Life and Letters*, p. 122

"Sheridan is short, broad-shouldered, and of an iron frame. Very short legs and small feet and naturally cannot be a good horseman." —David Hunter Strother, *A Virginia Yankee*, p. 286

"Sheridan attained the highest rank of anyone in my class. He was wholly unacquainted with books but was very observant and very energetic. I think his success was owing to a certain audacity and . . . a perfect indifference as to how many of his men were killed if he only carried his point." —David S. Stanley, *Memoirs*, p. 23

"Sheridan is like Grant, a persevering terrier dog and won't be shaken off. He too, is honest, modest, plucky and smart enough." —William T. Sherman, *Home Letters*, p. 314

"I believe Sheridan has no superior as a general, either living or dead, and perhaps not an equal . . . He has judgment, prudence, foresight, and power to deal with the dispositions needed in a great war." —Ulysses S. Grant, Sheridan *Memoirs*, 1:xv

"General Sheridan was not inclined to serve under any other commander but Grant, and it became difficult to humor him in this without embarrassing other operations." —Joshua Lawrence Chamberlain, *Passing of the Armies*, p. 101

"He pushes on, carrying his flanks and rear with him—rushing, flashing, smashing. He transfuses into his subordinates the vitality and energy of his purpose; transforms them into part of his own mind and will. He shows the power of a commander—inspiring both confidence and fear. He commanded our admiration, but we could discriminate: we reserved room for question whether he exhibited all the qualities essential to a chief commander . . ." —Joshua Lawrence Chamberlain, *Passing of the Armies*, p. 154

"Grant had not said Sheridan was great, until after he had become President, and then it was right to praise a good servant; and then it was a good idea to call Sheridan equal to Napoleon: and Sheridan, being his inferior, it was equal to saying he was superior to Napoleon. But that is all very well while he is content to be his servant, but if he attempted to ride over him. What would you do if a servant should ride over you? Wouldn't you object?" —Jefferson C. Davis, *Generals in Bronze*, p. 54

"Sheridan lacks judgment and administrative ability. He is impulsive, but his intentions are honest . . ." —Gideon Welles, *Diary*, 2:570

"His short but compact frame looked able to do or to endure all that was necessary in a soldier; his large and strikingly developed head and close shorn locks, his ruddy face and black twinkling eye were full of character; while his expression, generally jovial, but quickly changing to stern determination or magnificent intensity . . . a something in look, and gesture, and expression, that told you when he was in earnest—these gave him a magnetic influence over individuals and masses, which none but men of genius exercise, and which in a commander is invaluable." —Adam Badeau, *Military History of Ulysses S. Grant*, 2:500

"[H]e was a pisant . . . and lacked the spirit of a thoroughbred; he had physical courage, but I do not think he had moral courage. I do not like the way he acted in regard to Warren . . . I think he did it to please Grant." —John M. Schofield, *Generals in Bronze*, p. 245

"Probably no living soldier was ever more terrible in battle than Sheridan. With the first smell of powder he became a blazing meteor . . . The rather small short, heavily built man rose to surpassing stature in his stirrups, to the sublimity of heroism in action; and infused a like spirit in his troops . . . Absolutely fearless himself, with unwavering faith in his cause and his plans, he always raised the courage and faith of others, to the level of his own . . ." —Sylvanus Cadwallader, *Three Years with Grant*, p. 305

"He is a Major-General, and is an energetic and very brave officer. This command, however, is a very large one, larger than he ever had before. I have little doubt, that, for field-service, he is superior to any officer there." —Theodore Lyman, *Meade's Headquarters*, p. 210

"Gen. Sheridan, the new Chief of Cavalry [is] a small broad shouldered, squat man, with black hair & square head. He is of Irish parents, but looks very like a Piedmontese." —Theodore Lyman, *Meade's Army*, p. 122

"Whoever should undertake to rate Sheridan's capacity must remember that he has risen to every task that has yet been set him . . . he has proved equal to every emergency and every command . . . Certainly it may . . . be said of him that he is the most uniformly successful soldier of the war . . . In person Sheridan was short, muscular, and deep-chested . . . His head is disproportionately large, and the developments back of the ears are enormous, to the great inconvenience of his hatter. His temperament is sanguine; his hair is dark, shading off into the color of his full beard, which is reddish; and his face 'is flushed, not with wine, but with life' . . . he is an unassuming, chatty companion, . . . fond of a joke or a story, and the ideal of . . . 'a good fellow.'" —Whitelaw Reid, *Ohio in the War*, 1:556–557

"Sheridan was, above everything, a man of genius; of fiery enthusiasm; of magnetic influences; exciting and receiving impulses; with a concentrated force that nothing could withstand." —Adam Badeau, *Military History of Ulysses S. Grant*, 3:496

THOMAS W. SHERMAN Major general. West Point (1836). Seminole and Mexican War veteran. Division command, Army of the Ohio, Army of the Gulf.

"General 'Tim' Sherman of artillery fame . . . was in command and his record was of the best. His habits were good, his technical knowledge great, his experience varied and extensive, and his character above reproach. With a handsome and impressive figure, flashing blue eyes, martial bearing, austere manners, and a voice that startled you like an electric shock, he was deservedly regarded as one of the ablest, most self-reliant, and most promising officers in the regular army ... But not withstanding his high and masterful qualities, he turned out to be a martinet of violent and ungovernable temper, poorly qualified to train and to command volunteers." —James H. Wilson, *Under the Old Flag*, p. 68–69

"I think Sherman is doing his best and understand what he is about. He wants certain attributes to give him influence and to impress favorably those around him—he wants dress and address—is impatient and reticent where he ought not to be, may not be a commander in chief, but is a soldier, every inch of him." —Samuel F. DuPont, *Civil War Letters*, 1:293

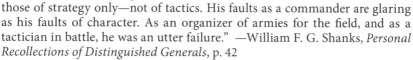

WILLIAM T. SHERMAN Major general.
West Point (1840). Brigade command, Army of the Potomac. Commander of Union forces in Kentucky, 1861. Division, corps, and army command, Army of the Tennessee. Commander, Military Division of the Mississippi.

"General Sherman's reputation as a soldier must rest entirely upon his strategic abilities. His successes were those of strategy only—not of tactics. His faults as a commander are glaring as his faults of character. As an organizer of armies for the field, and as a tactician in battle, he was an utter failure." —William F. G. Shanks, *Personal Recollections of Distinguished Generals*, p. 42

"His memory of details, of faces, of names and of seemingly unimportant events and circumstances was extraordinary in one whose mind was so engrossed upon great subjects and absorbing cares ..." —Benjamin Scribner, *How Soldiers were Made*, p. 31

"Sherman never ceased to grumble about the failure of his strategy and yet it was all his own inexcusable fault.... At the same time Sherman never gained the moral courage to fight a battle ... although he had a thousand chances. Partial affairs called battles, he ordered, but it was always by a fragment of his army. He never had the moral courage to order his whole army into a general engagement ... Knowing that he had a force superior to Johnston's ... Sherman would confront Johnston's entire line and then detach a small force, one or two divisions, never enough to achieve a great success, attack or threaten a flank, bring on partial engagement, get a lot of men killed, and effect nothing.... He liked to lay his failures on other's shoulders and, when the scapegoat attempted to explain or argue the case, he was never forgiven." —David S. Stanley, *Memoirs*, p. 182–183

"Sherman could easily be approached by any of his soldiers, but no one could venture to be familiar. His uniform coat, usually wide open at the throat, displayed a not very military black cravat and linen collar, and he generally wore low shoes and one spur." —Capt. Daniel Oakey, 2nd Mass, *Battles and Leaders*, 4:671

"Everything I saw of Sherman . . . increased my admiration for him. He was a very brilliant man and an excellent commander of a corps. Sherman's information was great, and he was a clever talker. He always liked to have people about who could keep up with his conversation, besides, he was genial and unaffected. I particularly admired his loyalty to Grant." —Charles A. Dana, *Recollections*, p. 57

"Sherman . . . impressed me much . . . He bore the stamp of true genius. Curiously natural, very fond of talking, there was about him nothing of the poseur. He was a delightful dinner-table companion, humorous, easy, striking, full of reminiscence. He and Humphreys, very different, but each great, were my two army ideals . . ." —Charles Francis Adams, *Autobiography*, p. 158

"Sherman's own knowledge of his own impulsive nature made him unduly distrustful of his own judgment when under great responsibility in emergencies, and this in spite of his unusual intellectual activity and his great confidence in his deliberately matured judgment . . . For this reason Sherman's capacity as a tactician was not by any means equal to his ability as a strategist. He lacked the element of confident boldness or audacity in action which is necessary to gain the greatest results by taking advantage of his adversary's blunders . . ." —John M. Schofield, *Forty-Six Years in the Army*, p. 341–342

"Sherman was tall, lithe, and active, with light brown hair, close-cropped sandy beard and moustache, and every motion and expression indicated eagerness and energy. His head was apt to be bent a little forward as if in earnest or aggressive advance, and his rapid incisive utterance hit off the topics

Major General William T. Sherman and Staff, 1864.

of discussion in a sharp and telling way. His opinions usually took a strong and very pronounced form, full of the feeling that was for the moment uppermost, not hesitating even at even a little humorous extravagance if it added point to his statement; but in such cases the keen eye took a merry twinkle accentuated by the crow-foot lines in the corner, so that the real geniality and kindliness that underlay the brusque exterior were sufficiently apparent. The general effect was a nature of intense, restless activity, both physical and mental." —Jacob Cox, *Reminiscences*, 2:203

"Sherman, like the rest of the ranking officers, lived in a tent. He was nervous and sleepless. Long after the rest of the company had gone to bed he would remain sitting on a camp stool, wrapped in a well worn army overcoat, leaning over the remains of the evening fire and seemingly pondering over the tremendous campaign before him. At times, for want of company, he would join the sentinel, walk alongside of him on his post, and, despite regulations, enter into long conversations with him." —David S. Stanley, *Memoirs*, p. 190

"General Sherman is proving himself a great general, and his movements from Chattanooga to the present demonstrate his ability as an officer. He has, undoubtedly, greater resources, a more prolific mind, than Grant, and perhaps as much tenacity if less cunning and selfishness." —Gideon Welles, *Diary*, 2:242

"As a corps and department commander, Sherman had no superior . . . He was pre-eminently a man of action, and exhibited his greatest qualities in aggressive movements and campaigns. The impetuosity of his character was exemplified whenever he was in supreme command . . . He was thoroughly subordinate and obedient to higher military authority . . . But he lacked Grant's superb equipoise. He often failed to control his temper." —Sylvanus Cadwallader, *Three Years with Grant*, p. 340–341

"He is a very remarkable-looking man, such as could not be grown out of America—the concentrated quintessence of Yankeedom. He is tall, spare, and sinewy, with a very long neck, and a big head at the end of same. The said big head is a most unusual combination . . . When a man is spare, with a high forehead, he usually has a contracted back to his head; but Sherman has a swelling 'fighting' back to *his* head, and all his features express determination, particularly the mouth, which is wide and straight, with lips that shut tightly together. He is a very homely man, with a regular nest of wrinkles in his face, which play and twist as he eagerly talks on each subject; but his expression is pleasant and kindly. But he believes in hard war." —Theodore Lyman, *Meade's Headquarters*, p. 327

"I had no confidence in Sherman, in as much as he had perverted the truth in a correspondence I had with him . . . I had discovered that it was his nature to do so to attain his objects." —St. John Richardson Liddell, *Liddell's Record*, p. 30

"Sherman was especially outspoken in giving his views, whether asked for or not; but having once freed his mind, verbally, or by letter . . . he dropped his contention there, and loyally and cheerfully, without hesitation or delay, and equally without grumbling or criticism, set vigorously about performing the duty assigned to him. It is but fair to add that Sherman always had decided views. He was . . . a man of great abilities and great attainments, not only in the art of war, but in nearly everything else." —James Harrison Wilson, *Battles and Leaders*, 5:124

"He is too warlike to be military . . . He is indeed warlike by nature, and his ardor often carries him beyond mere military rules—sometimes to evil, as at Kenesaw, sometimes to great glory, as in the march to the sea. Yet in many things he is devoted to the severest military methods. In moving, supplying and maneuvering great armies . . . he is without a rival or an equal. In the whole branch of the logistics of war he is the foremost General of the Country . . . As a strategist he has displayed inferior but still brilliant powers. He can not here be declared without a rival . . . His topographical knowledge was wonderful . . . In his plans there was often a happy mingling of audacity with system; of defiance of military methods in the conception with a skillful use of them in the execution." —Whitelaw Reid, *Ohio in the War*, 1:487–488

"General Sherman has been made a Major-General, a promotion he well deserves. You must not believe all the newspapers say of him; he is a splendid officer and a most excellent, good man. I have every confidence in him . . . A braver man I never saw . . ." —Thomas Kilby Smith, *Life and Letters*, p. 202

"Sherman is a martinet, but he is a soldier, every inch, and as brave as they make them . . . He's every inch a soldier and a gentleman and a chieftain . . . I have unlimited confidence in Sherman, who is a great man and a great general . . ." —Thomas Kilby Smith, *Life and Letters*, p. 235, 237

"The newspapers are savagely abusing Sherman—one of the most brilliant soldiers the country has produced, and, as I happen to know by a thousand evidences, one of the purest men in the land." —Ethan Allen Hitchcock, *Fifty Years in Camp and Field*, p. 476

JAMES SHIELDS Brigadier general. Politician and Senator.
Brigade commander in Shenandoah Valley, 1862.

"Gen. Shields was a brave man, but insincere, capricious, unballanced and aimless beyond self. Could do nothing as a subordinate & lacked judgment and honesty so essential to an independent command. Him we forced out of the service." —Alvin Voris, *A Citizen Soldier's Civil War*, p. 115

"He is certainly a man of pluck and enterprise and suits me better than anyone I have yet seen in the field." —David Hunter Strother, *A Virginia Yankee*, p. 17

DANIEL E. SICKLES Major general. Politician. Brigade,
division, and corps commander, Army of the Potomac.

"A Sickles would beat Napoleon in winning glory not earned. He is a hero without an heroic deed! Literally made by scribblers . . . I think a man as old

as Methusaleh would on his deathbed say he had to regret his short life, that he might see more of human character." —Alpheus Williams, *From the Cannon's Mouth*, p. 203

"This Daniel Sickles was the one who killed [Phillip Barton] Key in Washington some years ago. He has got credit for doing a great deal more fighting than he has ever done. New York correspondents have cracked him up where the credit for fighting was justly due to other brigades . . . But so it is." —Robert McAllister, *Civil War Letters*, p. 212

"Genl. Sickles supposed he was doing for the best; but he was neither born nor bred a soldier. But one can scarcely tell what may have been the motives of such a man—a politician, and some other things . . . a man after show, and notoriety, and newspaper fame, and the adulation of the mob!" —Frank Haskell, *Haskell of Gettysburg*, p. 117

FRANZ SIGEL Major general.
German revolutionary. Teacher. Division and corps command, Army of Virginia. Commander, Department of West Virginia.

"His hair and beard are tawny, his jaws and cheekbones square and angular, his eyes light blue, forehead narrow, and too small for his face. Small in stature and ungraceful. He had on a plain slouch hat and a major general's uniform . . . General Sigel . . . spoke English with more difficulty than I had supposed. He seemed also awkward and different . . . Sigel has the air to me of a military pedagogue, given to technical shams and trifles of military art, but narrow minded and totally wanting in practical capacity . . . I thought at one time or, rather, hoped that Sigel was honest and patriotic, but I have since been led to believe that he was a mere adventurer and connived at the dishonest practice of his set." —David H. Strother, *A Virginia Yankee*, p. 213, 222–223

"General Sigel is beaten and not the man for the command given him, I apprehend. He is always overwhelmed and put on the run." —Gideon Welles, *Diary*, 2:68

"He brought a splendid military reputation with him. He had bravely fought for liberty in Germany . . . he had been one of the foremost to organize and lead that force of armed men . . . that seemed suddenly to spring out of the pavements of St. Louis, and whose prompt action saved the city and the State of Missouri to the Union. On various fields . . . he had distinguished himself by personal gallantry as well as skillful leadership . . . General Sigel . . . possessed in a small degree that amiability of humor which will disarm ill-will and make for friendly comradeship. His conversation lacked the sympathetic element. There was something reserved, even morose, in his mien, which, if it did not discourage cheerful approach, certainly did not invite it . . . in Sigel's case it served to render the difficulties of his situation more difficult at critical periods." —Carl Schurz, *Reminiscences*, 2:348, 350

"He was a diminutive person, but well-knit, emaciated by his active career, feverish and sanguine of face, and . . . consuming with energy and ambition. As a General he was prompt to decide and do, and his manner of dealing with Confederate property was severer than that of any American . . . He preferred to fight by retreating, and if pursued, generally unmasked his guns and made massacre with the scattered opponents." —George A. Townsend, *Campaigns of a Non-Combatant*, p. 233

"It is rumored but not confirmed that General Sigel has arrived . . . I hope this is so. I have great faith in that General and his fighting." —James A. Garfield, *The Wild Life of the Army*, p. 96

"I am more perplexed to reach a satisfactory judgment concerning General Sigel than any other man I know. I halt between two veins—one leading me to earnest admiration of high qualities, the other to a sad contempt of his charlatanry and unfounded pretensions. On the whole . . . I think he has been overestimated and I shall not be greatly surprised, though much grieved, to find that his fame will grow less hereafter." —James A. Garfield, *The Wild Life of the Army*, p. 315

JOSHUA SILL
Brigadier general. West Point (1853). Brigade commander, Army of the Ohio, and Army of the Cumberland. Killed at Stones River, December 1862.

"Sill was one of Sheridan's brigade commanders [at Stones River]. Sill was a practical man, of great resources, energy, and courage, small of stature, and compactly built. He was beloved and admired in the army for his great courtesy, kindness and good sense." —William F. G. Shanks, *Personal Recollections of Distinguished Generals*, p. 137

"Rather small and delicate in person, gentle and refined in manner, he had about him little that answered to the popular notion of a soldier . . . Under his modest and scholarly exterior I quickly discerned a fine temper in the metal that made his after career no enigma to me . . ." —Jacob Cox, *Reminiscences*, 1:26–27

"Sill's modesty and courage were exceeded only by a capacity that had already been demonstrated in many practical ways." —Philip H. Sheridan, *Memoirs*, 1:209

"In every sphere of military duty to which he was called he proved himself a thorough soldier, a skillful officer, and an honorable gentleman . . . Of slight frame, mild and pleasing address, of sterling and extraordinary merit both as a soldier and a scholar, yet reserved almost to a fault—from modesty, not from pride—he seemed to court obscurity rather than notoriety. The simplicity and kindness of his manners, his perfect and stainless integrity, and the singular purity of his life, endeared him beyond measure to all who were happy enough to know him . . ." —Whitelaw Reid, *Ohio in the War*, 1:920

JAMES R. SLACK Brevet major general. Lawyer and politician. Brigade commander, Army of the Mississippi, Army of the Gulf.

"Slack is a solid, steady man, brave, thorough, and sensible, but will never set the river afire. His education is poor, but he would make a respectable brigadier general . . ." —Charles A. Dana, *Recollections*, p. 64

ADAM J. SLEMMER Brigadier general. West Point (1850). Acting inspector general, Department of the Ohio.

"He was a man of marked character . . . His failing health prevented his taking the prominent part in the war that his abilities warranted, but I have retained . . . a pleasing impression of his character and a respect for his military knowledge and talents." —Jacob Cox, *Reminiscences*, 1:123

HENRY SLOCUM Major general. West Point (1852). Seminole War veteran. Lawyer and politician. Brigade, division, and corps command, Army of the Potomac; corps command, Army of the Tennessee.

"Slocum is small, rather spare, with black straight hair, and beard, which latter is unshaven and thin, large full, quick black eyes, white skin, sharp nose, wide cheek bones, and hollow cheeks and small chin. His movements are quick and angular—and he dresses with a sufficient degree of elegance." —Frank Haskell, *Haskell of Gettysburg*, p. 133

"Slocum does not seem to me a very large man. He seems, peevish, irritable, fretful. Hooker says he is all that on account of his digestive apparatus being out of repair. Hooker does not speak unkindly of him; while he never mentions Hooker but to attack him." —John Hay, *Inside Lincoln's White House*, p. 86

ANDREW JACKSON SMITH Major general. West Point (1838). Brigade, division, and corps commander, Army of the Tennessee.

"An old cavalry officer of the regular service. He is intrepid to recklessness, his head is clear though rather thick, his disposition honest and manly, though given to boasting and self-exaggeration of a gentle and innocent kind. His division is well cared for, but is rather famous for slow instead of rapid marching . . . He is a good officer to command a division in an army corps, but should not be intrusted with any important independent command." —Charles A. Dana, *Recollections*, p. 64–65

CHARLES F. SMITH Brigadier general.

West Point (1825). Mexican War veteran. Brigade and division commander, Army of the Tennessee. Died at Savannah, Tennessee, April 25, 1862.

"Although a strict disciplinarian, he was a favorite with all the soldiers of his command. He was six feet tall, spare, straight, with a heavy white mustache and close cut gray hair. His personality was that of the ideal soldier, and his appearance on parade or elsewhere, elicited the applause of soldiers." —Augustus L. Chetlain, *Recollections of Seventy Years*, p. 82–83

"He was a person of superb physique, very tall, perfectly proportioned, straight, square-shouldered, ruddy-faced, with eyes of perfect blue. And long snow-white mustaches. He seemed to know the army regulations by heart, and caught a tactical mistake, whether of command or execution, by a kind of mental coup d'oeil. He was naturally kind, genial, communicative, and never failed to answer when information was sought of him ..." —Lew Wallace, *Battles and Leaders*, 1:405

"By reputation he was the best all-around officer in the regular army—a disciplinarian, stern, unsympathetic, an ogre to volunteers, but withal a magnificent soldier of the old school of Winfield Scott." —*Lew Wallace: An Autobiography*, 1:338

"General Halleck unquestionably deemed General C.F. Smith a much fitter officer for the command of all the forces in the military district than I was ... Indeed I was rather inclined to this opinion myself at that time ... His personal courage was unquestioned, his judgment and professional acquirements were unsurpassed, and he had the confidence of those he commanded as well as those over him." —Ulysses S. Grant, *Personal Memoirs*, 1:328–29

GILES A. SMITH Major general. Businessman. Brigade and division commander, Army of the Tennessee.

"Giles Smith is one of the very best brigadiers in Sherman's corps ... He only requires the chance to develop into an officer of uncommon power and usefulness. There are plenty of men with generals' commissions who in all military respects are not fit to tie his shoes." —Charles A. Dana, *Recollections*, p. 66

JOHN E. SMITH Major general. Jeweler. Brigade and division commander, Army of the Tennessee.

"General John E. Smith ... with much less intellect than [Isaac F.] Quinby, has a great deal better sense, with a firmness of character, a steadiness of hand, and a freedom from personal irritability and jealousy which must soon produce the happiest effect upon the division. Smith combines with these natural qualities

of a soldier and commander a conscientious devotion not merely to the doing but also to the learning of his duty, which renders him a better and better general every day. He is also fit to be intrusted with any independent command where judgment and discretion are as necessary as courage and activity, for in him all these qualities seem to be happily blended and balanced." —Charles A. Dana, *Recollections*, p. 69–70

MORGAN L. SMITH Brigadier general. Riverboatman and soldier. Brigade and division commander, Army of the Tennessee.

"This name of Smith ... attaches to too many good men and true, to say nothing of the damned rascals who also inherit it. There are four colonels, one a Kirby Smith from Ohio. There is your friend, E. Kirby Smith of Southern notoriety, and now ... I have been brigaded with Morgan L. Smith, the hero of Fort Donaldson. He is a dashing, fighting man, and we have an eminently fighting brigade ... but a man by the name of Smith might as well attempt to pluck bright honor from the pale-faced moon as to win fame." —Thomas Kilby Smith, *Life and Letters*, p. 208

WILLIAM F. "BALDY" SMITH Major general. West Point (1845). Engineer. Brigade, division, and corps commander, Army of the Potomac.

"He was one of those distinguished men of the old army whose sharp tongue and sententious speech had done much to make him enemies in high place and to mar his immediate career. He was popular with his subordinates, for he was a conscientious, painstaking, and industrious officer who spared no effort to keep his soldiers in good condition or to lead them successfully, no matter how great the difficulties..." —James H. Wilson, *Under the Old Flag*, p. 271

"Now I think Smith was an efficient soldier in many respects—although it would seem that I have every cause to dislike the man in every relation of life. But he had one inevitable regular army failing ...'interminable reconnoissances'— waiting and waiting, not going at a thing when he was told, but looking all around to see if he could not do something else than what he was told to do, or do it in a different way from what he was told." —Benjamin Butler, *Butler's Book*, 2:687

"Here ... I first beheld 'Baldy' Smith, a short, quite portly man, with a light-brown imperial and shaggy mustache, a round, military head, and the look of a German officer, altogether." —Theodore Lyman, *Meade's Headquarters*, p. 140

"'Baldy Smith' was a kind man to his subordinates, and had the soul of a great soldier in him. He was, at times, a perfect Ishmaelite to his superior officers, as they found out to their cost. I have seen him handle his division in a way that Napoleon would have loved, and yet sometimes, when the pall of superior authority fell over him, he was a dreadful kicker. He wrecked the chance of a greater name in these ways." —Thomas W. Hyde, *Following the Greek Cross*, p. 117

WILLIAM SOOY SMITH Brigadier general. West Point (1853). Brigade and division commander, Army of the Tennessee.

"He is one of the best officers in that army. A rigid disciplinarian, his division is always ready, and always safe. A man of brains, a hard worker, unpretending, quick, suggestive, he may also be a little crotchety, for such is his reputation; but I judge that he only needs the opportunity to render great services." —Charles A. Dana, *Recollections*, p. 67

JOHN WILSON SPRAGUE Brevet major general. Businessman. Brigade and division commander, Army of the Tennessee.

"J.W. Sprague was distinguished in the Army of the Tennessee for decided ability as a general, and meritorious conduct which he showed at all times, and for his dignity of carriage and thought . . ." —Oliver O. Howard, *Autobiography*, 2:218

"General Sprague is a man of fine personal appearance, tall, straight, and well-proportioned. His character as a soldier is unimpeachable, and his influence with his regiment, and afterward with his brigade, was almost unbounded. No one who knew him as a soldier, failed to esteem and love him. He was always prompt, efficient, and brave." —Whitelaw Reid, *Ohio in the War*, 1:866

JULIUS STAHEL Major general. Hungarian revolutionary. Brigade and division commander, Army of Virginia. Cavalry division commander, Army of the Shenandoah.

"In the General's room I saw a little fellow, rather insignificant, looking for all the world like a traveling clerk in dress and figure. General Sigel introduced him to me as Major General Stahel . . . Major General Stahel was a Hungarian exile, a very young man of mild and polite manners. He was said to be a scion of Hungarian nobility, which his very unpretending manner indicated. He was also said to have been teaching a dancing school in New York when the War broke out. He got his commission when the fury for foreigners was at its height . . . Stahel is a very fancy cavalry officer who has never done anything in the field and never will do anything. He is entirely too mild and amiable for any such position." —David Hunter Strother, *A Virginia Yankee*, p. 217, 223

DAVID S. STANLEY
Major general. West Point (1852). Brigade, division and corps commander, Army of the Mississippi and Army of the Cumberland.

"Maj. Gen. Stanley has served in the same army with myself since 1862 . . . In the discharge of his duties in the various positions held by him . . . he has given entire satisfaction . . . A more cool and brave commander would be a difficult task to find . . . Stanley is an officer of acknowledged ability, industrious and faithful in the discharge of any duty, alive to the interests of government, as well as the welfare of the troops under his command . . ." —George H. Thomas, in Stanley, *Personal Memoirs*, p. 218–219

"Stanley was a great soldier. His only trouble was he used to drink, which to a certain extent retarded his advancement." —James H. Wilson, *Generals in Bronze*, p. 275

"A more cool and brave commander would be a difficult task to find, and though he has been a participant in many of the most sanguinary engagements of the war, his conduct has, on all occasions, been so gallant and marked that it would almost be an injustice to him to refer to any isolated battle field." —George H. Thomas, in *Ohio in the War*, 1:798

JOHN C. STARKWEATHER
Brigadier general. Lawyer. Brigade commander, Army of the Cumberland.

"Gen. Starkweather had a powerful voice, which could be heard at a great distance. The rebel soldiers used to imitate him and repeat his commands to each other, and seemed to find great amusement in it." —Benjamin Scribner, *How Soldiers were Made*, p. 119

JAMES B. STEEDMAN
Major general. Printer. Brigade and division commander, Army of the Cumberland.

"Chattanooga was commanded by General James Steadman, the most thorough specimen of a political general I met during the war. He always managed to hold commands where there were emoluments. At this time [Chattanooga 64] he was living in very high style, holding a gay court. The Princess Salm Salm was his guest . . . Steadman was dead in love with the woman, and such an idiot that I could not get any work out of him. In fact he was so taken up with making love to the Princess and drinking champagne that it was difficult to see this great potentate of Chattanooga . . . Steadman allowed

no woman around—wife or otherwise—unless he kept them himself."
—David S. Stanley, *Memoirs*, p. 190–191

"General Steedman's career during the war was highly honorable . . . He was a bold, energetic fighter, and his voice was always for fight. He never belonged to the school of delaying Generals. His troops had unbounded confidence in and admiration for him. Personally he is warm-hearted and generous, careless as to appearance, and often neglectful of his own interests; hearty in his ways, with the free-and-easy manners of the people among whom he grew up. He never betrays a friend. Politically he is shrewd, and . . . unscrupulous." —Whitelaw Reid, *Ohio in the War*, 1:788

FREDERICK STEELE   Major general. West Point (1843).
Brigade and division commander in western theater.

"He is a gentlemanly, pleasant fellow . . . every one says that he handles troops with great coolness and skill in battle. To me his mind seems to work in a desultory way, like the mind of a captain of infantry long habituated to garrison duty at a frontier post. He takes things in bits, like a gossiping companion, and never comprehensively and strongly, like a man of clear brain and a ruling purpose. But on the whole I consider him one of the best division generals in the army, yet you can not rely on him to make a logical statement, or to exercise any independent command." —Charles A. Dana, *Recollections*, p. 65–66

ISAAC I. STEVENS   Brigadier general. West Point (1839).
Mexican War veteran. Brigade commander, Army of Virginia. Killed at Chantilly, September 1, 1862.

"He was short and rather stout, with a swarthy complexion and very bright dark eyes. He was a man of superior abilities and of marked skill and courage. His extreme political opinions . . . made it somewhat difficult for him to secure such a position in the army as one of his capacity might well have expected . . . A more zealous and faithful officer never lived." —John Pope, *Battles and Leaders*, 2:493

JOHN D. STEVENSON   Brevet major general. Lawyer. Mexican
War veteran. Brigade and division commander, Army of the Tennessee.

"He is a person of much talent, but a grumbler. He was one of the oldest colonels in the volunteer service, but because he had always been an antislavery man all the others were promoted before him. This is still one of his grounds for discontent . . . Thus all the world will not go to suit him." —Charles A. Dana, *Recollections*, p. 68

THOMAS G. STEVENSON   Brigadier general. Brigade and division commander in 9th Corps. Killed at Spotsylvania Court House, May 10, 1864.

"General Stevenson is stunning ... A thorough soldier, jolly and pleasant and very entertaining, very kind and considerate—everything that could be wished." —Charles J. Mills, *Through Fire and Blood*, p. 67

CHARLES P. STONE   Brigadier general. West Point (1845). Mexican War veteran. Brigade commander in Virginia and in Department of the Gulf.

"[He]was an efficient officer and one of the most agreeable gentlemen socially I ever met in my service during the war. He was remarkably well informed in regard to all branches of the service, particularly the staff departments ... He was familiar with the records of all the old army officers of that time, and their most striking characteristics. He was very kind and considerate in assisting us ..." —Benjamin Grierson, *A Just and Righteous Cause*, p. 198

"He was a most charming and amiable gentleman; honest, brave, a good soldier, though occasionally carried away by his chivalrous ideas. He was very unfortunate, and was as far as possible from meriting the sad fate and cruel treatment he met with." —George B. McClellan, *McClellan's Own Story*, p. 139

GEORGE STONEMAN   Brevet Major general. West Point (1846). Brigade and division command, Army of the Potomac; Cavalry command, Army of the Potomac, and Army of the Ohio.

"General Stoneman was a tall, thin man, full bearded, with large eyes. He had an air of habitual sadness, or gravity approaching it, and was commonly reputed to have an irritable temper ..." —Jacob Cox, *Reminiscences*, 2:139

"General Stoneman was a large man, with short gray whiskers and gray hair and a strikingly bronzed red face." —Frederick L. Hitchcock, *War from the Inside*, p. 202

EDWIN H. STOUGHTON   Brigadier general. West Point (1859). Brigade commander, Army of the Potomac.

"I found General Stoughton one of the handsomest men I have ever met, well educated, his manners very refined, and only 24 years of age. He has not seen much service, and when I tell you that his brother, only 19 years old, commands his former regiment, you may rest assured he has friends high in authority." —Alexander Hays, *Letters*, p. 298

"Stoughton had the reputation of being a brave soldier, but a fop. He dressed before a looking-glass as carefully as Sardanapalus* did when he went into battle." —John S. Mosby, *Memoirs*, p. 176

WILLIAM K. STRONG   Brigadier general. Merchant and politician. Command of Benton Barracks and District of Cairo.

"General Strong had been a merchant . . . but had been urged on by the Secretary of War for the commission of a brigadier-general . . . He was a good, kind-hearted gentleman, boiling over with patriotism and zeal. I advised him what to read and study . . . and could hear him practise in his room the words of command, and tone of voice . . ." —William T. Sherman, *Personal Memoirs*, 1:247

DAVID STUART   Brigadier general. Lawyer. Brigade and division commander, Army of the Tennessee.

"General Stuart has been my near, dear, and most intimate friend . . . Of splendid genius, most liberal education, wonderful accomplishments, as scholar, orator, lawyer, statesman, and now soldier. With the courage and chivalry of a knight of old, and the sweetness and fascination of a woman, he won me to his heart . . ." —Thomas Kilby Smith, *Life and Letters*, p. 283

SAMUEL D. STURGIS   Brevet major general. West Point (1846). Mexican War veteran. Brigade and division commander, Army of the Potomac. Cavalry commander, western theater.

"The advent of General Sturgis at Memphis was not creditable to himself, nor reassuring to those who must be his subordinates—but on the contrary, extremely discouraging. He was a stranger to them, entirely unknown to the troops assigned to his command, and had no knowledge whatever of the country through which he was to operate. Upon his arrival at Memphis . . . he had a protracted drunken spree for nearly two weeks, during which he smashed looking glasses, crockery and furniture to his heart's content, kicking up 'high jinks' generally, until his condition became notorious." —Benjamin Grierson, *A Just and Righteous Cause*, p. 235

"He was a handsome fellow, with full, round features, sharp black eyes, and curly black hair and mustache. He had been seated but a few minutes when he noticed a bottle of whiskey on the table and a glass which had been placed there as camp hospitality for any one that wanted it, but had apparently been neglected . . . The judgment of his superiors and of those who knew him well was made severer by the knowledge of his weakness in this respect . . ." —Jacob Cox, *Reminiscences*, 2:117–118

---

* *Sardanapalus was the last king of Assyria, seventh century BC. He was renowned for his decadent lifestyle and self-indulgence.*

JEREMIAH C. SULLIVAN Brigadier general. Lawyer
and naval officer. Brigade commander, Army of the Valley; commander, Department of Memphis.

"No one knew anything about the enemy, no scouts out about the country. It was sufficient to account for all this by the fact that Gen. Sullivan was in command. For, in addition to his many other shortcomings, he lacked physical courage." —George Crook, *Autobiography*, p. 122

EDWIN V. SUMNER Major general. Career army officer.
Indian and Mexican War veteran. Division and corps commander, Army of the Potomac.

"He was remarkable for two military virtues: an exact obedience to orders and a rigid enforcement of discipline. If two methods were presented, one direct and the other indirect, he always chose the direct; if two courses opened, the one doubtful and leading to safety, the other dangerous and heroic, he was sure to choose the heroic at whatever cost." —Oliver O. Howard, *Autobiography*, 1:181

"Old General Sumner is a fine old officer, it is true. But then Banks is a nobody and citizen, although as good a politician as he is a bad soldier. Keyes, a gentlemanly man . . . was a mere Professor at West Point, during the War of Mexico. Heintzelman was in Mexico, but not in a single battle . . . His Division was the worst in the Army. McDowell should never have been made a high General, for he had never commanded a soldier. He was on the Rio Grande, but was not in any battle." —Philip Kearny, *Letters from the Peninsula*, p. 52

"General E.V. Sumner was one of the best instructed line officers in the army. His bravery was beyond dispute, and his untiring energy was never more remarkable than when he crossed the Chickahominy and came into action to assist Couch . . ." —Erasmus Keyes, *Fifty Years Observations*, p. 470

"He was a man of great soldierly qualities, but so brusque in manner as to be rude at times, and there were many people who disliked him. Yet he was a man truthful, honest and kindhearted." —David S. Stanley, *Memoirs*, p. 42

"He was an old man and tried officer; perfectly honest; as brave as a man could be; conscientious and laborious. In many respects he was a model soldier. He was a man for whom I had a very high regard . . . He was a very valuable man, and his soldierly example was of the highest value in a new army. A nation is fortunate that possesses many such soldiers as . . . Edwin V. Sumner." —George B. McClellan, *McClellan's Own Story*, p. 138

"General Sumner was an old man—must have been nearly seventy—gray, and his color indicated advanced age, though he seemed quite vigorous. He went about very quietly and without display. He had a singular habit of dropping his under jaw, so that his mouth was partially open much of the time." —Frederick L. Hitchcock, *War from the Inside*, p. 40

"'Old Bull Sumner' . . . is a most appropriate nick-name. Owing to his incompetence to fill so large a post as corps commander, we lost the chance to destroy Johnston's army at Williamsburg last May . . . But the old soldier was as honest as the day, and simple as a child. The fault was not so much his, as of those who put him and kept him in such a place . . . He was one of those whom every one must hate to find fault with; yet whose removal from the command of a corps was generally looked on as a relief . . ." —Charles S. Wainwright, *A Diary of Battle*, p. 174

GEORGE SYKES Major general. West Point (1842). Seminole and Mexican War veteran. Brigade, division, and corps commander, Army of the Potomac.

"General Sykes is being pitched into heavily by all the papers; but he did as well as he ever did, or ever will do. He don't really know what is best to do in a trying time, and all our present corps commanders are bad ones— poor ones, not wicked ones . . . I think him much to blame for Porter's not attacking in the last Bull Run fight and for one or two other serious failures. I have no better opinion of the others—all honest and well meaning, but not fit for generals." —Gouverneur K. Warren, *Life and Letters*, p. 148

"Sykes is a small, rather thin man, well dressed and gentlemanly, brown hair and beard which he wears full, with a red, pinched, rough looking skin, feeble blue eyes, large nose, with the general air of one who is weary, and little ill natured." —Frank Haskell, *Haskell of Gettysburg*, p. 133

"General Sykes looks a little like the photograph of General [Nathaniel] Lyon and has a very thick head of hair, which stands up like Traddle's.* He is a mild, steady man, and very polite . . ." —Theodore Lyman, *Meade's Headquarters*, p. 9

"General George Sykes [was] a Southerner by birth, and my roommate at West Point—a man admired by all for his honor, courage, and frankness, and particularly endeared to me by his social qualities." —Daniel Harvey Hill, *Battles and Leaders*, 2:359

ALFRED H. TERRY Major general. Lawyer. Brigade, division, and corps commander, Army of the James.

"He is a gentleman in manners and education, traveled, of fair military abilities, and rose steadily from his colonelcy by a faithful discharge of duty—ever ready, without any special ambition or thirst for distinction but doing everything from a sense of duty." —Samuel F. P. DuPont, *Civil War Letters*, 3:428

"General Alfred H. Terry came into the army as a volunteer without a military education. His way was won without political influence up to an

Tommy Traddles is an orphan in Charles Dickens's David Copperfield.

important separate command . . . His success there was most brilliant . . . He is a man who makes friends of those under him by his consideration of their wants and their dues. As a commander, he won their confidence by his coolness in action and by his clearness of perception in taking in the situation under which he was placed at any given time." —Ulysses S. Grant, *Personal Memoirs*, 2:540–541

"Terry had no staff, wore no spurs, and we do not think he owned a sword. He had a well-formed head, full of sense, which served him in lieu of feathers, sword, boots, spurs and staff—of which a General can have too many." —David Dixon Porter, *Naval History of the Civil War*, p. 711

GEORGE H. THOMAS Major general.
West Point (1840). Seminole and Mexican War veteran. Brigade, division, corps, and army commander, Army of the Cumberland.

"No one has ever accused Thomas of being a genius either militarily or otherwise. He neither plans campaigns with the aptitude and originality of Sherman, nor fights battles with the vigor and abandon of Sheridan. Thomas' successes have been obtained by long service and patient industry, and he is an example of what may be accomplished by the unremitting toil of a practical man. He is possessed naturally of that good, clear sense . . . common sense. He has never been brilliantly educated and is neither a brilliant thinker nor converser." —William F. G. Shanks, *Personal Recollections of Distinguished Generals*, p. 77–78

"He has all the gravity and solemnity . . . of a Washington. Never pays a compliment unless he means it. An officer of great purity and most devoted to his duties, so much so that for four years he has never left the field . . ." —Alpheus Williams, *From the Cannon's Mouth*, p. 391

"It is hard to fix upon any prominent trait . . . in a man so cool and unemotional as Thomas . . . He was great in defensive operations and in no case was he ever driven from any position . . . His mind seemed to work slowly, but the results of his deliberate thought were always sound . . . I presume he had the natural ambition of a soldier . . . but if he did have it, he certainly never betrayed it to his closest observers . . ." —John Pope, *Memoirs*, p. 94

"While modest and unassuming beyond most men, Thomas was also conscious of his own great qualities, and knew that as a commander he was head and shoulders above Logan, or any other volunteer officer . . . He was an upright Christian gentleman, as well as great soldier." —James F. Rusling, *Men and Things I Saw*, p. 105

"Although a Virginian and a slaveholder, he decided that under his oath of office his allegiance was due to the United States, and that when he swore to 'defend the United States against all their enemies and opposers whomsoever,'

SLOCUM. THOMAS. MCPHERSON. ROUSSEU. SHERMAN. HOWARD. KILPATRICK.

ARMY OF THE WEST.

Carte de visite depicting General Sherman and his corps commanders in 1864.

he meant that and nothing less. He was faithful and true in small things and great actions. He never sacrificed a man to his own glory. He fought only where a commensurate good could be reasonably expected. He was never rash or careless of the lives of his men . . . He was a plain, simple, sincere, and honest man. He was just to all, and in all things." —William P. Carlin, *Memoirs*, p. 123

"General Thomas did not possess in a high degree the activity of mind necessary to foresee and provide for all the exigencies of military operations, nor the mathematical talent required to estimate 'the relations of time, space, motion, and force' involved in great problems of war. His well-known high qualities in other respects obscured these imperfections from the great majority of those who surrounded him during the war . . ." —John M. Schofield, *Forty-Six Years in the Army*, p. 242

"He was certainly an officer of the very highest qualities, soldierly and personally. He was a man of the greatest dignity and character . . . At the same time he was a delightful man to be with; there was no artificial dignity about Thomas. He was a West Point graduate, and very well educated. He was very set in his opinions, yet he was not impatient with anybody—a noble character." —Charles A. Dana, *Recollections*, p. 124–125

"General Thomas . . . was large and solidly stout, with an air of dignified quiet and deliberation. His full beard was not of so stubby a cut as Sherman's, his countenance was almost impassive, and the lines of his brow gave an air of sternness. His part in the conversation was less, his words much fewer and less expressive, but always clear and intelligent. His manner was kindly, but rather reserved, and one felt that his acquaintance must be gradually cultivated. His reputation for cool intrepidity and stubborn tenacity could not be excelled, and no soldier could approach him without a deep interest and respect that was not diminished by his natural modesty of demeanor . . . His intellect was strong and broad, and his mind had been expanded by general reading . . . He was a noble model of patriotic devotion to country, and of the private virtues that make a great citizen." —Jacob Cox, *Reminiscences*, 2:204–205

"Of all those met . . . none impressed me as did George H. Thomas . . . His full, knightly figure and leonine face somehow told me of the soldierly soul of the man . . . he . . . developed into the best beloved of the Western army." —*Lew Wallace: An Autobiography*, 1:311–312

"General Thomas' characteristics are much like those of my father. While I was under his command he placed confidence in me, and never changed it. Quiet, manly, almost stern in his deportment, an honest man, I trusted him . . ." —Oliver O. Howard, *Autobiography*, 2:45

"He has a fine, soldierly appearance, and my impressions are that he has, intellectually and as a civilian, as well as a military man, no superior in the service. He has been no courtly carpet officer, to dance attendance at Washington during the War, but has nobly done his duty." —Gideon Welles, *Diary*, 2:382

"General Thomas is an officer of the regular army; the field is his home; the tent his house, and war is his business. He regards rather coolly . . . the applications of volunteer officers for leaves of absence. Why should not they be as contented as himself?" —John Beatty, *The Citizen Soldier*, p. 304

"Gen. Thomas was an undesirable person to approach if you had nothing to say. There was no lounging and twaddle in about his office; no slopping of toddies over his desk; if you had no point to make pertinent for his action, he would fix those cold gray eyes of his upon you, and, with his immobile countenance, so embarrass and confuse you that you would wish yourself far away. But, on the contrary, if your matter was within the scope of his appropriate duties, he would give you his undivided attention . . . but would patiently hear what you had to say, and dispatch your business then and there . . . he was considerate with the humblest private soldier; he was truthful, sincere and even-tempered, and it was traits like these that begot confidence, respect and love which . . . were manifested toward him by his men." —Benjamin Scribner, *How Soldiers were Made*, p. 116–117

"I had become greatly attached to him, and had acquired that respect and admiration which was felt by all who had ever come in contact with him. 'Old Pap Thomas,' as we all loved to call him, was more of a father than a commander to the younger officers who served under his immediate command, and he possessed their warmest affection." —Horace Porter, *Campaigning with Grant*, p. 12

"Older than any of his compeers . . . a Virginian by birth, but of unswerving loyalty, he was full of noble qualities. He had none of the excitable imagination and fervid passion of Sherman, none of the dashing genius or the personal magnetism of Sheridan, but possessed not a few traits in common with Grant. His judgment was sound, his patience untiring, his courage never shaken, his endurance inexhaustible . . . he was always calm and collected, and though ordinarily quiet and even gentle, like him he could be resolute when necessary, and was then immovable by friend or foe." —Adam Badeau, *Military History of Ulysses S. Grant*, 3:178–179

LORENZO THOMAS Major general. West Point (1823).
Seminole and Mexican War veteran. Adjutant general's office.

"General Lorenzo Thomas, of Delaware, was also a graduate of West Point . . . I think that there was not entire confidence felt in his loyalty, or . . . he was suspected of Southern sympathies. For that reason, perhaps, but perhaps, also, because he was earnestly loyal, he became so violent in his patriotism and so malevolent toward all who were not so violent and unreasonable as himself as to induce the suspicion that he was doing it all for effect." —John Pope, *Memoirs*, p. 202

"He was the ranking Adjutant General in the United States Army, and never worked harmoniously with Secretary Stanton of the War department. His obstinacy and intractability were a constant source of irritation to the latter, who could brook no opposition to his own will." —Sylvanus Cadwallader, *Three Years with Grant*, p. 60

ALFRED T. A. TORBERT   Brevet major general. West Point (1855). Cavalry division commander, Army of the Potomac.

"Torbert had disappointed me on two important occasions … and I mistrusted his ability to conduct any operations requiring much self-reliance." —Philip H. Sheridan, *Memoirs*, 2:112

"General Torbert of the New Jersey brigade was a very handsome man and the best-dressed officer in the army. He had magnificent horses, a saddle which was said to have cost five hundred dollars, with accoutrements to match, and when he passed a reviewing stand it usually caused a sensation." —Thomas W. Hyde, *Following the Greek Cross*, p. 180–181

ZEALOUS B. TOWER   Brevet major general. West Point (1841). Engineer. Mexican War veteran. Brigade command, Army of Virginia.

"He is a man of very superior abilities, zealous, and full of spirit and élan, and might easily have expected to serve his country in a much higher position than the one that he held . . ." —John Pope, *Battles and Leaders*, 2:489

EDWARD D. TOWNSEND   Brigadier general. West Point (1837). Mexican and Seminole War veteran. Adjutant general of the U.S. Army.

"A quiet, well-read, high-toned gentleman, to be trusted in all things, both a judicious friend and a sound advisor . . . He was a loyal man and a true man in every sense and . . . no man ever questioned his integrity or the purity of his motive." —John Pope, *Memoirs*, p. 202

"Gen. E.D. Townsend … was obsequious and time-serving—knew which side of his bread was buttered—and became a plastic instrument for executing Stanton's high-handed and tyrannical administration . . ." —Sylvanus Cadwallader, *Three Years with Grant*, p. 60–61

JOHN B. TURCHIN   Brigadier general. Russian army officer. Brigade and division command, Army of the Cumberland.

"A dumpy, fat Russian, with short legs, he could sit on a horse as upon a chair but, when it came to a gallop or a full charge, he was afraid of falling off and of being run over. A perfectly cold-blooded foreigner, he did not care a fig what became of me or the few men who followed me. He did not care to be jostled in a rush of cavalry for anybody's health. I had no faith in him . . ." —David S. Stanley, *Memoirs*, p. 137

"Turchin … was a Russian, an educated officer who had served in the Russian staff corps. An excellent soldier in many respects, his ideas of discipline were, unfortunately, lax, and in the summer of 1862 he was court-martialed for allowing his men to pillage a town in Tennessee." —Jacob Cox, *Reminiscences*, 1:436

"From the accounts we had heard of him and his doings we had expected to meet as fierce and brutal a Muscovite as the dominions of the Czar could produce. But though he is a Russian by birth and education, yet when he came into court we met a fine manly figure with broad expansive forehead, mild blue eye[s] with an unusual depth of piercing intelligence which at once won respect." —James A. Garfield, *The Wild Life of the Army*, p. 123

JOHN W. TURNER Brevet major general. West Point (1855). Division commander, Army of the James.

"He had graduated at West Point. He was my chief commissary, and afforded me very great and efficient aid in seeing to the provisioning not only of the army, but of a large portion of the people of New Orleans . . . he was an intelligent and capable military officer, and possessed a further qualification—he was a good business man." —Ben Butler, *Butler's Book*, 2:894

DANIEL TYLER Brigadier general. West Point (1819). Division command, Army of the Potomac.

"General Tyler was a graduate of the Military Academy, and, though past sixty years of age, his activity and fitness for command were not impaired, while in the army he had been distinguished for his knowledge of his profession and employed on various important duties. He was a man of high character." —Erasmus Keyes, *Fifty Years' Observations*, p. 432

"Gen. Tyler . . . was a graduate of West Point . . . & had resigned after distinguished service & had been equally distinguished in civil life for intellect, energy, & character. He seems to have been little infected with the 'fire & fall back' idea & to have great faith in a bold policy . . ." —E. P. Alexander, *Fighting for the Confederacy*, p. 45

ERASTUS B. TYLER Brigadier general. Businessman. Brigade commander, Army of the Potomac.

"Few have been more exposed to danger than General Tyler, and yet he has singularly escaped serious personal injury . . . General Tyler had been for many years a temperate man, even to the extent of total abstinence. He maintained these principles in the army, and succeeded by his example in suppressing, to a great extent, the use of intoxicating liquors among the men of his command. Integrity, firmness, and kindness of heart have secured for him popularity in every department of the army in which he served, and the obedience, respect, and affection of his men." —Whitelaw Reid, *Ohio in the War*, 1:833

HECTOR TYNDALE   Brevet major general. Businessman.
Brigade commander, Army of the Potomac; Army of the Tennessee.

"When I first saw General Tyndale, with his proud mien, his keen eye, his severely classic features framed in a brown curly beard, it struck me that so Coriolanus might have looked . . . He was a few years older than I, and had already a remarkable record behind him . . . Although without an academic education, his appearance and conversation were those of a man of culture. His was the natural refinement of a mind animated with high ideals, pure principles, perfect honesty of intelligence, a chivalrous sense of honor, and . . . artistic instinct. He had been a warm anti-slavery man, but not an extreme abolitionist . . . As a strict disciplinarian, he was . . . at first not popular with his soldiers, but they gradually perceived that his apparent sternness sprang from an overruling sense of duty and a conscientious care for their welfare . . ."
—Carl Schurz, *Reminiscences*, 3:53–54

EMORY UPTON   Brevet major general. West Point (1856). Brigade
commander, Army of the Potomac. Cavalry division commander, Military Division of the Mississippi.

"Upton . . . was the only one . . . who thoroughly mastered that branch of the military. He always made proper provision for success, for reenforcements, for cooperating movements and for all contingencies that could be foreseen . . . no other corps or division commander on either side ever equaled Upton . . . He was a military enthusiast and student of extraordinary ability, courage, and judgment, and, young as he was, I have never doubted . . . he was the best all-around soldier of his day."   —James H. Wilson, *Under the Old Flag*, p. 181

FERDINAND VAN DERVEER   Brigadier general. Lawyer.
Mexican War veteran. Brigade commander, Army of the Cumberland.

"General Van Derveer possessed many of the most valuable characteristics of an officer. Though never 'spoiling for a fight,' he was always anxious for any duty that would tell on the operations of the campaign. He was quick to seize upon all the features of a position—for fortifications, attacks, pickets. He always paid special attention to selecting comfortable camps; gave personal attention to every thing connected with the well-being of his troops; always had the best transportation, and took pride in keeping it in prime order; knew all his men by name, and generally had a joke that each would appreciate when he met him; had the faculty of organizing his men so as to gain speed in field-work of all kinds; was so unceasingly vigilant, that from the day he entered the field a surprise to his camp would have been an impossibility. In action he was a cool and close observer. He was always close along the fighting line, always on horseback, and generally exposed more than any of his men." —Whitelaw Reid, *Ohio in the War*, 1:892–893

JAMES S. WADSWORTH Brevet major general. Lawyer and politician. Brigade and division command, Army of the Potomac. Mortally wounded in the Wilderness, May 6, 1864.

"Wadsworth was a gallant New York officer, and a brave old gentleman, with gray hair and side whiskers; he wore a glazed [India rubber] cover on his cap. He seemed cheerful and in good spirits . . ." —Gen. Joseph Hayes, *Generals in Bronze*, p. 137

"Wadsworth having been defeated in his efforts to be governor of New York gets the First Division as a balm . . . I know nothing of his natural ability, but it ought to be very great, as he knew nothing of military matters before the war, is not a young man, and has had no experience in battle to entitle him to so high a position." —Charles Wainwright, *Diary of Battle*, p. 149

"General Wadsworth was a wealthy, middle-aged man from the lovely Genessee Valley, New York . . . but considered it his patriotic duty to raise some battalions for the army and did so, placing himself at their head. The government showed him all honor, conferring at once high rank." —G. Moxley Sorrel, *Recollections of a Confederate Staff Officer*, p. 138

"He should, by good right and fair-dealing, have been at this moment Governor of New York . . . No purer or more single-minded patriot than Wadsworth has shown himself in this war. He left home and comforts and wealth to fight the battles of the Union." —Gideon Welles, *Diary*, 2:27

LEW WALLACE Major general. Lawyer, Mexican War veteran. Division commander, Army of the Tennessee; corps commander, eastern theater.

"Gen. 'Lew' Wallace . . . looks like a second rate opera singer with his huge moustache & theatrical air." —Theodore Lyman, *Meade's Army*, p. 311

WILLIAM T. WARD Brigadier general. Lawyer, politician and Mexican War veteran. Brigade and division commander, Army of the Tennessee.

"He is the roughest looking old fellow I ever saw . . . he wore a blue private's overcoat, dirty and almost ragged, a black hat that looked as if its owner had been in a 'free fight' and had received several punches in the head . . . In person he was short, stocky, almost corpulent. From beneath his battered hat, long, iron-gray, uncombed locks depended nearly to his chin on one side, while the other side was cut so short as to be scarcely visible under the hat—a string of iron-gray whiskers ran under his chin . . . and the face bronzed almost to Indian darkness gave him the appearance of an old Western trapper or California gold digger." —Harvey Reid, *The View from Headquarters*, p. 97–98

GOUVERNEUR K. WARREN
Major general. West Point (1850). Engineer. Brigade, division, and corps commander, Army of the Potomac.

"Fancy a small, slender man, with a sun burnt face, two piercing black eyes, and withal bearing a most ludicrous resemblance to Mary Pratt! He was dressed in a double-breasted blouse, buttoned awry, a pair of soldier's pantaloons, rather too short, and a very old little straw hat ... Such is the personnel of one of the very best generals in the Army of the Potomac! He is a most kind man, and always taking care of hysterical old Secesh ladies and giving them coffee and sugar. As to Secesh MALES, in the army, he is a standing terror to them." —Theodore Lyman, *Meade's Headquarters*, p. 26

"He was younger than the other corps commanders . . . His hair was jet black; and so were his sharp eyes, which put life into his darkly sallow face. He was a thinnish man with a liking for big horses, and he wore full uniform, sash and all, when he rode into action; a rather odd figure." —Abner R. Small, *The Road to Richmond*, p. 126

"He strikes me as the most original officer that [I] have seen; a small, dried up, pointed nose, though still young man, with a restless black eye, like a weasel's, and a body and mind that seem full of watch-maker's springs. He has a broad New York accent and is by no means particular in grammar. His conversation shows that his mind is extremely ready and sure on all points. The reputation of a great fighter goes with him." —Theodore Lyman, *Meade's Army*, p. 29

"General Warren is a small man, about thirty-five years old, dark complexioned, with black eyes, and long, straight black hair; he has the look of an Indian, and evidently is of a nervous temperament." —Charles Wainwright, *A Diary of Battle*, p. 338–339

"There were two prominent generals in front of Richmond whom I instinctively distrusted—[Gouverneur K.] Warren and [Benjamin F.] Butler ... Warren forfeited the high estimation in which Grant once held him. He was egotistical. His caution was excessive. His distrust of everyone's judgment which ran counter to his own was universal. He lacked many qualities of a great commander." —Sylvanus Cadwallader, *Three Years with Grant*, p. 202

"[Col. Charles S.] Wainwright was here, greatly disgusted, as is everyone else, with Warren—a very loathsome, profane ungentlemanly & disgusting puppy in power—it seems as if he and Meade were trying to see how much their Officers will bear in the way of injustice and insult." —Marsena Patrick, *Inside Lincoln's Army*, p. 381

"The glory of having saved Little Round Top was beginning to break around him . . . but however keen and full may have been his inward joy . . . it altered not his bearing—which was that of the thoughtful, modest scholar rather than the soldier—nor did it kindle any vanity in look or speech. It may have accounted, however, for the manifestation of what seemed to me a queer sense of humor, namely, his laughing and laughing again while alone in his tent over a small volume of 'limericks' . . . He would repeat them at almost every meal . . . and wonder that they did not seem nearly so amusing to others as they did to him." —Morris Schaff, *The Wilderness*, p. 30

"Meade has a fearful temper & Warren has been so puffed & elated & swelled up, that his arrogance & insolence are intolerable . . ." —Marsena R. Patrick, *Inside Lincoln's Army*, p. 317

"He was a man of fine intelligence, great earnestness, quick perception, and could make his dispositions as quickly as any officer, under difficulties where he was forced to act. But I had before discovered a defect which was beyond his control . . . He could see every danger at a glance before he had encountered it. He would not only make preparations to meet the danger which might occur, but he would inform his commanding officer what others should do while he was executing his move." —Ulysses S. Grant, *Memoirs, Battles and Leaders*, 4:723

"No officer in this army exceeds Genl Warren in personal gallantry, in activity, in zeal and sleepless energy, nor in devotion to his duties. The defect with Genl Warren consists in too great reliance on his own judgment and in an apparent impossibility on his part to yield his judgment so as to promptly execute orders, where these orders should happen not to receive his sanction or be in accordance with his views." —George G. Meade, *Meade papers*, Pennsylvania Historical Society

"I always classed General Warren among the best of the general officers in the Army of the Potomac." —Henry Heth, *Memoirs*, p. 180

"Our new commander, General Warren, is a perfect gentleman and soldier, though young—such as I like to serve with." —Alexander Hays, *Letters*, p. 484

"We have the bullyest little general in the army and his name is Warren. I will venture a prophecy on him—that he will in time command us all, although he is my junior by ten years." —Alexander Hays, *Letters*, p. 506

"Warren is a man of the right sort, and I am getting to like him much. I consider that his management of the Corps . . . has been able and judicious— it has certainly been eminently successful. Such men as he are required to end this War—men who will not hesitate to strike when a chance occurs, and who will hanker after a chance, and run forward to meet it." —Frank Haskell, *Haskell of Gettysburg*, p. 225

"He was well capable of organizing an entire plan of battle on a great field. He would have been an admirable chief of staff of the army, where brains outweigh temperament. He could see the whole comprehensively and adjust the parts subordinate to it. But he had a certain ardor of temperament which, although it brought him distinction as a subordinate commander, seemed to work against him as a corps commander. It led him to go in personally with a single division of brigade, when a sharp fight came on. Doing this when having a larger command, one takes the risk of losing grasp on the whole." —Joshua Lawrence Chamberlain, *Passing of the Armies*, p. 154

"Warren had a habit—which he had grown out of now—of making judgments on things he did not thoroughly understand." —Martin Thomas McMahon, *Generals in Bronze*, p. 84

"Such a soldier as G.K. Warren must have been a marked man, and have risen to high command in any war the world ever saw." —Charles A. Page, *Letters*, p. 183

"Some people say he is a selfish man, but he is certainly the most tender-hearted of our commanders. Almost all officers soon grow callous in the service; not unfeeling, only accustomed, and unaffected by the suffering they see. But Warren feels it a great deal, and that and the responsibility, and many things of course not going to suit him, all tend to make him haggard." —Theodore Lyman, *Meade's Headquarters*, p. 147

"Warren's military ability, which was great, did not exactly take the direction of command of troops. He seemed unable to 'spread himself' over more than division, and he had the incorrigible error of trying to do each thing *himself*, putting no faith in his subordinates. It was this that ruined him . . . His great strength was as a field engineer and perhaps chief of staff; to discern proper routes, put troops in position; discriminate points of attack and defence. He was a man of sleepless energy, activity and study—his mind never still; a master of his art, and of daring spirit; but promotion was too rapid and in the wrong direction." —Theodore Lyman, *Meade's Army*, p. 356

"General Warren has been in one of his pets all yesterday and today, as ugly and cross-grained as he could be. One would suppose that a man in his position would be ashamed to show that kind of temper . . . He has pitched into his staff officers most fearfully, cursing them up and down as no man has a right to do . . ." —Charles S. Wainwright, *A Diary of Battle*, p. 396

"Warren's gallantry and patriotism were beyond all question; his abilities were marked, and his subordination was undoubted; and yet all were wasted by this one quality of intellectual, or rather moral feebleness. He could not put doubts out of his mind, and concentrate all his energies into a moment of action, leaving to others, above and below him, the responsibilities that belonged to them. While he was cautiously maneuvering, the critical moment passed. He developed his line when he should have assaulted, and skirmished and felt the enemy till the enemy either escaped or fortified in his presence; and when he was quite ready, there was often no occasion for readiness." —Adam Badeau, *Military History of Ulysses S. Grant*, 2:184

"General Warren is now in his element: so far as I can learn he is his own officer of the trenches, and commander of the working parties. There is nothing that he likes so much as overseeing work . . . He is a queer mixture . . . I am becoming more than ever convinced that he has a screw loose, and is not quite accountable for all his freaks . . ." —Charles S. Wainwright, *A Diary of Battle*, p. 436

"Warren's difficulty was twofold: when he received an order to do anything, it would at once occur to his mind how all the balance of the army should be engaged so as properly to co-operate with him. His ideas were generally good, but he would forget that the person giving him orders had thought of others at the time he had of him . . . when he did get ready to execute an order, after giving most intelligent instructions to division commanders, he would go in with one division, holding the others in reserve until he could superintend their movements in person also . . . His difficulty was constitutional and beyond his control. He was an officer of superior ability, quick perceptions, and personal courage to accomplish anything that could be done with a small command." —Ulysses S. Grant, *Personal Memoirs*, 2:214–215

"Warren never seemed to appreciate the tremendous importance, in battle, of time. He elaborated, and developed, and prepared, as carefully and cautiously and deliberately in the immediate presence of the enemy as if there was nothing else to do, and, while he was preparing and looking out for his flanks, the moment in which victory was possible usually slipped away." —Adam Badeau, *Military History of Ulysses S. Grant*, 3:464–465

"He was a man of fine intelligence, great earnestness, quick perception, and could make his dispositions as quickly as any officer, under difficulties where he was forced to act. But I had before discovered a defect which was beyond his control, that was very prejudicial to his usefulness in emergencies . . . He could see every danger at a glance before he had encountered it. He would not only make preparations to meet the danger which might occur, but he would inform his commanding officer what others should do while he was executing his move." —Ulysses S. Grant, *Personal Memoirs*, 2:445

CADWALLADER C. WASHBURN Major general. Lawyer and politician. Cavalry commander 13th Corps, division commander, Army of the Gulf.

"Gen. Washburn was not only an able military man, but possessed of unusual administrative ability and great business experience, which gave him an advantage over the ordinary military officer. His wise and conservative administration of affairs, in his district, soon became apparent. It can in truth be said that his administration covering the greater part of a year, was not only successful, but a 'clean one,' all of which was well known and appreciated at Washington." —Augustus L. Chetlain, *Recollections of Seventy Years*, p. 102

"He is brave, steady, respectable; receives suggestions and weighs them carefully; is not above being advised, but acts with independence nevertheless. His judgment is good, and his vigilance sufficient . . . I don't find in him . . .

that effort to learn the military art which every commander ought to exhibit ... Washburn's whole soul is not put into the business of arms ... But he is a good man, and above the average of our generals ..." —Charles A. Dana, *Recollections*, p. 72

ALEXANDER S. WEBB Brevet major general. West Point (1855). Staff service. Brigade and division command, Army of the Potomac.

"General Webb is a good piece of luck, as successor to General Humphreys. He is very jolly and pleasant, while, at the same time, he is a thorough soldier, wide-awake, quick and attentive to detail. In fact, I believe him much better for the place than Gen. H. from the very circumstance that he was such a very superior man, that General Meade would take him as a confidential adviser ... My only objection to General Webb is that he continually has a way of laughing in a convulsive manner, by drawing in his breath, instead of letting it out—the which goes to my bones." —Theodore Lyman, *Meade's Headquarters*, p. 307

"I look upon Webb as one of the most conscientious, hard-working and fearless young officers that we have." —Charles S. Wainwright, *A Diary of Battle*, p. 333

GODFREY WEITZEL Major general. West Point (1855). Engineer. Brigade, division, and corps command, Army of the Gulf; corps command, Army of the James.

"A West Pointer, and a lieutenant of engineers, had been for some time Butler's chief military adviser, and had lately been made a brigadier general of volunteers. About twenty-six years old, with a stature of six feet four inches, he was a man of attractive and imposing presence." —John William De Forest, *A Volunteer's Adventures*, p. 53

"Godfrey Weitzel, chief engineer upon Butler's staff, is a curious man. Endowed with a wonderful nous, located in a big head, set on a long neck, atop of a long body, swung along by pendulum legs, he is—Godfrey Weitzel, and there is none other. Would there were, for the sake of the country, and every one a brigadier general." —Charles A. Page, *Letters*, p. 132–133

"Gen. Weitzel ... an intelligent, Saxon looking man with light eyes and beard. He was negligent in dress and I venture to guess, is better at his trade of engineer, than as a field fighter." —Theodore Lyman, *Meade's Army*, p. 299–300

"General Weitzel will always be honored for his share in the suppression of the great rebellion. His skill as an engineer commanded the confidence of his corps and of the army. He succeeded better than most engineers in the command of troops in the field; and his reputation as a good corps General was undisputed. He was also free from many of the prejudices of the regular army, particularly with reference to the capacity of negro troops ... His appearance and bearing denote his German descent." —Whitelaw Reid, *Ohio in the War*, 1:795

JULIUS WHITE Brigadier general. Lawyer. Brigade and division commander, Army of the Potomac and 9th Corps.

"I like him very much ... He is a very kindly, pleasant person, rather Western, but gentlemanly and is taking hold of the division in a very satisfactory manner... He is rather lazy... but on the whole satisfactory, and immensely preferable to his predecessor whom I hope never to meet again." —Charles J. Wills, *Through Blood and Fire*, p. 145, 148

"There was nothing strikingly military about his looks, but he was mounted on a handsome black horse, was handsomely uniformed, with an untarnished sabre, immaculate gloves and boots, and had a staff fittingly equipped." —Henry Kyd Douglas, *I Rode with Stonewall*, p. 162

ORLANDO B. WILCOX Brevet major general. West Point (1847). Engineer. Brigade and division command, Army of the Potomac.

"The command ... devolves on Brig. Gen. Wilcox, who is considered a fair officer, but who doesn't show it by his management at present, which consists for the most part in doing nothing at all, with the exception of spasmodic intervals, when piles of orders come out, and which he expects to have executed in somewhat less than no time." —Charles J. Mills, *Through Blood and Fire*, p. 69

SETH WILLIAMS Brevet major general. West Point (1842). Mexican War veteran. Assistant adjutant general and inspector general, Army of the Potomac.

"I never met a better bureau officer ... He thoroughly understood the working of the adjutant-general's department, was indefatigable in the performance of his duty, made many and valuable suggestions as to the system of returns, reports, etc., and thus exerted a great influence in bringing about the excellent organization of the Army of the Potomac. He was thoroughly honest and a gentleman; he was, if anything, too modest, for he would probably have accomplished more had he possessed more self-reliance. He won universal regard by his kind and considerate manner towards those with whom he was officially brought in contact. I never knew a more laborious and conscientious man." —George B. McClellan, *McClellan's Own Story*, p. 141

"He is an odd looking man, with close-cut sandy red hair, a large, massive head & jaw and a face that looks as if it loved a joke. His aspect is not at all military, and reminds one rather of an expressman. His ability is said to be very great, which seems probable." —Theodore Lyman, *Meade's Army*, p. 29

"Seth Williams [was] a very quiet, modest man, but a master of the minutest details of every department and an indefatigable worker. It was said his chief could wake him in the middle of the night and get from his memory a correct answer as to the number of men fit for duty in any one of the hundreds of regiments in the army . . ." —Frederick L. Hitchcock, *War from the Inside*, p. 32

THOMAS WILLIAMS Brigadier general. West Point (1837). Black Hawk War, Seminole War, and Mexican War veteran. Brigade commander, Army of the Gulf. Killed at Baton Rouge, August 5, 1862.

"He is a weak, incompetent, wrong-headed, passionate man. He has not given one order correctly since he first attempted to drill us. His pretensions are disgusting. What could have induced the President to appoint such a worthless brigadier? I have been under his command quite long enough." —Eleazer Paine, *A Wisconsin Yankee*, p. 45

"Brigadier-General Thomas Williams . . . was a man of many idiosyncrasies, and outside of his staff was cordially disliked for his severe treatment of the men." —Rush C. Hawkins, *Battles and Leaders*, 1:639

JAMES H. WILSON Major general. West Point (1860). Engineer. Cavalry division commander, Army of the Potomac; chief of cavalry, Military Division of the Mississippi.

"He was a brilliant man intellectually, highly educated, and thoroughly companionable." —Charles A. Dana, *Recollections*, p. 62

"He had just come from Grant's command and was made at once Sherman's Chief of Cavalry. He was young, intelligent and very ambitious . . . he set to work very energetically to reorganize and remount the cavalry which was to remain in Tennessee. Wilson did this well . . ." —David S. Stanley, *Memoirs*, p. 190

THOMAS J. WOOD Major general. West Point (1845). Brigade, division, and corps commander, Army of the Cumberland.

"His intelligence and activity were very marked, and his courage was of the cool indomitable character most highly prized in divisions of a great army. Of medium height, solid but not large build, dark hair and complexion, high forehead, he was a noticeable man in any assemblage of officers. A fluent talker, attentive to polite forms of speech as well as of conduct, he was liked and respected throughout the army . . ." —Jacob Cox, *Reminiscences*, 2:160

"I am unfortunately under the immediate command of General Wood, a very narrow, impetuous, proslavery man in whose prudence and patriotism and brains I have but very little confidence, and a shamefully rough, blasphemous man, quite destitute of fine or manly feelings." —James A. Garfield, *The Wild Life of the Army*, p. 90

WILLIAM E. WOODRUFF   Colonel. Lawyer and soldier.

"Col. Woodruff, of Kentucky, . . . for some reason claimed to be a brigadier general, was assigned . . . to the command of a division temporarily . . . I told Colonel Woodruff that I didn't believe he was a brigadier general . . . For two months Colonel Woodruff exercised the command of a brigadier general . . . After the battle of Stones River . . . it was discovered that he was neither a brigadier general or an officer of any grade." —William P. Carlin, *Memoirs*, p. 70–71

CHARLES R. WOODS   Brevet major general. West Point (1852). Brigade and division command, Army of the Tennessee.

"General Woods is portly in appearance, rather slow in movements and in conversation. He gives those who meet him the impression of a steady, solid, judicious, and trustworthy person, rather than one of special brilliancy. General Sherman once spoke of him as a 'magnificent officer.' Before the war his political sympathies were conservative and democratic." —Whitelaw Reid, *Ohio in the War*, 1:843

JOHN E. WOOL   Major general. Veteran of War of 1812 and Mexican War. Commander middle department, 8th Corps and Department of the East.

"With regular troops of long standing in the service . . . General Wool was a capable and most efficient officer, but with volunteers he had little sympathy and less influence. Indeed, General Wool had few elements of personal popularity and was almost without friends in the army . . . however . . . full credit was given him as a soldier, even by his enemies . . . He was a Democrat from policy before and during the war, but an intensely loyal man both from principle and feeling. He was short and slender, very agile and vivacious, with dark hair and eyes and a perfectly beardless and mustacheless face." —John Pope, *Memoirs*, p. 196

"Wool had a reputation as a gallant officer in the War of 1812, rather lowered by his weak demeanor at Buena Vista. He was a notorious old gambler and won a great deal of money from young Lieutenants in the Army. Whilst Inspector General of the Army, his method of drawing mileage finally compelled a remodeling of the law . . . No wonder he could leave eighty thousand dollars to put a grand monument over his tomb." —David S. Stanley, *Memoirs*, p. 34–35

"With volunteers General Wool's reputation was that of a martinet, prim, formal and stern to an offensive degree. They said he would not allow himself the compliment of a serenade; that he was always in uniform, with a leather stock about his neck and epaulets on his shoulders; that he received his visitors capped, booted, and spurred; that he began his business at daybreak, and ate with his sword on; some believed he even slept with his sword. In short, there was no limit to the general's unpopularity. I found him an agreeable gentleman, kind and sympathetic . . ." —*Lew Wallace: An Autobiography*, 1:163–164

HORATIO G. WRIGHT   Major general. West Point (1841).
Engineer. Commander, Department of the Ohio, 1862, Army of the Ohio, 6th Corps, Army of the Potomac.

"Wright was another engineer officer, well educated, of good, solid intellect, with capacity for command, but no special predilection for fighting." —Charles A. Dana, *Recollections*, p. 191

"We have all smiled out here at Brigadier General Wright being made a *Major General*, the most incompetent, though a very worthy man, of all the brigadiers that came out—and recently defeated on James Island." —Samuel F. DuPont, *Civil War Letters*, 2:205

FAMOUS CONFEDERATE COMMANDERS OF THE CIVIL WAR, 1861-'65.

Postwar lithograph of prominent Confederate generals. Premium for The Pivotal Battle of the Civil War.

CONFEDERATE GENERALS

EDWARD PORTER ALEXANDER Brigadier general.
West Point (1857), Confederate signal officer and engineer, chief of ordnance, Army of Northern Virginia

"General E.P. Alexander . . . was a many-sided character—an engineer of the highest abilities, an artillerist of great distinction, a good reconnoitering officer and an enthusiastic sportsman besides." —G. Moxley Sorrel, *Recollections of a Confederate Staff Officer*, p. 260

RICHARD H. ANDERSON Lieutenant general. West Point
(1842), Mexican War veteran, division, and corps commander, Army of Northern Virginia

"Major General Richard H. Anderson, of South Carolina, had been a captain of cavalry in the United States Army and was rather an interesting character. His courage was of the highest order, but he was indolent. His capacity and intelligence excellent, but it was hard to get him to use them. Withal, of a nature so true and lovable that it goes against me to criticize him. He had served well as a brigadier general . . . and had shown commendable prudence and intelligent comprehension . . . He was a very brave man . . . but of a rather inert, indolent manner for commanding troops in the field, and by no means pushing or aggressive . . . He seemed to leave the corps much to his staff, while his own meditative disposition was constantly soothed by whiffs from a noble, cherished, meerschaum pipe . . . He was a short, thick, stocky figure, with good features and an agreeable expression." —G. Moxley Sorrel, *Recollections of a Confederate Staff Officer*, p. 128, 242–243

"Gen. Dick Anderson was as pleasant a commander to serve under as could be wished, & was a sturdy & reliable fighter." —E. P. Alexander, *Fighting for the Confederacy*, p. 365

LOUIS A. ARMISTEAD   Brigadier general. Expelled from West Point, 1836. Mexican War veteran. Brigade commander, Army of Northern Virginia. Killed at Gettysburg.

"If ever there was a man absolutely without fear, it was Armistead." —Henry Heth, *Memoir*, p. 56

TURNER ASHBY   Brigadier general. Farmer and businessman. Commanded Stonewall Jackson's cavalry in 1862 Shenandoah Valley Campaign. Killed at Harrisonburg.

"General Ashby was a man of striking personal appearance, about five feet ten inches tall, with a well-proportioned figure, graceful and compact, black eyes, black hair, and a flowing black beard. His complexion was of the darkest brunette . . . His face was placid, not stern; even his smile was shadowed with a tinge of melancholy . . . His face did not flush in battle or under excitement . . . He often smiled, rarely laughed. His eye was gentle, peaceful; in battle it did not sparkle fitfully but burned steadily beneath his dark brows . . . Riding his black stallion, he looked like a knight of the olden time . . ." —Henry Kyd Douglas, *I Rode with Stonewall*, p. 82

"Meek as a child in peace, fierce as a tiger in battle, night and day in the saddle, ever restless and watchful, always in advance when danger threatened. To see him ride to the front in the crisis of battle . . . waving his sword . . . was a sight which none will forget who witnessed it." —An English Combatant, *Battlefields of the South*, p. 290–291

"Ashby has played his part handsomely . . . displaying a great deal of personal boldness and military tact . . . with his small force." —David Hunter Strother, *A Virginia Yankee*, p. 17

"You could see from his dress, his firm tread, his open and frank glance, that he was a thorough soldier—indeed he always 'looked like work'—but under the soldier, as plainly was the gentleman." —John Esten Cooke, *Wearing of the Gray*, p. 61

PIERRE G. T. BEAUREGARD

General. West Point (1838). Engineer, Mexican War veteran, commanded Confederate forces at Charleston, First Manassas, 1861; Army of Tennessee, 1862; Richmond & Petersburg defenses, 1864–1865.

"General Beauregard . . . is a man of middle height, about forty-seven years of age. He would be very youthful in appearance if not for the color of his hair, which is much grayer than his earlier photographs represent. Some persons account for the sudden manner in which his hair turned gray by allusions to his cares and anxieties during the last two years; but the real and less romantic reason is to be found in the rigidity of the Yankee blockade, which interrupts the arrival of articles of toilet. He has a long straight nose, handsome brown eyes, and a dark mustache without whiskers, and his manners are extremely polite. He is a New Orleans creole, and French is his native language." —Arthur J. L. Fremantle, *Three Months in the Southern States*, p. 195–196

"He is a man of brilliant talents, of wonderful vivacity and is at once an able man and a delightful companion . . . Beauregard was too impulsive and quick-tempered to be a prudent or safe counselor and too restless and enterprising to be satisfied with any condition except that of constant action . . . He has all the genial polished manners, all the vivacity and impulse of the French Creole, without his indolent habits of body and mind. Of all restless, energetic men whom I have known, General Beauregard is one of the foremost." —John Pope, *Memoirs*, p. 207–208

". . . A good man, but lacking in indomitable energy and purpose for a commander of an Army. I mean General Beauregard. He is a man with French impulses, but devoid of English resolution and tenacity. I regard and respect him sincerely." —St. John Richardson Liddell, *Liddell's Record*, p. 67–68

"The General is a small, compact man, about thirty-six years of age, with a quick and intelligent eye and action, and a good deal of the Frenchman in his manner and look." —William Howard Russell, *My Diary North & South*, p. 56

"He is a small man, with a sallow complexion, a heavy black moustache, and closely cut hair. With the left hand in his trowsers pocket, a cigar in his mouth, a buttoned-up coat, and small cap, he is the exact type of a French engineer, and could not anywhere be mistaken for a civilian. He is jaunty in his gait, dashing in manner, and evidently takes delight in the circumstance of war. It must be confessed his modesty is equal to his merit—he is not imperious or overbearing, bears great respect for his brother officers of the old service, and is never seen to such advantage as when standing on an earthwork, and giving orders, or conversing with animated gesture." —An English Combatant, *Battlefields of the South*, p. 32

"General Beauregard was patriotic, but too impulsive and of too limited capacity for an army commander. He would have made a fine corps commander, and should never have ranked any higher." —William C. Oates, *The War Between the Union and the Confederacy*, p. 309

"I think Gen. B. had more courtesy of manner than any of the other generals with whom I ever served. He was of medium size or a very trifle short, but compactly built, quick & alert, of fine carriage & aspect, & of unusual strength & activity. His age must have been about 45 . . . His hair was black, but a few months afterward when some sorts of chemicals & such things became scarce it began to come out quite gray." —E. P. Alexander, *Fighting for the Confederacy*, p. 38

"Gen. Beauregard had more about him of what I would call military technique than any of our Confederate generals. He was very particular in the observance of all military routines, traditions, & methods, in keeping up scouting & secret service & in requiring reports & preserving office records. His records . . . would do credit to the staff of any European nation . . ." —E. P. Alexander, *Fighting for the Confederacy*, p. 424–425

"He was simply a great soldier, and a finished gentleman. Once in his presence, you would not be apt to deny his claim to both of these characters. The nervous figure, the gaunt, French, fighting, brunette countenance, deeply bronzed by sun and wind—these were the marks of the soldier. The grave, high-bred politeness; the ready, courteous smile; the kindly and simple bearing, wholly free from affectation and assumption—these were the characteristics of the *gentilhomme* by birth and habit, by nature as by breeding." —John Esten Cooke, *Wearing of the Gray*, p. 82–83

BARNARD BEE Brigadier general. West Point (1845), Mexican War veteran. Killed at First Manassas.

"I was always a great admirer of Bee; he was as gallant a soldier as ever drew a sword, and a splendid man in every respect . . . had Bee lived, he would have made a great name for himself, and attained the highest rank in the army." —Henry Heth, *Memoirs*, p. 137

"Bee was one of the most admirable soldiers of that day. Six feet in stature, he was every inch a soldier, and as gentle as he was brave. He was distinguished always for his delicate consideration for others, as for his manly and noble bearing in personal danger." —Dabney H. Maury, *Recollections of a Virginian*, p. 24

BRAXTON BRAGG Full general. West

Point (1837); Seminole and Mexican War veteran. Commanded coastal defenses in 1861; Army of Tennessee 1862–1864; military advisor to Jefferson Davis, 1864–1865.

"Bragg was a remarkably intelligent and well-informed man, professionally and otherwise. He was also thoroughly upright. But he was possessed of an irascible temper and was naturally disputatious. A man of the highest moral character and the most correct habits, yet in the old army he was in frequent trouble. As a subordinate he was always on the lookout to catch his commanding officer infringing upon his prerogatives; as a post commander he was equally vigilant to detect the slightest neglect, even of the most trivial order." —Ulysses S. Grant, *Battles and Leaders*, 3:710

"Bragg's manner made him malignant enemies and indifferent callous friends . . . He had such poor judgment of character . . . that I have known him to overlook men whose actions and zeal entitled them to wiser consideration, and it became the general belief that not service or enterprise entitled men to credit and promotion, but favoritism only." —St. John Richardson Liddell, *Liddell's Record*, p. 116–117

"This officer is in appearance, the least prepossessing of the Confederate officers. He is very thin; he stoops, and has a sickly, cadaverous, haggard appearance, rather plain features, bushy black eyebrows which unite in a tuft at the top of his nose, and a stubby iron gray beard; but his eyes are bright and piercing. He has the reputation of being a rigid disciplinarian and of shooting freely for insubordination. I understand he is rather unpopular on this account, and also by reason of his acerbity of manner." —Arthur J. L. Fremantle, *Three Months in the Southern States*, p. 145–146

"This officer . . . was a noted artillerist, and would possibly have done greater execution in directing the movements of field batteries, which was a specialty, than in directing the movements of an army or handling it in battle. General Bragg was undoubtedly a man of ability, but his health was bad, and unfortunately his temper was no better." —John B. Gordon, *Reminiscences of the Civil War*, 126

"I knew Bragg. His reputation was that of a martinet. He was a severe disciplinarian; a good soldier, and a hard fighter." —Thomas L. Crittenden, *Battles and Leaders*, 3:633

"Tall and erect, with thick, bushy eyebrows and black, fierce eyes, with harsh features and a most forbidding countenance, he possessed, or was possessed, by the most sullen and devilish temper that ever afflicted a human being. Kindly feeling or soft sentiment of any kind fled before his frown and those subject to his authority retired from his presence with almost equal celerity and relief. I do not think he could ever have had warm friends. Indeed, he seemed even to detest himself, if one might judge from the dissatisfied expression which continually sat enthroned on his face and yet the South produced no more capable general than he . . . Had his temper and his manners been such as to make friends and not enemies, it is hard to say how great might have been his success . . . " —John Pope, *Memoirs*, p. 78

"General Bragg . . . almost unrivalled as a subordinate and lieutenant, could never have become a great commander. He was lacking in the quick, fertile, and accurate conception and broad comprehension which makes the successful strategist; he was not an able tactician. So far from inspiring, as nearly all great captains have done, confidence and love in those who followed them, General Bragg aroused sentiments the very reverse. His temper was austere and even morose, his manner was repellant, his very look and bearing suggested in others distrust of his judgment, and doubt of successful achievement." —Basil W. Duke, *Reminiscences*, p. 298

"Longstreet . . . told the President . . . that General Bragg was incompetent to manage an army or put men into a fight; that his intentions were all good, but he knew nothing of the business . . ." —W. W. Blackford, *Letters from Lee's Army*, p. 221

"There was no man in either of the contending armies who was General Bragg's superior as an organizer and a disciplinarian, but when he was in the presence of an enemy he lost his head." —Henry Heth, *Memoirs*, p. 168

"Bragg was an able officer and considered by [President Jefferson] Davis as the best of his generals. He had been unfortunate. He had the great fault of being easily led astray or turned aside by petty side issues. Not foreseen in his original program, they completely upset him in trying moments and ruined *all* his well laid plans. In a word, he was no tactician to execute his own strategic combinations." —St. John Richardson Liddell, *Liddell's Record*, p. 97–98

"I have always regarded him as one of the best organizers of an army and disciplinarians that I ever met with, and he possessed many of the qualities essential to a commander. Full of energy, indefatigable in his labors, firm and impartial as an administrative officer, he was no respecter of person or rank, and punished a delinquent, be he the general next below him, or the meanest soldier in the ranks, the one with as little hesitation as the other. A terror to all quarter-masters and commissaries . . . I think that the army under his command . . . was in a higher state of efficiency whilst he ruled than ever before or after . . . He was not, however, a great general; made many mistakes . . . Personally, I learned to like him . . . he certainly was excited by the purest patriotism, and one of the most honest and unselfish officers of our army." —Arthur Middleton Manigault, *A Carolinian Goes to War*, p. 158

"Possessing experience in and talent for war, he was the most laborious of commanders, devoting every moment to the discharge of his duties. As a disciplinarian he far surpassed any of the senior Confederate generals; but his method and manner were harsh, and he could have won the affections of his troops only by leading them to victory. He furnished a striking illustration of the necessity of a healthy body for a sound intellect. Many years of dyspepsia had made his temper sour and petulant; and he was intolerant to a degree of neglect of duty, or what he esteemed to be such, by his officers." —Richard Taylor, *Destruction and Reconstruction*, p. 100

"General Bragg was a good soldier, but in no respect a great captain. He could organize and adapt the means by which an end might be attained, but he could not design or accomplish the end. He could plan to a certain extent, or partially execute a plan formulated by another, but seemed incapable of pursuing any plan to its consummation. He evinced undaunted and determined courage as a subordinate, but was subject, when in chief command and feeling entire responsibility, to sudden and apparently uncontrollable starts of timidity . . . [I]t was a misfortune for the Confederacy . . . that he was advanced from the position of lieutenant to that of leader." —Basil Duke, *Reminiscences*, p. 338

"He was celebrated through all the Confederate armies as a stern disciplinarian . . . But I don't think Gen. Bragg inspired any enthusiasm in his men . . . he certainly never impressed me as a man of intellectual power—as a cool & clear thinker, at all. And to be entirely frank there were some who did not hesitate openly to say that he was simply muddle headed & especially that he never could understand a map, & that it was a spectacle to see him wrestle with one, with one finger painfully holding down his own position." —E. P. Alexander, *Fighting for the Confederacy*, p. 307

"He was silent and reserved and seemed gloomy and despondent. He had grown prematurely old since I saw him last, and showed much nervousness. His relations with his next in command (General Polk) and with some of the others of his subordinates were known not to be pleasant. His many retreats, too, had alienated the rank and file from him, or had at least taken away that enthusiasm which soldiers feel for the successful general, and which makes them obey his orders without question, and thus wins for him other successes." —D. H. Hill, *Battles and Leaders*, 3:639

JOHN C. BRECKINRIDGE Major general. Lawyer. Vice president of the United States under James Buchanan, brigade and division commander in the Army of Tennessee; Confederate secretary of war, 1864–1865.

"This illustrious statesman . . . was fast winning his way to distinction in his new role of Confederate soldier . . . Tall, erect, and commanding in physique, he would have been selected in any martial group as a typical leader . . . he exhibited in a marked degree the characteristics of a great commander. He was fertile in resource, and enlisted and held the confidence and affection of his men, while he inspired them with enthusiasm and ardor. Under fire and in extreme peril he was strikingly courageous, alert, and self-poised." —John B. Gordon, *Reminiscences of the Civil War*, p. 192

"While his reputation in the Confederate was good, and he was ranked among the best of those who held high but subordinate rank, it was not what I think it should have been. Nature had endowed him generously in all respects, giving him an unusually handsome and commanding presence, a rare and most persuasive eloquence, and a manner singularly attractive. With extremely brilliant qualities, he possessed also a profound sagacity—a judgment acute and seldom at fault in any manner upon which he was adequately informed . . . he had . . . the military aptitude and soldierly instincts which . . . make the successful captain." —Basil Duke, *Reminiscences*, p. 176

"He had unquestionably a remarkable sagacity in all matters pertaining to actual warfare, a rare military aptitude. His courage and resolution were superb. I have never . . . witnessed an indifference to danger so absolutely calm and imperturbable as I have seen him display under very extraordinary exposure to personal peril. His chief defect as a soldier . . . was a strange indolence or apathy which at times assailed him . . . When thoroughly aroused he acted with tremendous vigour, as well as indomitable decision; but he needed to be spurred to action, and without some special incentive was often listless and lethargic." —Basil Duke, *Reminiscences*, p. 193

SIMON BOLIVAR BUCKNER Lieutenant general.
West Point (1844). Mexican War veteran. Brigade, division, and corps commander, Army of Tennessee.

"Buckner I had known as a cadet at West Point; he was greatly beloved in the regiment, was an accomplished officer and gentleman." —Henry Heth, *Memoirs*, p. 97

"Being the best drill officer in the service, he had organized and disciplined the best division of troops in the Army of Tennessee. I learned to estimate this man highly for his many good qualities, affable, high-toned, and able, though not brilliant. He lacked only constancy of purpose to have made him a more prominent figure in the war. I thought him to be impatient with superiors and yet lacking in energy when left to himself . . . Buckner was somewhat captious." —St. John Richardson Liddell, *Liddell's Record*, p. 37

ABRAHAM BUFORD Brigadier general. West Point (1841). Mexican War veteran, served under N. B. Forrest.

"Buford was the most accomplished swearer I had ever seen up to that time— I had not met General [William S.] Harney . . . Buford was a Kentuckian and devoted to blooded horses and racing." —Henry Heth, *Memoirs*, p. 82

BENJAMIN FRANKLIN CHEATHAM Major general. Mexican War veteran and major general of militia. Brigade, division, and corps commander, Army of Tennessee.

"I met Major-General Cheatham, a stout, rather rough looking man, but with the reputation of 'a great fighter.' It is said he does all the necessary swearing in the 1st *corps d'armée*, which General Polk's clerical character incapacitates him from performing." —Arthur J. L. Fremantle, *Three Months in the Southern States*, p. 147

CHARLES CLARK Brigadier general. Mississippi legislator and Mexican War veteran. Brigade commander Army of Tennessee.

"General Clarke, of Mississippi . . . spoke with sense and firmness of the present troubles, and dealt with the political difficulties in a tone of moderation which bespoke a gentleman and a man of education and thought. He had also served in the Mexican War, and had the air and manner of a soldier." —William Howard Russell, *My Diary North & South*, p. 163

PATRICK R. CLEBURNE Major general. Veteran of British army. Lawyer. Brigade and division commander, Army of Tennessee. Killed at Franklin.

"Physically General Cleburne was of a striking appearance . . . he was six feet in height, of spare build, with broad shoulders and erect carriage. In his large gray eyes the gleam of sympathy and the sparkle of humor were most often seen and they grew dark and stern in danger or battle . . . The most pronounced characteristic of the man . . . was his courage. He had indeed, the lion's heart. He was absolutely indifferent to danger and was as cool when exposed to it as in the most peaceful moments of his life . . . He went where duty called, calm and determined . . . and in the performance of it, his mind and his arm acted with the rapidity and force of lightning." —Judge L. H. Mangum, *Cleburne and His Command*, p. 78–79

Cleburne "was a blunt, impassive, rather heavy man ... who only needed the flames of battle to kindle his dull features, to stir the depths of his strong nature and to show forth a soldier for stoutness of heart, for stubbornness of fight, for shining valor and forgetfulness of self rarely to be matched." —Archer Anderson, *Cleburne and His Command*, p. 35

"When Cleburne's Division defended, no odds broke its lines; where it attacked, no numbers resisted its onslaught, save only once, and there is the grave of Cleburne." —William J. Hardee, *Cleburne and His Command*, p. 64

"While it cannot be claimed that he possessed the genius of [Stonewall] Jackson ... he had the same dauntless temper and patient, unflagging energy, the same conscientious, almost fanatical devotion to duty, and an equally combative inclination as a soldier ... I cannot remember that I ever saw an officer who was so industrious and persistent in his efforts properly to drill and instruct the men under his command. He took great interest in everything connected with tactics ... and was occupied from morning until night in superintending squad, company, and battalion drill, guard mounting, inspection, and ... everything mentioned in the books or that he could conceive of." —Basil Duke, *Reminiscences*, p. 68–69

"He is the son of a doctor ... at the age of seventeen he ran away from home, and enlisted in Her Majesty's 41st Regiment of foot ... He then bought his discharge and emigrated to Arkansas, where he studied law ... By his distinguished services ... [he has] been appointed to command of a division ... he is now thirty-five years of age; but, his hair having turned grey, he looks older." —Arthur J. L. Fremantle, *Three Months in the Southern States*, p. 153–154

"Cleburne was resentful, exceedingly ambitious, friendly to those useful to him, until they stood in the way of his advancement. Then he did not hesitate to shake them off. He was brave and considerate in danger, but slow to conception. He was ever ready, however, to learn by the experience of others and closely applied the lessons he had received in actual service in the field. He studied well the business he had on hand always and applied his resources well." —St. John Richardson Liddell, *Liddell's Record*, p. 161

"Major General Cleburne had been distinguished for his admirable conduct upon many fields ... He was a man of equally quick perception and strong character ... He possessed the boldness and the wisdom to earnestly advocate, at an early period of the war, the freedom of the negro and the enrollment of the young and able-bodied men of that race." —John B. Hood, *Advance and Retreat*, p. 296

"Of his personal appearance he might have been proud, as he was considered the handsomest man in the country. He was six feet high, spare made, long of arm and length of limb, his features fine cut and well shaped. He was a great beau with the girls. His small head was covered with a coat of sleek black hair, which he trained with good taste. He was of dark complexion, with a haughty, self sufficient air." —Edward Nash, *Biographical Sketches of Cleburne and Hindman*, p. 40

"He had not the genius of some of our generals, but he possessed in its place a well balanced mind, with strong common sense. He affected neither sumptuousness of living nor brilliance of style. There was the same simplicity in his language when general as when a private . . . He seemed utterly unconscious of the petty ambitions which so disturb the happiness of others, but moved straight forward in the path of duty, without any concern for himself." —H. G. Bunn, in Nash, *Biographical Sketches of Cleburne and Hindman*, p. 196

THOMAS R. R. COBB Brigadier general. Lawyer, ardent secessionist from Georgia. Brigade commander, Army of Northern Virginia. Killed at Fredericksburg.

"I had learned to esteem him warmly, as I believe every one did who came to know his great intellect and his good heart . . . he was a religious enthusiast, and being firmly convinced that the South was right, believed that God would give us a visible sign that Providence was with us, and daily prayed for His interposition on our behalf." —Lafayette McLaws, *Battles and Leaders*, 3:940

SAMUEL COOPER Full general. West Point (1815). Veteran of the Seminole and Mexican wars. Highest ranking Confederate general.

"General Cooper . . . was a native of New York and . . . had neither interest in the South nor sympathy with its purpose to break up the Union. He went because his wife's family were Southern . . . In point of fact, he deserted his post while still Adjutant General of the Army . . . I have not been able to believe that a man with so high a reputation for honor as he had before could have been guilty of such a breach of trust . . . He went and with that departure went all his reputation, all the honor and all the happiness of his life." —John Pope, *Memoirs*, p. 201

GEORGE B. CRITTENDEN Major general. West Point (1832). Veteran of Blackhawk War, Texas War, and Mexican War.

"General George B. Crittenden is a Kentuckian, about fifty-five years of age . . . he is generally considered to be an excellent and reliable officer when free from the influence of alcohol and gay company. . . . This vice is too prevalent among talented men of the South." —T.E.C., *Battlefields of the South*, p. 128

"Mr. Davis has made some very bad appointments, & Genl. Crittenden's, I expect, was one. I believe Genl C. to be a brave and a true man, but he has not the ability such as I think requisite for a Major General. He is an intemperate man, which is his greatest fault . . . those who know him say he can not indulge at all without drinking to excess. I made his acquaintance here, and was very much pleased with him as a gentleman, but thought he was a man of ordinary ability." —Thomas Goree, *Longstreet's Aide*, p. 73

"The particulars of the late Battle near Somerset, Ky. are coming in, & what a great victory it was for us; yet it seems to me that it was managed badly by the Rebels. It is reported that the rebel Genl. Crittenden was in command and *drunk*—As he was an inveterate drunkard when in our army, I suppose the report is true." —Franklin Archibald Dick, *Troubled State*, p. 51

JUBAL A. EARLY Lieutenant general.
West Point (1837). Seminole War veteran, lawyer.
Brigade, division, and corps commander, Army of
Northern Virginia.

"Jubal Early, brigadier general, was one of the ablest soldiers in the army. Intellectually he was perhaps the peer of the best for strategic combinations, but he lacked ability to handle troops effectively in the field; that is, he was deficient in tactical skill. His irritable disposition and biting tongue made him anything but popular . . . his appearance was quite striking, having a dark, handsome face, regular features and deep piercing eyes. He was the victim of rheumatism, and although not old was bent almost double, like an aged man. Of high scholarly and fine political attainments, he never married, but led the life of a recluse in Virginia . . ." —G. Moxley Sorrel, *Recollections of a Confederate Staff Officer*, p. 50

"Early . . . was equally queer and brave, a man of more ability than Ewell, but not near so good a soldier. He posed too much and always recalled to me Plato's speech to Diogenes, that 'he echoed his vanity by his rags.' He had quite a reputation as a division commander but failed completely as a corps commander . . . He continued to pose after the war, and was very harsh in his criticism of men who certainly did as good service as he did." —John Haskell, *The Haskell Memoirs*, p. 18

"Of all the generals . . . in the Army of Northern Virginia, there were none . . . after the death of Stonewall Jackson, who possessed the essential qualities of a military commander to a greater extent than Early. With a mind clear, direct, and comprehensive . . . with a boldness to attack that approached rashness and a tenacity in resisting that resembled desperation, he was yet on the field of battle not equal to his own intellect or decision . . . he received with impatience . . . either advice or suggestion from his subordinates. Arbitrary, cynical, with strong prejudices, he was personally disagreeable; he made few admirers or friends either by his manners or his habits . . . If he had a tender feeling, he endeavored to conceal it and acted as though he would be ashamed to be detected in doing a kindness; yet many will recall . . . that his heart was naturally full of loyalty and tenderness." —Henry Kyd Douglas, *I Rode with Stonewall*, p. 33

"He was not the great Military Chieftain that his admirers claim him to have been; nor was he the Military Imbecile such as his enemies have described him as being. He was unquestionably a patriot, and a Soldier of marked ability.

As a strategist he was superb; as a tactician he was some times at fault. Seen in the light of defeat his faults are magnified and his virtues minimized." —Cullen Andrews Battle, *Third Alabama*, p. 140

"General Jubal A. Early ... was an able strategist and one of the coolest and most imperturbable of men under fire and in extremity. He had, however, certain characteristics which militated against his achieving the greatest successes ... he lacked ... official courage, or what is known as the courage of ones convictions ... General Early possessed other characteristics peculiarly his own ... his indisposition to act upon suggestions submitted by subordinates and his distrust of the accuracy of reports by scouts ... General Early was a bachelor, with a pungent style of commenting on things he did not like; but he had a kind heart and he was always courteous to women." —John B. Gordon, *Reminiscences of the Civil War*, p. 317–318

"I have feared our friend Early wd not accomplish much because he is such a *Godless* man. He is a man who utterly sets at defiance all moral laws & such a one heaven will not favour." —Walter Taylor, *Lee's Adjutant*, p. 177

"He opposed the secession of Virginia ... but when the war began he went with his people ... When he got thoroughly into secession and war he was one of the most earnest and uncompromising rebels in the entire South ... He never cared much for society—never married, but was quite an interesting conversationalist. He was a man of the highest integrity and condemned in unmeasured terms whatever he thought was wrong, despised false pretense and hypocrisy. He was of the highest courage and a skilful general in strategy, but too slothful in execution." —William C. Oates, *The War Between the Union and the Confederacy*, p. 385

"Early proved himself a remarkable corps commander. His greatest quality perhaps was the fearlessness with which he fought against all odds & discouragements." —E. P. Alexander, *Fighting for the Confederacy*, p. 397

"General Early is an excellent officer and ought to be a Major General. He is dissatisfied, as well he may be, and talks sometimes of going out to join Bragg. He is very able and very brave and would be an acquisition in your part of the world." —Richard S. Ewell, *Old Bald Head*, p. 122

"General Early ... appeared to be a person of middle age; was nearly six feet in height; and, in spite of severe attacks of rheumatism, could undergo great fatigue. His hair was dark and thin, his eyes bright, his smile ready and expressive, though somewhat sarcastic. His dress was plain gray, with few decorations ... what most impressed those who were thrown with him, was that satirical, sometimes cynical humour, and the force and vigour of his conversation. His voice was not pleasing, but his 'talk' was excellent. His intellect was evidently strong, combative, aggressive in all domains of thought; his utterance direct, hard-hitting, and telling ... Sarcastic and critical, he was criticised in return, as a man of rough address, irascible temperament, and as wholly careless whom he offended." —John Esten Cooke, *Wearing of the Gray*, p. 99, 101

NATHAN G. "SHANKS" EVANS Brigadier general. West Point (1848). Brigade commander, Army of Northern Virginia.

"Gen. Evans . . . had he done his duty could have captured the whole lot with little or no trouble. He is very much censured for not attacking . . . but the truth of the matter is . . . that he got a little drunker than usual, and was consequently not in a condition to do anything. . . . General Evans is one of the bravest men I ever saw, and is no doubt a good officer when sober, but he is unfortunately nearly always under the influence of liquor." —Thomas Goree, *Longstreet's Aide*, p. 51

"Evans was very restless . . . He is about forty years of age with a head of the cast of Tom Moore's; slightly bald; small restless black eyes; heavy black mustaches; and when he smiles displays incomparable teeth; he has a quick, cunning and snappish look although his manner is polished and polite. His countenance looks like one who dissipates occasionally; he is of medium stature, angular in his movements, never happy but when in the saddle—a perfect soldier in everything, and 'swears like a trooper.'" —An English Combatant, *Battlefields of the South*, p. 59

"N.G. Evans ('Shank' Evans) . . . was a rather marked character. A regular soldier, he had served well in Mexico, and at Manassas . . . had done exceedingly well with a small command, a good eye, and quick decision . . . Evans was reputedly difficult to manage and we found him so." —G. Moxley Sorrel, *Recollections of a Confederate Staff Officer*, p. 93

"General Evans had a military education, and started into the war brilliantly, but on account of his intemperate habits never won any promotion, and several years after the war died at midway, Ala . . . in utter poverty. He had been teaching school there." —William C. Oates, *The War Between the Union and the Confederacy*, p. 65–66

RICHARD S. EWELL Lieutenant general. West Point (1840). Mexican War veteran. Brigade, division, and corps commander, Army of Northern Virginia.

"He is rather a remarkable looking old soldier; with a bald head, a prominent nose and a rather haggard, sickly face; having so lately lost his leg above the knee, he is still a complete cripple, and falls off his horse occasionally . . . he used to be a great swearer . . . but since his late marriage, he has 'Joined the Church.'" —Arthur J. L. Fremantle, *Three Months in the Southern States*, p. 284

"Ewell was one of the most eccentric characters, and . . . one of the most interesting that I have ever known . . . It was most interesting to note the change that came over the spirit of this formerly irascible old bachelor . . . Ewell had become a husband and was sincerely devoted to Mrs. Ewell. He never seemed to realize, however, that her marriage to him had changed her

name, for he proudly presented her to his friends as 'My wife, Mrs. Brown, sir.'"
—John B. Gordon, *Reminiscences of the Civil War*, p. 157–158

". . . He was of a singular modesty. Bright prominent eyes, a bomb shaped, bald head and a nose like that of Francis of Valois, gave him a striking resemblance to a woodcock; and this was increased by a birdlike habit of putting his head on one side to utter his quaint speeches. He fancied he had some mysterious internal malady, and would eat nothing but frumenty . . . His nervousness prevented him from taking regular sleep, and he passed nights curled around a campstool, in positions to dislocate an ordinary person's joints . . . With a fine tactical eye on the battle field, he was never content with his own plan until he had secured the approval of another's judgment, and chafed under the restraint of command, preparing to fight with the skirmish line."
—Richard Taylor, *Destruction and Reconstruction*, p.37

"General Ewell . . . had in many respects the most unique personality I have ever known. He was a compound of anomalies, the oddest, most eccentric genius in the Confederate army. He was my friend . . . No man had a better heart or a worse manner of showing it. He was in truth as tender and sympathetic as a woman, but, even under slight provocation, he became externally as rough as a polar bear, and the needles with which he pricked sensibilities were more numerous and keener than porcupines' quills."
—John B. Gordon, *Reminiscences of the Civil War*, p. 38

"I saw a good deal . . . of Ewell, who was a queer character, very eccentric, but upright, brave and devoted. He had no very high talent, but he did all that a man of courage and moderate capacity could." —John Haskell, *The Haskell Memoirs*, p. 18

"General Ewell became a very distinguished soldier, and justly so. To uncommon courage and activity he added a fine military instinct, which could make him a good second in command in any army." —G. Moxley Sorrel, *Recollections of a Confederate Staff Officer*, p. 47

"Ewell was a first-class lieutenant, but he did not have enough confidence in himself to make him successful with an independent command . . . He hesitated . . . Therein was Ewell's deficiency as a general. He had a splendid tactical eye, capable of grand military conceptions, and once resolved quick as lightning to act, yet he was never quite confident of his judgment and sought the approval of others before he would execute." —William C. Oates, *The War Between the Union and the Confederacy*, p. 90, 202

JOHN B. FLOYD
Major general. Mexican War veteran. Lawyer and politician. Secretary of War for President James Buchanan. Abdicated command of Confederate forces at Fort Donelson.

"John B. Floyd, Gideon J. Pillow and Simon B. Buckner. Of these, the first was ranking officer, and he was at the time under indictment by a grand jury at Washington for malversation as Secretary of War . . . and for complicity in an embezzlement of public funds . . . The second officer had a genuine military record; but it is said of him that he was of a jealous nature, insubordinate and quarrelsome . . . there is little doubt that the junior of the three commanders was the fittest . . . He was their equal in courage; while in devotion to the cause and to his profession of arms, in tactical knowledge, in military bearing, in the faculty of getting the most service out of his inferiors, and inspiring them with confidence in his ability—as a soldier in all the higher meanings of the word—he was greatly their superior." —Lew Wallace, *Battles and Leaders*, 1:401

"I had a long talk with General Lee and expressed to him my views as to Floyd's ability to exercise an independent command. I told him if Floyd was given an independent command, it would be merely a question of time when it would be captured; that I did not think the Confederacy could afford to lose three or four thousand men, simply to gratify the ambition of a politician who was as incapable of taking care of his men or fighting them, as a baby." —Henry Heth, *Memoirs*, p. 156

"He had, as Secretary of War, given great offense to the North by the shipping of arms from the northern arsenals to the South, some months before secession. He was charged with having been in collusion with the enemies of the Government under which he held office, and with treachery. At Donelson he was the senior officer in command. When the other brigadiers refused to fight any longer, he brought off his own men and left the others to surrender to Grant. This was regarded as a breach of discipline, and Jefferson Davis relieved him of his command." —John S. Mosby, *Memoirs*, p. 18–19

"His comprehensive views of the military policy of the Confederate Government inspired me with respect . . . Although no soldier by profession, I thought Floyd would have been better . . . supervising and directing the general conduct of the war. Why he was overlooked by Mr. Davis I could not understand." —St. John Richardson Liddell, *Liddell's Record*, p. 54

"General Floyd . . . was a man of talent enough for any civil position, was no soldier and, possibly, did not possess the elements of one. He was further unfitted for command, for the reason that his conscience must have troubled him and made him afraid. As Secretary of War he had taken a solemn oath to maintain the Constitution of the United States and to uphold the same against all its enemies. He had betrayed that trust." —Ulysses S. Grant, *Personal Memoirs*, 1:308–309

NATHAN BEDFORD FORREST

Lieutenant general. Planter and slave-trader. Cavalry commander, Army of Tennessee. Independent commander of cavalry.

"His command knew him to be a man of powerful mind, active and energetic, great will-power, keen perception, quick to act, full of strategy, with cool, daring bravery, his whole soul in the cause, his tactics common sense . . .

when asked 'how do you manage to whip all of your battles?' He replied, 'By getting there first with the most men . . .'" —Major Gilbert Rambaut, *As They Saw Forrest*, p. 57

"General Forrest, as a commander, was in many respects, the negative of a West Pointer. He regarded evolution, maneuvers and exhaustive cavalry drill an unnecessary tax upon men and horses. He cared nothing for tactics further than the movement by twos or fours in column . . . from column into line, dismounting, charging and fighting . . . these simple movements proved sufficient." —John W. Morton, *As They Saw Forrest*, p. 271

"Forrest is the very devil and I think he has got some of our troops under cower. I have two officers at Memphis that will fight all the time . . . I will order them . . . to go out and follow Forrest to the death if it takes 10,000 lives and breaks the Treasury. There will never be peace in Tennessee until Forrest is dead . . ." —William T. Sherman, *Official Records*, 1:39 pt. 2, p. 121

"Forrest, the backwoodsman, the farmer, and the slave-dealer, knew nothing of 'grand strategy,' but he was at once a shrewd, able man of business, and at the same time thoroughly acquainted with the common-sense tactics of the hunter and the Western pioneer . . . The *art* of war was an instinct in him . . . His favorite maxim was 'War means fighting, and fighting means killing.' Hence it was, his track was usually marked with blood, and the dead bodies of his enemies were the records he left of fierce charges down roads, and of Federal camps or bivouacs taken by surprise." —General Viscount Garnet Wolseley, *As They Saw Forrest*, p. 33

"N.B. Forrest, the 'wizard of the saddle' . . . was one of the unique figures of the war . . . who, in my estimation, exhibited more native untutored genius as a cavalry leader than any man of modern times." —John B. Gordon, *Reminiscences of the Civil War*, p. 127

"General Forrest has very much the appearance of a gentleman. He is a middle-sized, dark complexioned man of over forty years of age—wears black mustache and closely trimmed chin whiskers which, with his hair, are slightly sprinkled with gray. He wore . . . a dark blue U.S. military overcoat over his uniform, and a 'shocking bad' black wool hat without ornament of any kind . . . His uniform coat was gray with double row of buttons, arranged by twos like our Brigadiers. The insignia of rank of a Brigadier general is three stars on the coat collar each surrounded with a wreath . . ." —Harvey Reid, *The View from Headquarters*, p. 49

"Gen. Nathan B. Forrest was one of the ablest cavalry officers developed on either side, especially for partisan warfare. Bold and reckless, almost to a fault, he often accomplished by sheer audacity and celerity of movement, what could never have been done in any other way. His thorough topographical knowledge of the country enabled him to take advantage of every road and bridle path . . . and thus avail himself of the most desirable places for offensive and defensive fighting . . . He was quick to take advantage of our errors, and the exact moment in which to strike." —Sylvanus Cadwallader, *Three Years with Grant*, p. 39

"It is thought by some that had Forrest been thoroughly educated, he would have been a greater general than he was . . . But there abounded in his makeup so much good sense, so much energy, so much fertility of resource, as made us feel he was born for war, and that his native gift raised him above the aid of education. His intuition led him directly to the essence of every question, and while he perceived the true objects of war no less quickly and clearly, and pursued them with no less vigor than [Stonewall] Jackson did, he had vastly more fertility of resource than that great captain ever evinced, and when main force and direct attack failed of success he often won it by stratagem and finesse." —Dabney H. Maury, *Battles and Leaders*, 5:13

RICHARD B. GARNETT Brigadier general. West Point
(1841). Seminole and Mexican war veteran. Brigade commander, Army of Northern Virginia. Killed at Gettysburg.

"Old Dick is a fine fellow, a brave, splendid soldier . . . He is as sensitive and proud as he is fearless and sweet-spirited, and has felt more keenly than most men would Old Jack's censure of him at the battle of Kernstown . . ." —George E. Pickett, *The Heart of a Soldier*, p. 62

ROBERT S. GARNETT Brigadier general. West Point (1841).
Mexican War veteran. First general to die in the war, killed at Corrick's Ford.

"Garnett was a Virginian who had graduated at the Military Academy five years before McClellan. He had won his laurels in the Mexican campaign and afterward against the Indians . . . he was considered an excellent officer, a rigid disciplinarian, and, in consequence of many soldierly traits, had at one time been appointed commandant of the Cadet Corps at West Point." —Fitzhugh Lee, *General Lee*, p. 113–114

"Garnett . . . was a dashing man, & ambitious. He would have played a good part, & made an active enterprising General . . . His capacity was very moderate as a scholar, but he had studied men and manners." —Josiah Gorgas, *The Journals of Josiah Gorgas*, p. 42

"He served in Mexico . . . and was conspicuous for gallantry and good conduct . . . When Western Virginia was invaded, he offered his services to go to her defense . . . how bravely he struggled against adverse fortune, and how gallantly he died in the discharge of his duty . . ." —Jefferson Davis, *Rise and Fall*, 1:338–339

STATES RIGHTS GIST Brigadier general. Harvard Law
School graduate. Brigadier general of South Carolina Militia. Brigade commander, Army of Tennessee. Killed at Franklin.

"General States Rights Gist is a South Carolinian, only thirty-two years of age, and although not educated as a soldier, he seems easily to have adapted himself to the military profession. He looks a determined man and he takes responsibility very coolly." —Arthur J. L. Fremantle, *Three Months in the Southern States*, p. 113

JOSIAH GORGAS   Brigadier general. West Point (1841). Chief of ordnance of the Confederate States.

"The chief of ordnance was General J. Gorgas, a man remarkable for his scientific attainment, for the highest administrative capacity and moral purity, all crowned by zeal and fidelity to his trust, in which he achieved results greatly disproportioned to the means at his command." —Jefferson Davis, *Rise and Fall*, 1:481

DANIEL C. GOVAN   Brigadier general. Gold miner and planter. Brigade commander, Army of Tennessee.

"A More gallant leader and brave soldier never smelt gunpowder, and the general had numerous opportunities of smelling the sulphorous smoke . . . I have often heard Gen. Cleburne speak in the highest terms of Gen. Govan. . . . Govan added another laurel to the brow of Arkansas." —H. G. Bunn, *Biographical Sketches of Cleburne and Hindman*, p. 211

THOMAS GREEN   Brigadier general. Lawyer. Veteran of the Texas War and Mexican War. Cavalry division commander in District of West Louisiana.

"Upright, modest, and with the simplicity of a child, danger seemed to be his element, and he rejoiced in combat. His men adored him, and would follow wherever he led; but they did not fear him, for, though he scolded at them in action, he was too kind-hearted to punish breaches of discipline. In truth he had no conception of the value of discipline in war . . ." —Richard Taylor, *Destruction and Reconstruction*, p. 178

"Major General Tom Green is nearly six feet high, rather stoop-shouldered; his face is rather rounding, with a short, grizzly beard. His troops had unbounded confidence in him, and believed whatever he did was right, and that is everything . . . His career as a soldier has been a brilliant record of dashing exploits—of noble victories . . . There are men who are soldiers by inspiration. Green is one." —J. P. Blessington, *Walker's Texas Division*, p. 184–185

MAXCY GREGG   Brigadier general. Lawyer. Mexican War veteran. Brigade commander, Army of Northern Virginia. Killed at Fredericksburg.

"His hair is grey; he has full whiskers and moustaches and a ruddy complexion; in person he is thick-set, of medium height, and jocular in his manner. His uniform looked the worse for wear, even the three stars upon his throat being dingy and ragged, while his common black felt hat would not bring half a dollar at any place in times of peace. But he is well mounted and armed . . ." —An English Combatant, *Battlefields of the South*, p. 333

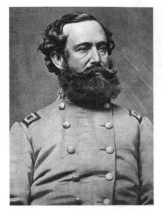

WADE HAMPTON Lieutenant general. South Carolina legislator and landowner. Brigade, division and Cavalry Corps commander, Army of Northern Virginia.

"This officer had served from the very beginning of the war with high distinction, had proved himself a careful, vigilant, as well as enterprising cavalry leader, and possessed the confidence of the cavalry troops . . . General Hampton was of fine presence, a bold horseman, a swordsman, and of the most undaunted courage." —G. Moxley Sorrel, *Recollections of a Confederate Staff Officer*, p. 249

"Of this eminent soldier, I will say that . . . I always regarded him as a noble type of courage and manhood—a gentleman and soldier 'to the finger nails' . . . You saw at a glance the race from which he sprang, and the traits of heart and brain which he brought to the hard contest." —John Esten Cooke, *Wearing of the Gray*, p. 51

ROGER W. HANSON Brigadier general. Lawyer and Mexican War veteran. Brigade commander, Army of Tennessee. Killed at Stones River.

"No officer was more liked and respected by the Kentucky soldiers, or possessed more thoroughly the confidence of his superiors on command . . . Hanson had many noble traits of character, was brave, candid, and truthful, and sincerely scorned dissimulation or pretense of any kind. His personal appearance was singular and striking. In stature, below the medium height, his form was strong and massive but ungraceful. His keen gray eyes and florid complexion indicated a sanguine temperament, and every feature of his face was expressive of energy and determination." —Basil Duke, *Reminiscences*, p. 138–139

"Hanson was a large fat man. But as all (even the blind) could see, he possessed the soul of a hero, true as steel to his purposes, sincere and unsophisticated as a child, the very man whom all honest and good people would flock to for advice, friendship, and protection. The man drew me to him by his *natural* nobility of nature." —St. John Richardson Liddell, *Liddell's Record*, p. 105

WILLIAM J. HARDEE

**Lieutenant general. West Point (1838).
Author of *Rifle and Light Infantry Tactics*.
Brigade, division, and corps commander,
Army of Tennessee.**

"Was not a very prominent personage during the war and made little mark in its history. He was a genial gentleman, of good address and rather of reserved manners; an officer accomplished in all the details of service . . . He was a good tactician . . . [but] was never considered a man of large ability . . ." —John Pope, *Memoirs*, p. 81

"He is a fine soldierlike man, broad-shouldered and tall. He looks rather like a French officer . . . He bears the reputation of being a thoroughly good soldier and he is the author of the drill book still in use by both armies. . . . Until quite lately he was the commanding officer of the military college at West Point. He distinguished himself at the battles of Corinth and Murfreesborough . . . he is a widower, and has the character of being a great admirer of the fair sex." —Arthur J. L. Fremantle, *Three Months in the Southern States*, p. 138–139

"This officer, who was an accomplished tactician, had made a record which many thought indicated abilities of a high order, fitting him for chief command of the Western army." —John B. Gordon, *Reminiscences of the Civil War*, p. 127

" . . . Surpassed by none in ability and soldierly quality in command of a corps, he shrunk from the burden of chief responsibility for a campaign and declined the permanent appointment . . . Hardee was in person and bearing a good type of the brilliant soldier and gentleman. Tall and well formed, his uniform well fitting and almost dandyish, his manner genial and easy, his conversation at once gay and intelligent, it would be hard to find a more attractive companion, or one with whom you would be put more quickly at ease." —Jacob Cox, *Reminiscences*, 2:179–180, 525

"A close friend of his family, I never ceased to be interested in his career. By his uniform courtesy he won the regard of all associates . . . By 1861 he had grown gray in service; he had given to the army his light infantry tactics; he had also won enviable distinction in the Mexican War, and probably no name was more familiar to the people at large than his." —Oliver O. Howard, *Autobiography*, 1:101

"An educated soldier of large experience, Hardee was among the best of our subordinate generals, and, indeed, seemed to possess the requisite qualities for supreme command; but this he steadily refused, alleging his unfitness for responsibility. Such modesty is not a common American weakness, and deserves to be recorded." —Richard Taylor, *Destruction and Reconstruction*, p. 215–216

"Hardee, who has charge of the defences of Mobile . . . is an agreeable, delicate-looking man, scarcely of middle age, and is well-known in the State as the author of *The Tactics*, which is, however, merely the translation of the French manual of arms. He does not appear to be possessed of any great energy or capacity, but is, no doubt, a respectable officer." —William Howard Russell, *My Diary North & South*, p. 110

"Whilst General Hardee had, perhaps, no superior as a corps commander during retreat in presence of an enemy, or in defensive operations, he was wanting in that boldness requisite for offensive warfare . . . Long and gallant service had . . . endeared him to his troops, and, because of further demoralization which I feared might ensue in the event of his removal, I decided to retain him in command." —John B. Hood, *Advance and Retreat*, p. 186–187

"I believe that by getting rid of Hardee, the one most dangerous element of discord is put out of the way, and the others will be so overruled that they will be powerless, and now instead of being split into factions intent on the personal aggrandisement of particular individuals; or striving to detract from the merit of some rival chieftain, they will unite in advancing the public good & in driving our enemies away. How any one can be patriotic under the leadership of Hardee is beyond my comprehension." —Lafayette McLaws, *A Soldier's General*, p. 243

PAUL OCTAVE HEBERT   Brigadier general. West Point (1840). Commanded Department of Texas and Sub-district of North Louisiana.

"General Hebert is a good-looking creole. He was a West-Pointer, and served in the old army, but afterwards became a wealthy sugar-planter. He used to hold Magruder's position as commander-in-chief in Texas, but has now been shelved . . . He is extremely down upon England for not recognizing the South." —Arthur J. L. Fremantle, *Three Months in the Southern States*, p. 87

AMBROSE POWELL HILL   Lieutenant general. West point (1847). Brigade, division, and corps commander, Army of Northern Virginia. Killed at Petersburg.

"Hill was a very pleasant, attractive man, quite good looking and rather dandified in his dress, which was always a blue, blouse shirt of broadcloth, with very conspicuous insignia of his rank and a treble row of large gold buttons. He was a stylish horseman, always well mounted, and presented a very pleasing appearance. I don't think very much was expected of him beyond being a creditable soldier but he was next year appointed major general . . . and made for himself and his command a brilliant reputation." —John Haskell, *The Haskell Memoirs*, p. 16–17

"Hill was a West Point man of medium height, a light, good figure, and most pleasing soldierly appearance. He surely handled his division on all occasions with great ability and courage and justly earned his reputation, When Lee created the Third army Corps . . . it was thought Hill did not realize in that high position all that was hoped of him." —G. Moxley Sorrel, *Recollections of a Confederate Staff Officer*, p. 83

"As a division commander he had few equals. He was quick, bold, skillful, and tenacious when the battle had begun . . . he did his work dashingly and well. In the Second Corps he gained his chief glory and deserved the reputation he had. It cannot be said he added to it when he commanded a corps. Perhaps . . . after Jackson too much was expected of him." —Henry Kyd Douglas, *I Rode with Stonewall*, p. 147

DANIEL HARVEY HILL Lieutenant general. West Point (1842). Mexican War veteran. Brigade and division commander, Army of Northern Virginia. Corps commander, Army of Tennessee.

"Hill was a small, delicate man, rather bent, and cursed with dyspepsia, which seemed to give color to his whole being. He was . . . a capable, well read soldier, and positively about the bravest man ever seen. He seemed not to know peril and was utterly indifferent to bullets and shell, but with all these qualities, was not successful. His backbone seemed a trifle weak. He would take his men into battle, fight furiously . . . and then something weakened him . . . his attack would be apt to fail and his first efforts go unrewarded. His speech was bitter . . . he was accustomed to sneer at cavalry . . . But Hill had brains, and rose . . . He was really a good man, but of sharp prejudice and intemperate language." —G. Moxley Sorrel, *Recollections of a Confederate Staff Officer*, p. 54

"He was the hero of Bethel, Seven Pines, South Mountain, and the hardest fighter at Sharpsburg. His record was as good as that of 'Stonewall' Jackson, but, not being a Virginian, he was not so well advertised." —James Longstreet, *From Manassas to Appomattox*, p. 332

"Hill was an old army officer, trained at West Point, but teaching when the war began. He was a man of considerable capacity and always seemed to go from choice into the most dangerous place he could find on the field. He was as earnest in his Puritan beliefs as Stonewall Jackson, who was his brother-in-law, and greatly resembled Jackson in many other ways; perhaps he imitated him. He had a high and well deserved reputation as a hard fighter." —John Haskell, *The Haskell Memoirs*, p. 40

"General Hill . . . had always borne the unenviable reputation . . . of having his own way and doing things only as pleased him, and, were it otherwise, throwing obstacles in the way . . ." —Arthur Middleton Manigault, *A Carolinian Goes to War*, p. 123

"D.H. Hill is still before Washington N.C., and has alarmed the enemy . . . Did they know Hill as well as we do they would be little alarmed. He can never achieve a success, tho' he might I suppose blunder upon one, as other short witted people do." —Josiah Gorgas, *The Journals of Josiah Gorgas*, p. 62

"I fear General [D. H.] Hill is not entirely equal to his present position. An excellent executive officer, he does not appear to have much administrative ability. Left to himself, he seems embarrassed and backward to act." —Robert E. Lee, *Wartime Papers*, p. 258

"Col. Hill who had charge of the Military School at Charlotte has command here. He is an able officer of the Army and a very fine man." —William Dorsey Pender, *One of Lee's Best Men*, p. 17

THOMAS C. HINDMAN Major general.
**Mexican War veteran. Arkansas Congressman.
Division commander, Army of Tennessee.**

"Hindman was a man of genius and could have commanded a department, or have been a minister of war; but he could not command an army in the field, or plan and execute a battle." —Thomas L. Snead, *Battles and Leaders*, 3, 450

"Hindman had been a successful politician, and was in congress at the breaking out of the war. He was a forcible and attractive speaker, and, indeed, a really able man. His energy was extraordinary, and his temper as impetuous as his courage. While arbitrary and imperious in his dealings with those who opposed him, or whom he deemed his enemies, he was much admired and liked by his friends . . . he was very popular with the Arkansas troops, and his influence over them was greater . . . than that of any other officer." —Basil Duke, *Reminiscences*, p. 59

"He had the reputation of being a desperate fighter, good disciplinarian, but a scheming, maneuvering, political general, with whom it was dangerous to come in contact. Morally, he stood deservedly low in the opinions of most of the officers of the Army, but he was certainly a man of talent, and the cunningest, most slippery intriguer that I ever met with." —Arthur Middleton Manigault, *A Carolinian Goes to War*, p. 78

"While in congress, Hindman was regarded the most brilliant speaker and the most forcible reasoner of his age, locking horns with the best talent the north could send against him. . . . Hindman was after the Napoleonic stripe, both in civil and military tactics . . . and those of my readers who admire the bold dash of the French general, not always balanced by mature

judgment and unselfish feeling, will admire the character of Gen. Hindman."
—Charles Nash, *Biographical Sketches of Cleburne and Hindman*, p. 63

THEOPHILUS H. HOLMES Lieutenant general. West Point (1829). Brigade and division commander, Army of Northern Virginia. Commander, Trans-Mississippi Department.

"I, who knew him from our schoolboy days, who served with him in garrison and in the field, and with pride watched him as he gallantly led a storming party up a rocky height at Monterey, and was intimately acquainted with his whole career during our sectional war, bear willing testimony to the purity, self-abnegation, generosity, fidelity, and gallantry which characterized him as a man and a soldier." —Jefferson Davis, *Rise and Fall*, 2:144

JOHN BELL HOOD Full general. West Point (1853). Brigade and division commander, Army of Northern Virginia. Corps and army commander, Army of Tennessee.

"General Hood . . . is a tall, thin, wiry looking man, with a grave face and light colored beard, thirty three years old and is accounted one of the best and most promising officers in the army." —Arthur J. L. Fremantle, *Three Months in the Southern States*, p. 247

"I knew Hood to be a great, large hearted, large sized man, noted a great deal more for his fine social and fighting qualities than for any particular scholastic acquirements . . ." —Milo Hascall, *Personal Recollections of Stone River*, p. 2

"As a division or corps commander, there were very few men in either army who were superior to Hood; but his most intimate associates and ardent admirers in the army never regarded him as endowed with those rare mental gifts essential to the man who was to replace Gen. Joseph E. Johnston. To say that he was as brave and dashing as any officer of any age would be the merest commonplace tribute to such a man; but courage and dash are not the sole or even the prime requisites of the commander of a great army." —John B. Gordon, *Reminiscences of the Civil War*, p. 127–128

"Hood is a good fighter, very industrious on the battle field, careless off, & I have had no opportunity of judging of his action, when the whole responsibility rested upon him. I have a high opinion of his gallantry, earnestness & zeal." —Robert E. Lee, *The Wartime Papers of R. E. Lee*, p. 821–822

"John B. Hood was a jolly good fellow, a little discouraged at first by unexpected hard work; but he fought his way manfully to the end. He was not quite so talented as some of his great associates in the Confederate army, but he was a tremendous fighter when occasion offered." —John M. Schofield, *Forty-Six Years in the Army*, p. 14–15

"As a commander of a brigade, division, and corps, Hood had proved himself an aggressive, bold, determined, and careful fighter, perhaps a shade too sanguine, and disposed to assume that subordinates would carry instructions into effect as fully as he would have done if in their place . . . He was physically as active as he had been in the early years of the war; but he was an excellent horseman and could ride nearly as well as most men who have two legs and two arms . . . As an army commander his orders were judicious and well-timed in the operations around Atlanta . . ." —Gustavus W. Smith, *Battles and Leaders* 4:335

"Major General John B. Hood's appearance was very striking; in age only 34, he had a personality that would attract attention anywhere. Very tall and somewhat loose-jointed; a long, oval face shaded by a yellowish beard, plentiful hair of same color, and voice of great power and compass. With very winning manners, he is said to have used these advantages actively for his own advancement. But apart from that, his services in the field were of the best." —G. Moxley Sorrel, *Recollections of a Confederate Staff Officer*, p. 127

"Hood is a new man and a fighter and must be watched . . . as he is reckless of the lives of his men." —William T. Sherman, *Home Letters*, p. 304

"Johnston was cautious, wary, flexible, full of expedients; Hood was incautious, blunt, strong-willed, and fearless of Sherman's strategy. He was not the general to execute any plan but his own . . ." —Oliver O. Howard, *Autobiography*, 1:605

"Gen. Hood was indeed a brave man, if not a courageous one, and he couched his lance at the enemy wherever he met him, whether in the guise of a windmill or the helmet of Mambrino . . . Gen. Hood was a noble commander of a division . . . but as the commander of an army . . . he was too impulsive . . . Hood was a fighter; but he was not able by reason of his wounds to undergo the labor devolving on a commander constantly marching and fighting, often without supplies." —Samuel G. French, *Two Wars*, p. 272, 303

"Hood's exhibition of generalship whilst with the army, and up to the time of his promotion to its command, had proved him unfitted for the command of a corps, so that it is not surprising that as their leader, the army received the announcement with very bad grace, and with no little murmuring." —Arthur Middleton Manigault, *A Carolinian Goes to War*, p. 256

"He was a splendid leader in battle, and as a brigade or division commander unsurpassed; but, arrived at higher rank, he seems to have been impatient of control . . . Unwillingness to obey is often interpreted by governments into capacity to command." —Richard Taylor, *Destruction and Reconstruction*, p. 217

"When Johnston was removed . . . Hood, a *tolerable* division Commander, and a *very poor Corps* Commander, was appointed. He issued a *flaming, fighting, boastful,* braggart address . . . He fought three battles around Atlanta and was worse *whipped & easier,* and worse *outflanked* than has ever been anybody during this war, not even excepting his prototypes (the *braggarts,* Pope & Hooker)." —Thomas J. Goree, *Longstreet's Aide*, p. 140

"He is a splendid-looking, dignified man of about forty-five years, possessing a melodious and powerful voice, and has the look of a dashing officer, and is much beloved." —An English Combatant, *Battlefields of the South*, p. 341

"I . . . inquired of General [John M.] Schofield . . . about Hood, as to his general character etc., and learned that he was bold even to rashness, and courageous in the extreme; I inferred the change of commanders meant 'fight.'" —William T. Sherman, *Personal Memoirs*, 2:72

BENJAMIN HUGER

Major general. West Point (1825). Mexican War veteran. Division commander, Army of Northern Virginia. Inspector of artillery, Trans-Mississippi department.

"General Huger had been a distinguished officer in the Mexican war, where he had served on the staff of General [Winfield] Scott . . . Both he and General [John B.] Magruder made some great blunders during the seven days fight around Richmond and were relieved from their commands. General Huger never again had a command, and I think General [Edmund Kirby] Smith made a great mistake when he gave Magruder one." —William Boggs, *Military Reminiscences*, p. 61

"Major-General Benjamin Huger appears to be near sixty years of age. He is of medium height, thick-set, and stout; full face, ruddy complexion, with grey hair, heavy grey moustaches, grey eye, slow of speech and motion, evidently slow of thought, and sits his horse uneasily. Like most of our generals, his uniform is much worn, and far from imposing . . . He is brave to a fault, but that does not compensate for the want of a quick, penetrating intellect, and rapidity of movement." —An English Combatant, *Battlefields of the South*, p. 360

THOMAS J. "STONEWALL" JACKSON

Lieutenant general. West Point (1846). Mexican War veteran. Brigade, division and corps commander, Army of Northern Virginia. Mortally wounded at Chancellorsville.

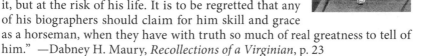

"Old Jack was very clumsy in his horsemanship and with his sword, and we were painfully anxious as we watched him leaping the bar and cutting at heads. He would do it, but at the risk of his life. It is to be regretted that any of his biographers should claim for him skill and grace as a horseman, when they have with truth so much of real greatness to tell of him." —Dabney H. Maury, *Recollections of a Virginian*, p. 23

"I sought Jackson, whom I had never met . . . I had time to see a pair of cavalry boots covering feet of gigantic size, a mangy cap with visor drawn low, a heavy dark beard, and weary eyes—eyes I afterwards saw filled with intense but never brilliant light . . . If silence be golden, he was a bonanza. He sucked lemons, ate hardtack and drank water, and praying and fighting appeared to be his idea of the 'whole duty of man.' . . . where Jackson got his lemons 'no fellow could find out,' but he was rarely without one." —Richard Taylor, *Destruction and Reconstruction*, p. 49

"He urged the officers to call upon him for information about even the minutest details of duty, often remarking that it was no discredit to a civilian to be ignorant of military matters. He was a rigid disciplinarian, and yet as gentle and kind as a woman. He was the easiest man in our army to get along with pleasantly so long as one did his duty, but as inexorable as fate in exacting the performance of it; yet he would overlook serious faults if he saw they were the result of ignorance, and would instruct the offender in a kindly way. He was as courteous to the humblest private who sought an interview for any purpose as to the highest officer in his command. He despised superciliousness and self-assertion, and nothing angered him so quickly as to see an officer wound the feelings of those under him by irony or sarcasm." —John B. Imboden, *Battles and Leaders*, 1:122

"At Malvern Hill I learned the secret of Jackson's wonderful power and success as a soldier. It was due not only to his keen and quick perception of the situation in which he found himself at each moment in the rapidly changing scenes as the battle progressed or before it began, but notably to an implicit faith in his own judgment when once made up. He would formulate that judgment, risk his last man upon its correctness, and deliver the stunning blow, while others less gifted were hesitating and debating as to its wisdom and safety." —John B. Gordon, *Reminiscences of the Civil War*, p. 72

"Jackson's genius never shone when he was under the command of another. It seemed to be shrouded or paralyzed . . . He once wrote to Richmond requesting that he might have 'fewer orders and more men.' That was the keynote to his whole character. The hooded falcon cannot strike the quarry." —D. H. Hill, *Battles and Leaders* 2:389–390

"He studied carefully . . . all his own and his adversary's movements. He knew the situation perfectly, the geography, and the topography of the country, the character of the officers opposed to him, the number and material of his troops. He never joined battle without a thorough personal reconnaissance of the field." —D. H. Hill, *Battles and Leaders*, 3:642

"He grew to suggest the scholar, not the soldier: moderate height, stooped and awkward of gait, with eyes dark and intelligent, and face framed by a black beard . . . No great rider, he brought little elegance to a brown that had degenerated to a bony nag." —Justus Scheibert, *A Prussian Observes the American Civil War*, p. 2

"Lee has immortalized himself and Jackson added new laurels to his brow— not that I like to be under Jackson, for he forgets that one ever gets tired, hunger, or sleepy . . . Our men march and fight without provisions . . . Jackson would kill up any army by the way he marches and the bad management in the subsistence Dept." —William Dorsey Pender, *One of Lee's Best Men*, p. 171, 173

"I rejoice at Stonewall Jackson's death as a gain to our cause, and yet in my soldier's heart I cannot but see him the best soldier of all this war, and grieve at his untimely end . . . Those men of the South, who now maintain its existence were once, many of them my associates; and together we deplored the political debasement and malignity that was bringing on this war. The South has put its incendiaries down already; and the North, by its distress, recognizes its meed of worth, we shall be able to overpower them; and they will find a pitying foe in their distress. Now, as it stands, unrelenting cruelty would be practiced by a triumphant North, and so (as I believe) God delays our hour of triumph till, in the humility of our hearts, we can judge our enemies as He will judge us." —Gouverneur K. Warren, *Life and Letters*, p. 112

"Jackson . . . was a typical Roundhead. He was poorly dressed . . . he looked so though his clothes were made of good material. His cap was very indifferent and pulled down over one eye, much stained by weather and without insignia. His coat was closely buttoned up to his chin and had upon the collar the stars and wreath of a general. His shoulders were stooped and one shoulder was lower than the other . . . His face . . . is not handsome or agreeable and he would be passed by anyone without a second look, though anyone could see determination and will in his face by the most casual glance . . ." —W. W. Blackford, *Letters from Lee's Army*, p. 86

"He is a curious, wonderful man. No one seems to know much of him, not even those who are with him hourly. He has no social graces but infinite earnestness. He belongs to the class from which Cromwell's regiment was made except he has no religious hypocrisy about him. He is a zealot and has stern ideas of duty." —W. W. Blackford, *Letters from Lee's Army*, p. 96

"He was a striking looking man, rather stiff and awkward in his movements, both on foot and on horseback, always rather shabby in his appearance and badly mounted, at a time when fine horses and stylish uniforms were the rule. He was always courteous, but beyond a salute he had rarely anything to say . . . He was not only a great man, but one of the sternest Puritan nature, who would come as near as any man could to doing what he thought best, absolutely, regardless of whom it helped or hurt. And he did what he thought best from a military point of view; he certainly never doubted that he was right and the man who differed was wrong." —John Haskell, *The Haskell Memoirs*, p. 20, 22

"He was not egotistical and never volunteered opinions or advice to his superior in rank. If he were ambitious he kept it to himself and never gave vent to any desire of the kind. His whole soul, mind, and strength were addressed to the discharge of duty. He received his orders without question or comment, and executed them to the letter with superb ability. Lee told him what he wished done, leaving the details and manner of doing to him, and without doubt or question it was done as speedily as possible. When he fell, well might Lee exclaim that he had lost his right arm." —William C. Oates, *The War Between the Union and the Confederacy*, p. 187

"Though the suggestion of a smile always hung about his features, it was commonly said that it never fully developed . . . Standing, he was a graceful figure, five feet ten inches in height, with brown wavy hair, full beard, and regular features. At first glance his gentle expression repelled the idea of his severe piety, the full beard concealing the lower features . . . Mounted, his figure was not so imposing as that of the bold dragoon . . . He had a habit of raising his right hand, riding or sitting, which some of his followers were wont to construe into invocation for Divine aid . . . The fact is, he received a shot in that hand at First Bull Run, which left the hand under partial paralysis and the circulation through it imperfect. To relieve the pressure and assist the circulation he sometimes raised his arm." —James Longstreet, *From Manassas to Appomattox*, p. 191–192

"General Jackson was a bold leader . . . But he mingled with his boldness great prudence and judgment. He never went so far into danger that he could not get out again . . . If he played war as poker, he knew exactly when to bluff, and against whom; consequently he was never beaten." —Henry Kyd Douglas, *I Rode with Stonewall*, p. 62

"Gen. Jackson does not say much. He is quite deaf; spends most of his time in his room, by himself, except when in the saddle; but he is very pleasant and I like him much . . . I never knew a man more guarded in his speech in reference to others. I do not remember to have ever heard him say ought in derogation of anyone, at any time." —Jedediah Hotchkiss, *Make Me a Map of the Valley*, p. 18, 20

"'Stonewall' may be a very fine old gentleman, and an honest, good-tempered, industrious man, but I should admire him much more in a state of rest than continually seeing him moving in the front. And such a dry old stick, too! As for the uniform, he has none—his wardrobe isn't worth a dollar, and his horse is quite in keeping, being a poor lean animal of little spirit or activity . . . He is about thirty-five years old, of medium height, strongly built, solemn and thoughtful, speaks but little, and always in a calm, decided tone; and from what he says there is no appeal, for he seems to know every hole and corner of this Valley . . ." —An English Combatant, *Battlefields of the South*, p. 141–142

"For myself I think that the one defect in Gen. Jackson's character as a soldier was his religious belief. He believed, with absolute faith, in a personal God, watching all human events with a jealous eye to His own lorry—ready to reward those people who made it their chief care, & to punish those who forgot about it. And he specially believed that a particular day had been set aside every week for the praise of this God, & that a personal account was strictly kept with every man as to how he kept this day & that those who disregarded it need expect no favors, but that those who sacrificed all other considerations, however recklessly, to honoring Him by its observance, would be rewarded conspicuously." —E. P. Alexander, *Fighting for the Confederacy*, p. 96–97

"He was combative; his facial characteristics . . . have been compared to those of Julius Caesar and William of Normandy. Activity, vigilance, and restlessness were marked traits of his character. His thoughts were with God and his cause . . . Above others, on either side, Jackson understood the great value of celerity in military movements, and his infantry was termed 'foot cavalry.'" —Fitzhugh Lee, *General Lee*, p. 141–42

"Jackson was truly a modest man. He would blush like a schoolgirl at a compliment. He was easily confused in the presence of strangers, especially if they were ladies. It was well known that the noisy demonstrations which the troops always made when they saw him were painfully embarrassing to him." —D. H. Hill, *Battles and Leaders*, 5:137

"Old Jackson is no fool; he knows how to keep his own counsel, and does curious things, but he has method in his madness; he has disappointed me entirely." —Richard S. Ewell, *Old Bald Head*, p. 104–105

"That vigilant, enterprising, and patriotic soldier, General T.J. Jackson, whose steadiness under fire at the first battle of Manassas had procured for him the *sobriquet* of 'Stonewall' . . . was a West Virginian; and . . . possessed a well-deserved confidence among the people of that region. Ever watchful and daring in the discharge of any duty, he was intensely anxious to guard his beloved mountains of Virginia." —Jefferson Davis, *Rise and Fall*, 1:454

"Jackson was an apparently commonplace person, and his bearing neither striking, graceful, nor impressive. He rode ungracefully, walked with an awkward stride, and wanted ease of manner. He never lost a certain shyness in company . . . His bearing thus wanted ease; but, personally, he made a most agreeable impression by his delightfully natural courtesy." —John Esten Cooke, *Wearing of the Gray*, p. 41

MICAH JENKINS
Brigadier general. South Carolina Military Academy (1854). Brigade and division commander, Army of Northern Virginia. Killed in the Wilderness.

"He was one of the most estimable characters of the army. His taste and talent were for military service. He was intelligent, quick, untiring, attentive, zealous in discharge of duty, truly faithful to official obligations, abreast with the foremost in battle, and withal, a humble, noble Christian." —James Longstreet, *From Manassas to Appomattox*, p. 566

"He was a remarkable man, full of spirit and enthusiasm, and as full of the most resolute courage. He could lead a charge as dashingly as Murat and repel one as stubbornly as Ney. We lost him . . . because he thought when he fought only where he could go do to the enemy the most harm, never of himself." —John Haskell, *The Haskell Memoirs*, p. 66

"His was the most remarkable character I have ever known. Cold and impassive of aspect, he was tenderly affectionate and full of fire. Filled with conscientious scruples, he was at times cruelly unjust." —Dabney H. Maury, *Recollections of a Virginian*, p. 72

"Being himself absolutely fearless, and having unusual mental and moral, as well as physical, courage, he goes ahead on his own hook, asking no advice and resenting interference. He places no value on human life, caring for nothing so much as fighting, unless it be praying. Illness, wounds and all disabilities he defines as inefficiency and indications of a lack of patriotism . . . He never praises his men for gallantry, because it is their duty to be gallant and they do not deserve credit for doing their duty." —George E. Pickett, *The Heart of a Soldier*, p. 62–63

"He is highly educated in military matters, and far surpasses many of those political generals who are incessantly blundering among us . . . His conduct during the whole war in Virginia has marked him as a very superior officer . . . He is comparatively young, and can do more with raw troops, or recruits, than any officer I have seen in the field, rapidly bringing them up to a high state of efficiency . . . As a disciplinarian, he has few equals . . ." —An English Combatant, *Battlefields of the South*, p. 254

EDWARD "OLD ALLEGHENY" JOHNSON
Major general. West Point (1838) Seminole War and Mexican War veteran. Brigade and division commander, Army of Northern Virginia.

"He was a strongly built man of a stern and rather bad face, and was dressed in a double-breasted blue-grey coat, high riding boots and a very bad felt hat . . . His demeanor was dignified and proper." —Theodore Lyman, *Meade's Headquarters*, p. 111

"My association with him was satisfactory in the extreme, and I say without hesitation that he was the best Division commander I ever met with, a thorough soldier and capable officer. I have but little doubt that as a corps commander he would have proved himself far superior to others that I knew . . ." —Arthur Middleton Manigault, *A Carolinian Goes to War*, p. 251

ALBERT SIDNEY JOHNSTON Full general. West Point
(1826). Veteran of Black Hawk War, Texas Independence War and Mexican War. Commander of all Confederate forces west of the Alleghenies. Killed at Shiloh.

"Born in Kentucky, descended from an honorable colonial race . . . he was peculiarly fitted to command western armies . . . His character was lofty and pure, his presence and demeanor dignified and courteous . . . and he at once inspired the respect and gained the confidence of cultivated gentlemen and rugged frontiersmen." —Richard Taylor, *Destruction and Reconstruction*, p. 232

"He was a man who would not abandon what he deemed an important trust in the face of danger . . . he was a man of high character and ability.

His contemporaries at West Point, and officers generally who came to know him ... expected him to prove the most formidable man to meet that the Confederacy would produce. Nothing occurred in his brief command of an army to prove or disprove the high estimate that had been placed upon his military ability." —Ulysses S. Grant, *Battles and Leaders*, 1:483

"It is actually believed by many intelligent people that if he had lived, the fortunes of the Confederacy might ... have had a very different issue ... His military appointments and the impression of his military ability are based solely on Mr. Jefferson Davis. Except in Texas he was substantially an unknown man and the belief in his ability and his fitness for high military office was confined mainly to Mr. Jefferson Davis. So far as can be ascertained ... this record yet remains as the only practical foundation of the strange opinion of his great capacity as a military commander." —John Pope, *Memoirs*, p. 77, 78

"There was in his nature a stalwart manliness, a moral grandeur, shaping his action in every situation, and which, totally without harsh or imperious assertion, yet dominated ... all who approached him ... His manner and bearing ... were inexpressibly majestic ... He exercised control and leadership without effort, and under all circumstances displayed the inborn faculty of command." —Basil Duke, *Reminiscences*, p. 114

"The fall of Albert Sydney [*sic*] Johnston was probably a great loss to the Confederacy. He was a man of fine presence, a very dignified and polite man. His career in the war was too short to determine his place as a commander, but ... on that first day at Shiloh, he pushed the attacks in a manner that showed him as a very dangerous enemy, and the bullet that cut short his career was a very lucky one for the Union." —David S. Stanley, *Memoirs*, p. 97

"My impression of General Johnston was that he possessed a clear head, without brilliancy. He was comprehensive in his views, with an imperturbable equanimity of manner. Fully seeing the danger surrounding him, he went at his work with calm determination and unflinching tenacity. He hoped to win if possible at the start or to maneuver for better opportunity ... I was not impressed with the profundity of his combinations. It was his good common-sense views that struck me and won respect. I know no one whose good sense I valued so much." —St. John Richardson Liddell, *Liddell's Record*, p. 40

"Like Washington and Lee, he combined those singularly attractive qualities which inspired and held the love and confidence of his soldiers, while commanding the respect and admiration of the sages of West Point. In him more than in any other man at that period were centred the hopes of the Southern people." —John B. Gordon, *Reminiscences of the Civil War*, p. 125

"Every one who knew him had a high opinion of his ability. All of the Union generals and officers of the old army looked upon him as the ablest general on either side of the Civil War . . . He was sixty years old, but a tireless worker, gave close attention to details, neglected nothing, and had an eye to everything . . . He attended to all the details and never seemed tired nor lacking in confidence . . . In manner he was dignified, polite, and kind to all . . . he did not possess any oratorical gifts, spoke slowly and thoughtfully, and endeavored to use the words adapted to convey his precise meaning. His personal appearance and general deportment were such that whoever beheld him at once recognized him as a general of superb ability . . ." —William C. Oates, *The War Between the Union and the Confederacy*, p. 297, 307–308

"The president's infatuation for Johnston (A.S.) seems to be of the blindest and most unaccountable nature . . . It is very evident that Johnston (A.S.) has been badly out-generalled." —Richard S. Ewell, *Old Bald Head*, p. 74

"In his fall the great pillar of the Southern Confederacy was crushed, and beneath its fragments the best hope of the Southwest lay buried. A highly educated and richly endowed soldier, his varied experience embraced also civil affairs, and his intimate knowledge of the country and the people of the Southwest so highly qualified him for that special command that it was not possible to fill the place made vacant by his death. Not for the first time did the fate of an army depend upon a single man, and the fortunes of a country hang, as in a balance, on the achievements of a single army." —Jefferson Davis, *Rise and Fall*, 2:67–68

JOSEPH E. JOHNSTON   Full general.
West Point (1829). Seminole and Mexican War veteran. Commander, Army of Northern Virginia, 1861–1862; Department of the West, 1863; Army of Tennessee, 1863–1864.

"In appearance General Joseph E. Johnston is rather below the middle height, spare, soldierlike, and well set up; his features are good and he has lately taken to wear a grayish beard. He is a Virginian by birth and appears to be about fifty-seven years old. He talks in a calm, deliberate and confident manner . . . but he certainly possesses the power of keeping people at a distance when he chooses, and his officers evidently stand in great awe of him. He lives very plainly . . . he has undoubtedly acquired the entire confidence of all the officers and soldiers under him . . . General Johnston is a very well-read man, and agreeable to converse with." —Arthur J. L. Fremantle, *Three Months in the Southern States*, p. 116–17, 120

"He was . . . a short, spare man, very erect and alert, with an engaging countenance and cordial, unaffected manners. He was in addition a man of large ability . . . He was genial and kindly in his manners to young officers and was popular with them . . . Somehow we had taken up the notion that he had been generally . . . in love with someone and had a wide experience in sentimental affairs running on many years . . . He was one of the most energetic men I ever saw and did whatever he had to do with all his might, but he had an apparently uncontrollable craving to serve in all arms of service and in all positions in the army, which gave him the most diversified military career of any other officer." —John Pope, *Memoirs*, p. 206–207

"Joseph E. Johnston . . . was equal to all the elements of generalship to Lee . . . No officer or soldier who ever served under me will question the generalship of Joseph E. Johnston. His retreats were timely, in good order, and he left nothing behind." —William T. Sherman, *Battles and Leaders*, 4:252, 253

"I am inclined to think that General Joe Johnston was the ablest and most accomplished man that the Confederate armies produced. He never had the opportunity accorded to many others, but he showed wonderful power as a tactician and a commander. I do not think we had his equal for handling an army and conducting a campaign. General Lee was a great leader—wise, deep and sagacious. His moral influence was something wonderful. But he lost his poise in certain occasions . . . He was a great man, a born leader, a wise general, but I think Johnston was the most accomplished and capable commander we had." —James Longstreet, *Battles and Leaders*, 5:691–692

"I was informed that . . . General Joseph E. Johnston had been ordered to the command of the army in upper Georgia. I told them that . . . if I were to judge by his campaign on the peninsula or in Mississippi, we would soon hear of him at Atlanta and if not relieved, in the everglades of Florida. General Johnston's strategy seemed to be in permitting the enemy to keep him amused at one of his strategic points while they quietly turned both flanks and compelled him to fall back to the next one." —William R. Boggs, *Military Reminiscences*, p. 74

"Johnston was critical, controversial, and sometimes irritable by nature, very exact in his statements, and possessed of a wonderful memory. Few men read so much as he, and none I have ever seen retained so accurately facts and impressions, or were so careful in the selection of the words to express their views. It is not probable that any man in our country had ever studied the histories and biographies of wars and warriors as had Johnston." —Dabney H. Maury, *Recollections of a Virginian*, p. 146

"We have many rumors afloat . . . amongst them that Johnston has given Grant a good thrashing. I am almost tempted to believe it. I would do so if it were anyone but Johnston in command on our side. He is a very able man . . . but seems to so doubt the ability of his troops to carry out the plans his skill devises that he will not test it. No victory has ever been won without bringing about a fight." —W. W. Blackford, *Letters from Lee's Army*, p. 180

"Johnston . . . was reckoned second only to Lee . . . His military experience and knowledge were large, his mind eminently systematic, his judgment sound, his courage imperturbable. He was not sanguine in temperament, and therefore was liable to lack in audacity." —Jacob Cox, *Atlanta*, p. 26–27

"General Johnston was . . . regarded by many as the coming soldier of the Confederacy. He was an ideal soldier, in the prime of a vigorous life, about 47 or 48 years old, rather undersized, but the most soldierly looking man in the army. Very erect, he was a dashing horseman, with a rather stern, but handsome face, which could light up as brilliantly and look as kindly as it seemed possible for a face to look, yet it could change as suddenly to as stern and menacing expression as any face ever could. It was a true index to his character, which was as affectionate and warmhearted, but as quick and passionate, as any I ever met; yet his passion, which was sometimes of unseemly violence, was always as quickly followed by regret and acknowledgement so hearty and full that one could never harbor resentment against as true and right-minded a gentleman as ever lived." —John Haskell, *The Haskell Memoirs*, p. 6–7

"General Johnston was skilled in the art and science of war, gifted in his quick, penetrating mind and soldierly bearing, genial and affectionate in nature, honorable and winning in person, and confiding in his love. He drew the hearts of those about him so close that his comrades felt that they could die for him." —James Longstreet, *From Manassas to Appomattox*, p. 100

"General Joseph E. Johnston . . . was full bearded, dusty, and worn from long marching; a high-bred, stern-looking soldier of faultless seat and bearing in the saddle. I had the good fortune to know him well and most happily in the coming years." —G. Moxley Sorrel, *Recollections of a Confederate Staff Officer*, p. 19

"In the full vigor of mature manhood, erect, alert, quick, and decisive of speech, General Johnston was the beau ideal of a soldier. Without the least proneness to blandishments, he gained and held the affection and confidence of his men. Brave and impetuous in action, he had been often wounded, and no officer of the general staff of the old United States army had seen so much actual service with troops." —Richard Taylor, *Destruction and Reconstruction*, p. 42

"Next to Genl. Lee, he is the greatest *chieftain* in the Confederacy; in truth, he is superior to Genl. Lee in many respects. If he has not gained great victories, it is because he never had the force at his control, nor ever been properly supported by the President who dislikes him . . . Genl. Lee was forced back with far greater rapidity from the Rapidan to Richmond, than was Genl. Johnston from Dalton to Atlanta." —Thomas J. Goree, *Longstreet's Aide*, p. 140

"Few men that I have met . . . possess the same personal, purely personal influence. To my mind, he surpasses Genl. [Robert E.] Lee as far in the power of attaching his subordinates & his troops devotedly to himself as he does in

some other qualities of a great commander—or as he unfortunately falls short of him in that pliability & imperturbability of temper which alone could mould [Jefferson] Davis to his purposes. Johnston's defect was that he could not where a matter of *right* was concerned, look upon it as other than important."
—Campbell Brown, *Campbell Brown's Civil War*, p. 49–50

"His hair is grey, and cut close; his deep-set grey eyes are full of meaning; his features calm as those of a Jesuit; his complexion is ruddy; he wears military whiskers, and no moustaches; his uniform is of a grey color with facings of light orange, and stars on the throat. In manner he is decided and unequivocating; short, sharp, and dry in conversation; decision of character is plainly seen in the close-set lips: altogether, he is a spruce, neat, compact little man."
—An English Combatant, *Battlefields of the South*, p. 305

"He would have led men into action as gallantly as any soldier. But leading men into action is one thing, and ordering an Army into battle is another . . . He is a man of courage and ability, and a fine organizer of an army for the field; but he lacks the bold genius of Lee, and, consequently, will rarely, if ever, see sufficient chances in his favor—especially at the right time—to induce him to risk battle." —John B. Hood, *Advance and Retreat*, p. 156–157

"He was an officer of great executive ability. His discernment and foresight as to the plans, purposes, and contemplated movements of his adversary were fine. He was the most cautious of any of the Confederate generals. His policy was too Fabian . . . It was not due to a deficiency of courage, for he was surely a brave man. While it may be truly said that he never won a battle, it is equally true that he never lost one. Whenever his army was in great danger he extricated it with consummate skill." —William C. Oates, *The War Between the Union and the Confederacy*, p. 459

"I think Gen. Jos. E. Johnston was more the soldier in looks, carriage & manner than any of our other generals & in fact more than any man I ever met . . . His pictures . . . give an excellent idea of his strong & intellectual face. He was of medium stature but of most extraordinary strength, vigor & quickness . . . He was a great soldier. I used to think . . . that his one fault was impatience of detail. But to study his fine campaign in front of Sherman in 1864 would seem to imply that he was specially excellent in detail." —E. P. Alexander, *Fighting for the Confederacy*, p. 48–49, 89

"He became distinguished before his beard grew. In the Indian wars in Florida and in Mexico his coolness, address, soldierly bearing, daring deeds, and his many wounds made him famous. General Scott is reported to have said 'Johnston is a great soldier, but was unfortunate enough to get shot in nearly every engagement.' . . . his decision to fight under the flag of the South was hailed with delight by the Southern people . . ." —Fitzhugh Lee, *General Lee*, p. 101

"I am inclined to think General Joe Johnston was the ablest and most accomplished man that the Confederate armies produced. He never had the opportunity accorded to many others, but he showed wonderful power as a tactician and a commander. I do not think that we had his equal for handling an army and conducting a campaign." —James Longstreet, *Battles and Leaders*, 5:691

"General Johnston will never speak on official matters to but the person interested, dislikes to have a crowd about him, never mentions military matters when away from his office. Often rides off alone, never will have more than two with him. Has not much to say even to his best friends, and does not appear to care about dress, although he always dresses neatly & in a uniform coat—if you have business with him it is yes or no, without talking more than to a proper understanding of the subject." —Lafayette McLaws, *A Soldier's General*, p. 138–139

DAVID RUMPH JONES Major general. West Point (1846). Brigade and division commander, Army of Northern Virginia. Died in winter 1862–1863.

". . . a native of South Carolina and a West Pointer. He was a pleasant gentleman and a brave soldier, but never was distinguished. He was quite an invalid, and died in the winter of '62–'63 . . . he was devoted to red tape, and to give my position the appearance of having something to do he required all brigade commanders to come to me to get orders for everything." —John Haskell, *The Haskell Memoirs*, p. 28–29

"D.R. Jones . . . was . . . a very agreeable, lovable man, tall and stately, he made a brave appearance, and well merited the sobriquet of 'Neighbor Jones,' as they pleasantly called him at West Point . . . he could not figure with much success, his health being poor, and after Sharpsburg, was transferred to some easier service elsewhere, and soon after died." —G. Moxley Sorrel, *Recollections of a Confederate Staff Officer*, p. 50

JOSEPH B. KERSHAW Major general. Lawyer and Mexican War veteran. Brigade and division commander, Army of Northern Virginia.

"Major General Joseph B. Kershaw, a lawyer from South Carolina, was one of the most distinguished and efficient officers of the Virginia army . . . his steady courage and military aptitude invariably showing handsomely in the arduous service of his regiment . . . General Kershaw was of most attractive appearance, soldierly and handsome, of medium size, well set up, light hair and moustache, with clean-cut, high-bred, features." —G. Moxley Sorrel, *Recollections of a Confederate Staff Officer*, p. 228

ALEXANDER R. LAWTON Brigadier general. West Point (1839). Quartermaster general for the Confederate States Army.

"He had graduated from West Point in the class of '39 and entered the artillery . . . An admirable, well-rounded character, with many friends, Lawton was a leading man in municipal and State affairs for years. When the clash came in 1861 there was no doubt as to where he would stand ... he was immediately commissioned a brigadier general ... Lawton's abilities suggested him for administrative work, and he was made Quartermaster General." —G. Moxley Sorrel, *Recollections of a Confederate Staff Officers*, p. 181

ROBERT E. LEE Full general. West Point
(1829). Mexican War veteran. Commander, Army of Northern Virginia, 1862–1865.

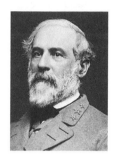

"I prefer Lee to [Joseph E.] Johnston—the former is too cautious and weak under grave responsibility—personally brave and energetic to a fault, he yet is wanting in moral firmness when pressed by heavy responsibility and is likely to be timid and irresolute in action." —George B. McClellan, *Civil War Papers*, p. 244–245

"His services on our coast defenses were known as able, and those who knew him in Mexico as one of the principal engineers ... knew that as a military engineer he was especially distinguished; but officers of the line are not apt to look to the staff in choosing leaders of soldiers, either in tactics or strategy. There were, therefore, some misgivings as to the power and skill for field service of the new commander." —James Longstreet, *From Manassas to Appomattox*, p. 112

"There can be no doubt that Lee is a man of very high character (which you may reconcile as you may with his abandonment of the flag). He carries on war in a merciful and civilized way, his correspondence is dignified and courteous, and his despatches are commonly (not always) frank and not exaggerated." —Theodore Lyman, *Meade's Headquarters*, p. 125

"Lee was elegantly dressed in full uniform, sword and sash, spotless boots, beautiful spurs and by far the most magnificent man I ever saw." —W. W. Blackford, *Letters from Lee's Army*, p. 86

"To my mind, General Lee was the only commander on either side who came near to getting all out of his resources that could be done without exhausting them and leaving nothing for the next step ... He alone would risk all when necessary, strike quick and run great dangers when he thought the end justified the risk, but he always kept a clear view of the next step or the next campaign." —John Haskell, *The Haskell Memoirs*, p. 24

"He had an apparent antipathy to anything partaking of pomposity and the vanity of war, but he had an utterly undue regard for the value of the elementary teaching of West Point and for the experience gained by the very small police duty of our miniature regular army. He failed to realize that while a military school is excellent for the training of drill masters ... it teaches little of military science in comparison with the hard experience of a single campaign." —John Haskell, *The Haskell Memoirs*, p. 55

"General Lee ... was the most aggressive man in his army. No one ever went to General Lee and suggested an aggressive movement who was not listened to attentively, and if convinced that there was a remote chance of striking the enemy a blow, was not permitted to make the attempt." —Henry Heth, *Memoirs*, p. 214–215

"General Lee was an unusually handsome man, even in his advanced life. He seemed fresh from West Point, so trim was his figure and so elastic his step. Out of battle he was as gentle as a woman, but when the clash of arms came he loved fight, and urged his battle with wonderful determination. As a usual thing he was remarkably well-balanced—always so, except on one or two occasions of severe trial when he failed to maintain his exact equipoise. Lee's orders were always well considered and well chosen. He depended almost too much on his officers for their execution." —James Longstreet, *Battles and Leaders*, 2:405

"When he took us in hand his full gray beard was growing, cropped close, and always well tended. An unusually handsome man ... the perfect poise of head and shoulders and limbs, the strength that lay hidden and the activity that his fifty-five years could not repress. Withal graceful and easy, he was approachable by all; gave attention to all in the simplest manner ... His eyes— sad eyes!—beaming the highest intelligence and with unvarying kindliness, yet with command so firmly set that all knew him for the unquestioned chief. He loved horses and had good ones ... The General was always well dressed ... the simplest emblems of his rank appearing ... he rarely wore his sword, but his binoculars were always in his hand ..." —G. Moxley Sorrel, *Recollections of a Confederate Staff Officer*, p. 67–68

"Lee was an aggressive general, a fighter. To succeed, he knew battles were to be won, and battles cost blood, and blood he did not mind in his general's work. Although always considerate and sparing of his soldiers, he would pour out their blood when necessary or when strategically advisable." —G. Moxley Sorrel, *Recollections of a Confederate Staff Officer*, p. 73–74

"Our estimate of General Lee was that he exemplified remarkable ability as a commander. In military sagacity and astuteness we recognized his superiority. In singleness of purpose, and patient persistence ... he was remarkable. In his constant care for his men, and especially in conduct after disaster he won our respect and in some ways our sympathy. We regarded him as a master in military economy, making best use with least waste of material. And in defensive operations we looked upon him as a skillful tactician, taking best advantage of a situation." —Joshua Lawrence Chamberlain, *Passing of the Armies*, p. 382

"In stature General Lee stood five feet ten inches, was of well-developed muscular figure, as trim as a youth, and weighed one hundred and seventy pounds. In features he was a model of manly beauty. His teeth were of ivory whiteness; his mouth handsome and expressive of frankness, kindness, and generosity. His nose and chin were full, regular, strong, and gave his face force and character ... As a commander he was much of the Wellington

'Up-and-at-'em' style. He found it hard, the enemy in sight, to withhold his blows." —James Longstreet, *From Manassas to Appomattox*, p. 287–288

"General Lee is . . . the handsomest man of his age I ever saw. He is fifty-six years old, tall, broad-shouldered, very well made, well set up—a thorough soldier in appearance; and his manners are most courteous and full of dignity. He is a perfect gentleman in every respect . . . he has none of the small vices, such as smoking, drinking, chewing, or swearing, and his bitterest enemy never accused him of the greater ones. He generally wears a well-worn long grey jacket, a high black felt hat, and blue trousers tucked into his Wellington boots. I never saw him carry arms; and the only mark of his military rank are the three stars on his collar . . . he himself is very neat in his dress and person . . ." —Arthur J. L. Fremantle, *Three Months in the Southern States*, p. 253–254

"Lee was not conscious of his strength, because his greatness of soul was derived from his goodness of heart, and it rested upon him with the ease and grace of a garment. His generosity induced him to overlook the frailty incident to humanity, and to forgive even disobedience in his lieutenants . . . he envied no one . . ." —Samuel G. French, *Two Wars*, p. 176

"Gen. Lee and I knew each other well in the days before the war. We had served together in Mexico and commanded against each other on the Peninsula. I had the highest regard for his ability as a commander, and knew that he was not a general to be trifled with or carelessly afforded an opportunity of striking a fatal blow." —George B. McClellan, *McClellan's Own Story*, p. 553–554

"Lee is, all agree, a stately-looking man; tall; erect and strongly built, with a full chest. His hair and closely trimmed beard, though thick, are now nearly white. He has a large and well-shaped head, with a brown, clear eye, of unusual depth. His face is sunburnt and rather florid. In manner he is exceedingly grave and dignified—this, I believe he always has . . . from his speech I judge he was inclined to wander in his thoughts. You would not have recognized a Confederate officer from his dress, which was a military blue overcoat, a high gray hat, and well-brushed riding boots." —Theodore Lyman, *Meade's Headquarters*, p. 360–361

"Of all the men I have seen, he was best entitled to the epithet of distinguished; and so marked was his appearance in this particular, that he would not have passed unnoticed through the streets of any capital. Reserved almost to coldness, his calm dignity repelled familiarity; not that he seemed without sympathies, but: that he had so conquered his own weaknesses as to prevent the confession of others before him . . . Indeed his character seemed perfect . . . His soldiers reverenced him and had unbounded confidence in him . . . Tender and protecting love he did not inspire: such love is given to weakness, not to strength." —Richard Taylor, *Destruction and Reconstruction*, p. 96

"General Lee was perhaps the most unassuming of great commanders. Responsibilities that clearly belonged to him as a soldier he met promptly and to the fullest extent; but he was the last man holding a commission in the Confederate army to assume authority about which there could be any

General Lee seated between his son, G. W. C. (Custis) Lee, left, and Lt. Colonel Walter H. Taylor, right. Photographed by Mathew Brady in the basement below the back porch of Lee's Franklin Street home in Richmond, Virginia, April 16, 1865.

question . . . Nothing could tempt him to cross the line separating his powers from those of the civil authorities. That line might be dim to others, but it was clear to him." —John B. Gordon, *Reminiscences of the Civil War*, p. 132

"If there is one man in either army, Federal or Confederate, who is, head & shoulders, far above every other one in either army in audacity that man is Gen. Lee, and you will soon have lived to see it. Lee is audacity personified. His name is audacity, and you need not be afraid of not seeing all of it you will want to see." —Joseph C. Ives, quoted by E. P. Alexander, *Fighting for the Confederacy*, p. 91

"General Lee was a great leader—wise, deep, and sagacious. His moral influence was something wonderful. But he lost his poise in certain occasions. No one who is acquainted with the facts can believe that he would have fought the battle of Gettysburg had he not been under great excitement . . . His great soul rose masterful within him when a crisis or disaster threatened. This tended to disturb his admirable equipoise . . . He was a great man, a born leader, a wise general . . ." —James Longstreet, *Battles and Leaders*, 5:691–692

"Speaking of Lee, he [Joseph Hooker] expressed himself slightingly of Lee's abilities. He says he was never much respected in the Army. In Mexico he was surpassed by all his Lieutenants. In the cavalry he was held in no esteem. He was regarded very highly by Gen. Scott. He was a courtier and readily recommended himself by his insinuating manner to the General whose petulant and arrogant temper has driven of late all officers of spirit and self esteem away from him . . . The strength of the rebel Army rests on the broad shoulders of Longstreet. He is the brain of Lee as Stonewall Jackson was his right arm. Before every battle he has been advised with. After every battle Lee may be found in *his* tent. He is a weak man and little of a soldier. He naturally rests on Longstreet who is a soldier, born." —Joseph Hooker, quoted by John Hay, *Inside Lincoln's White House*, p. 83

"The movement of General Lee against McClellan was a strategic enterprise of the most brilliant character, and at once demonstrated that he was a general of the highest order of genius." —Jubal A. Early, *Narrative of the War Between the States*, p. 90

"Robert E. Lee, gentleman, scholar, gallant soldier, great general, and true Christian . . . was of the highest type of manly beauty, yet seemingly unconscious of it, and so respectful and unassuming as to make him a general favorite before his great powers had an opportunity for manifestation. His mind led him to analytic rather than perceptive methods for obtaining results." —Jefferson Davis, *Battles and Leaders*, 6:91

"General Lee is rapidly regaining . . . the confidence of the army and the people as a skillful and even a dashing officer. The criterion in military matters is success and up to this hour the combinations of General Lee have been of the most marked, decided, and successful." —Lafayette McLaws, *A Soldier's General*, p. 148

"What we want is a military man capable of directing operations in the field everywhere. I think Lee is such a man. But can he, a modest man and a Christian, aspire to such a position?" —John B. Jones, *A Rebel War Clerk's Diary*, 1:107

"General Lee was not a man of hesitation, and they have mistaken his character who suppose caution was his vice. He was prone to attack, and not slow to press an advantage when he gained it." —Jefferson Davis, *Rise and Fall*, 2:152

"When we remember that if General Lee had taken sides against his own people and State, he could have been Commander-in-Chief of the armies of the United States, and that he had to abandon his great landed estate and palatial residence fronting Washington City . . . we can understand the unparalleled sacrifice this heroic general made in supporting and defending the cause of right. I can but feel that God made him one of the bravest, best, and most patriotic, as well as one of the greatest of men." —John H. Reagan, *Memoirs*, p. 194

"Lee was tall, large in form, fine in person, handsome in feature, grave and dignified in bearing; if anything, a little too formal. There was a suggestion of effort in his deportment; something that showed he was determined to die gracefully; a hint of Caesar muffling himself into his mantle." —Adam Badeau, *Military History of Ulysses S. Grant*, 3:604

"He wore blue military pants without suspenders and a short linen sack with no vest, a soft felt hat, and buff gauntlets. He had no insignia of rank about him, and carried neither sword, pistol or field glass . . . This was his usual style. He always was mounted on the same horse, and as he passed along his lines or through his army . . . he looked more like some planter . . . than like the conventional military chieftain." —Johnson Hagood, *Memoirs of the War of Secession*, p. 304

STEPHEN D. LEE Lieutenant general. West Point (1854). Artillery commander, Army of Mississippi; cavalry commander, Army of Mississippi; corps commander, Army of Tennessee.

"Lee is the pink of honor, in morals above the ordinary standard at least, in sobriety unquestionable, and in goodness of heart unequaled." —William Dorsey Pender, *One of Lee's Best Men*, p. 132

"He was a cadet lieutenant of my company when I was a plebe, was a splendid, handsome six footer, was always universally popular every where, was a natural-born soldier, & was one of the few young men who afterward deservedly rose by hard fighting to the rank of lieut. gen." —E. P. Alexander, *Fighting for the Confederacy*, p. 159

WILLIAM HENRY FITZHUGH "ROONEY" LEE Major general. Harvard graduate. Brigade commander of cavalry, Army of Northern Virginia.

"Lee is near my own age, a heavy set, but well-proportioned man, somewhat inclined to boast, not overly profound, and thoroughly impregnated with the idea that he is a Virginian and a Lee withal." —John Beatty, *The Citizen Soldier*, p. 470

THOMAS MULDRUP LOGAN Brigadier general. Graduate, South Carolina College. Brigade commander of cavalry, 1865.

"Logan was slight, slender, blue eyed, youthful looking & with such delicate features, that his college nickname, like 'the gallant Pelham's,' had been a girl's. Pelham's was Sally Pelham. Logan's was Molly Logan." —E. P. Alexander, *Fighting for the Confederacy*, p. 315

JAMES "OLD PETE" LONGSTREET
Lieutenant general. West Point (1842). Mexican War veteran. Brigade, division and corps commander, Army of Northern Virginia.

"General Longstreet is an Alabamian—a thickset, determined looking man, forty-three years of age. He was an infantry major in the old army and now commands the first corps de armee: he is never far from General Lee, who relies very much on his judgment. By the soldiers he is invariably spoken of as 'the best fighter in the whole army.'" —Arthur J. L. Fremantle, *Three Months in the Southern States*, p. 242

"He is about five feet eleven inches in height, and weighs about 200 pounds, has light hair . . . with blue eyes; has a florid complexion, and a very amiable, soft expression of countenance. He wears a large, heavy set of whiskers and moustache, which hides the lower part of his face. When on foot, and in citizens dress, he has a rather sluggish appearance, but he is exceedingly punctual and industrious. Whatever he has to do, he does well and quickly . . . The ladies all say he is the handsomest. He is always agreeable with the ladies." —Thomas J. Goree, *Longstreet's Aide*, p. 60

"He was brave, honest, intelligent, a very capable soldier, subordinate to his superiors, just and kind to his subordinates, but jealous of his own rights, which he had the courage to maintain. He was never on the lookout to detect a slight, but saw one as soon as anybody when intentionally given." —Ulysses S. Grant, *Personal Memoirs*, 2:87

"General Longstreet is one of the kindest, best hearted men I ever knew. Those not well acquainted with him think him short and crabbed, and he does appear so except in three places: 1st, when in the presence of ladies, 2nd, at the table, and 3rd, on the field of battle. At any of those places he has a complacent smile on his countenance, and seems to be one of the happiest men in the world." —Thomas J. Goree, *Longstreet's Aide*, p. 39

"He was one of the sturdiest fighters in the Southern Army, with, however, but little of that dash and energy which characterized the operations of 'Stonewall' Jackson . . . George H. Thomas and Longstreet were usually looked upon as slow and so they were—exceedingly slow at leaving any place where it was a matter of importance for them to remain. 'Stonewall' Jackson was a remarkable exception to the general rule. He had all the dash of the intrepid nervous leader combined with the sturdy, solid characteristics of the wheel horse." —John Gibbon, *Personal Recollections of the Civil War*, 292–293

"The reputation that Longstreet had as a fighting man was unquestionably deserved, and when in action, there was no lack of energy or of quickness of perception, but he was somewhat sluggish by nature, and I saw nothing in him to make me believe that his capacity went beyond the power to conduct a square hard fight. The power of combination, he did not possess, and whenever he had an independent command, he was unsuccessful . . ." —Francis W. Dawson, *Reminiscences of Confederate Service*, p. 129–130

"General Longstreet was a hard fighter and handled his troops with skill after he got into battle, but his tardiness of movement and want of energy became notorious in the latter years of the war . . ." —William C. Oates, *The War Between the Union and the Confederacy*, p. 289

"He is a very fine officer, and is as brave as Julius Caesar. His forte though as an officer consists, I think, in the seeming ease with which he can handle and arrange large numbers of troops, as also with the confidence and enthusiasm with which he seems to inspire them . . . In an action, if he is ever excited, he has a way of concealing it, and always appears as if he has the utmost confidence in his own ability to command and in that of his troops to execute. In a fight he is a man of but very few words, and keeps at all time his own counsels . . . He is very reserved and distant towards his men, and very strict, but they all like him." —Thomas J. Goree, *Longstreet's Aide*, p. 60

"Longstreet is a powerfully-built man, somewhat bald, about five feet ten inches high, with sandy hair and whiskers—the latter allowed to grow untrimmed. He possesses a fine bluish-gray eye, of great depth, penetration, and calculation; seldom speaks unnecessarily, seems absorbed in thought, and very quiet in manner." —An English Combatant, *Battlefields of the South*, p. 59

"General Longstreet . . . stands high as a very gallant soldier, he commands the centre—General [D. H.] Hill who commands Yorktown is a very determined officer, and stands high as a gentleman of pure character and great honesty of purpose." —Lafayette McLaws, *A Soldier's General*, p. 139

"I consider him a humbug—a man of small capacity, very obstinate, not at all chivalrous, exceedingly conceited, and totally selfish. If I can it is my intention to get away from his command." —Lafayette McLaws, *A Soldier's General*, p. 197

MANSFIELD LOVELL Major general. West Point (1842).
Mexican War veteran. Commander of New Orleans; corps commander Army of the West.

"I hope Genl. Lovell will not think that I would derogate from him when I say that my self-esteem was considerably elated, by finding that I was nearly as smart as he was. General Albert Sidney Johnston and General Polk were the only Major Generals I had seen up to this time, and I felt that I was rather small fry when I was with them, but Genl. Lovell was not much older than myself and as I said before not much smarter, and I began to think that I too, might wear three buttons, instead of pairs some day." —M. Jeff Thompson, *Civil War Reminiscences*, p. 134

"His military career, so far as it had any importance, ended with the catastrophe at New Orleans . . . He was full of self-conceit and self-appreciation and carried his admiration of himself almost to imbecility only reached by . . . General George B. McClellan. Farther than this man could not go . . . Lovell was a fine-looking man, fair in complexion and of graceful carriage. He was a generous man, too . . . He had the ability and the acquirement to have been a successful soldier, but I do not think he had the suavity of manner nor the kindly sympathy and forbearance necessary to enlist the willing service of troops, especially volunteer troops." —John Pope, *Memoirs*, p. 83–84

WILLIAM W. MACKALL Brigadier general. West Point
(1837). Seminole and Mexican War veteran. Department commander and chief of staff to Braxton Bragg.

"He was an army man out of West Point, and an able, accomplished soldier. He should have achieved much in the Confederate war, but circumstances were against him . . . He was of a high order of mind and of the finest and nicest elevation of character; there was something supercritical, however, that would stand in his way without reason." —G. Moxley Sorrel, *Recollections of a Confederate Staff Officer*, p. 71–72

JOHN B. "PRINCE JOHN" MAGRUDER Major
general. West Point (1830). Mexican War veteran. Commander Army of the Peninsula; District of Texas.

"General Magruder is a fine soldierlike man, of about fifty-five, with broad shoulders, a florid complexion and bright eyes. He wears his whiskers and mustaches in the English fashion and he was dressed in the Confederate grey uniform . . . He is a Virginian, a great talker . . . Magruder was an artilleryman, and has been a good deal in Europe . . ." —Arthur J. L. Fremantle, *Three Months in the Southern States*, p. 30–31

"He was a man remarkable for his humor and brilliant conversation . . . Prince John, as he was sometimes called was not at all scrupulous in his dealings with his tailors and tradesmen but laid them all under contribution without money. His humor consisted rather in exaggerated statements of his own position influence in the army etc, than in any play on words. Every thing he said and did in his own peculiar line occasioned great laughter." —Abner Doubleday, *My Life in the Old Army*, p. 232–233

"Major General Magruder is about forty years of age, thick-set, voluptuous in appearance, very dressy and dandified, 'showy' in his style and bearing, and nearly always mounted . . . He looks like a man too much given to dissipation, and is incapable of planning a battle, although very vigorous in fighting one." —An English Combatant, *Battlefields of the South*, p. 117

"He was known in the old Army as 'Prince John,' from the splendor of his appearance and his dress. Of commanding form and loving display, he had assembled a numerous staff, all, like himself, in the most showy uniforms. To these he added a fine troop of cavalry, and when the cavalcade at a full gallop inspected the thin lines of the Warwick, it was a sight for men and gods." —G. Moxley Sorrel, *Recollections of a Confederate Staff Officer*, p. 57

"General Magruder was a man of singular versatility. Of a boiling, headlong courage, he was too excitable for high command. Widely known for social attractions, he had a histrionic vein, and indeed was fond of private theatricals. Few managers could have surpassed him in imposing on an audience a score of supernumeraries for a grand army." —Richard Taylor, *Destruction and Reconstruction*, p. 93

"No one ever lived who could play off the Grand Seignior with a more lordly air than 'Prince John,' as Magruder was called. During the absence of Lee he kept up such a clatter that each of McClellan's corps commanders was expecting a special visit from the much-plumed cap and the once-gaudy attire of the master of ruses and strategy. He put on naturally all those grand and imposing devices which deceive the military opponent." —D. H. Hill, *Battles and Leaders*, 2:362

"General Magruder favors us with stampedes very generally—but we have become so much accustomed to his cry of wolf that it will be very difficult to arouse us from our apathy, even when the enemy does come— I have more to fear from that than from anything else . . . General Magruder is fond of dress parade and of company. Conceals nothing, and delights to have a crowd about him, to whom he converses freely upon any and all subjects. He never moves from his head quarters without having five or six aides & a dozen or more orderlies . . . General Magruder can talk twenty four hours incessantly." —Lafayette McLaws, *A Soldier's General*, p. 125, 138, 139

"General Magruder . . . was perhaps the most picturesque general officer of the Confederacy. Fond of display, punctilious in ceremonial, apt in the ruses of war, belligerent by temperament, he was withal a competent commander and an engineer of skill." —D. H. Hill, *Bethel to Sharpsburg*, 2:4

WILLIAM B. MAHONE: Major general. Graduate of Virginia Military Institute. Brigade and division commander, Army of Northern Virginia.

"Major General William B. Mahone was a Virginian, about forty years of age. His appearance arrested attention. Very small both in height and frame, he seemed a mere atom with little flesh . . . Sallow of feature, sharp of eye, and very active in movement was the General; in dress quite unconventional, he affected jackets rather than coats . . . A plaited brown linen jacket, buttoned to trousers, of same material . . . topped off by a large Panama straw hat of the finest and most beautiful texture, met our eyes, and I must say he looked decidedly comfortable . . . He was undoubtedly a general of very uncommon ability." —G. Moxley Sorrel, *Recollections of a Confederate Staff Officer*, p. 264–265

"I was led . . . to an officer mounted on a sorrel horse and wearing stars on the collar of his badly fitting coat. He was a cadaverous, dyspeptic-looking man, with nerves all over him and an eye as cold as a glacier. This, I was told, was 'Billy' Mahone." —Abner R. Small, *The Road to Richmond*, p. 156

HUMPHREY MARSHALL Brigadier general. West Point (1832). Mexican War veteran and Congressman. Brigade commander, Army of Tennessee.

"Intellectually he was a superior . . . a man of unusual ability. He was a ripe and astute lawyer and a politician of broad views and extensive information . . . A graduate of West Point, he was no doubt in his early life a good soldier . . . As brigadier general in the Confederate army he attained no special distinction, nor was he very actively employed. This was perhaps due . . . to physical incapacity. He was enormously corpulent . . . he ate frequent and prodigious meals . . . he would fall asleep while in the midst of a conversation, and sometimes while on his feet." —Basil W. Duke, *Reminiscences*, p. 143

"General Marshall personally was not adapted to mountain warfare, owing to his great size; nor was he qualified to command volunteers, being the most democratic of men. Moreover, his heart was tender as a woman's. For these reasons he could not enforce the rigorous discipline of an army. So well known was his leniency, that an officer of his staff made a standing offer to eat the first man the general should shoot for any crime." —Edward O. Guerrant, *Battles and Leaders*, 1:397

"He was an able and distinguished man and determined in his devotion to the Confederacy. He wished to do his full duty, but he appeared to feel that he could render more efficient service with a separate command than if trammeled by subordination to a superior commander; and his aversion to having any intervening power between himself and the President was apparent." —Joseph Wheeler, *Battles and Leaders*, 3:21

DABNEY H. MAURY Major general. West Point (1846). Mexican War veteran. Division commander, Army of Tennessee; commander Department of the Gulf, 1864.

"He is a very gentlemanlike and intelligent but diminutive Virginian . . . he was very civil . . . the family seems to be a very military one. His brother is captain of the Confederate steamer *Georgia*." —Arthur J. L. Fremantle, *Three Months in the Southern States*, p. 130–131

BENJAMIN McCULLOCH Brigadier general. Veteran of Texas War for Independence, and the Mexican War. Mortally wounded at Pea Ridge.

"McCulloch was a 'rough and ready' man, not at all speculative, but very practical, to the point, and rich in resources to reach it . . . He was a good fighter, energetic in battle, and quick in discerning danger or espying the weak point of his antagonist; an excellent organizer, disciplinarian, and administrator, indefatigable in recruiting and equipping troops. His care for them was proverbial, and his ability in laying out encampments was extraordinary . . ." —Franz Sigel, *Battles and Leaders*, 1:318

"He was a most kindly and gentle man, with a low, soft voice and very quiet, pleasing manners. Like all real frontiersmen, mountainmen and trappers, as well as scouts, he was a silent, uncommunicative man, who listened much but talked little. If he came to know you well and happened to like you, he would unbend to you and then become a very interesting companion . . . He was a fine specimen of the frontier scout and ranger . . . and belonged to a class which is produced no more." —John Pope, *Memoirs*, p. 196–197

JAMES McQUEEN McINTOSH Brigadier general. West Point (1849). Mexican War veteran. Killed at Pea Ridge.

"General McIntosh had been of the regular army . . . when McCulloch fell, McIntosh immediately took command of the division . . . He was greatly loved and admired for his dash and other soldierly qualities by those who were under his immediate command, and promised to make a mark had he lived." —H. G. Bunn, in Nash, *Biographical Sketches of Cleburne and Hindman*, p. 143–144

LAFAYETTE McLAWS Major general. West Point (1842). Mexican War veteran. Brigade and division commander, Army of Northern Virginia.

"He was an officer of much experience and most careful. Fond of detail, his command was in excellent condition, and his ground and position well examined and reconnoitered; not brilliant in the field or quick in movement . . . he could always be counted on and had secured the entire confidence of his officers and men." —G. Moxley Sorrel, *Recollections of a Confederate Staff Officer*, p. 127

JOHN HUNT MORGAN Brigadier general. Mexican War veteran. Businessman. Killed at Greeneville, Tennessee.

"He had the instinct of destructiveness, but was no general. A gambler by profession, he gambled on men's lives, and lost his own in a very rash venture.

He did more harm than good to the Confederate cause ... Morgan was the great raider of the war. He destroyed much property and disturbed railway service on many occasions, but he did the Confederacy much more harm than good, as his men were wholly undisciplined—were all thieves—and inflicted as much damage on their friends as on their enemies ... Even Morgan himself encouraged plundering." —David S. Stanley, *Memoirs*, 122, 221–222

"Morgan's reputation as a soldier was a peculiar one. He had made a number of raids which showed a good deal of boldness in the general plan and a good deal of activity in the execution, but it cannot be said that he showed any liking for hard fighting. Like boys skating near thin ice, he seemed to be trying to show how close he could come to danger without getting in. A really bold front showed by a small body of brave men was usually enough to turn him aside ... Morgan achieved notoriety by the showy temerity of his distant movements, but nobody was afraid of him in the field at close quarters." —Jacob Cox, *Reminiscences*, 1:495

"Morgan was beyond all men adapted to independent command ... His energy never flagged, and his invention was always equal to the emergency. Boldness and caution were united in all that he undertook. He had a most remarkable aptitude for promptly acquiring a knowledge of any country in which he was operating ... he was enabled easily to extricate himself from difficulties. The celerity with which he marched, the promptness with which he attacked or eluded a foe, intensified the confidence of his followers, and kept his antagonists always in doubt and apprehension." —Basil W. Duke, *Battles and Leaders*, 6:315–316

JEAN JACQUES ALFRED ALEXANDER MOUTON
Brigadier general. West Point (1850). Brigade commander, Army of Tennessee, and Taylor's Department. Killed at Mansfield.

"Major General Mouton ... was a noble looking man, of fine, dignified appearance. He was a courteous, refined gentleman, and a brave officer." —J. P. Blessington, *Walker's Texas Division*, p. 184

JOHN C. PEMBERTON Lieutenant
general. West Point (1837) Mexican War veteran. Commanded Department of Mississippi and Eastern Louisiana.

"General Pemberton showed a great deal of ability in his defense of Vicksburg ... and won the respect of his opponents by his zeal and fidelity to his cause, to say nothing of his spirit of endurance." —David Dixon Porter, *Naval History of the Civil War*, p. 301

"General Pemberton . . . was a soldier *per se*, and would have taken his inspiration from 'orders' from Richmond and not from the people and civil authorities by whom he was surrounded. These he had not the tact to conciliate and use, and, for their military opinions, entertained and sometimes exhibited a most professional contempt . . . General Pemberton made few friends in Charleston, from his unfortunate want of tact and brusquerie of manner. He was not to the taste of people at that time particularly disposed to be critical of military men . . ." —Johnson Hagood, *Memoirs of the War of Secession*, p. 70, 100

WILLIAM DORSEY PENDER Major general. West Point (1854). Brigade and division commander, Army of Northern Virginia. Mortally wounded at Gettysburg.

"Pender is an excellent officer, attentive, industrious, & brave. He has been conspicuous in every battle, & I believe wounded in all of them." —Robert E. Lee, *The Wartime Papers of R. E. Lee*, p. 489

WILLIAM NELSON PENDLETON Brigadier general. West Point (1830). Chief of Artillery, Army of Northern Virginia.

"It does seem preposterous and absurd to me . . . the idea of such an old granny as Pendleton presuming to give a lecture or knowing anything about the battle of Gettysburg—Although nominally Chief of Artillery, yet he was in the actual capacity of Ordnance Officer, and, as I believe, miles in the rear. I know that I did not see him on the field during the battle. It was a notorious fact . . . that he was almost entirely ignored by Genl. Lee . . . " —Thomas Goree, *Longstreet's Aide*, p. 159

"As much as I esteem & admire Genl [William N.] Pendleton, I would not select him to command a corps in this army. I do not mean to say by that he is not competent, but from what I have seen of him, I do not know that he is. I can spare him . . ." —Robert E. Lee, *The Wartime Papers of R. E. Lee*, p. 783

JAMES JOHNSTON PETTIGREW Brigadier general. Professor at Naval Observatory in Washington. Brigade and division commander, Army of Northern Virginia. Killed at Falling Waters.

"He was a North Carolinian . . . His reputation for genius went back to his college days . . . Pettigrew had studied military science very earnestly, and spent some time in Europe trying to see active service . . . He was a singularly charming man, whose men were devoted to him and felt the most implicit confidence in him. I had never previously met him, but soon fell under the influence of his charm and was devoted to him ever after . . . Pettigrew seemed to have every attribute of a great soldier, uniting with the brightest mind and an active body a disposition which made him the idol of his men and a courage which nothing could daunt. He was so full of theoretical knowledge that I think it really impaired his usefulness . . . but experience . . . would have corrected that . . ." —John Haskell, *The Haskell Memoirs*, p. 40–41, 52

GEORGE E. PICKETT Major

general. West Point (1846). Mexican War veteran. Brigade and division commander, Army of Northern Virginia.

"A singular figure indeed! A medium sized, well-built man, straight, erect, and in well-fitting uniform, an elegant riding whip in hand, his appearance was distinguished and striking. But the head, the hair were extraordinary. Long ringlets flowed loosely over his shoulders, trimmed and highly perfumed; his beard likewise was curling and giving out the scents of Araby . . . Pickett became very friendly, was a good fellow, a good brigadier." —G. Moxley Sorrel, *Recollections of a Confederate Staff Officer*, p. 48

"I first met him as a cadet at West Point . . . He served with distinguished valor in Mexico . . . In memory I can see him, of medium height, of graceful build, dark, glossy hair, worn almost to his shoulders in curly waves, of wondrous pulchritude and magnetic presence . . . He was devoted to his martial profession . . . He was of an open, frank, and genial temperament, but he felt very keenly the distressing calamities entailed upon the beloved sunny South . . ." —James Longstreet, *The Heart of a Soldier*, p. 27–28

"Perhaps there is no doubt that he was the best infantry soldier developed on either side during the Civil War . . . He was of the purest type of the perfect soldier, possessing manly beauty in the highest degree; a mind large and capable of taking in the bearings of events under all circumstances; of that firm and dauntless texture of soul that no danger or shock of conflict could appall or confuse; full of that rare magnetism which could infuse itself into masses of men . . . ; his perception clear; his courage of that rare proof which rose to the occasion; his genius for war so marked that his companions all knew his mind worked clearer under fire . . . than even at mess-table . . ." —George B. McClellan, *The Heart of a Soldier*, p. 28

"General Pickett . . . wears his hair in long ringlets, and is altogether rather a desperate-looking character." —Arthur J. L. Fremantle, *Three Months in the Southern States*, p. 253

GIDEON J. PILLOW Brigadier general. Lawyer. Mexican War veteran. Second in command to John B. Floyd at Fort Donelson.

"If I had captured [General Pillow], I would have turned him loose, I would rather have him in command of you fellows than as a prisoner." —Ulysses S. Grant to Simon B. Buckner, *Century Magazine*, April, 1897, p. 944

"General Pillow is a small, compact, clear-complexioned man, with short grey whiskers, cut in the English fashion, a quick eye, and a pompous manner of speech; and I had not been long in his company before I heard of Chapultepec and his wound, which causes him to limp a little in his walk, and gives him inconvenience in the saddle. He wore a round black hat, plain blue frock coat, dark trousers, and brass spurs on his boots; but no signs of military rank." —William Howard Russell, *My Diary North & South*, p. 162

"He is a man of energy and ability and were he content to *serve* would I think be very useful; but his great ambition leads him to seek commands to which his military status is hardly equal. To a General by whom he would be controlled he would be very useful." —Josiah Gorgas, *The Journals of Josiah Gorgas*, p. 92

"Pillow, a brave and competent but vain commander . . . wrote or caused to be written to home newspapers extravagant accounts of his own personal prowess. These letters, disparaging his equals and superiors, were received in the army with much condemnation and ridicule." —Ethan Allen Hitchcock, *Fifty Years in Camp and Field*, p. 318

CAMILLE ARMAND JULES MARIE, PRINCE DE POLIGNAC Major general. French Army officer. Division commander in Taylor's army.

"A gallant and accomplished Frenchman . . . He belonged to the princely family of that name . . . and it certainly never furnished a braver or more creditable representative. But, while the general spoke English fluently . . . he was addicted, when excited, to a multitude of imprecatory ejaculations. In plain truth, 'he would swear like a trooper.'" —Basil Duke, *Reminiscences*, p. 132

"The Texans swore that a Frenchman, whose very name they could not pronounce, should never command them, and mutiny was threatened . . . Polignac, by his coolness under fire, gained the confidence of his men, as he soon gained their affections by his care and attention. They got on famously, and he made soldiers out of them." —Richard Taylor, *Destruction and Reconstruction*, p. 153–154

LEONIDAS POLK   Lieutenant general. West Point (1827). Bishop of Louisiana. Corps commander, Army of Tennessee. Killed at Pine Mountain.

"Lieutenant-General Leonidas Polk, Bishop of Louisiana . . . is a good looking gentlemanlike man, with all the manners and affability of a 'grand Seigneur.' He is fifty-seven years old—tall, upright and looks much more the soldier than the clergyman . . . he is very rich . . . He is much beloved by the soldiers on account of his great personal courage and agreeable manners . . . In his clerical capacity I have always heard him spoken of with the greatest respect." —Arthur J. L. Fremantle, *Three Months in the Southern States*, p. 140

"General Polk had been Bishop in the Protestant Episcopal Church in Tennessee before the war, but he had received a military education in early life . . . His influence was large and his example influenced a multitude of followers . . . A higher military rank was given him than his experience or abilities as a soldier would alone have warranted . . ." —Jacob D. Cox, *Atlanta*, p. 98

"A pure and lofty character, nothing but the most self-sacrificing, patriotic convictions, and almost peremptory wishes of the Executive had him lay down his great Episcopal station and duties and take to arms. His training at West Point had well prepared him for the stern efforts in the field awaiting Southern men. Throughout his army career he was never without a desire to put by his sword and take up again his dearly loved people, his Bishop's staff, for prayer and strength and consolation in their many trials and sufferings . . . Of commanding presence and most winning address, he served with distinction and renown . . . he had won to himself the abiding affection and confidence of all officers and men whom he commanded." —G. Moxley Sorrel, *Recollections of a Confederate Staff Officer*, p. 188

"Gen. Polk had been an Episcopal bishop, and enjoyed the best the land afforded. The mating songs of the birds disturbed not his morning repose . . . He was a valiant trencherman, but when the repast was over he threw aside the surplice. The priest became warrior when he girded on his saber, and sallied forth a paladin in the strife." —Samuel G. French, *Two Wars*, p. 190

"He was truly a good man, lofty in sentiment, gallant and enthusiastic in the cause. He possessed all the requisites of a great soldier, except strategy and tactical combinations. His name alone carried great weight in the army . . ." —St. John Richardson Liddell, *Liddell's Record*, p. 100–101

"General Leonidas Polk was a prince among men and an officer of marked ability. He was a bishop of the Episcopal Church. His character was beautiful in its simplicity and strength." —John B. Gordon, *Reminiscences of the Civil War*, p. 79

STERLING PRICE Major general.
Lawyer and Congressman. Mexican War veteran.
Army commander in Trans-Mississippi Department.

"Price had ... military experience in the Mexican War, which circumstance, combined with his political position, his irreproachable personal character and sincere devotion to the cause which he embraced ... had made him the military head of the secession forces in the state. Brave, and gifted with the talent of gaining the confidence and love of his soldiers, he was undoubtedly the proper man to gather around him and hold together the heterogeneous military forces; but ... he seldom could rise above the effectiveness of a guerrilla chief, doing business on a large scale and almost on his own account." —Franz Sigel, *Battles and Leaders*, 1:318–319

"He was a man of decided ability as a citizen and a public man, had had some military experience in the Mexican War and exercised the completest influence over the troops he led from Missouri ... Personally and publicly, few men ... stood higher in public opinion or commanded such entire confidence in his state. His integrity was unquestioned and unquestionable, his judgment deliberate and unimpassioned and his manners genial and unsympathetic. His bearing was very dignified, without being in the least haughty or forbidding." —John Pope, *Memoirs*, p. 84

"A man of distinction and high standing as a statesman and politician ... As a military man he was a decided failure. He was made a major-general and always had large commands, but invariably his schemes and plans failed, until finally the Rebs lost all confidence in him." —David S. Stanley, *Memoirs*, p. 69

"It is impossible for any one who knew him personally to mention his name without some tribute to his exceeding kindness of heart and grandeur of character. He impressed all who approached him with the conviction that he was a good, as well as a great, man." —Basil Duke, *Reminiscences*, p. 53

"In person, General Price is very farmer-like. No one would suppose his predilections to be martial. He is more than fifty years of age, about five feet ten inches in height, strongly made, thick-set, and inclined to obesity. He has a large, round face,, of a ruddy complexion, short-cut grey hair, small and restless grey eyes. In his movements he is slow; in manners extremely social and unpretending, a plain, out-spoken man, true as steel, and an unflinching patriot ... Whatever may have been achieved was due more to the indomitable energy and reckless bravery of his men, than to any great display of consummate generalship." —An English Combatant, *Battlefields of the South*, p. 139

"General Price possessed an extraordinary power to secure the personal attachment of his troops, and to inspire them with a confidence which served in no small degree as a substitute for more thorough training. His own enthusiasm and entire devotion to the cause he served were infused throughout his followers, and made them all their country's own." —Jefferson Davis, *Rise and Fall*, 1:428

ROGER A. PRYOR Brigadier general. Lawyer and congressman. Brigade commander, Army of Northern Virginia.

"Roger Pryor, a Virginian and brigadier, was formerly Congressman from Virginia and distinguished himself in the halls of legislation more by his combativeness than eloquence . . . he is a young man, rather thin and tall, with a feminine face, delicate moustaches, and long black hair. He is veritably one of the 'fire-eaters' and with a brigade of Mississippians once under his command . . . he has made his name famous." —An English Combatant, *Battlefields of the South*, p. 116

GABRIEL J. RAINS Brigadier general. West Point (1827). Seminole and Mexican War veteran. Brigade commander, Army of Northern Virginia. Explosives expert.

"It was our good fortune to have a valuable man whose military education and scientific knowledge had been supplemented by practical experience in a large manufactory of machinery. He, General G.W. Rains . . . when his native State North Carolina, seceded from the Union and joined the Confederacy, true to the highest instincts of patriotism . . . [he] only asked where he could be most useful. The expectations which his reputation justified, caused him to be assigned to the task of making a great powder-mill . . ." —Jefferson Davis, *Rise and Fall*, 1:475

STEPHEN D. RAMSEUR Major general. West Point (1860). Brigade and division commander, Army of Northern Virginia. Mortally wounded at Cedar Creek.

"He was a most gallant and energetic officer whom no disaster appalled, but his courage and energy seemed to gain new strength in the midst of confusion and disorder." —Jubal A. Early, *A Memoir of the Last Year of the War*, p. 112

ROSWELL S. RIPLEY Brigadier general. West Point (1843). Brigade commander, Army of Northern Virginia.

"He is a jovial character, very fond of the good things of this life; but it is said that he never allows this propensity to interfere with his military duties, in the performance of which he displays both zeal and talent. He has the reputation of being an excellent artillery officer, and although by birth a Northerner, he is a red-hot and indefatigable rebel." —Arthur J. L. Fremantle, *Three Months in the Southern States*, p. 179

Was "an officer of distinguished ability, great energy, and fertile in resource; no more accomplished artillery officer could have been found in either army." —Samuel Jones, *New Annals*, p. 228

ROBERT E. RODES   Major general. VMI (1848). Brigade and division commander, Army of Northern Virginia. Mortally wounded at Winchester, 1864.

"In Major General Rodes I had to regret the loss not only of a most accomplished, skillful, and gallant officer, upon whom I placed great reliance, but also of a personal friend, whose counsels had been of great service to me . . . He fell at his post, doing a soldier's and patriot's duty to his country, and his memory will long be cherished by his comrades." —Jubal A. Early, *A Memoir of the Last Year of the War*, p. 91

THOMAS L. ROSSER   Major general. Resigned from West Point 1861. Brigade and division commander, Army of Northern Virginia.

"To my mind, there were few officers in the service who had as much military genius as he had. Instinctively, he seemed to know what was best to do, and how to do it. It appeared almost impossible to tire him, or to break him down . . ." —Francis W. Walker, *Reminiscences of Confederate Service*, p. 139

DANIEL RUGGLES   Brigadier general. West Point (1833). Veteran of Seminole and Mexican wars. Division commander, Army of Tennessee.

"Another general . . . was among our passengers—a dirty-faced, frightened-looking young man, of some twenty-three or twenty-four years of age, redolent of tobacco, his chin and shirt slavered by its foul juices, dressed in a green cutaway coat, white jean trousers, strapped under a pair of prunella slippers, in which he promenaded the deck in an Agag-like manner, which gave rise to a suspicion of bunions or corns. This strange figure was topped by a tremendous black felt sombrero, looped up at one side by a gilt eagle, in which was stuck a plume of ostrich feathers, and from the other side dangled a heavy gold tassel. This decrepit young warrior's name was Ruggles, or Struggles, who came from Arkansas . . ." —William Howard Russell, *My Diary North & South*, p. 163–164

WILLIAM READ SCURRY Brigadier general. Mexican War
veteran. Cavalry commander in Trans-Mississippi. Killed at Jenkins Ferry.

"General Scurry . . . is very amusing, and is an admirable mimic . . . In peace times he is a lawyer. He was a volunteer major in the Mexican war, and distinguished himself very much in the late campaigns in New Mexico and Arizona, and at the recapture of Galveston." —Arthur J. L. Fremantle, *Three Months in the Southern States*, p. 64

EDMUND KIRBY SMITH Full general.
West Point (1845). Mexican War veteran. Commander
of Trans-Mississippi Department.

"He went West and the evidence as to his service is conflicting. He was a man of high character but mediocre ability. There was so much less fighting in the Trans-Mississippi area, that, like the one-eyed man in the country of the blind, anyone who was there was a great leader . . ." —John Haskell, *The Haskell Memoirs*, p. 19

"He is a Floridian by birth, was educated at West Point, and served in the United States cavalry. He is only thirty-eight years old; and he owes his rapid rise to a lieutenant-general to the fortunate fact of having just fallen, just at the very nick of time, upon the Yankee flank at the first battle of Manassas. He is a remarkably active man, and of very agreeable manners; he wears big spectacles and a black beard." —Arthur J. L. Fremantle, *Three Months in the Southern States*, p. 81

GUSTAVUS W. SMITH Major general. West Point (1842).
Mexican War veteran. Wing commander in Army of Northern Virginia;
Secretary of War 1862; commander of Georgia State Militia.

"Major-General G.W. Smith was one of the highest standing of the West Point classes, and, like others of the Engineers, had a big name to help him in the position to which he had suddenly been called . . ." —James Longstreet, *From Manassas to Appomattox*, p. 103

"General Smith . . . was a graduate of West Point who had served with some distinction as a lieutenant of engineers in the Mexican War . . . For some reason he came South with a wonderful military reputation and was at once appointed major general . . . General Smith had imperfectly recovered from a stroke of paralysis . . . It is probable that he was prevented by that attack from fulfilling the expectations of his friends, as he never rendered service to justify his reputation, though he certainly was a gallant gentleman of high intelligence and courage." —John Haskell, *The Haskell Memoirs*, p. 9

"General Gustavus W. Smith . . . had been twice brevetted for gallantry and merit in the Mexican War. He was a self-respecting, dignified man of marked ability. He had left the army, and was trying out his skill in civil pursuits . . . when the secession outburst took him south." —Oliver O. Howard, *Autobiography*, 2:72

"I had always been a great friend of Gen. G.W. & believed him a great soldier. In the Mexican War he . . . had had an unusual amount of hard & close fighting, & he came out of that war with several brevets, & a reputation for person gallantry second to none in the army. But, some how, in our war, the fates were against him. He started with high rank but never had a chance in battle . . ." —E. P. Alexander, *Fighting for the Confederacy*, p. 88

"General G.W. Smith . . . is most decidedly a reserved man on all military matters—although away from that topic he is as free as a boy. He is a classmate of mine, and has always been distinguished for his talents and sound judgment. It is supposed that he has considerable influence over General Johnston and the only one that has." —Lafayette McLaws, *A Soldier's General*, p. 139

CLEMENT H. STEVENS Brigadier general. Banker. Built coastal fortifications in South Carolina. Commanded brigade in Army of Tennessee. Mortally wounded at Peach Tree Creek.

"Clement C. Stevens . . . raised a regiment . . . was promoted to a brigade and died in battle in the Western Army. General Stevens was a man of high character and intelligence, and earned the reputation of a most excellent officer." —Johnson Hagood, *Memoir of the War of Secession*, p. 36

JAMES EWELL BROWN STUART Lieutenant general. West Point (1854). Brigade, division and Cavalry Corps commander, Army of Northern Virginia. Mortally wounded at Yellow Tavern, 1864.

"[Stuart] was a gallant figure to look at. The gray coat buttoned to the chin; the light French saber balanced by the pistol in its black holster; the cavalry boots above the knee, and the brown hat with its black plume floating above the bearded features, the brilliant eyes, and the huge mustache, which curled with laughter at the slightest provocation—these made Stuart the perfect picture of a gay cavalier." —John Esten Cooke, *Wearing of the Gray*, p. 175

"Stuart, endowed by nature with the gifts that go to make a perfect cavalryman, improved and cultivated through years of active warfare, experience, and discipline, was the embodiment of all that goes to make up the ideal soldierly character—the bold, dashing dragoon . . . Through all the vicissitudes of

war he held his troopers beside him peerless in prowess and discipline."
—James Longstreet, *From Manassas to Appomattox*, p. 573

"J.E.B. Stuart was cut out for a cavalry leader. In perfect health, but thirty-two years of age, full of vigor and enterprise, with the usual ideas imbibed in Virginia concerning State Supremacy, Christian in thought and temperate by habit, no man could ride faster, endure more hardships, make a livelier charge, or be more hearty and cheerful while so engaged. A touch of vanity, which invited the smiles and applause of the fair maidens of Virginia, but added to the zest and ardor of Stuart's parades and achievements." —Oliver O. Howard, *Autobiography*, 1:380

"He was a remarkable mixture of a green, boyish, undeveloped man, and a shrewd man of business and a strong leader. To hear him talk no one would think that he could ever be anything more than a dashing leader of a very small command, with no dignity and much boastful vanity. But with all that he was a shrewd, gallant commander . . . He was a good looking man, coarse in feature and figure, but powerful and enduring, of immense energy, and as coolly brave an individual as ever lived." —John Haskell, *The Haskell Memoirs*, p. 19

"General Stuart was a stoutly-built man, rather above the middle height, of a most frank and winning expression, the lower part of his face covered with a thick brown beard, which flowed over his breast. His eye was quick and piercing, of a light blue in repose, but changing to a darker tinge under high excitement. His whole person seemed instinct with vitality his movements were alert, his observations keen and rapid, and altogether he was to me the model of a dashing cavalry leader." —Heros Von Borcke, *Memoirs*, 1:21–22

"Stuart was a graduate of West Point and . . . had won distinction and had been wounded in an Indian fight. At the beginning of the war he was just twenty-eight years old. His appearance—which included a reddish beard and a ruddy complexion—indicated a strong physique and great energy. In his work on the outposts Stuart soon showed that he possessed the qualities of a great leader of cavalry. He never had an equal in such service. He discarded the old maxims and soon discovered that in the conditions of modern war the chief functions of cavalry are to learn the designs and to watch and report the movements of the enemy." —John S. Mosby, *Memoirs*, p. 31

"He is commonly called Jeb Stuart, on account of his initials; he is a good-looking, jovial character, exactly like his photographs. He has certainly accomplished wonders, and done excellent service in his peculiar style of warfare. He is a good and gallant soldier, though he sometimes incurs ridicule by his harmless affectation and peculiarities . . . he also departs considerably from the severe simplicity of dress adopted by other Confederate generals; but no one can deny that he is the right man in the right place." —Arthur J. L. Fremantle, *Three Months in the Southern States*, p. 293

"General Stuart was a great cavalry commander . . . He was a great soldier, but a born cavalryman, dashing, fearless, clearheaded, enterprising, brilliant . . . Fond of how and with much personal vanity, craving admiration in the parlor as well as on the field, with a taste for music and poetry and song, desiring as much the admiration of handsome women as of intelligent men, with full appreciation of his own well-won eminence . . . did not detract from his personal popularity or his great usefulness." —Henry Kyd Douglas, *I Rode with Stonewall*, p. 280

"The soul of this brilliant cavalry commander was as full of sentiment as it was of the spirit of self-sacrifice. He was as musical as he was brave. He sang as he fought." —John B. Gordon, *Reminiscences of the Civil War*, p. 99

"Stuart himself wore no insignia of command: a common black felt hat, turned down in front and up behind; a heavy black overcoat, tightly buttoned; elegant riding-boots covering the thigh; a handsome sabre, carelessly slung by his side, and a heavy pair of Mexican spurs . . . Thickset, full-faced, close-cut hair, and ruddy complexion, he looked more like Ainsworth's 'gentleman of the road' than a young, daring cavalry chief of thirty summers." —An English Combatant, *Battlefields of the South*, p. 305

RICHARD TAYLOR Lieutenant general. Planter, politician, and son of President Zachary Taylor. Division commander in 1862 Shenandoah Valley Campaign; commander of District of West Louisiana; Department of Alabama and Mississippi.

"Major General Dick Taylor is of middle stature, with a compact, well-knit frame. His face is rectangular, but almost bronze . . . He has a glorious pair of dark eyes, that scintillate beneath his heavy brows and dark hair. A heavy, curved mustache covers his well formed mouth. Such is his appearance, and his fighting qualities are in accordance. As a soldier, he has been wonderfully successful. Though some of his movements savored of rashness, when calmly weighed, they showed good judgment and military genius that conceived them. When once he forms an opinion, he acts upon it with an unbending, uncompromising resolve." —J. P. Blessington, *Walker's Texas Division*, p. 184

"General Dick Taylor was eternally vigilant; he never missed an opportunity of annoying Banks, attacking and capturing outposts and threatening his communications." —William Boggs, *Military Reminiscences*, p. 70

"General Taylor was one of the most accomplished men I ever met; he had been a great reader, and remembered what he read, thoroughly posted in politics, science, art, finance, and the current literature of the day, and was the most charming raconteur I ever encountered." —Henry Heth, *Memoirs*, p. 210

"Taylor was a great general and a man of high attainments, which qualified him for civil as well as military functions. He never had a fair opportunity to show what a general he really was . . . He was a noble man, of high courage, a generous heart, a fine soldier, an accomplished gentleman and devoted Southerner." —William C. Oates, *The War Between the Union and the Confederacy*, p. 452

ROBERT A. TOOMBS Brigadier general. Lawyer and politician. Brigade commander, Army of Northern Virginia.

"General Robert Toombs was quite conspicuous. Everyone knows that that luminous intellect embraced no soldier's talent. It might have been so with study, but the Georgian was for once and all a politician, and in the wrong shop with a sword and uniform on . . . He was a great lawyer and a good politician, but in the wrong place when posing as a soldier." —G. Moxley Sorrel, *Recollections of a Confederate Staff Officer*, p. 53, 94

"He was a loud, boisterous man, with many attractive qualities and a brilliant, if disorderly, character and intellect. He had a great contempt for West Pointers and a great dislike for Mr. Davis . . . He was no soldier and had no business in the army, but he took good care of his men and did the best he could. He was deserving of much more credit than some who have a higher name in history for their war record." —John Haskell, *The Haskell Memoirs*, p. 17–18

"Toombs is a malcontent. Scarcely a man has contributed more than Toombs to the calamities that are upon us . . . I have ever considered him a reckless and audacious partisan, an unfit leader in public affairs, and my mind has not changed in regard to him. Toombs, however, was never a sycophant." —Gideon Welles, *Diary*, 1:428

"Mr. Toombs . . . is unquestionably one of the most original, quaint, and earnest of the Southern leaders, and whose eloquence and power as a debater are greatly esteemed by his countrymen. He is something of an Anglo-maniac, and an Anglo-phobist—a combination not unusual in America . . ." —William Howard Russell, *My Diary North & South*, p. 101

"General Toombs, our Georgia fire-eater, was given to criticizing pretty severely all the officers of the regular army who had joined their fortunes with those of the Confederacy. He was hot-blooded and impatient, and chafed at the delays of the commanders in their preparations for battle. His general idea was that the troops went out to fight, and he thought they should be allowed to go at it at once." —William B. Taliaferro, *Battles and Leaders*, 2:525–526

"Mr. Toombs was a man of massive intellect, strong will, and of very clear and deep convictions on public questions. He was the peer of the ablest in the Senate of the United States." —John H. Reagan, *Memoirs*, p. 108

ISAAC R. TRIMBLE   Major general. West Point (1822). Brigade and division commander, Army of Northern Virginia.

"He was a charming old fellow, kindly and brave, but cranky. He never would give anyone his proper military title, and sometimes rather provoked General Johnston . . . by calling him always 'Mr.' Johnston." —John Haskell, *The Haskell Memoirs*, p. 18

"Gen. Isaac R. Trimble was a Marylander, a West Pointer and an old army officer. Although sixty-five years old, after the riot in Baltimore in 1861 . . . he came to Richmond and offered his services to the Confederacy. He was made a brigadier and assigned to the command of our brigade. He was unsurpassed for cool bravery." —William C. Oates, *The War Between the Union and the Confederacy*, p. 142

DAVID E. TWIGGS   Major general. Veteran of the War of 1812 and the Mexican War. Commander, District of Louisiana.

"General Twiggs . . . had the reputation of being the greatest master of the art of sarcasm in the old army. As he resigned at the beginning of the war to join the Confederacy, who by the way, seemed to have no use for him, his name is only known . . . by his disgraceful order, while still in our service, for all the troops under his command in Texas to at once surrender to the enemy . . ." —Abner Doubleday, *My Life in the Old Army*, p. 215

"He was in every respect a marked man. Tall and bulky with a highly florid face and bald head, wearing habitually a countenance half cynical, half humorous and altogether malicious and with a tongue of venom, he held all the young men and many of the old men in constant apprehension of some malicious or ill-natured remark. He seemed to delight in mishaps or mortifications to others and never failed to assist people to them whenever he could. He was a man of keen judgment and remarkable ability and might have been one of the foremost men in the nation if only he could have rid himself of two or three distinctive traits of character which brought to grief all of his undeniable talent and capacity." —John Pope, *Memoirs*, p. 197

EARL VAN DORN   Major general. West Point (1842). Veteran of Mexican War. Commander, Army of the West. Murdered by a jealous husband in 1863.

"A Small handsome man, the very picture of a thorough cavalryman, he enjoyed a high reputation from service in Mexico and against the Indians." —G. Moxley Sorrel, *Recollections of a Confederate Staff Officer*, p. 49

Upon his death, "the character of the general was discussed, and the common opinion was clearly expressive of condemnation. Little or no regret was felt for a man whose willful violation of social rights led him to such an inglorious end. He had started with the full confidence and favor of the people and President." —St. John Richardson Liddell, *Liddell's Record*, p. 121

"Van Dorn was a classmate of mine at West Point . . . He was very sentimental, and always in love with somebody, and his sentimentality was not only the great weakness of his character, but it was the direct cause . . . of his violent and tragical death. He possessed very moderate abilities, indeed so moderate that it was with difficulty he managed to graduate . . . Indeed, we all feared . . . that he might not pass his examination at all . . . None of his classmates in their wildest flights in his behalf, ever predicted any more successful career than that incident to the dull routine of army service . . . Considering Van Dorn's limited abilities and meager intellectual endowments, he certainly succeeded in reaching and holding far higher positions than his friends believed him capable of reaching." —John Pope, *Memoirs*, p. 82, 83

"He was a dashing soldier, and a very handsome man, and his manners were graceful and fascinating. He was slight of stature and his features were almost too delicately refined for a soldier, but this defect, if it was a defect, was converted into a charm by the martial aspect of his mustache and imperial, and by an exuberant growth of brownish hair." —Thomas L. Snead, *Battles and Leaders*, 1:275

"General Earl Van Dorn was . . . the most remarkable man the State of Mississippi has ever known . . . and was one of the most attractive young fellows in the army . . . His figure was lithe and graceful, his stature did not exceed five feet six inches, but his clear blue eyes, his firm set mouth, with white strong teeth, his well cut nose with expanding nostrils, gave assurance of a man whom men could trust and follow." —Dabney H. Maury, *Annals of the Civil War*, p. 460

"He was an educated soldier, had served with marked distinction in the war with Mexico . . . He was among the first to leave the service of the United States, and came to offer his sword to Mississippi . . . Gentle as he was brave, and generous, freely sharing all the dangers and privations top which his troops were subjected, he possessed . . . both the confidence and affection of his men." —Jefferson Davis, *Rise and Fall*, 2:389

JOHN G. WALKER   Major general. Mexican War veteran. Brigade and division commander (cavalry), Army of Northern Virginia. Commanded Department of West Louisiana.

"His presence was always hailed with the wildest enthusiasm by both officers and soldiers . . . No commander could surpass him. Devoid of ambition, incapable of envy, he was brave, gallant, and just." —J. P. Blessington, *Walker's Texas Division*, p. 73

"Major General John G. Walker is a man of slight frame, and apparently delicate constitution; of a grave, pleasing demeanor, and of most affable and courteous manner. He is kind and courteous to all, without compromising his dignity. He was beloved by his officers, almost adored by his men. As a general, Walker is calm and cautious; does everything by rule; leaves nothing to chance. He makes his arrangements for battle with caution and foresight . . . nothing disturbs or unnerves him." —J. P. Blessington, *Walker's Texas Division*, p. 184

WILLIAM H. T. WALKER Major general. West Point
(1837). Seminole and Mexican War veteran. Division and reserve corps commander, Army of Tennessee. Killed at Atlanta, 1864.

"I am sorry to see that a good deal of dissatisfaction is being manifested in the army with President Davis on account of some of his appointments. In consequence . . . one of the best generals in the army has resigned and gone home. This is Brigadier general W.H.T. Walker of Georgia. He was an old army officer, has been in the service for more than 20 years, and carried more lead than any man in the army, having been shot in nine different engagements, the most of the times through the body." —Thomas Goree, *Longstreet's Aide*, p. 51

"Brig. Gen'l, W.H.T. Walker of Georgia [was] an officer educated at West Point and distinguished by much severe service in the Seminole and Mexican wars. Gen. Walker had been desperately wounded on several occasions, but recovered, as he said, 'to spite the doctors,' although the permanent evidences of his sufferings remained in a painfully spare frame and a pale cadaverous complexion, which always suggested a ghost on horseback." —Henry Handerson, *Yankee in Gray*, p. 33

"General Walker [was] a fierce and very warlike fire-eater, who was furious at having been obliged to evacuate Jackson after having only destroyed four hundred Yankees." —Arthur J. L. Fremantle, *Three Months in the Southern States*, p. 117

"General Walker was well-known to be a crackbrained fire-eater, always captious or caviling about something whimsical and changeable and hardly reliable . . . though otherwise I regarded him as honorable and high-strung in all engagements. We were very friendly but constantly differed in our views." —St. John Richardson Liddell, *Liddell's Record*, p. 137

"Always a martyr to asthma, he rarely enjoyed sleep but in a sitting posture; yet he was as cheerful and full of restless activity as the celebrated Earl of Peterborough . . . His ability as an instructor, and his lofty, martial bearing, deeply impressed his new brigade and prepared it for its stern work . . . his character . . . was one of the strangest I have met. No enterprise was too rash to awaken his ardor, if it necessitated daring courage and self-devotion." —Richard Taylor, *Destruction and Reconstruction*, p. 22–23

JOSEPH WHEELER   Major general.
West Point (1859). Cavalry corps commander, Army of Tennessee.

"A small, slight man, very quick and alert in his movements, quite young, only recently from West Point, he had just earned great distinction as a cavalry leader of our western army." —G. Moxley Sorrel, *Recollections of a Confederate Staff Officer*, p. 200

WILLIAM HENRY CHASE WHITING   Major general.
West Point (1845). Brigade and division commander, Army of Northern Virginia; and Wilmington, North Carolina. Mortally wounded at Fort Fisher, 1865.

"General Whiting . . . was apprehensive of bayous and parallels . . . Though of brilliant highly cultivated mind, the dark side of the picture was always more imposing with him." —James Longstreet, *From Manassas to Appomattox*, p. 113

"He was a West Point officer, having graduated far ahead of his class in every branch taught there. He started his career with a prestige which he did not fully sustain, though he made a fine reputation. His friends, however, thought that he did not get the chances or the rank to which he was entitled. He was probably the finest engineer in the army, and would probably have done more brilliant service if kept on staff duty. But he was very ambitious and very brave, and the line of distinction was as a commander in the field." —John Haskell, *The Haskell Memoirs*, p. 32

LOUIS T. WIGFALL   Brigadier general. Lawyer and politician.
Brigade commander, Army of Northern Virginia.

"A good type of the men whom the institutions of the country produce or throw off—a remarkable man, noted for his ready, natural eloquence; his exceeding ability as a quick, bitter debater; the acerbity of his taunts; and his readiness for a personal encounter." —William Howard Russell, *My Diary North & South*, p. 63

CHARLES S. WINDER   Brigadier general. West Point (1850).
Commanded Stonewall Brigade, Army of Northern Virginia. Killed at Cedar Mountain.

"General Winder was handsome and attractive in person, graceful on horseback or off, polished in address, dignified and courteous in manner, with a will as inflexible as that of Jackson himself . . . He was the most brilliant of the many valuable officers Maryland gave to the Confederacy . . ." —Henry Kyd Douglas, *I Rode with Stonewall*, p. 126

JONES M. WITHERS   Major general. West Point (1835). Veteran of Creek and Mexican wars. Division commander in Army of Tennessee.

"General Withers, at his own request, was . . . relieved of his command, his health failing . . . We parted from him with regret, for although . . . he was personally unpopular, but very little confidence also was felt in his military ability, he had latterly changed and improved very much, and had on several occasions shown much skill and good judgment, and was now regarded by his command with affection and much good-will, and as an officer he was well thought of, in spite of general mistakes which at an earlier period he had committed." —Arthur Middleton Manigault, *A Carolinian Goes to War*, p. 78

FELIX K. ZOLLICOFFER
Brigadier general. Journalist. Veteran of Seminole War. Department of East Tennessee commander. Killed at Mill Springs, 1862.

"Felix K. Zollicoffer had held many State offices . . . and was almost idolized by his people . . . though he had neither military training nor military education. He did not know how to drill a squad, but he was brave, and acted on what he deemed common sense. His men were raw militia, but all patriotic, believed in Zollicoffer, and would follow him anywhere." —William C. Oates, *The War Between the Union and the Confederacy*, p. 300–301

COMPOSITE QUOTES

"[W]illiam S.] Rosecrans is of medium height and stout, not quite as tall as [Alexander M.] McCook, and not nearly so heavy. McCook is young and very fleshy. [Lovell H.] Rousseau is by far the handsomest man in the army; tall and well proportioned, but possibly a little too bulky. R.S. Granger is a little man, with a heavy, light sandy mustache. [Thomas] Wood is a small man, short and slim, with dark complexion and black whiskers. Crittenden, the major general, is a spare man, medium height, lank, common sort of face, well whiskered. Major General [David S.] Stanley, the cavalryman, is of good size, gentlemanly in bearing, light complexion, brown hair. McCook and Wood swear like pirates and affect the rough and ready style. Rousseau is given to profanity somewhat and blusters occasionally. Rosecrans indulges in an oath now and then . . . Crittenden . . . swears like a trooper . . . He is a good drinker; and the same can be said of Rousseau. Rosecrans is an educated officer, who has rubbed much against the world and has experience. Rousseau is brave, but knows little of military science. McCook is a chucklehead. Wood and Crittenden know how to blow their own horns exceedingly well. Major General [George H.] Thomas is tall, heavy, sedate; whiskers and grayish beard. Puts on less style than any of those named, and is a gentlemanly, modest, reliable soldier." —John Beatty, *The Citizen Soldier*, p. 235

Wartime broadside depicting the prominent leaders of the Confederacy.

"Buell is our best soldier. Halleck the ablest man. Grant very brave but not brilliant. Thomas, slow, cool & methodic. I don't think much of Pope or McClernand." —William T. Sherman, *Sherman at War*, p. 62

"At the beginning of the war I was asked the question, 'Who of the Federal officers are most to be feared?' I replied, 'Sherman, Rosecrans and McClellan. Sherman has genius and daring, and is full of resources. Rosecrans has fine practical sense, and is of a tough, tenacious fiber. McClellan is a man of talents, and his delight has always been in the study of military history and the art and science of war.' Grant was not once thought of . . ." —D. H. Hill, *Battles and Leaders*, 3: 638

"[Charles S.] Winder, [George B.] Anderson, and [Samuel] Garland, probably the most promising of all our young brigadiers, fell fighting for the cause they loved. [John F.] Reynolds, one of the noblest of mankind, fell doing his duty on his side at Gettysburg. [George] Sykes, as the friend of [George B.] McClellan, never received the recognition which his knightly qualities demanded. Worst of all, [Fitz John] Porter, who commanded on the field the most creditable to the Federal arms, received that condemnation so much worse than death from the country he had served faithfully and loyally." —D. H. Hill, *Battles and Leaders* 2:361

"The changes in our army had been numerous. General McPherson had been killed; both [John M.] Palmer and [Joseph] Hooker gone off in a pet— Hooker because he was not put in command of the Army of Tennessee, and Palmer because he was directed to take orders from [John M.] Schofield. Many of the political generals, finding the place too strong for them, had gone to the rear to look after their political fences. [John A.] Logan returned to Illinois to make speeches. I wonder if he ever thought then of being immortalized in bronze as a great general." —David S. Stanley, *Memoirs*, p. 184

"You can have no idea of the disgust felt here towards the Government. Unable to run the army themselves, they take away McClellan . . . they cashier Fitz John Porter, one of the best general officers we have; and now relieve Burnside, one of our best corps commanders, ridiculously displaced by these very men; Sumner, the hardest fighter and best man to take or hold a position in the whole army, and Franklin, on the whole considered the ablest officer we have—all this that Hooker may be placed in command, a man who has not the confidence of the army and who in private character is well known to be—I need not say what." —Charles Francis Adams Jr., *A Cycle of Adams Letters*, 1:250

"Neither Rosecrans, Sherman nor Grant ever understood the true uses of cavalry. Each of these commanders was given to sending cavalry upon aimless raids, invariably resulting in having their cavalry used up and accomplishing nothing. Generals Thomas and Sheridan had more correct views of cavalry and used it

1862 engraving entitled "Our Generals," featuring prominent Union leaders.

to protect flanks, to keep themselves in order for battle, and then . . . threw the whole cavalry force upon the enemy's flank at the critical period of the battle . . . This is the true application of cavalry." —David S. Stanley, *Memoirs*, p. 132

"My division commanders . . . were dictated by [James A.] Garfield, and worse could not be found. [John B.] Turchin, a fat, short-legged Russian, who could not ride a horse, and Robert Mitchell, a politician, always thinking of the votes he could make in Kansas. Two such cavalry subordinates were never before imposed on a cavalry commander." —David S. Stanley, *Memoirs*, p. 135

"[John A.] Dahlgren and [Montgomery] Meigs were both intelligent officers and in their specialties among the first of their respective positions, but neither of them was endowed with the fighting qualities of [David G.] Farragut or [Philip H.] Sheridan, and in that time of general alarm . . . they were not the men to allay panic or tranquillize the government officials. They were prudent, cautious men, careful to avoid danger, and provide the means to escape from it." —Gideon Welles, *Diary* 1:62

"Old Jo Johnston himself is a perfect wheel horse. . . . [W]hen Genl Johnston had difficulties before him, he always put his mind to work to find a solution for them, and if he could not find one, it bothered him terribly. G. W. Smith saw all the difficulties, and appreciated them, but if he could not solve them, he gave himself no further trouble . . . But Genl Beauregard . . . would always try and counteract any difficulty that he could not get around by digging in the ground, and by throwing up fortifications." —Thomas J. Goree, *Longstreet's Aide*, p. 61

"[John] Newton, who commands the 6' (while Sedgwick commands the two Corps) does not, I think, amount to very much. [John] Sedgwick, I *fear*, is not enough of a General for that position—He is a good honest fellow & that is all, I do not think his officers have very much confidence in him—[Daniel] Sickles & the most of his crew, are poor—very poor concerns, in my opinion . . ." —Marsena R. Patrick, *Inside Lincoln's Army*, p. 237–238

"Sickles and Doubleday. A pretty team!—Rascality and Stupidity. I wonder which hatches the most monstrous chicken." —Charles S. Wainwright, *A Diary of Battle*, p. 325

"The tall, angular, dignified gentleman with compressed lips and a 'character' nose, was General [William F.] Barry, Chief of Artillery. The lithe, severe, gristly, sanguine person, whose eyes flashed even in repose, was General Stoneman, Chief of Cavalry. The large, sleepy-eyed, lymphatic, elderly man, clad in dark, civil gray, whose ears turned up habitually as from deafness, was Prince de Joinville, brother to Louis Philippe, King of France. The little man with red hair and beard, who moved quickly and who spoke sharply, was Seth Williams, Adjutant-General. The stout person with florid face, large, blue eyes, and white, straight hair, was General [Stewart] Van Vliet, Quartermaster-General. And the man at the table, was General Marcy, father-in-law to McClellan, and Executive officer of the army." —George A. Townsend, *Campaigns of a Non-Combatant*, p. 96–97

"General Logan had taken command of the Army of the Tennessee by virtue of his seniority . . . but I did not consider him equal to the command of three corps. Between him and General [Francis P.] Blair there existed a natural rivalry. Both were men of great courage and talent, but were politicians by nature and experience, and it may be for this reason they were mistrusted by regular officers . . . I regarded both Generals Logan and Blair as 'volunteers,' that looked to personal fame and glory as auxiliary and secondary to their political ambition, and not as professional soldiers." —William T. Sherman, *Personal Memoirs*, 2:85–86

"Buell opposes Bragg & Pope, Jackson. Pope is morally worthless, Jackson is a just and upright man, & in earnest. Providence will help the righteous man who puts his shoulder to the wheel. Between Bragg & Buell there is little to choose on the score of morality. Both are like the common run of humanity." —Josiah Gorgas, *The Journals of Josiah Gorgas*, p. 50

"Our war has developed no great cavalry officer. [George] Stoneman has good points but does not fulfill his early promise. [Alfred] Pleasanton is splendid, enterprising and brave—but full of mannerisms and weaknesses. [John] Buford is far superior to any others in all the qualities of a great rider. But none of them approach the ideal." —Joseph Hooker, quoted by John Hay, *Inside Lincoln's White House*, p. 82

"I submit to you . . . it would . . . be well to promote [Richard S.] Ewell & A.P. Hill. The former is an honest, brave soldier, who had always done his duty well. The latter I think . . . is the best soldier of his grade with me." —Robert E. Lee, *The Wartime Papers of R. E. Lee*, p. 488

"I believe Hooker is a good soldier; the danger he runs is of subjecting himself to bad influences, such as Dan Butterfield and Dan Sickles, who, being intellectually more clever than Hooker, and leading him to believe they are very influential, will obtain an injurious ascendancy over him and insensibly affect his conduct . . . Such gentlemen as Dan Sickles and Dan Butterfield are not the persons I should select as my intimates, however worthy and superior they may be." —George G. Meade, *Life and Letters*, 1:351, 354

"Sherman ... is as quick as lightning, the most rapid thinker, actor, writer, I ever came in contact with—proud and high-spirited as an Arab horse. Grant is slow and cautious, and sure and lucky. They are both good men. Men you would admire if you knew them, and men who upon first blush you would be marvelously deceived in ..." —Thomas Kilby Smith, *Life and Letters*, p. 340

"McClellan was not Scott's first choice for general-in-chief of the army, to succeed him on his retirement ... He remarked that he should feel quite easy to turn over his responsibilities to Halleck as major-general, commanding the army. While General Scott held McClellan in high estimation for some junior command, he preferred Halleck, as being ten years older, and therefore presumably having riper judgment, besides having known accomplishments in theoretical knowledge of military law and practice." —Edward D. Townsend, *Anecdotes of the Civil War*, p. 62

"I don't care whether McClellan or Burnside commands the army, if the commander is only a capable man, but I still believe the former is the best general we have. No one has proved himself better yet." —Robert Gould Shaw, *Blue-eyed Child of Fortune*, p. 259

"Burnside who attacked on H[ancock]'s left didn't make much. He is a d'd humbug—Warren who is a ditto did about the same ..." —Oliver Wendell Holmes Jr., *Touched with Fire*, p. 116

"A McClellan in the army was lamentable, but a combination of McClellan and Buell was deplorable." —Abraham Lincoln, in Engle, *Don Carlos Buell*, p. 278

"Sheridan's lieutenants were well chosen. [Alfred T. A.] Torbert had already distinguished himself as an infantry commander; [David M.] Gregg had come from the regular cavalry and possessed the confidence of whole corps for good judgment and coolness; [James H.] Wilson ... was very quick and impetuous; [Wesley] Merritt was a pupil of the Cooke-Buford school, with cavalry virtues well proportioned ... [George A.] Custer was the meteoric sabreur; [John B.] McIntosh, the last of a fighting race; [Thomas C.] Devin, the 'Old War Horse'; [Henry E.] Davies, polished, genial, gallant; [George H.] Chapman, the student-like; Irvin Gregg, the steadfast." —Theo Rodenbrough, *Battles and Leaders*, 4:188

"Being on the staff, I saw all the Generals and all the movements. There was Benham, an old hen, cackling round, insulted by messages from angry Brigadiers sent through boyish aids, and he himself mainly anxious for cover, indecisive, and many thought, frightened. There was [Horatio] Wright, a little excited at times but growing genial and kindly as the fire grew hot. There was your friend, [Isaac] Stevens, dirty and excited, but clear headed and full of fight, with a dirty straw hat on his head and his trousers above his knees from the friction of riding. And finally, there was handsome Bob Williams astride of his big horse . . . the long sabre hanging from the saddle-brow and his eyes beaming, sparkling and snapping according to the turn of the fight. In the hottest fire he grew genial . . . " —Charles Francis Adams Jr., *A Cycle of Adams Letters*, 1:157

"He is a man of great ability, very calm, practical, earnest, and cold, devoted to the Union—a soldier, and something more. [Robert E.] Lee is considered the ablest man on the [Confederate] side, but he is slow and timid. 'Joe' Johnson is their best strategist. [Pierre G. T.] Beauregard is nobody and nothing—so think they at headquarters. All of them together are not equal to Halleck . . ." —William Howard Russell, *My Diary North & South*, p. 251

"As to Heintzelman, a very commonplace individual of no brains, or whose limited apportionment was long since ossified in the small details of an Infantry garrison . . . There are at least one hundred Brigadier Generals, who are not required . . . Old General [Edwin V.] Sumner is a fine old officer, it is true. But then, [Nathanial P.] Banks is a nobody and citizen, although as good a politician as he is a bad soldier. [Erasmus D.] Keyes, a gentlemanly man, and a good friend of mine, was a mere professor at West point, during the War of Mexico." —Phil Kearny, in *Until Antietam: The Life and Letters of Major General Israel B. Richardson*, p. 125

"McClernand is an old politician who looks to self-aggrandizement, and is not scrupulous of the means. Grant is brave, honest & true, but not a Genius. [James B.] McPherson is a fine soldier & Gentleman. [Frederick] Steele, [John A.] Logan & others are good soldiers, but [Frank] Blair is a 'disturbing element.' I wish he was in Congress or a Bar Room, anywhere but our army." —William T. Sherman, *Sherman at War*, p. 109

"General [J. E. B.] Stuart, one of the healthiest, stoutest, bravest, and most dashing men in the army, does not touch a drop, neither does he smoke or chew . . . I wish that all the officers of our army were half so abstemious, but it is not the case. Generals [Joseph E.] Johnston & [P. G. T.] Beauregard, Major General Gustavus W. Smith, [Edmund] Kirby Smith, [Earl] Van Dorn, [James] Longstreet and [Thomas J.] Jackson are comparatively temperate men, but Brig. Genls. [Arnold] Elzey, [Nathan] Evans & [Louis T.] Wigfall are always more or less under the influence of liquor, and very often real drunk, and for this reason they are not safe generals, for no man, when under the influence of liquor, can or will act with discretion. I would not detract from the noble dead, but from all I can learn, both Genls. [Barnard] Bee and [Francis S.] Bartow went themselves, and carried their men into places on 21st July which they could and would have avoided, had they been entirely from under the influence of liquor." —Thomas Goree, *Longstreet's Aide*, p. 53

"John B. Floyd and Henry Wise were appointed brigadier generals in the Confederate Army. Each of these gentlemen had occupied prominent positions; each had been governor of his state; Floyd was Mr. Buchanan's Secretary of War; Wise had been minister to one of the South American States and a prominent member of Congress from Virginia. Floyd and Wise were rival politicians, and hated each other as only rival politicians can . . . I think their most ardent admirers will acknowledge, that those two men, Floyd and Wise, were out of place as general officers, exercising independent commands, and it was a mistake in ever bringing them together . . ." —Henry Heth, *Memoirs*, p. 151, 160

APPENDIX A:
MAPS

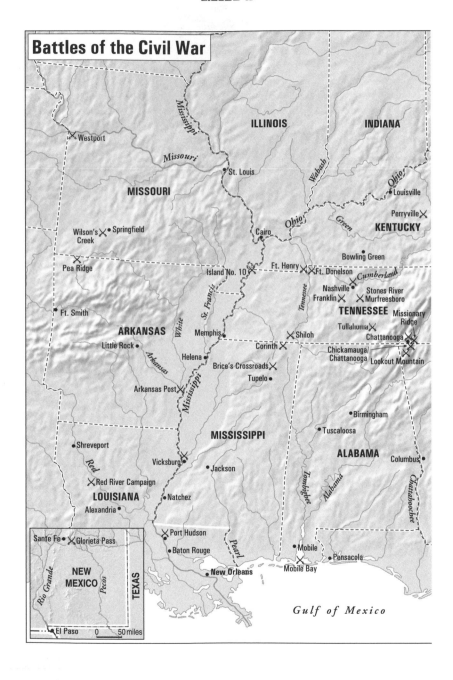

Battles of the Civil War

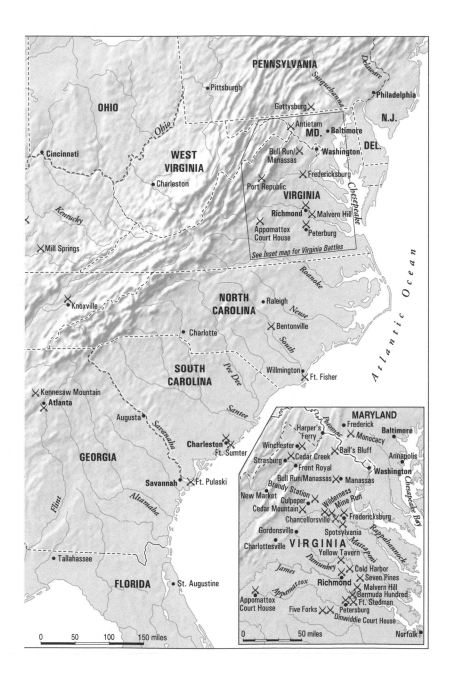

PENNSYLVANIA

Delaware

Susquehanna

•Pittsburgh

OHIO

Gettysburg×

•Philadelphia

N.J.

Ohio

Antietam×
MD. •Baltimore

DEL.

•Cincinnati

WEST
VIRGINIA

Bull Run/× •Washington
Manassas

•Charleston

×Fredericksburg

Chesapeake

Kentucky

Port Republic

VIRGINIA

Richmond× ×Malvern Hill

×
Appomattox
Court House •Peterburg

See Inset map for Virginia Battles

×Mill Springs

Roanoke

Atlantic Ocean

•Knoxville

NORTH
CAROLINA

•Raleigh

Nense

×Bentonville

•Charlotte

South

SOUTH
CAROLINA

Pee Dee

Willmington•
×Ft. Fisher

×Kennesaw Mountain
•Atlanta

Augusta•

Santee

Savannah

Charleston×
Ft. Sumter

GEORGIA

Flint

Savannah• ×Ft. Pulaski

Altamaha

•Tallahassee

FLORIDA

•St. Augustine

0   50   100   150 miles

MARYLAND

Potomac

•Frederick

Harper's
Ferry

×Monocacy Baltimore•

Winchester• ×Ball's Bluff •Annapolis

Strasburg• •Cedar Creek

Front Royal• •Washington

Bull Run/Manassas× •Manassas

Brandy Station•

New Market• Culpeper• ×Wilderness
Cedar Mountain• •Mine Run

Chancellorsville• •Fredericksburg

Gordonsville• Spotsylvania•

Charlottesville• VIRGINIA

Yellow Tavern•

James Pamunkey ×Cold Harbor
×Seven Pines

Richmond• ×Malvern Hill
×Bermuda Hundred
×Ft. Stedman

Appomattox
Court House Five Forks× ×Petersburg
Dinwiddie Court House

0   50 miles Norfolk•

Mattaponi

Rappahannock

Chesapeake Bay

ANTIETAM

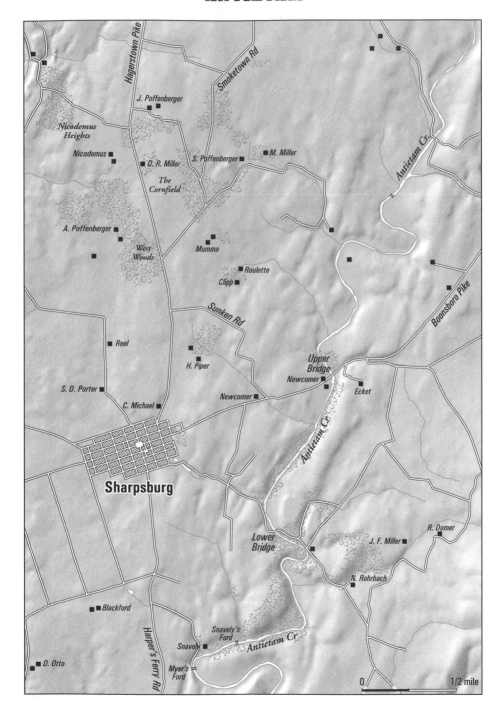

BULL RUN

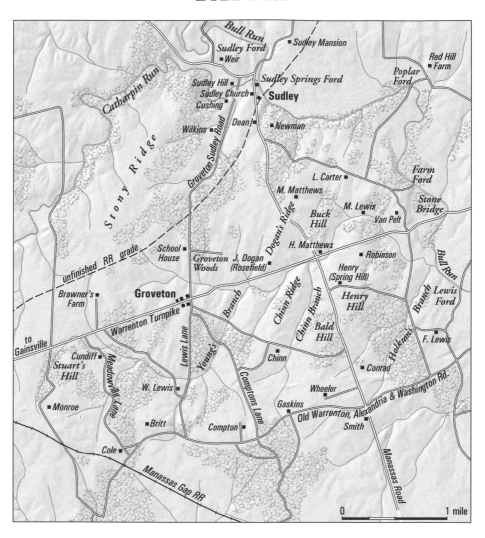

GETTYSBURG

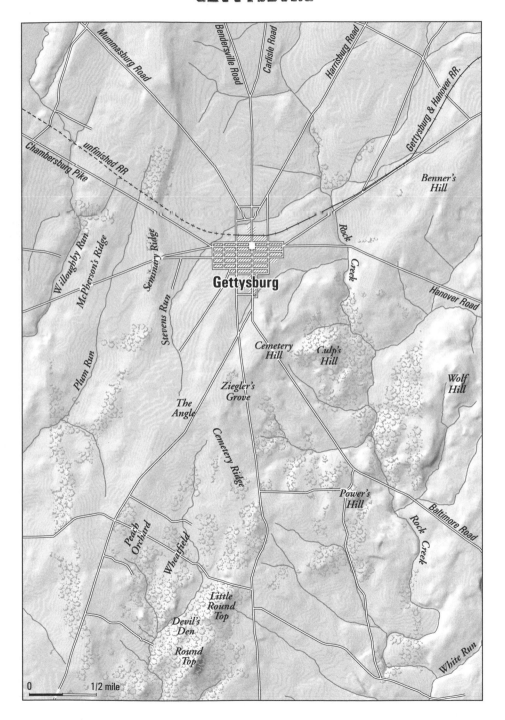

Gettysburg

Mummasburg Road

Bendersville Road

Carlisle Road

Harrisburg Road

Gettysburg & Hanover RR.

Chambersburg Pike

unfinished RR

Benner's Hill

Willoughby Run

McPherson's Ridge

Seminary Ridge

Stevens Run

Rock Creek

Hanover Road

Plum Run

Cemetery Hill

Culp's Hill

Wolf Hill

Ziegler's Grove

The Angle

Cemetery Ridge

Power's Hill

Baltimore Road

Rock Creek

Peach Orchard

Wheatfield

Little Round Top

Devil's Den

Round Top

White Run

0　　1/2 mile

SEVEN DAYS

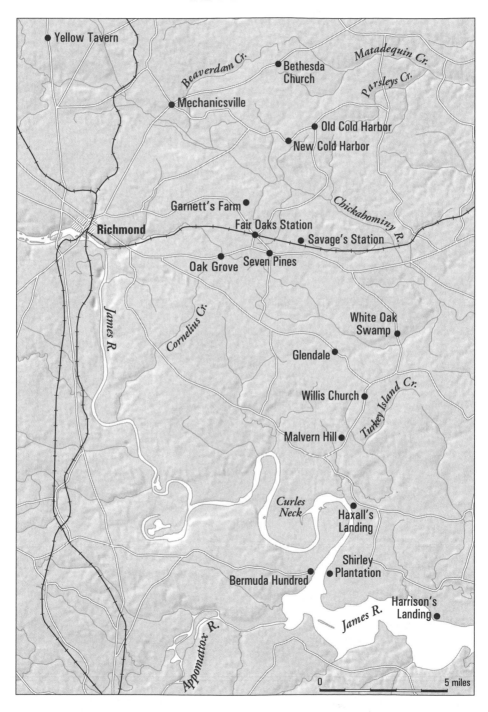

Yellow Tavern

Beaverdam Cr.

Matadequin Cr.

Bethesda
Church

Parsleys Cr.

Mechanicsville

Old Cold Harbor

New Cold Harbor

Garnett's Farm

Chickahominy R.

Richmond

Fair Oaks Station

Savage's Station

Oak Grove

Seven Pines

James R.

Cornelius Cr.

White Oak
Swamp

Glendale

Willis Church

Turkey Island Cr.

Malvern Hill

*Curles
Neck*

Haxall's
Landing

Shirley
Plantation

Bermuda Hundred

Harrison's
Landing

James R.

Appomattox R.

0   5 miles

APPENDIX B:
THE CONTRIBUTORS

Charles Francis Adams Jr., U.S.A., grandson of President John Quincy Adams, colonel of 1st Massachusetts Cavalry

Edward Porter Alexander, C.S.A., brigadier general, chief of artillery of Longstreet's Corps, Army of Northern Virginia

Daniel Ammen, rear admiral, USN

Archer Anderson, C.S.A., lieutenant colonel, from Virginia

Anonymous English Combatant, a British military observer known only as T.E.C.

Adam Badeau, U.S.A., colonel and brevet brigadier general; military secretary on the staff of Ulysses S. Grant

Francis C. Barlow, U.S.A., brevet major general, division commander

Cullen Andrews Battle, C.S.A., brigadier general, from Alabama

John Beatty, U.S.A., brigadier general, from Ohio

David Bell Birney, U.S.A, major general, commanded Tenth Corps

Charles M. Blackford, C.S.A., captain, 2nd Virginia Cavalry, staff officer for Stonewall Jackson

William W. Blackford, C.S.A., captain 1st Virginia Cavalry, engineer and staff officer

J. P. Blessington, C.S.A., private, 16th Texas Infantry

William R. Boggs, C.S.A., brigadier general, chief of staff for E. Kirby Smith

G. Campbell Brown, C.S.A., major, on the staff of Confederate Lt. Gen. Richard S. Ewell

Irving A. Buck, C.S.A., adjutant to Gen. Patrick R. Cleburne

Don Carlos Buell, U.S.A., major general, commander of the Army of the Ohio

H. G. Bunn, C.S.A., colonel, 4th Arkansas Infantry

Benjamin F. Butler, U.S.A., major general, commander, Army of the James

Sylvanus C. Cadwallader, war correspondent, *Chicago Times*, and *New York Herald*

William P. Carlin, U.S.A., major general, division commander, Army of the Cumberland

Joseph B. Carr, U.S.A., major general, division commander, Army of the Potomac

Joshua L. Chamberlain, U.S.A., brevet major general, brigade commander,
    Army of the Potomac

Augustus L. Chetlain, U.S.A., brevet major general

Cyrus B. Comstock, U.S.A., brevet brigadier general, staff engineer for
    Ulysses S. Grant

Phillippe d'Orleans, Comte de Paris, U.S.A., captain on staff of George B. McClellan

John Esten Cooke, C.S.A., captain, volunteer aide on staff of J. E. B. Stuart

Darius Couch, U.S.A., major general, corps commander, Army of the Potomac

Jacob D. Cox, U.S.A., brigadier general, Army of the Cumberland, corps commander

Thomas L. Crittenden, U.S.A., major general, division and corps commander

George R. Crook, U.S.A., major general, commander Dept. of West Virginia

Edward E. Cross, U.S.A., colonel, 5th New Hampshire Volunteer Infantry

George A. Custer, U.S.A., brevet major general, cavalry division commander

Charles A. Dana, newspaperman, assistant secretary of war

Jefferson Davis, president, Confederate States of America

Jefferson C. Davis, U.S.A., major general, corps commander, Army of the Tennessee

Francis W. Dawson, C.S.A., lieutenant, assistant ordnance officer for
    James Longstreet

John W. DeForest, U.S.A., writer, captain 12th Connecticut Volunteer Infantry

Regis De Trobriand, U.S.A., brevet major general, brigade and division commander

Franklin Archibald Dick, U.S.A., assistant adjutant general to Nathaniel Lyon

Grenville M. Dodge, U.S.A., major general, corps commander,
    Army of the Tennessee

Abner Doubleday, U.S.A., major general, brigade and division commander,
    Army of the Potomac

Henry Kyd Douglas, C.S.A., brigadier general, served on staff of Stonewall Jackson

Basil W. Duke, C.S.A., brigadier general, brother-in-law of John Hunt Morgan

Samuel F. P. DuPont, rear admiral, USN

Jubal A. Early, C.S.A., lieutenant general, corps commander,
Army of Northern Virginia

Richard S. Ewell, C.S.A. lieutenant general, corps commander,
Army of Northern Virginia

Josiah M. Favill, U.S.A., lieutenant, 57th New York Infantry

Arthur J. L. Fremantle, colonel of the Coldstream Guards, British Army Observer

Samuel G. French, C.S.A., major general, division commander, Army of Tennessee

James B. Fry, U.S.A., brevet major general, chief of staff for Irvin McDowell and
Don Carlos Buell

Charles Augustus Fuller, U.S.A., lieutenant, 61st New York Infantry

J. S. Fullerton, U.S.A., brevet major general, aide-de-camp to Maj. Gen. Gordon
Granger, military secretary to President Andrew Johnson

James A. Garfield, U.S.A., major general, Army of the Cumberland, chief of staff for
William S. Rosecrans

John W. Geary, U.S.A., major general, division commander

John Gibbon, U.S.A., major general, division and corps commander,
Army of the Potomac

John B. Gordon, C.S.A., major general, division and corps commander,
Army of Northern Virginia

Thomas J. Goree, C.S.A., captain, aide on staff of James Longstreet

Josiah Gorgas, C.S.A., brigadier general, chief of ordnance for the Confederacy

Ulysses S. Grant, lieutenant general, general in chief of the Union armies, 1864–1865

Benjamin H. Grierson, U.S.A., brevet major general, cavalry division commander

Edward O. Guerrant, U.S.A., assistant adjutant general to Gen.
Humphrey Marshall

Johnson Hagood, C.S.A., brigadier general

Henry W. Halleck, U.S.A., major general, chief of staff, United States Army

Cyrus Hamlin, U.S.A., son of Vice President Hannibal Hamlin, brevet major general,
aide-de-camp to John C. Fremont

Henry E. Handerson, C.S.A., major, 9th Louisiana Infantry, adjutant general

Frank A. Haskell, U.S.A., colonel, aide-de-camp to John Gibbon

Milo S. Hascall, U.S.A., brigadier general, brigade and division commander

William J. Hardee, C.S.A., lieutenant general, corps commander, Army of Tennessee

Benjamin Harrison, U.S.A., brigadier general, Army of the Cumberland

Herman Haupt, U.S.A., brigadier general, commander U.S.M.R.R.

Rush C. Hawkins, U.S.A., brevet brigadier general, 6th Pennsylvania Cavalry

John Hay, secretary to President Abraham Lincoln

Alexander Hays, U.S.A., brevet major general, brigade commander,
    Army of the Potomac

Joseph Hayes, U.S.A., brigadier general, brigade commander, Army of the Potomac

William B. Hazen, U.S.A., major general, brigade and division commander

Hans C. Heg, U.S.A., colonel, 15th Wisconsin Volunteer Infantry

Henry Heth, C.S.A., major general, division commander, Army of Northern Virginia

Daniel Harvey Hill, C.S.A., lieutenant general, division and corps commander

Ethan Allen Hitchcock, U.S.A., major general, advisor to secretary of war

Frederick L. Hitchcock, U.S.A., staff officer, 132nd Pennsylvania Infantry, colonel
    25th U.S.C.T.

Oliver Wendell Holmes Jr., U.S.A., brevet colonel, 20th Massachusetts, aide-de-camp
    to Horatio Wright

John Bell Hood, C.S.A., lieutenant general, corps and army commander

Jedediah Hotchkiss, C.S.A., topographical engineer for Stonewall Jackson

Oliver O. Howard, U.S.A., major general, corps and army commander

Thomas W. Hyde, U.S.A., lieutenant colonel, provost marshall of the 6th Corps,
    Army of the Potomac

John D. Imboden, C.S.A., brigadier general

Joseph C. Ives, C.S.A., captain, staff officer for President Jefferson Davis

Richard W. Johnson, U.S.A., major general, division commander,
    Army of the Cumberland

Phillip Kearny Jr., U.S.A., major general, division commander, Army of the Potomac

R. M. Kelley, U.S.A., colonel

Erasmus D. Keyes, U.S.A., major general, corps commander, Army of the Potomac

Gustave P. Koerner, U.S.A., lieutenant governor of Illinois, colonel and aide-de-camp to John C. Fremont

Evander M. Law, C.S.A., brigadier general, Army of Northern Virginia

Fitzhugh Lee, C.S.A., major general, cavalry division commander, Army of Northern Virginia

Robert E. Lee, C.S.A., general, commander Army of Northern Virginia

St. John Richardson Liddell, C.S.A., brigadier general, chief of staff to Braxton Bragg

Abraham Lincoln, president of the United States

Thomas L. Livermore, U.S.A., colonel, staff officer, Army of the Potomac

John A. Logan, U.S.A., major general, corps commander, Army of the Tennessee

James Longstreet, C.S.A., lieutenant general, commanding the 1st Corps, Army of Northern Virginia

Judge L. H. Mangum, C.S.A., law partner and aide-de-camp of Patrick R. Cleburne

Arthur Middleton Manigault, C.S.A., brigadier general, Army of Tennessee

Dabney H. Maury, C.S.A., major general

Theodore Lyman III, U.S.A., lieutenant colonel, and volunteer aide-de-camp to Maj. Gen. George Gordon Meade

George G. Meade, U.S.A., major general, commander of the Army of the Potomac, 1863–1865

Robert McAllister, U.S.A., brevet major general, division commander

George B. McClellan, U.S.A., major general, commander, Army of the Potomac

Lafayette McLaws, C.S.A., major general, division commander, Army of Northern Virginia

Martin T. McMahon, U.S.A., brevet major general, aide-de-camp to John Sedgwick

Nelson A. Miles, U.S.A., major general, brigade and division command, Army of the Potomac

Charles J. Mills, U.S.A., major

John W. Morton, C.S.A., artillerist under Nathan B. Forrest

John S. Mosby, C.S.A., colonel, partisan ranger, served on staff of J. E. B. Stuart

Frederick C. Newhall, U.S.A., lieutenant colonel, 6th Pennsylvania Cavalry, assistant adjutant general on the staff of Philip H. Sheridan

John Newton, U.S.A., major general, corps commander, Army of the Potomac

John G. Nicolay, secretary to President Abraham Lincoln

Oliver W. Norton, U.S.A., bugler, 83rd Pennsylvania Infantry

Daniel Oakey, U.S.A., captain, 2nd Massachusetts Volunteers

William C. Oates, C.S.A., colonel, 15th Alabama Infantry

James R. O'Beirne, U.S.A., brevet brigadier general

Charles A. Page, war correspondent

Eleazer A. Paine, U.S.A., brigadier general

John M. Palmer, U.S.A., major general, corps commander

Marsena R. Patrick, U.S.A., brevet major general and provost marshal general of the Army of the Potomac

William Dorsey Pender, C.S.A., major general, division commander, Army of Northern Virginia

George E. Pickett, C.S.A., major general, division commander, Army of Northern Virginia

Alfred Pleasanton, U.S.A., brevet major general, cavalry commander, Army of the Potomac

John Pope, U.S.A., major general, commander, Army of the Mississippi, Army of Virginia

David Dixon Porter, Admiral, USN

Horace Porter, U.S.A., brevet brigadier general, staff of Ulysses S. Grant

Gilbert V. Rambaut, C.S.A., major, staff of Nathan B. Forrest

John H. Reagan, postmaster general of the Confederate States of America

Harvey Reid, U.S.A., headquarters clerk, 22nd Wisconsin Infantry

Whitelaw Reid, journalist, war correspondent for the *New York Herald Tribune*

James Clay Rice, U.S.A., brigadier general, brigade commander, Army of the Potomac

Israel B. Richardson, U.S.A., major general, division commander, Army of the Potomac

William S. Rosecrans, U.S.A., major general, commander, Army of the Cumberland

James F. Rusling, U.S.A., colonel, quartermaster, 3rd Army Corps

William Howard Russell, war correspondent for *The Times* of London

Morris Schaff, U.S.A., lieutenant, staff officer under G. K. Warren

Justus Scheibert, captain, Prussian observer

John M. Schofield, U.S.A., major general, corps commander, Army of the Cumberland

Carl Schurz, U.S.A., major general, division commander, Army of the Potomac

Benjamin F. Scribner, U.S.A., brigadier general, Army of the Cumberland

John Sedgwick, U.S.A., major general, commander Sixth Army Corps

William F. G. Shanks, war correspondent for the *New York Times*

Robert Gould Shaw, U.S.A., colonel 54th Massachusetts Volunteer Infantry

Philip H. Sheridan, U.S.A., major general, cavalry commander, Army of the Potomac

William T. Sherman, U.S.A., major general, commander, Army of the Tennessee

Franz Sigel, U.S.A., major general, corps commander

Abner R. Small, U.S.A., major, 16th Maine Volunteers

Gustavus W. Smith, C.S.A., major general, commander, Army of Northern Virginia

William F. Smith, U.S.A., major general, corps commander

Thomas L. Snead, C.S.A., major, chief of staff to Sterling Price

G. Moxley Sorrel, C.S.A., brigadier general, chief of staff to James Longstreet

George T. Stevens, U.S.A., surgeon of the 77th New York Volunteers, Sixth Corps

David Hunter Strother, U.S.A., colonel, chief of staff to David Hunter

Alfred Sully, U.S.A., brigadier general

C. C. Suydam, U.S.A., colonel, Army of the Potomac

Richard Taylor, C.S.A., lieutenant general, commander, Army of Western Louisiana

Walter H. Taylor, C.S.A., lieutenant colonel, assistant adjutant general,
    Army of Northern Virginia

William B. Taliaferro, C.S.A., major general, division commander,
    Army of Northern Virginia

Lorenzo Thomas. U.S.A., brevet major general, adjutant general of the
United States Army

M. Jeff Thompson, C.S.A., brigadier general, Missouri State Guard

Edward D. Townsend, U.S.A., major general, assistant adjutant general of the
United States Army

George Alfred Townsend, war correspondent for the *New York Herald*

Emory Upton, U.S.A., brevet major general, brigade and division commander,
Army of the Potomac

Heros Von Borcke, C.S.A., lieutenant colonel, staff of J. E. B. Stuart

Alvin C. Voris, U.S.A., brevet major general

James Franklin Wade, U.S.A., brigadier general

Charles S. Wainwright, U.S.A., colonel, chief of artillery, 5th Corps,
Army of the Potomac

Lewis Wallace, U.S.A., major general, division and corps commander

Gouverneur K. Warren, U.S.A., major general, commander of the 5th Corps,
Army of the Potomac

Alexander S. Webb, U.S.A., brevet major general, chief of staff, Army of the Potomac

Stephen Minot Weld, U.S.A., colonel

Gideon Welles, United States secretary of the Navy

Orlando B. Willcox, U.S.A., major general, division commander,
Army of the Potomac

Alpheus S. Williams, U.S.A., major general

James Harrison Wilson, U.S.A., major general

APPENDIX C:
THE BATTLES

Antietam

U.S.A.: Francis Barlow, Ambrose Burnside, Jacob D. Cox, Lysander Cutler, William B. Franklin, William French, George Gordon, Winfield S. Hancock, George Hartsuff, Joseph Hooker, Nathan Kimball, Joseph Mansfield, George B. McClellan, George G. Meade, Thomas F. Meagher, John Newton, Robert Potter, Israel Richardson, James Ricketts, John Sedgwick, Truman Seymour, Daniel Sickles, William F. Smith, Samuel Sturgis, Edwin Sumner, Alfred Torbert, Orlando Willcox

C.S.A.: E. P. Alexander, Jubal Early, Nathan Evans, Maxcy Gregg, A. P. Hill, D. H. Hill, John B. Hood, Thomas J. Jackson, D. R. Jones, Joseph Kershaw, Alexander Lawton, Robert E. Lee, Stephen D. Lee, James Longstreet, William Mahone, Lafayette McLaws, William D. Pender, William N. Pendleton, George Pickett, Roger Pryor, Stephen D. Ramseur, Roswell Ripley, Robert Rodes, J. E. B. Stuart, Robert Toombs

Arkansas Post

U.S.A.: John A. McClernand, William T. Sherman, Andrew J. Smith, Frederick Steele

Atlanta

U.S.A.: Francis P. Blair, James Brannan, John Corse, Jacob D. Cox, Jefferson C. Davis, Grenville Dodge, William B. Hazen, Joseph Hooker, Allen Hovey, Oliver O. Howard, Hugh Judson Kilpatrick, Mortimer Leggett, John A. Logan, John McArthur, James B. McPherson, George Morell, Emerson Opdycke, Peter J. Osterhaus, John Palmer, Orlando M. Poe, Thomas E. G. Ransom, Lovell Rousseau, John Schofield, William T. Sherman, Henry Slocum, Giles A. Smith, John E. Smith, David Stanley, George Stoneman, George Thomas, John Turchin

C.S.A.: Benjamin F. Cheatham, Patrick Cleburne, Daniel Govan, William J. Hardee, T. C. Hindman, John B. Hood, Joseph E. Johnston, Leonidas Polk, Gustavus Smith, Clement Stevens, W. H. T. Walker, Joseph Wheeler

Ball's Bluff

U.S.A.: Edward Baker, Charles Stone

C.S.A. Nathan Evans

Bentonville

U.S.A.: William P. Carlin, Jefferson C. Davis, Peter J. Osterhaus, William T. Sherman, Henry Slocum

C.S.A.: Braxton Bragg, William J. Hardee, Joseph E. Johnston, Roswell Ripley

Bermuda Hundred

U.S.A.: Benjamin Butler, Quincy Gillmore, George Hartsuff, John Martindale, Gershom Mott, E. O. C. Ord, William F. Smith, Alfred Terry, Godfrey Weitzel

C.S.A.: W. H. C. Whiting

Brandy Station

U.S.A.: John Buford, George Custer, Wesley Merritt, Alfred Pleasonton

C.S.A.: J. E. B. Stuart

Brice's Crossroads

U.S.A.: Samuel Sturgis

C.S.A.: Nathan B. Forrest

Bristoe Station

U.S.A.: Alexander Hays, William H. Morris, Gouverneur K. Warren

C.S.A.: A. P. Hill

Bull Run

U.S.A.: Louis Blenker, Ambrose Burnside, Orris Ferry, William B. Franklin, Charles Griffin, John Hartranft, Samuel Heintzelman, Oliver O. Howard, Irvin McDowell, Thomas F. Meagher, Israel Richardson, James Ricketts, William T. Sherman, Henry Slocum, George Sykes, Daniel Tyler

C.S.A.: P. G. T. Beauregard, Barnard Bee, Jubal Early, Nathan Evans, Richard S. Ewell, Wade Hampton, Thomas J. Jackson, Joseph E. Johnston, D. R. Jones, Joseph Kershaw, James Longstreet, William N. Pendleton, Robert Rodes, Thomas Rosser, Edmond Kirby Smith, Clement Stevens, J. E. B. Stuart

Second Battle of Bull Run

U.S.A.: David Birney, John Buford, Joseph B. Carr, Lysander Cutler, John Gibbon, George Gordon, Charles Griffin, Cuvier Grover, George Hartsuff, Herman Haupt, Alexander Hays, Samuel Heintzelman, Philip Kearny, Rufus King, Irvin McDowell, Robert Milroy, George Morell, Gershom Mott, John Pope, Fitz John Porter, Robert Potter, Jesse Reno, John F. Reynolds, James Rice, Robert Schenck, Carl Schurz, Truman Seymour, Franz Sigel, Isaac Stevens, Samuel Sturgis, George Sykes, Alfred Torbert, Gouverneur K. Warren

C.S.A.: T. R. R. Cobb, Jubal Early, Nathan Evans, Richard S. Ewell, Maxcy Gregg, D. H. Hill, John B. Hood, Thomas J. Jackson, Micah Jenkins, D. R. Jones, Joseph Kershaw, Robert E. Lee, Stephen D. Lee, James Longstreet, William Mahone, Lafayette McLaws, William D. Pender, William N. Pendleton, George Pickett, Roger Pryor, J. E. B. Stuart, Robert Toombs, Isaac Trimble

Cedar Creek

U.S.A.: George Crook, Thomas Devin, James Ricketts, Philip H. Sheridan, Alfred Torbert, Horatio Wright

C.S.A.: Jubal Early, Stephen D. Ramseur, Thomas Rosser

Cedar Mountain

U.S.A.: Nathaniel Banks, John Buford, John Geary, George Gordon, Robert Potter, James Ricketts

C.S.A.: Maxcy Gregg, A. P. Hill, Thomas J. Jackson, Isaac Trimble

Chancellorsville

U.S.A.: William T. H. Brooks, Daniel Butterfield, Joseph B. Carr, Darius Couch, Lysander Cutler, Alfred Duffie, William French, John Geary, David M. Gregg, Charles Griffin, Winfield S. Hancock, Joseph Hooker, Oliver O. Howard, Andrew Humphreys, Hugh Judson Kilpatrick, Robert McAllister, George G. Meade, Wesley Merritt, Gershom Mott, Thomas Neill, John Newton, Alfred Pleasonton, John F. Reynolds, James Rice, David A. Russell, Carl Schurz, John Sedgwick, Daniel Sickles, Henry Slocum, George Stoneman, Alfred Torbert

C.S.A.: Richard H. Anderson, Jubal Early, Richard S. Ewell, A. P. Hill, Thomas J. Jackson, Robert E. Lee, William Mahone, William D. Pender, William N. Pendleton, Stephen D. Ramseur, Robert Rodes, Thomas Rosser, J. E. B. Stuart

Charleston

U.S.A.: Quincy Gillmore, Truman Seymour, Thomas Stevenson

C.S.A.: P. G. T. Beauregard

Chickamauga

U.S.A.: John Beatty, James Brannan, William P. Carlin, Thomas L. Crittenden, Jefferson C. Davis, James Garfield, Gordon Granger, Charles Harker, William B. Hazen, Richard Johnson, William H. Lytle, Alexander McCook, Daniel McCook, Emerson Opdycke, Joseph J. Reynolds, William S. Rosecrans, Lovell Rousseau, Philip H. Sheridan, John Starkweather, George Thomas, John Turchin, Ferdinand Van Derveer, Thomas Wood

CSA: E. P. Alexander, Braxton Bragg, Patrick Cleburne, Nathan B. Forrest, D. H. Hill, T. C. Hindman, John B. Hood, James Longstreet, Lafayette McLaws, Leonidas Polk, Clement Stevens, W. H. T. Walker, Joseph Wheeler

Cold Harbor

U.S.A.: John Gibbon, Ulysses S. Grant, Winfield S. Hancock, John Martindale, George G. Meade, Thomas Neill, William F. Smith

C.S.A.: Jubal Early, Joseph Kershaw, Robert E. Lee, William Mahone, William N. Pendleton, George Pickett, Robert Rodes

Corinth

U.S.A.: William P. Carlin, Augustus L. Chetlain, Gordon Granger, Ulysses S. Grant, Henry Halleck, Edward Hatch, Stephen A. Hurlbut, Thomas McKean, E. O. C. Ord, John Pope, William S. Rosecrans, Philip H. Sheridan, William T. Sherman, David Stanley, John D. Stevenson, George Thomas

C.S.A.: P. G. T. Beauregard, Braxton Bragg, Dabney Maury, Sterling Price, Daniel Ruggles, Earl Van Dorn

Dinwiddie Court House

U.S.A.: George Custer, Philip H. Sheridan

C.S.A.: George Pickett, Thomas Rosser

Five Forks

U.S.A.: Romeyn Ayres, Samuel Crawford, George Custer, Charles Griffin, Philip H. Sheridan, Gouverneur K. Warren

C.S.A.: Robert E. Lee, W. H. F. Lee, George Pickett, Thomas Rosser

Fort Donelson

U.S.A.: Augustus L. Chetlain, Ulysses S. Grant, Jacob Lauman, Michael Lawler, John A. Logan, John McArthur, John McClernand, Georg McGinnis, Thomas E. G. Ransom, Charles F. Smith, John E. Smith

C.S.A.: Simon B. Buckner, John B. Floyd, Nathan B. Forrest, Roger Hanson, Gideon Pillow

Fort Fisher

U.S.A.: Benjamin F. Butler, Alfred Terry, Godfrey Weitzel

C.S.A. W. H. C. Whiting

Fort Pulaski

U.S.A.: Quincy Gillmore, Alfred Terry

Fort Stedman

 U.S.A.: John Hartranft, John Parke

Fort Sumter

U.S.A.: Robert Anderson, John Foster

C.S.A.: P. G. T. Beauregard, Charles S. Winder

Franklin

U.S.A.: Jacob D. Cox, Nathan Kimball, Emerson Opdycke, John Schofield, David Stanley

C.S.A.: Benjamin F. Cheatham, Patrick Cleburne, Nathan B. Forrest, States Rights Gist, John B. Hood, Stephen D. Lee, Joseph Wheeler

Fredericksburg

U.S.A.: David Birney, William T. H. Brooks, Ambrose Burnside, Joseph B. Carr, William B. Franklin, John Gibbon, Winfield S. Hancock, Joseph Hooker, Oliver O. Howard, Andrew Humphreys, Henry Hunt, Nathan Kimball, Robert McAllister, George G. Meade, Thomas F. Meagher, Thomas Neill, John Newton, Orlando M. Poe, John F. Reynolds, John C. Robinson, John Sedgwick, Daniel Sickles, William F. Smith, Samuel Sturgis, Edwin Sumner, Alfred Torbert, James Wadsworth, Orlando Willcox

C.S.A.: E. P. Alexander, T. R. R. Cobb, Jubal Early, Maxcy Gregg, A. P. Hill, John B. Hood, Thomas J. Jackson, Joseph Kershaw, Robert E. Lee, James Longstreet, William Mahone, Lafayette McLaws, William D. Pender, William N. Pendleton, George Pickett, J. E. B. Stuart

Gettysburg

U.S.A.: Francis Barlow, David Birney, John Buford, Daniel Butterfield, Joseph B. Carr, Samuel Crawford, George Custer, Lysander Cutler, Thomas Devin, William French, John Geary, John Gibbon, David M. Gregg, Charles Griffin, Winfield S. Hancock, Alexander Hays, Oliver O. Howard, Henry Hunt, Hugh Judson Kilpatrick, Robert McAllister, George G. Meade, Wesley Merritt, William H. Morris, John Newton, Alfred Pleasonton, John F. Reynolds, James Rice, James Ricketts, John C. Robinson, Carl Schurz, John Sedgwick, Daniel Sickles, Henry Slocum, George Sykes, Alfred Torbert, James Wadsworth, Gouverneur K. Warren, Alexander Webb

C.S.A.: E. P. Alexander, Louis A. Armistead, Jubal Early, Richard S. Ewell, Richard B. Garnett, Wade Hampton, A. P. Hill, John B. Hood, Edward Johnson, Joseph Kershaw, Robert E. Lee, James Longstreet, William Mahone, Lafayette McLaws, William D. Pender, William N. Pendleton, James J. Pettigrew, George Pickett, Robert Rodes, J. E. B. Stuart, Isaac Trimble

Glorieta Pass

U.S.A.: Edward S. Canby,

C.S.A.: Thomas Green, William Scurry

Island No. 10

U.S.A.: Gordon Granger, Edward Hatch, John Palmer, John Pope, James Slack, David Stanley

C.S.A.: William Mackall

Kennesaw Mountain

U.S.A.: Francis P. Blair, Jefferson C. Davis, Charles Harker, Oliver O. Howard, Richard Johnson, Daniel McCook, William T. Sherman, George Thomas

C.S.A.: Benjamin F. Cheatham, Patrick Cleburne, William J. Hardee, Joseph E. Johnston

Knoxville

U.S.A.: Ambrose Burnside, Milo Hascall, William B. Hazen, John M. Parke, Orlando M. Poe, Robert Potter, Orlando Willcox

C.S.A.: E. P. Alexander, Micah Jenkins, James Longstreet, Lafayette McLaws

Lookout Mountain

U.S.A: William P. Carlin, John Geary, Joseph Hooker

Malvern Hill

U.S.A.: Francis Barlow, Henry Hunt, John Martindale, George B. McClellan, Fitz John Porter, John Sedgwick

C.S.A.: D. H. Hill, Theophilus Holmes, Joseph Kershaw, Robert E. Lee, James Longstreet, John Magruder, William Mahone, Lafayette McLaws, William N. Pendleton, Stephen D. Ramseur, W. H. C. Whiting

Manassas (See Bull Run)

Mill Springs
U.S.A. Robert McCook, George Thomas

C.S.A. George Crittenden, Felix Zollicoffer

Mine Run
U.S.A.: William French, George G. Meade, William H. Morris, Gershom Mott, Thomas Neill, John Sedgwick, George Sykes, Gouverneur K. Warren

C..S.A.: Robert E. Lee

Missionary Ridge
U.S.A.: John Beatty, Francis P. Blair, William P. Carlin, Jefferson C. Davis, John Geary, Gordon Granger, Ulysses S. Grant, Joseph Hooker, Richard Johnson, Emerson Opdycke, Peter J. Osterhaus, John Palmer, Philip H. Sheridan, William T. Sherman, Giles A. Smith, John E. Smith, John Starkweather, George Thomas, John Turchin, Thomas Wood

C.S.A.: Braxton Bragg, Benjamin F. Cheatham, Patrick Cleburne, Leonidas Polk

Mobile Bay
 U.S.A.: David G. Farragut

Murfreesboro (See Stones River)

Nashville
U.S.A.: Jacob D. Cox, Edward Hatch, Nathan Kimball, John McArthur, Robert Milroy, John Schofield, David Stanley, James Steedman, George Thomas, Thomas Wood

C.S.A.; Benjamin F. Cheatham, John B. Hood, Stephen D. Lee, Joseph Wheeler

Pea Ridge
U.S.A.: Grenville Dodge, Franz Sigel

C.S.A.: Dabney Maury, Benjamin McCulloch, James McIntosh, Sterling Price, Earl Van Dorn

Perryville
U.S.A.: Don Carlos Buell, William P. Carlin, Ebenezer Dumont, James Fry, Charles Harker, William B. Hazen, William H. Lytle, Alexander McCook, Lovell Rousseau, Philip H. Sheridan, John Starkweather, James Steedman, George Thomas, Thomas Wood

C.S.A.: Braxton Bragg, John C. Breckinridge, William J. Hardee, Humphrey Marshall, Leonidas Polk, Edmond Kirby Smith, Joseph Wheeler, Jones Withers

Petersburg

U.S.A.: Romeyn Ayres, David Birney, Ambrose Burnside, Samuel Crawford, Lysander Cutler, John Gibbon, Ulysses S. Grant, Charles Griffin, Winfield S. Hancock, Andrew Humphreys, Henry Hunt, James Ledlie, John Martindale, Robert McAllister, George G. Meade, John Parke, Robert Potter, David Russell, Truman Seymour, William F. Smith, Alfred Terry, Gouverneur K. Warren, Orlando Willcox, James H. Wilson

C.S.A.: E. P. Alexander, P. G. T. Beauregard, Jubal Early, Richard S. Ewell, A. P. Hill, Joseph Kershaw, Robert E. Lee, William Mahone, William N. Pendleton, George Pickett, Robert Rodes

Port Hudson

U.S.A.: George Andrews, Nathaniel P. Banks, Cuvier Grover, Thomas W. Sherman, Godfrey Weitzel

Red River Campaign

U.S.A.: Nathaniel P. Banks, William Emory, William B. Franklin, James Slack, Andrew J. Smith, Frederick Steele

C.S.A.: Camille Armond de Polignac, William Scurry, Richard Taylor, John Walker

Seven Days

U.S.A.: Winfield S. Hancock, Joseph Hooker, Philip Kearny, George B. McClellan, George G. Meade, George Morrell, Alfred Pleasonton, Fitz John Porter, Israel Richardson, John C. Robinson, John Sedgwick, Daniel Sickles, William F. Smith, George Stoneman, Edwin Sumner, George Sykes, Gouverneur K. Warren

C.S.A.: T. R. R. Cobb, Jubal Early, Richard S. Ewell, A. P. Hill, D. H. Hill, Theophilus Holmes, John B. Hood, Benjamin Huger, Thomas J. Jackson, Micah Jenkins, Joseph Kershaw, Alexander Lawton, Robert E. Lee, Stephen D. Lee, James Longstreet, John Magruder, William Mahone, Lafayette McLaws, William D. Pender, William N. Pendleton, George Pickett, Roger Pryor, Stephen D. Ramseur, Roswell Ripley, Thomas Rosser, J. E. B. Stuart, Richard Taylor, Robert Toombs, Isaac Trimble, W. H. C. Whiting

Seven Pines

U.S.A.: Alexander Hays, Samuel Heintzelman, Oliver O. Howard, George B. McClellan, Fitz John Porter, Edwin Sumner

C.S.A.: Jubal Early, John B. Hood, Benjamin Huger, Joseph E. Johnston, James Longstreet, James J. Pettigrew, Robert Rodes, Gustavus Smith, W. H. C. Whiting

Shiloh

U.S.A.: Jacob Ammen, Don Carlos Buell, Augustus L. Chetlain, Thomas L. Crittenden, Ulysses S. Grant, Allen Hovey, Stephen A. Hurlbut, Edward Kirk, Jacob Lauman, Mortimer Leggett, John McArthur, John McClernand, George McGinnis, William Nelson, Thomas E. G. Ransom, William T. Sherman, John E. Smith, David Stuart, Lew Wallace

C.S.A.: P. G. T. Beauregard, Braxton Bragg, John C. Breckinridge, Benjamin F. Cheatham, Patrick Cleburne, Nathan B. Forrest, William J. Hardee, Albert S. Johnston, Leonidas Polk, Daniel Ruggles, Jones Withers

Spotsylvania

U.S.A.: Romeyn Ayres, Francis Barlow, David Birney, Ambrose Burnside, Samuel Crawford, Lysander Cutler, John Gibbon, Ulysses S. Grant, Charles Griffin, Winfield S. Hancock, John Hartranft, James Ledlie, Robert McAllister, George G. Meade, William H. Morris, Gershom Mott, Thomas Neill, Robert Potter, James Rice, James Ricketts, John C. Robinson, David Russell, John Sedgwick, Thomas Stevenson, Emory Upton, Gouverneur K. Warren, Orlando Willcox, Horatio Wright

C.S.A.: E. P. Alexander, Richard H. Anderson, Jubal Early, Richard S. Ewell, A. P. Hill, Edward Johnson, Joseph Kershaw, Robert E. Lee, William Mahone, Stephen D. Ramseur, Robert Rodes

Stones River

U.S.A.: William P. Carlin, Jefferson C. Davis, Charles Harker, Milo Hascall, William B. Hazen, Richard Johnson, Edward Kirk, Alexander McCook, William S. Rosecrans, Lovell Rousseau, Philip H. Sheridan, Joshua Sill, David Stanley, John Starkweather, James Steedman, George Thomas, Thomas Wood, William Woodruff

C.S.A.: Braxton Bragg, John C. Breckinridge, Benjamin F. Cheathm, Patrick Cleburne, Nathan B. Forrest, Roger Hanson, William J. Hardee, John H. Morgan, Leonidas Polk, Joseph Wheeler, Jones Withers

Tullahoma

U.S.A.: William P. Carlin, Jefferson C. Davis, Richard Johnson, Alexander McCook, William S. Rosecrans, Lovell Rousseau, David Stanley, James Steedman, George Thomas

C.S.A.: Braxton Bragg, Patrick Cleburne, Leonidas Polk, Joseph Wheeler

Vicksburg

U.S.A.: Francis P. Blair, Eugene A. Carr, John M. Corse, Ulysses S. Grant, Edward Hatch, Francis Herron, Nathan Kimball, Jacob Lauman, Michael Lawler, John A. Logan, John McArthur, John McClernand, George McGinnis, James B. McPherson, E. O. C. Ord, Peter J. Osterhaus, David D. Porter, Thomas E. G. Ransom, William T. Sherman, Andrew J. Smith, John E. Smith, David Stuart

C.S.A.: States Rights Gist, Joseph E. Johnston, Stephen D. Lee, John C. Pemberton, Clement Stevens, W. H. T. Walker

Westport

U.S.A.: James Blunt

C.S.A.: Sterling Price

Wilderness

U.S.A.: Romeyn Ayres, Francis Barlow, David Birney, Ambrose Burnside, Samuel Crawford, Lysander Cutler, John Gibbon, Ulysses S. Grant, Charles Griffin, Winfield S. Hancock, Alexander Hays, Robert McAllister, George G. Meade, William H. Morris, Gershom Mott, Thomas Neill, Robert Potter, James Ricketts, John C. Robinson, David Russell, John Sedgwick, Emory Upton, James Wadsworth, Gouverneur K. Warren, Orlando Willcox, James H. Wilson, Horatio Wright

C.S.A.: E. P. Alexander, Richard H. Anderson, Jubal Early, Richard S. Ewell, A. P. Hill, Micah Jenkins, Edward Johnson, Joseph Kershaw, Robert E. Lee, James Longstreet, William Mahone, Robert Rodes, J. E. B. Stuart

Wilson's Creek

U.S.A.: Eugene A. Carr, Francis Herron, Nathaniel Lyon, John Schofield, David Stanley, Frederick Steele, Samuel Sturgis

C.S.A. Sterling Price

Winchester

U.S.A.: George Crook, George Custer, David Russell, Philip H. Sheridan, Alfred Torbert, Emory Upton

C.S.A.: Jubal Early, Robert Rodes

Yellow Tavern

U.S.A.: George Custer, Philip H. Sheridan

C.S.A.: Wade Hampton, J. E. B. Stuart

BIBLIOGRAPHY

Adams, Charles F., *Charles Francis Adams 1835–1915, An Autobiography* (Houghton Mifflin Co., Boston and New York, 1916)

Agassiz, George R., editor, *Meade's Headquarters 1863–1865: Letters of Colonel Theodore Lyman from The Wilderness to Appomattox*, (The Atlantic Monthly Press, Boston, 1922)

Alexander, E. P., *Military Memoirs of a Confederate*, (Morningside Bookshop, Dayton, 1990)

Anders, Curt, *Henry Halleck's War*, (Guild Press of Indiana, Carmel, 1999)

Badeau, Adam, *Military History of Ulysses S. Grant, From April, 1861 to April, 1865*, three volumes, (D. Appleton and Company, New York, 1882)

Beatty, John, *The Citizen Soldier*, (Wilstach, Baldwin & Co., Cincinnati, 1879)

Beck, Brandon H., editor, *Third Alabama! The Civil War Memoir of General Cullen Andrews Battle, C.S.A.*, (University of Alabama Press, Tuscaloosa, 2000)

Blackford, Charles M., *Letters from Lee's Army, or Memoirs of Life in and out of The Army in Virginia During the War between the States*, (Charles Scribners Sons, New York, 1947)

Blair, William A., editor, *A Politician Goes to War: The Civil War Letters of John White Geary*, (The Pennsylvania State University Press, University Park, 1995)

Blegen, Theodore C., *The Civil War Letters of Colonel Hans Christian Heg*, (Norwegian-American Historical Association, Northfield, 1936)

Blessington, J. P., *The Campaigns of Walker's Texas Division*, (State House Press, Austin, 1994)

Boggs, William R., *Military Reminiscences of Gen. Wm. R. Boggs, C.S.A.*, (The Seeman Printery, Durham, 1913)

Buck, Irving A., *Cleburne and His Command*, (Broadfoot Publishing Co., Wilmington, 1987)

Burlingame, Michael, editor, *With Lincoln in the White House, Letters, Memoranda, and Other Writings of John G. Nicolay, 1860–1865*, (Southern Illinois University Press, Carbondale, 2000)

Burlingame, Michael and John R. Turner Ettlinger, editors, *Inside Lincoln's White House, The Complete Civil War Diary of John Hay*, (Southern Illinois University Press, Carbondale, 1999)

Butler, Benjamin, *Butler's Book*, (A. M. Thayer & Co., Boston, 1892)

Byrne, Frank L., editor, *The View from Headquarters: Civil War Letters of Harvey Reid*, (State Historical Society of Wisconsin, Madison, 1965)

Byrne, Frank L., and Andrew T. Weaver, editors, *Haskell of Gettysburg: His Life and Civil War Papers*, (Kent State University Press, Kent, 1989)

Cadwallader, Sylvanus, *Three Years with Grant as Recalled by War Correspondent Sylvanus Cadwallader*, (Alfred A. Knopf, New York, 1956)

Carter, Gari, editor, *Troubled State: Civil War Journals of Franklin Archibald Dick*, (Truman State University Press, 2008)

Chamberlain, Joshua L., *The Passing of the Armies*, (Morningside Bookshop, Dayton, 1991)

Chance, Joseph E., editor, *My Life in the Old Army: The Reminiscences of Abner Doubleday*, (Texas Christian University Press, Fort Worth, 1998)

Chetlain, Augustus L., *Recollections of Seventy Years*, (The Gazette Publishing Co., Galena, 1899)

Colburn's United Service Magazine and Naval and Military Journal, (London, 1862)

Cooke, John Esten, *Wearing of the Gray*, (Kraus Reprint Co., Millwood, 1977)

Cox, Jacob, *Military Reminiscences of the Civil War*, (Charles Scribner's Sons, New York, 1900)

Cox, Jacob D., *Atlanta* (Charles Scribner's Sons, New York, 1882)

Cozzens, Peter, and Robert I. Girardi, editors, *The Military Memoirs of General John Pope*, (University of North Carolina Press, Chapel Hill, 1998)

Cozzens, Peter & Robert I. Girardi, editors, *The New Annals of the Civil War*, (Stackpole Books,

Mechanicsburg, 2004)

Cozzens, Peter, editor, *Battles & Leaders of the Civil War*, Volume 5, (University of Illinois Press, Urbana, 2002)

Cozzens, Peter, editor, *Battles & Leaders of the Civil War*, Volume 6, (University of Illinois Press, Urbana, 2004)

Cummer, Clyde L., *Yankee in Gray: The Civil War Memoirs of Henry E. Handerson with a Selection of his Wartime Letters*, (The Press of Western Reserve University, U.S.A., 1962)

Cutrer, Thomas W., editor, *Longstreet's Aide: Major Thomas J. Goree*, (University Press of Virginia, Charlottesville, 1995)

Dana, Charles A., *Recollections of the Civil War*, (University of Nebraska Press, Lincoln, 1996)

Davis, Jefferson, *The Rise and Fall of the Confederate Government*, two volumes, (D. Appleton and Company, New York, 1881)

Davis, Oliver Wilson, *Life of David Bell Birney, Major-general United States Volunteers*, (King & Baird, Philadelphia, 1867)

Dawson, Francis W., *Reminiscences of Confederate Service, 1861–1865*, (Louisiana State University Press, Baton Rouge, 1980)

De Forest, John William, edited by James H. Croushore, *A Volunteer's Adventures, A Union Captain's Record of the Civil War*, (Yale University Press, New Haven, 1946)

Dinces, Bruce J., and Shirley A. Leckie, editors, *A Just and Righteous Cause, Benjamin H. Grierson's Civil War Memoir*, (Southern Illinois University Press, Carbondale, 2008)

Douglas, Henry Kyd, *I Rode with Stonewall*, (University of North Carolina Press, Chapel Hill, 1980)

Duke, Basil, *Reminiscences of General Basil W. Duke*, (Doubleday, Page & Co., Garden City, 1911)

Duncan, Russell, editor, *Blue-eyed Child of Fortune: The Civil War Letters of Colonel Robert Gould Shaw*, (University of Georgia Press, Athens, 1992)

Early, Jubal A., *General Jubal Anderson Early, Autobiographical Sketch and Narrative of the War Between the States*, (Broadfoot Publishing Co., Wilmington, 1989)

Early, Jubal A., *A Memoir of the Last Year of the War for Independence in the Confederate States of America*, (Charles W. Button, Lynchburg, 1867)

Eby, Cecil D., Jr., *A Virginia Yankee in the Civil War: The Diaries of David Hunter Strother*, (University of North Carolina Press, Chapel Hill, 1961)

Engle, Stephen D., *Don Carlos Buell, Most Promising of All*, (University of North Carolina Press, Chapel Hill, 1999)

Engle, Stephen D., *Yankee Dutchman: The Life of Franz Sigel*, (University of Arkansas Press, Fayetteville, 1993)

Ewing, Joseph H., *Sherman at War*, (Morningside Bookshop, Dayton, 1992)

Favill, Josiah, *The Diary of a Young Officer Serving with the Armies of the United States During the War of the Rebellion*, (R. R. Donnelly and Sons, New York, 1909)

Fehrenbacher, Don E., editor, *Abraham Lincoln, Speeches and Writings, 1859–1865*, (The Library of America, Camp Hill, 1989)

Fleming, George T., *The Life and Letters of Alexander Hays, Brevet Colonel United States Army, Brigadier General and Brevet Major General United States Volunteers*, (Gilbert Adams Hays, Pittsburg, 1919)

Ford, Worthington Chauncey, editor, *A Cycle of Adams Letters 1861–1865*, two volumes, (Houghton Mifflin Company, Boston, 1920)

Fremantle, Col. Arthur J. L., *Three Months in the Southern States*, (William Blackwood and Sons, Edinburgh, 1863)

French, Gen. Samuel G., *Two Wars: An Autobiography of Gen. Samuel G. French*, (Confederate Veteran, Nashville, 1901)

Fuller, Charles Augustus, *Personal Recollections of the War of 1861*, (New Job Printing House, Sherburne, N.Y., 1906)

Gallagher, Gary W., editor, *Fighting for the Confederacy: The Personal Recollections of General Edward Porter Alexander*, (University of North Carolina Press, Chapel Hill, 1989)

Gibbon, John, *Personal Recollections of the Civil War*, (Morningside Bookshop, Dayton, 1988)

Girardi, Robert I. and Nathaniel Cheairs Hughes Jr., *The Memoirs of Brigadier General William Passmore Carlin, U.S.A.*, (University of Nebraska Press, Lincoln, 1999)

Gold, David M., *Cyrus Hamlin's Civil War: Letters of the Vice President's Son on the Civil War and Reconstruction*, (Heritage Books, Westminster, 2011)

Gordon, John B., *Reminiscences of the Civil War*, (Charles Scribner's Sons, New York, 1903)

Grant, Ulysses S., *Personal Memoirs of U.S. Grant*, (Charles L. Webster & Company, New York, 1885)

Hagood, Johnson, *Memoirs of the War of Secession from the Original Manuscripts of Johnson Hagood, Brigadier, C.S.A.*, (Jim Fox Books, Camden, 1997)

Hamlin, Percy Gatling, *"Old Bald Head" (General R. S. Ewell): The Portrait of a Soldier and The Making of a Soldier, Letters of General R. S. Ewell*, (Ron R. Van Sickle Military Books, Gaithersburg, 1988)

Hascall, Milo S., *Personal Recollections and Experiences Concerning the Battle of Stone River*, (Times Publishing Co, Goshen, 1889)

Haskell, John, edited by Gilbert Govan and James W. Livingood, *The Haskell Memoirs*, (G. P. Putnam's Sons, New York, 1960)

Hassler, William W., editor, *One of Lee's Best Men: The Civil War Letters of General William Dorsey Pender*, (University of North Carolina Press, Chapel Hill, 1999)

Haupt, Herman, *Personal Reminiscences of General Herman Haupt*, (Wright and Joys Co., Milwaukee, 1901)

Hayes, John D., editor, *Samuel Francis DuPont, A Selection from his Civil War Letters*, three volumes, (Cornell University Press, Ithaca, 1969)

Hazen, William B., *A Narrative of Military Service*, (Blue Acorn Press, Huntington, 1993)

Henry, Robert S., *As They Saw Forrest*, (Broadfoot Publishing Co., Wilmington, 1987)

Heth, Henry, edited by James L. Morrison, *The Memoirs of Henry Heth*, (Greenwood Press, Westport, 1974)

Hill, D. H., *Bethel to Sharpsburg*, two volumes, (Broadfoot Publishing Co., Wilmington, 1992)

Hitchcock, Ethan Allen, *Fifty Years in Camp and Field, Diary of Major-General Ethan Allen Hitchcock, U.S.A.*, edited by W. A. Croffut, PhD, New York: G. P. Putnam's Sons, 1909

Hitchcock, Frederick L., *War From the Inside*, (J. B. Lippincott Company, Philadelphia, 1904)

Holden, Walter, William E. Ross & Elizabeth Slomba, editors, *Stand Firm and Fire Low: The Civil War Writings of Colonel Edward E. Cross*, (University Press of New England, Hanover, 2003)

Holzer, Harold, editor, *Lincoln on War, Our Greatest Commander-in-Chief Speaks to America*, (Algonquin Books, Chapel Hill, 2011)

Hood, John B., *Advance and Retreat*, (Blue and Gray Press, Secaucus, 1985)

Howard, Oliver O., *Autobiography of Oliver Otis Howard*, (The Baker & Taylor Co., New York, 1907)

Howe, M. A. DeWolfe, editor, *Home Letters of General Sherman*, (Charles Scribner's Sons, New York, 1909)

Howe, M. A. DeWolfe, editor, *Touched with Fire: Civil War Letters and Diary of Oliver Wendell Holmes, Jr.*, (Harvard University Press, Cambridge, 1946)

Hughes, Nathaniel C., Jr., editor, *Liddell's Record, St. John Richardson Liddell, Brigadier General, C.S.A.*, (Morningside, Dayton, 1985)

Humphreys, Andrew A., *The Virginia Campaign of '64 and '65: The Army of the Potomac and the Army of the James*, (Charles Scribner's Sons, 1902)

Hutton, Paul Andrew, editor, *The Custer Reader*, (University of Nebraska Press, Lincoln, 1992)

Hyde, Samuel C., Jr., *A Wisconsin Yankee in Confederate Bayou Country, The Civil War Reminiscences of a Union General, Halbert Eleazer Paine*, (Louisiana State University Press, Baton Rouge, 2009)

Hyde, Thomas W., *Following the Greek Cross or Memories of the Sixth Army Corps*, (University of South Carolina Press, Columbia, 2005)

Johnson, Robert U. & Clarence C. Buel, *Battles and Leaders of the Civil War*, four volumes (The Century Company, New York, 1884–1887)

Johnson, Richard W., *A Soldier's Reminiscences in Peace and War*, (J. B. Lippincott Press, Philadelphia, 1886)

Johnston, Joseph E., *Narrative of Military Operations, Directed During the Late War Between the States*, (Indiana University Press, Bloomington, 1959)

Jones, John B., *A Rebel War Clerk's Diary*, two volumes, (J. B. Lippincott and Co., Philadelphia, 1866)

Jones, Terry L., editor, *Campbell Brown's Civil War, With Ewell and the Army of Northern Virginia*, (Louisiana State University Press, Baton Rouge, 2001)

Jordan, David M., *"Happiness is Not My Companion," The Life of General G. K. Warren*, (Indiana University Press, Bloomington, 2001)

Keyes, Erasmus D., *Fifty Years' Observation of Men and Events. Civil and Military*, (Charles Scribner's Sons, New York, 1884)

Koerner, Gustave, edited by Thomas J. McCormack, *Memoirs of Gustave Philipp Korner, 1809–1896*, two volumes, (The Torch Press, Cedar Rapids, 1909)

Lamm, Alan K., PhD, "Oliver O. Howard: Bentonville's Controversial 'Christian General,'" in *The Battle Cry*, Vol. 9, Issue 1, Fall 2004, The Official Newsletter of the Bentonville Battleground Historical Association.

Lee, Fitzhugh, *General Lee*, (Broadfoot Publishing Co., Wilmington, 1989)

Logan, John A., *The Volunteer Soldier of America*, (The Scholar's Bookshelf, Cranberry, 2006)

Longstreet, James, *From Manassas to Appomattox*, (J. B. Lippincott, Philadelphia, 1908)

Lowe, David W., editor, *Meade's Army: The Private Notebooks of Lt. Col. Theodore Lyman*, (Kent State University Press, Kent, 2007)

Mason, Jack C., *Until Antietam: The Life and Letters of Major General Israel B. Richardson, U.S. Army*, (Southern Illinois University Press, Carbondale, 2009)

Maury, Dabney H., *Recollections of a Virginian in the Mexican, Indian, and Civil Wars*, (New York: Charles Scribner's Sons, 1894)

McClellan, George B., *McClellan's Own Story*, (Charles L. Webster and Co., New York, 1887)

McClure, A. K., *The Annals of the Civil War Written by Leading Participants North and South*, (Morningside, Dayton, 1988)

McClure, A. K., *Abraham Lincoln and Men of War-Times*, (The Times Publishing Company, Philadelphia, 1892)

Meade, George Gordon, *The Life and Letters of George Gordon Meade Major-General United States Army*, two volumes (Charles Scribner's Sons, New York, 1913)

Michie, Peter S., *The Life and Letters of Emory Upton*, (D. Appleton & Co., New York, 1885)

Miles, Nelson A., *Serving the Republic: Memoirs of the Civil and Military Life of Nelson A. Miles, Lieutenant-General, United States Army*, (Harper & Brothers Publishers, New York, 1911)

Mills, Charles J., compiled and edited by Gregory A. Coco, *Through Blood and Fire, The Civil War Letters of Major Charles J. Mills, 1862–1865*, (Gregory A. Coco, Gettysburg, 1982)

Morris, Roy, Jr., *The Life and Wars of General Phil Sheridan*, (Crown Publishers, New York, 1992)

Mosby, John S., edited by Charles Wells Russell, *The Memoirs of Colonel John S. Mosby*, (Little, Brown and Co., Boston, 1917)

Mushkat, Jerome, editor, *A Citizen Soldier's Civil War: The Letters of Brevet Major General Alvin C. Voris*, (Northern Illinois University Press, DeKalb, 2002)

Nash, Charles Edward, *Biographical Sketches of Gen. Pat Cleburne and Gen. T. C. Hindman*, (Morningside Bookshop, Dayton, 19770

Nevins, Allan, editor, *A Diary of Battle: The Personal Journals of Colonel Charles S. Wainwright, 1861–1865*, (Stan Clark Military Books, Gettysburg, 1962)

Newell, Clayton R., and Charles R. Shrader, *Of Duty Well and Faithfully Done, A History of the Regular Army in the Civil War*, (University of Nebraska Press, Lincoln, 2011)

Oates, William C., *The War Between the Union and the Confederacy*, (Morningside Bookshop, Dayton, 1974)

Oeffinger, John C., editor, *A Soldier's General, The Civil War Letters of Major General Lafayette McLaws*, (University of North Carolina Press, Chapel Hill, 2002)

Page, Charles A., *Letters of a War Correspondent*, (L. C. Page & Company, Boston, 1899)

Palmer, John M., *Personal Recollections of John M. Palmer*, (The Robert Clarke Company, Cincinnati, 1901)

Pellicano, John M., *"Well Prepared to Die" The Life of Brigadier General James Clay Rice*, (Fredericksburg, VA, 2007)

Philadelphia Weekly Times, The Annals of the Civil War Written by Leading Participants North and South, (Morningside Bookshop, Dayton, 1988)

Pickett, George E., and La Salle Corbell Pickett, *The Heart of a Soldier*, (Seth Moyle, New York, 1913)

Porter, David Dixon, *The Naval History of the Civil War*, (Castle Books, Secaucus, 1984)

Porter, Horace, *Campaigning with Grant*, (The Century Co., New York, 1907)

Reagan, John H., *Memoirs, with Special Reference to Secession and the Civil War*, (The Neale Publishing Company, New York, 1906)

Reid, Whitelaw, *Ohio in the War: Her Statesmen, Her Generals and Soldiers*, two volumes, (Moore, Wilstach, and Baldwin, New York, 1868)

Robertson, James I., Jr., editor, *The Civil War Letters of General Robert McAllister*, (Rutger's University Press, New Brunswick, 1965)

Rusling, James F., *Men and Things I Saw in Civil War Days*, (Eaton and Mains, New York, 1899)

Russell, William Howard, edited by Fletcher Pratt, *My Diary North & South*, (Harper & Brothers, New York, 1954)

Samito, Christian G., editor, *"Fear Was Not in Him," The Civil War Letters of Major General Francis C. Barlow, U.S.A.*, (Fordham University Press, New York, 2004)

Schaff, Morris, *The Battle of the Wilderness*, (Houghton Mifflin, Co., Boston, 1910)

Schiller, Herbert M., *Autobiography of Major General William F. Smith 1861–1864*, (Morningside, Dayton, 1990)

Schmidt, Martin F., editor, *General George Crook, His Autobiography*, (University of Oklahoma Press, Norman, 1960)

Schofield, John M., *Forty-Six Years in the Army*, (University of Oklahoma Press, Norman, 1998)

Scott, Robert G., *Forgotten Valor: The Memoirs, Journals & Civil War Letters of Orlando B. Willcox*, (Kent State University Press, Kent, 1999)

Schurz, Carl, *The Reminiscences of Carl Schurz*, three volumes, (Doubleday, Page & Co., New York, 1907, 1908)

Scribner, Benjamin F., *How Soldiers were Made*, (Blue Acorn Press, Huntington, 1995)

Sears, Stephen W., *The Civil War Papers of George B. McClellan, Selected Correspondence 1860–1865*, (Ticknor and Fields, New York, 1989)

Sedgwick, John, *Correspondence of John Sedgwick*, (Butternut and Blue, Baltimore, 1999)

Shanks, William F. G., *Personal Recollections of Distinguished Generals*, (Harper & Brothers, New York, 1866)

Sheridan, Philip H., *Personal Memoirs of P. H. Sheridan, General United States Army*, two volumes, (Charles Webster & Company, New York, 1888)

Sherman, William T., *Memoirs of Gen. W. T. Sherman, Written by Himself*, (Charles L. Webster & Co., New York, 1891)

Small, Harold A. and Earl J. Hess, editors, *The Road to Richmond: The Civil War Letters of Major Abner R. Small of the 16th Maine Volunteers*, (Fordham University Press, New York, 2000)

Smith, Walter George, *Life and Letters of Thomas Kilby Smith, Brevet Major General, United States Volunteers, 1820–1887*, (G. P. Putnam's Sons, New York, 1898)

Smith, William F., edited by Herbert M. Schiller, *Autobiography of Major General William F. Smith, 1861–1864*, (Morningside, Dayton, 1990)

Smith, William Farrar, *From Chattanooga to Petersburg Under Generals Grant and Butler*, (The Riverside Press, Cambridge, 1893)

Sparks, David S., editor, *Inside Lincoln's Army: The Diary of Marsena Rudolph Patrick, Provost Marshal General, Army of the Potomac*, (Thomas Yoseloff, New York, 1964)

Stanley, David S., *Personal Memoirs of Major-General David S. Stanley*, (Harvard University Press, Cambridge, 1917)

Stanton, Donald J., Goodwin F. Berquist, and Paul C. Bowers, *The Civil War Reminiscences of General M. Jeff Thompson*, (Morningside, Dayton, 1988)

Stevens, George T., *Three Years in the Sixth Corps*, (S. R. Gray Publishers, Albany, 1866)

Styple, William B., editor, *Our Noble Blood: The Civil War Letters of Major General Regis de Trobriand*, (Belle Grove Publishing, Kearny, 1997)

Styple, William B., *Letters from the Peninsula: The Civil War Letters of General Philip Kearny*, (Belle Grove Publishing, Kearny, 1988)

Styple, William B., editor, *Generals in Bronze: Interviewing the Commanders of the Civil War*, (Belle Grove Publishing Company, Kearny, 2005)

Sully, Langdon, *No Tears for the General: The Life of Alfred Sully, 1821–1879*, (American West Publishing Company, Palo Alto, 1974)

Sumner, Merlin E., editor, *The Diary of Cyrus B. Comstock*, (Morningside, Dayton, 1987)

Taylor, Emerson G., *Gouverneur Kemble Warren, the Life and Letters of an American Soldier, 1830–1882*, (Houghton, Mifflin Co., Boston, 1932)

Taylor, Richard, *Destruction and Reconstruction*, (D. Appleton and Company, New York, 1879)

Tower, R. Lockwood, editor, *Lee's Adjutant: The Wartime Letters of Colonel Walter Herron Taylor; 1862–1865*, (University of South Carolina Press, Columbia, 1995)

Tower, R. Lockwood, editor, *A Carolinian Goes to War: The Civil War Narrative of Arthur Middleton Manigault*, (University of South Carolina Press, Columbia, 1988)

Townsend, Edward D., *Anecdotes of the Civil War in the United States*, (D. Appleton and Company, New York, 1884)

Townsend, George Alfred, *Campaigns of a Non-Combatant*, (Blelock and Company, New York, 1866)

Trautmann, Frederic, *A Prussian Observes the American Civil War: The Military Studies of Justus Scheibert*, (University of Missouri Press, Columbia, 2001)

Von Borcke, Heros, *Memoirs of the Confederate War for Independence*, (Morningside Bookshop, Dayton, 1985)

Wallace, Lew, *Lew Wallace: An Autobiography*, (Harper & Brothers, New York, 1906)

Warner, Ezra J., *Generals in Blue*, (Louisiana State University Press, Baton Rouge, 1964)

Warner, Ezra J., *Generals in Gray*, (Louisiana State University Press, Baton Rouge, 1959)

Weld, Stephen M., *War Diary and Letters of Stephen Minot Weld 1861–1865*, (Massachusetts Historical Society, Boston, 1979)

Welles, Gideon, edited by Edgar T. Welles, *Diary of Gideon Welles in Three Volumes*, (Houghton Mifflin Co., New York, 1911)

Westcott, Allan, editor, *Mahan on Naval Warfare, Selections from the Writings of Rear Admiral Alfred T. Mahan*, (Little, Brown and Co., Boston, 1918)

Wiggins, Sarah Woolfolk, editor, *The Journals of Josiah Gorgas*, 1857–1878, (University of Alabama Press, Tuscaloosa, 1995)

Wilson, James H., *Under the Old Flag*, (Greenwood Press, Westport, 1912)

Wistar, Isaac Jones, *Autobiography of Isaac Jones Wistar 1827–1905, Half a Century in War and Peace*, (Harper & Brothers Publishers, New York, 1914)

Wittenberg, Eric J., editor, *With Sheridan in the Final Campaign against Lee, by Lt. Col. Frederick C. Newhall, Sixth Pennsylvania Cavalry*, (Louisiana State University Press, Baton Rouge, 2002)

INDEX